PENGUIN BOOKS

ON THE RECORD

Guy Oseary got his start managing bands while still in high school. At seventeen, he began working at what would become Maverick Records. Within years, he became Madonna's partner in the record label and in Maverick Films and Television. Today Oseary is also a principal partner in Untitled Entertainment, one of the leading talent management companies in Hollywood. This is his second book.

ON THE RECORD

Over 150 of the Most Talented People in Music
Share the Secrets of Their Success

Guy Oseary

Foreword by **Steven Tyler**

Edited by **Brandon Panaligan**

Illustrations by Miles Donovan

PENGUIN BOOKS

PENGUIN BOOKS

Published by the Penguin Group

Penguin Group (USA) Inc., 375 Hudson Street, New York, New York 10014, U.S.A.

Penguin Group (Canada), 10 Alcorn Avenue, Toronto, Ontario, Canada M4V 3B2 (a division
of Pearson Penguin Canada Inc.)

Penguin Books Ltd, 80 Strand, London WC2R 0RL, England

Penguin Ireland, 25 St Stephen's Green, Dublin 2, Ireland (a division of Penguin Books Ltd)

Penguin Books (Australia), 250 Camberwell Road, Camberwell, Victoria 3124, Australia
(a division of Pearson Australia Group Pty Ltd)

Penguin Books India Pvt Ltd, 11 Community Centre, Panchsheel Park, New Delhi – 110 017, India

Penguin Group (NZ), cnr Airborne and Rosedale Roads, Albany, Auckland, New Zealand
(a division of Pearson New Zealand Ltd)

Penguin Books (South Africa) (Pty) Ltd, 24 Sturdee Avenue, Rosebank, Johannesburg 2196,
South Africa

Penguin Books Ltd, Registered Offices: 80 Strand, London WC2R 0RL, England

First published in Penguin Books 2004

10 9 8 7 6 5 4 3 2 1

Copyright © Guy Oseary, 2004
Illustrations copyright © Miles Donovan, 2004
All rights reserved

Library of Congress Cataloging-in-Publication Data

Oseary, Guy.
   On the record : over 150 of the most talented people in music share the secrets of their
success / by Guy Oseary ; edited by Brandon Panaligan.
      p.   cm.
   ISBN 0-14-200304-2
   1. Music trade—United States.   2. Music—Bio-bibliography.   3. Music—Social aspects.
   I. Panaligan, Brandon.   II. Title.

   ML3790.O83 2004
   780'.92'2—dc22   2004048211

Printed in the United States of America
Set in Preface
Designed by Daniel Lagin

This book is dedicated to every kid with a big dream, from one of their own.

Foreword

BY STEVEN TYLER

Music meant everything to me as a kid, and it helped save me from many hard times. When I lost everything later in my career, music once again saved me and helped me find a way through the darkness. I can remember as a young boy watching my dad play the piano. I didn't know what it was, but I saw joy and magic all around him. I know now that it's "soul." I think that was passed on from my dad to me through music. I've been doing this a long time, but I still have that lust and desire to create new music. It's like when they told Christopher Columbus the world was flat, he said, "Just give me a fucking boat . . . I gotta see for myself!" That's what music is every day . . . uncertain, passionate, mystical, sexual, spiritual, and most of all . . . fun! I see babies and old people in wheelchairs still groovin' to music. It's the one thing we've all got that's universal. No country, no color, no war, no peace . . . just music. It's here forever, and I'm blessed to be a small part of it. Even when I'm long gone and taking the dirt nap, I know the birds will be singing "Dream On."

Contents

Introduction

When I was twelve years old, I was fortunate enough to meet Morrissey of the Smiths. I will never forget what it felt like when the front man of one of my favorite bands took the time to sign my copy of *The Queen Is Dead* album with these words: "To Guy . . . Be Lucky!"

I *have* been very lucky, and music is a huge reason why. Through music, I have been able to see the world and fulfill so many of my earliest dreams. In fact, music has given me a life that I could hardly even have imagined growing up. A life in music has also provided me a very real sort of education. I've had the good luck to meet some of the most successful people in this business—important artists, label heads, producers, managers, and attorneys—and over the years I've had the good fortune to hear their stories and learn firsthand so many of the valuable lessons they have to share.

I'm not sure when I first knew that I wanted to spend my life around music, but I do remember badgering my father repeatedly to buy me my very first album—*The Gambler* by Kenny Rogers. My dad struck a tough but fair deal with me—if I learned my times table, then he would get me the album. I like to think this was a deal that paid off quite well for both of us.

Ultimately, nobody gets where they're going in this life without a lot of help from many people. It takes a village to make a rock star, or even someone like me who is lucky enough to spend so much of my life in their good company. Three people in the music business made a particularly strong impact on my life and helped get me on my path.

The first person is Freddy DeMann. When I was sixteen, Freddy brought me into what was to become Maverick. I was managing bands at the time and was told that at some point there would be a record company for which I could find bands. I was given an office and a phone and—most importantly—my first chance to shine. There was no pay, but that didn't matter. All I really wanted—all I could really hope for—was that first shot. Freddy wasn't much for words of advice—he was more of a watch-and-learn type of guy. With someone like Freddy, you could learn so much by his example. He let me stay in the room when he made calls. He allowed me to be the fly on his wall. He gave me a chance to soak up as much information as possible, and in the beginning at least, being a sponge can be a very good thing. We had some great times together back then, and I can never forget what Freddy did for me.

The second person is Madonna. I first met Madonna when I was still a teen and everything was new to me. She grabbed me by the hand and took the time to introduce me to a whole new world. Madonna's world was filled with ideas, art, culture, music, drama, beauty, and seemingly endless possibility. Madonna is a shining example of someone who had a big dream and transformed it into a global reality. Just being around Madonna inspires people, and she responds to people who challenge themselves and have their own point of view. She cannot stand mediocrity. She pushes you to be your best, but she pushes no one harder than she pushes herself. She has been the true light of my life. To me, she is family, and more than anything, I've wanted to make her proud.

When I was nineteen, Madonna also introduced me to the third person who has been a guide for me, David Geffen. We became fast friends, and David was from the beginning very patient with me, taking the time to explain many of the fine points of this business. It was a thrill and an honor to learn from the best. Every year since we've known each other, I sit down with him on my birthday. He puts me in my place and tells me things that others won't. David has taught me so many great lessons, and he has never wanted anything in return but to see me be successful.

In my life, I've been lucky in countless ways, but none more so than in having such teachers.

There is one more person I must mention here—my friend Anthony Kiedis. For me, Anthony has been less like a teacher and more like a brother. He instinctively knows exactly how to keep me honest, taking me to task when I richly deserve it. Since we first met back when I was nineteen, Anthony's always been there for me. He has also allowed me to witness up close the rise of the Red Hot Chili Peppers, a class act that stands as an inspiring example of how artists can reach the top while being totally true to themselves. Whatever you do with your life, you'll be really lucky if you have a friend like this—someone whom you can learn with and learn from, laughing through most of it.

Because I have been so fortunate, I'm often asked by others for my advice on how to get in the business and how to stay in it. *On the Record* is my attempt to share what I've learned from the very best—those remarkable recording artists and behind-the-scenes players who have basically taught me everything that I know. This is a book full of their stories and their often hard-earned and now priceless wisdom.

When I was first starting out, I wanted to learn as much as I could about this world, so I bought every book on music that I could find. Most of what was available then was filled with advice on music publishing, royalties, contracts, deal terms, etc. Today, as chairman of a label, I know full well these areas remain important. But for a kid with a big dream—exactly the sort traditionally drawn to this business—that simply wasn't enough. All the legal and technical terms were almost a turnoff when I hungered for so much more than simply that. Somehow wherever I looked, I never found an introduction to the world of music that spoke to me in the same way the music itself did, a book that communicated with me on my own terms. I also never found a guidebook to this world written directly by the people who made it to where I so wanted to be and lived to tell.

With all that in mind, I decided to put this book together. *On the Record* is a journey into the hearts and minds of some of the most talented and successful people in music. This is an all-ages club with artists and behind-the-scenes legends from many parts of our music world, all coming together on some common ground. What unites all of them—from Pavarotti to Chuck D, from Quincy Jones to Britney Spears—is a love of music and a willingness to share some of their knowledge with the rest of us. My hope is that whether you're trying to break into this business or you are simply a passionate fan of music, the stories and points of view gathered here will inspire, educate, and entertain you. Here's your chance to get the lowdown from the remarkable individuals who've already made it to the top, whether it's Bono or Burt Bacharach, Dick Clark or Alicia Keys.

Everyone in the book was asked the same twelve questions that explore their influences, their inspirations, and their regrets. From their answers you'll learn who helped shape them, who their mentors were, what their favorite songs and albums are, as well as what lessons they'd like to pass down. For me, this book itself has been an education. These people who have already taught me so much taught me some new lessons with their open and thought-provoking responses.

For me—and I hope now for you—*On the Record* is more than simply a collection of interviews about the music business. This is a book that comes from the heart and speaks to our dreams. It's about success and happiness. It's about trials and tribulations. It's about business and strategy. It's about preparation and luck. It's about creativity and genius. It's about failure and regret. It's about faith and perseverance.

It's about life.

Be lucky,

Guy Oseary
BEVERLY HILLS
2004

ON THE RECORD

ARTISTS

Christina Aguilera

Did you have a mentor or someone who inspired you? If so, what have you learned from that person?

Strong women have always inspired me. Women who aren't afraid to push boundaries, speak their minds, and be free of inhibitions. My mother has been my biggest inspiration, for her ability to remain strong no matter what life may bring her way. She has taught me to always believe in myself and to follow my heart.

What was your very first job in the music industry, and how did you get it?

I started out singing at local pool and block parties around my hometown in Pittsburgh when I was six and seven years old. My first job as a professional was as a "mousketeer" on the *Mickey Mouse Club* when I was thirteen years old. I kept my eyes open for any opportunities and found an open audition in the local newspaper for the show.

What was your first big break? The first great thing that ever happened to you . . .

From word of mouth, after shopping around for a record deal, I landed the opportunity to sing the song "Reflection" in the Disney movie *Mulan* when I was sixteen. That got me my deal with RCA records.

What elements of your job make you want to go to work every day?

Creating and performing music is my passion. To be able to share my music with the world is a blessing. There is nothing else I would rather be doing with my time.

What qualities most helped you get to where you are today?

Passion, drive, and focus. I have always known what I wanted to do with my life, and I never let anything or anyone get in the way of that dream.

If you knew everything at the beginning of your career that you know now, what would you have done differently?

Of course I've had to learn the hard way that show business is truly a *business,* and that people will quickly smile in your face as long as you're putting fast cash in your pocket, then stab you in the back as soon as you're not looking.

But as much as that hurts at times, I wouldn't do anything differently. Through falling hard, I've gained so much strength, knowledge, and courage to get myself back on my feet—I've learned lessons I wouldn't have otherwise.

What is your greatest lesson learned?

I have learned to trust my own instincts and be unafraid to act on them.

What are some of your favorite albums?

Revolver, the Beatles

Nevermind, Nirvana

Thriller, Michael Jackson

Ready to Die, the Notorious B.I.G.

Physical Graffiti, Led Zeppelin

Did you have any posters on your bedroom walls as a kid? Of whom?

Paula Abdul, Milli Vanilli (they fooled me), Michael Jackson, and Whitney Houston. They all came from my teenybop magazines.

What are some great shows you've seen?

It's funny, but I was never able to see concerts growing up. I was always busy performing myself. It was not until recently that I was able to attend other shows. I just saw Prince, which was amazing.

What are some of your favorite songs?

"Kashmir," by Led Zeppelin, "At Last," by Etta James, and my all-time favorite is "Imagine," by John Lennon

List up to ten things that could be helpful to someone breaking into the business.

1. Trust and believe in your love and talent for music.
2. Know this is what you want to dive into. Don't do it for the wrong reasons.
3. Be as knowledgeable in your talent, skill, and art as possible.
4. Expect challenges and disappointments. Brave them fearlessly.
5. Don't listen to negative people or unconstructive criticism.
6. Be open to other opinions and criticism.

7. Don't care. Go for it.

8. Don't lip sync. Be a true artist and do it from the heart.

9. Learn how to hold a microphone. Don't sell out to those cheesy headset mics. You're working a stage, not a drive-thru. Comfort is key onstage. It's a place where you can truly be free.

10. Never forget, bottom line—it's all about the music!

Andre 3000

OUTKAST

Did you have a mentor or someone who inspired you? If so, what have you learned from that person?

I learned from the music of Parliament/Funkadelic, Prince, James Brown, Jimi Hendrix, and Kraftwerk. What's important to me about these artists—and how I judge whether an album is good or great—is this question: If this artist never existed, what would music sound like today? All of these artists have taken the genre of music they were in and pushed it to the limits. If you listen to any other album that came out around the same time, or in the same genre, their music sounded completely different. They weren't restrained to a category; they weren't in a box, bound to a certain thing. So if you're an up and coming artist, I think it's important to know that you *don't* have to do a certain thing. People forget that music is about expression, and to put limits on an expression is kind of bad.

What was your very first job in the music business, and how did you get it?

The first job was being in Outkast. We were just a group from Atlanta and had been working toward it for a while when we met with a couple of producers, including a group called Organized Noise. They had ties with LaFace, so we hooked up with L.A. Reid from LaFace, and they signed our group. So it was a mixture of talent and "who you know." The "who you know" helps out sometimes, but if you don't know anybody, just keep performing until you make a name and people want to come and see your show. Then people will want to be in business with you, so it's not like you're trying to shake down record companies.

What was your first big break? The first great thing that ever happened to you . . .

It would have to be after we put out the first album and started to go on tour. We started to talk to people who were buying albums. It was our first album, so we would invite people back to the hotel, and just talk, drink, and smoke with the people. They would talk to us about the music, and how it affected their lives. We thought we were just making some music, so that was the first time we realized something else was going on. Someone else had to tell it.

What elements of your job make you want to go to work every day?

The chance that there's always something new to do. That's the only thing that keeps me going, and it's actually where the 3000 part of my name comes from. When we started out I was just "Andre" from the group Outkast. Then, as I started to produce songs, and got more into the music itself and the concept behind making albums, I quickly learned that I get bored really fast. The only way I can stay excited is to try new things and do things I haven't done before. To always look forward, toward the future. That's where the 3000 comes from.

What qualities most helped you get to where you are today?

I think they're defects really. My attention span is really short, and I get bored *fast*. There have been so many times when I actually wanted to quit doing it, to quit the business. The only thing that has kept me going is trying to be a new group every time. Finding something to do that is interesting. Finding something I haven't done. In general, I think it's not a great thing to have a short attention span or to get bored fast, but it's worked for the music though. . . .

Reinventing myself comes naturally. For me to make a song like "Hey Ya" again would be to sell out. It would be bullshit, because I've done it, and I know how to do it. So even when I go to places to produce or write, I have to be doing something new or I feel like I'm not growing.

That doesn't stop me from listening to my old material. It feels like I'm listening to some other group. Even now, "Hey Ya" is five years old to me. It's like it's not even me. I did "Hey Ya" two or three years before it came out.

If you knew everything at the beginning of your career that you know now, what would you have done differently?

Don't sell your publishing.

If you're down and out, and don't have any money, you could maybe sell off *some* of it.

But if you can hold off, you should. If you know you're gonna be great, if you feel like you're gonna be great—then hold off. You can always sell it later if you want to, or make some kind of deal later. Selling it early may not be a good thing—we just didn't know those things.

What is your greatest lesson learned?

This comes from watching people's careers. Don't ever do something so great for too long. If you do something so great for so long, when you do something else, people won't like you, because they *love* you for what you have done before. If you show variety, you won't always have to do the same thing. I think that would be torture, to have to do the same thing over and over again for a lifetime.

What are some of your favorite albums?

Niggaz4life, N.W.A.

The Low End Theory, A Tribe Called Quest

Sign O' the Times, Prince

Are You Experienced?, Jimi Hendrix
   Experience

A Love Supreme, John Coltrane

Any album by Anita Baker

The Ramones, the Ramones

Did you have any posters on your bedroom walls as a kid? Of whom?

I was never into music as a kid. I drew and painted, and that's what I was into. I liked music, and I listened to the radio, but I was never like a "music head." I didn't have any heroes, and I didn't think I was going to be doing music until I was in tenth grade or so.

What are some great shows you've seen?

The Hives were great.

Goodie Mob's live show after *Soul Food.*

I've seen a lot of great performances on tape, such as Parliament/Funkadelic in 1976 and Sly Stone.

What are some of your favorite songs?

"Adore," Prince

"One Nation Under a Groove,"
   Parliament/Funkadelic

"Giant Steps," John Coltrane

"Electric Relaxation," A Tribe Called Quest

"I Wanna Be Your Boyfriend," the Ramones

"Mongoloid," Devo

List up to ten things that could be helpful to someone breaking into the business.

- Know your worth. If you don't know your worth, people can and will buy you for anything.
- There are a couple of great books out there about publishing, about scales. Read them. The more knowledge you have, and the more research you do, the better off you are when you start meeting with people.
- The history of music is important. Learn what other artists have gone through. Learn who was the first person to own their masters. Learn from people's mistakes.
- Read biographies—you'll definitely learn something. You may even learn not to party every night.

Fiona Apple

Did you have a mentor or someone who inspired you? If so, what have you learned from that person?

I wouldn't say that I have a mentor, but there are people who have guided me by example; people whom I've observed long-term who keep me interested. Also, it's important to know that not all of those people set good examples, and I don't even necessarily like all of them. But, they are interesting and inspiring—most everything is.

What was your very first job in the music industry, and how did you get it?

My first job was making my first album, and it came about in a very Cinderella-like way: The first demo I ever handed out got me a record deal.

What was your first big break? The first great thing that ever happened to you . . .

My first break and the first great thing to happen to me couldn't possibly be one and the same. However, my first break led to meeting a whole lot of people whom I really love, and that is the greatest thing to happen to me, and it's ongoing.

What elements of your job make you want to go to work every day?

Nothing makes me want to work every day, and I don't.

What qualities most helped you get to where you are today?

I believe I have a lot of good qualities, but the ones that got me where I am today probably lean more toward the needy and the angry!

If you knew everything at the beginning of your career that you know now, what would you have done differently?

I would have enjoyed myself more and maybe extended myself a little more to the other aspects of record-making. Of course, I can still do that.

What is your greatest lesson learned?

My father once said that he wasn't afraid of earthquakes because he knew there was nothing he could do about them anyway. I said that's exactly why I am afraid. I don't know if it's a lesson, but I'm trying to learn to do what I can in the areas in which I have power, and to let go and stop worrying when there's simply nothing to be done. Worry and freedom are difficult to reconcile.

What are some of your favorite albums?

The Lion and the Cobra, Sinéad O'Connor
Anything by John Lennon, Mahalia Jackson, or Fred Astaire

Did you have any posters on your bedroom walls as a kid? Of whom?

Just the Beatles' *Let it Be* poster.

What are some great shows you've seen?

Well, of course Jon Brion at Largo, and I once saw Evelyn Glennie, and that was—and I'm using this word correctly, Mama—*awesome!*

What are some of your favorite songs?

I find the favorite song question impossible to answer. It's kind of like trying to pick your favorite word. My mind just goes blank; it's too overwhelming.

List up to ten things that could be helpful to someone breaking into the business.

■ Surround yourself with people you like to be around, people you admire, and you will have a much better chance of enjoying yourself and doing better work.
■ Take your time in trusting even the sweetest of colleagues.
■ Don't waste your time looking at record company people as "The Man." They're all just people. Some you'll like to be around, some you won't.
■ Take your time working when you need to—the work is the reason for it all. There are so many opinions out there; if you don't feel solid with your work, any one of them can sway you.
■ Be kind.

Burt Bacharach

Did you have a mentor or someone who inspired you? If so, what have you learned from that person?

What got me into music, what really hooked me in, was Dizzy Gillespie and that whole era of Charlie Parker, Thelonius Monk, big band. It was just incredible. I used to hear them on Fifty-second Street. I'd get a phony ID card and listen to them in the bars there. Dizzy was a hero of mine. On the classical side it was Ravel, Debussy, and the French Impressionists. As far as a teacher, I studied with Darius Milhaud, and he taught me to never, ever be afraid of something melodic. Melody was good. Others in my class were writing very extreme music, and I would come in with something that was very simple and had a melody. He encouraged it.

What was your very first job in the music industry, and how did you get it?

My first job in the music industry was playing piano at a couple of bars in Cape Cod. I got fired from the first job and moved to a lesser job for the rest of the summer. My first job in the major part of the music industry was conducting for Vic Damone, and that lasted about three or four weeks. I got fired there too.

What was your first big break? The first great thing that ever happened to you . . .

Certainly the exposure of conducting for acts, whether it was Vic Damone or Dietrich. I saw a lot of the world that way. Of course, there's nothing like having a hit song when you've been trying to have a hit for a year and a half.

What elements of your job make you want to go to work every day?

Being in touch with music is what I was meant to do. It's discipline. The best part of the whole job is going and making the record of the song that you wrote. That's where it all lives or dies— in the studio. You either make it right, or it doesn't come out right, and then it doesn't matter about the song. All the elements have to be working for you.

What qualities most helped you get to where you are today?

Talent helps for sure, and hard work. I go for 100 percent in just about everything that I do. It can drive me crazy. It's a discipline that can make me nuts, because I can look at the little pimples on the record that no one else sees. Maybe in the end it won't make any difference at all, but that's who I am.

If you knew everything at the beginning of your career that you know now, what would you have done differently?

I don't think much. It just took its course. I studied serious, contemporary classical composing. I wouldn't have done anything differently, except maybe taking time to smell the roses a little bit more. Through a lot of the period when things were exciting it was "finish a project and on to the next."

What are some of your favorite albums?

I've always gravitated to Brazilian music. I would say albums by Ivan Lins, Djavan, and Milton Nascimento.

Did you have any posters on your bedroom walls as a kid? Of whom?

I don't remember, but maybe football players.

What are some great shows you've seen?

I don't see a lot of shows. I never did. Some shows are really hard to listen to, with the music cranked up so loud. It's like getting hit in the stomach. It's kind of tough.

What are some of your favorite songs?

"House Is Not a Home"
"Alfie"

List up to ten things that could be helpful to someone breaking into the business.

Learn how to read music. Learn how to write it down when you're riding on a plane and you hear something in your head. Write the notes down on a piece of music paper. Learn the rules, to be able to break the rules.

Chester Bennington

LINKIN PARK

Did you have a mentor or someone who inspired you? If so, what have you learned from them?

I'm not really sure I had a mentor, as far as music is concerned, but I was always involved in things like sports and other team activities. I learned to really like the applause and the attention, and working with a team as well. That's been a big part of being with Linkin Park, always being part of a team.

What was your very first job in the music industry, and how did you get it?

My first gig was when I was fifteen or so. There were two rival fraternities that were across the street from each other on corners. They were always fighting and feuding. I wasn't in either of them—I wasn't *that* much of a team player! They decided that to make friends and bridge the gap between them they would have a big block party. So they invited my band Grey Days to play, and they paid us like fifteen hundred bucks to play the gig. That was a huge deal, that paid for a lot of shit—new strings, rehearsal space.

We were supposed to play for about three hours, so we learned over seventy cover songs. We also played three original songs, and after about two hours, when we started playing "Smells Like Teen Spirit," the place went completely insane. Fighting broke out and spread throughout the two thousand people that were there and into both houses across the street. It turned to rioting, and the cops came with their big shields and helmets and beanbag shotguns.

We had some security guards at the time, mostly friends of ours wearing shirts with our band's name and SECURITY written on them. One of our security guys was a small jock guy who was friends with the drummer. He was about four inches shorter than me, but I saw him throw an ASU linebacker out of the mosh pit. He just picked him up. It was pretty awesome . . .

That was the first time I was paid for it, and it was pretty cool and a pretty big deal to me at the time, getting more than fifty bucks to play my friend's backyard party or something.

What was your first break? The first great thing that ever happened to you . . .

I was working at a place called Diversified Information Services Corporation. The only thing musical about that place was the sound of the scanner. I got a call from Scott Harrington, who asked me to audition for a band that was looking for a singer. My first question was, "*How* did you find me???"

What elements of your job make you want to go to work every day?

Definitely the creative aspect is something you can get addicted to. You're doing something you really like, you start seeing that other people like it to, and it just keeps you going. There's an indescribable connection between the audience and a band. Once you get onstage, and you see the people singing along, with emotions as strong or greater than the ones you are singing with, you get a rush from it. You just have to keep going back; it's a longing.

If you knew everything at the beginning of your career that you know now, what would you have done differently?

I don't know if I'd do anything differently, as I'm in a pretty good place right now.

What is your greatest lesson learned?

The greatest lesson I've learned—not only for a musician but for anybody who has something they really want to do—is not to go seek advice from people who haven't tried it. They'll just tell you it's impossible. If you go to your parents, well, maybe if your dad is a guitar player or used to be in a band, if you tell him you're really interested in doing it, he's more qualified to say "Yeah, go for it dude," or "Watch out for scumbag promoters," or "Stay out of the drug scene." If he's been there and tried, he's probably someone you can rely on. But if he's a dentist, and he doesn't understand the music that you're into, or listen to the music that you listen to . . . he's probably not going to have anything to say that matters for what you're trying to do. Finding those people to get advice from is really difficult. I've always relied on my own willpower to ba-sically prove to everybody that it *is* possible and that I am talented enough. I loved it so much there was nothing else I wanted to do. It's been that obvious to me, ever since I was about thir-teen years old. So I guess the moral of the story is if you really want to do something, and you believe in yourself, go for it, and don't listen to anyone who'll try to convince you otherwise.

What are some of your favorite albums?

This is the hardest question—ever—because there are so many records that I like so much, so my top five is probably different every time I answer this question. Off the top of my head . . .

Milo Goes to College, the Descendents   *Led Zeppelin I,* Led Zeppelin
Walk Among Us, the Misfits   *Black Celebration,* Depeche Mode
Incesticide, Nirvana   *Sgt. Pepper's Lonely Hearts Club Band, the Beatles*

Did you have any posters on your bedroom walls as a kid? Of whom?

I had a wall-sized poster of Depeche Mode from *Black Celebration.* I had lots of posters of guys surfing waves, and people in half-pipes. There was always lots of garbage in my room. Lots of STP stickers, because I love Stone Temple Pilots. They're probably my favorite band ever—I've probably seen them twenty times, on my own that is, before I toured with them and got to see them every night. Lots of Doors posters—in high school I listened a lot to the Doors, Zeppelin, and Black Sabbath.

What are some great shows you've seen?

My first show I saw was this birthday show for one of the first AM alternative rock stations. It was called the *Q-Fest* and Front 242 played. It was awesome; those guys were maniacs.

Best show I've ever seen in my life was Pearl Jam, Nirvana, and the Red Hot Chili Peppers. Each of them was respectively out supporting the best records of our time—*Blood Sugar Sex Magik, Nevermind,* and *Ten.* I saw it in the basketball coliseum on the Arizona State University campus. There was a mosh pit on the side, in the arena area, but we were up in the seats and we tore all of the seats out and were moshing on the side, on the steps. It was kind of dope. I remember getting tossed down ten rows because I was surfing at such an angle when some guy threw me. I just went down from row 42 to row 33.

Lollapalloza, 1992, the year Pearl Jam played with Ministry, Ice Cube.

What are some of your favorite songs?

This is easier than the records question, because when I think of records, I think of the *whole.* What can I listen to from beginning to end? But songs . . . I can mix up songs all day.

"Summertime Rolls," Jane's Addiction off of *Nothing's Shocking.* It's killer.
"Hey Jude," the Beatles
"Waiting Room," Fugazi
"Let's Stay Together," and almost every song on *Al Green's Greatest Hits.* You put on that song and you know what time it is. You can never lose with that song.
"Everlong," Foo Fighters. Inside our band, we always joke, "Why couldn't we have written that song?"
I don't want to be a dick by naming one of my own songs, but I think "Breaking the Habit" is one of my favorite songs. People are probably gonna think "what a jerk!" but it's a good song.
The theme from the original *Mario Brothers.*
"Happy Birthday"
The song that Ernie sings on the *Sesame Street Sing-Along* about loving under the sea. I've seen three-hundred-pound men cry to that song.

List up to ten things that could be helpful to someone breaking into the business.

I think the most important thing today, because technology is so wonderful and can take us to places that we'd never imagined going before (without the help of record companies), is the fact that you can distribute your own music to everybody on the planet for nothing. It's a really cool thing. If you're smart about it, take your time and write, rather than spending thousands of dollars buying cabinets to fill up some crappy rehearsal space, jamming all day with the hope that one day you'll play live. Go invest in ProTools, learn how to use it, and learn how to write songs. Write songs that you're so in love with that you can't wait to play them for people. Then when you share them with people who are close to you, and they love it and want to give it to their friends, you can start telling people about it, get it up on a Web site, give it away on MP3, and very simply, start building your fan base that way. Start making tapes. Burn copies and copies of your CDs and send them to your fans in Tucson or out in Maine. Because of the Web, we had fans all over the world before any record company ever wanted to look at us. I think it's a really great tool for a band to use in a positive way to promote their band. Today, you don't make your money selling records. You make your money playing shows, and you're gonna be much better off with a strong fan base, regardless of whether or not you have the push of your record company. Getting out there and playing shows is the only way you're going to be able to pay your bills for a long time.

Don't ever sign merchandising deals, especially for touring. Don't sign it away to people. That's how I kept food on my table for the last three and a half years. It's a little extra gravy, because someone's going to want a piece of everything. But they don't have to have everything. Let them share in things that you know are impossible for you to do on your own. You know you can make merch—you can go through some company and buy fifty thousand t-shirts and take them on the road with you. Sell them on the road, and pay somebody a percentage of what you make, but then you take the rest home. Only sign retail deals.

Keep on your publishing too. Don't fuck around with that! Michael Jackson is not known for spending millions of dollars a month because he's sold a lot of records—it's because he owns half of one of the largest publishing companies on the planet. That's where you earn your money.

Bono

Did you have a mentor or someone who inspired you? If so, what have you learned from that person?

U2's manager, Paul McGuinness, has had the most pivotal role in the way my creative life has been structured. At the beginning he encouraged the band to share equally our publishing and recording income, because money is the thing that breaks most bands up. Also, the ego of a group should be a collective one; songs should make the album because they are the best, not because someone has invested time and pride in them. In U2 we argue about the good and the very good all the time—we never argue about what's great. Another thing Paul McGuinness hardwired into our thinking was a sense of having to take responsibility for the commerce as well as the art. If you value your gift you should know how to bodyguard it. U2 was always much more independent than any of the so-called indie bands. We went to our record company for advice, not a plan.

I am often asked how U2 got to own all of its recordings and publishing (we lease them to Universal). Well, it was an extraordinary thing that Paul fought for and the great and gracious Chris Blackwell, founder of Island Records, acceded to. But in the end, we paid for it with lower royalties on some of our best-selling work. This autonomy stuff is expensive.

What was your very first job in the music business, and how did you get it?

U2 is the only job I have ever had. I got to be a singer not because I could sing, but because I was worse at everything else. I was driven to Larry Mullen's house on the back of Reggie Manuel's fast bike, aged sixteen, because he thought I had enough "front" if only he could get me there. On the journey something changed in me. . . . God pulled up beside us at the traffic lights and told me if I could stay truthful with my maker, he'd always put petrol in my tank.

What was your first big break? The first great thing that ever happened to you . . .

The breaks came when we were ready for them . . . slowly . . . your ears don't bleed if you move slowly up the rock face, they just pop a bit.

What elements of your job make you want to go to work every day?

Maybe you can't change the world in three and a half minutes, but you can change your own world.

What qualities most helped you get to where you are today?

Insecurity. It's hard to get anywhere interesting without it.

If you knew everything at the beginning of your career that you know now, what would you have done differently?

I saw a picture of myself at twenty-one recently at one of Anton Corbijn's exhibitions, so young, so naive . . . the face was wide open, no goggles, just eyes ready to read and to be read. Naïveté is so powerful. If I could meet my first face again—and I'm sad I can't—I would whisper into my ear six words: *"Don't second guess, you are right."* Maybe two others: *"Break rhyme."*

What is your greatest lesson learned?

The greatest lesson I haven't learned is the Christ story . . . it's so hard to get your head around the concept of grace. Karma is at the center of every religion. It is at the core of all physical laws: "an eye for an eye," "for every action an equal and opposite," etc., and yet grace interrupts it. Love thine enemy doesn't make much sense, but I know it's God's point of view.

What are some of your favorite albums?

Favorite albums change all the time for me. I associate pivotal records with pivotal moments. When I was twelve, John Lennon's *Imagine* and at thirteen, Bob Dylan's *The Times They Are a-Changin'*, brought to me the idea that the world is more malleable than you think. Nothing is set in concrete, or if it is, you should leave your initials in it before it dries. When I was fourteen, Leonard Cohen's *Songs from a Room* taught me religion and sex were not enemies. At fifteen, Neil Young's *After the Gold Rush* made me fancy girls in jeans who smelt of patchouli. The seventies also belonged to David Bowie's *Ziggy Stardust*, the Sex Pistols' *Never Mind the Bollocks*, Patti Smith's *Horses*. The Clash's *Sandinista!* taught me the most important lesson of my theatrical life—never look too comfortable on the stage. The performer that looks like they might follow you home, mug you, make out with you, rob a bank, or change the world with you is the one you can't stop watching. In the eighties, it was Ian Curtis from Joy Division's *Unknown Pleasures*, Talking Heads' *Remain in Light*, Bruce Springsteen's *Darkness on the Edge of Town*, Miles Davis's *In a Silent Way*. I was a late developer and a slow learner. I didn't know jazz was such a language; I wasn't sure what was being communicated. With Miles, I guess it was sex. With John Coltrane's *A Love Supreme*, the desire to worship your maker.

In the nineties, the Pixies went diggin' for fire on *Bossanova*. Every so often, somebody changes the game. Charles Thompson is one of twenty people in rock to do so. He opened the door that Kurt Cobain walked through. Nirvana might have been the fire he was digging for, although I much preferred the Pixies and Hole's *Live Through This*—a work of pure, white hot metal; the Verve's *Urban Hymns,* Massive Attack's *Blue Lines,* and Oasis's *What's the Story Morning Glory?* Oasis upped the melodic ante. Not since Roy Orbison have bridges sounded so like choruses, choruses sounded so like choruses, middle eights sounded so like choruses. Liam Gallagher's voice rings true. Noel Gallagher is capable of anything. If he can be himself, he is more interesting than the people he would like to be.

In the zeros, Eminem's "Lose Yourself," Trent Reznor's "Hurt," performed by Johnny Cash. The White Stripes, *Elephant,* an oddly romantic album, where values of the past feel sort of futuristic . . . like we might need them in the future. I just realized I've left out the dance music that kept me alive in the nineties, the hip-hop that so raised the game for the last ten years. Public Enemy, *It'll Take a Nation of Millions to Hold Us Back,* Dr. Dre, Wyclef Jean, Lauryn Hill and the Fugees, and if you don't believe in God, there's Beyoncé. On that subject, how can I not mention Willie Nelson's *Teatro* and Wynnona Judd singing gospel on *The Heart of America* tour.

And lastly, with a red face, I have to 'fess up to staying two hours in a greasy spoon somewhere listening to the Bee Gees' greatest hits. I literally couldn't leave; they left me in a puddle. Maybe it was a bad day at the office, or maybe they proved the rule that genius is only recognized when it's well-dressed. I shouldn't have been surprised.

Did you have any posters on your bedroom walls as a kid? Of whom?

I still have Who posters up in my bedroom.

I still have a poster of David Bowie's *Hunky Dory*. At fourteen, I thought he was a duo. Marc Bolan and Alice Cooper might explain the art of gobbledygook lyrics and wild exhibitionism. They were on my wall, too, as was John Lennon's only command, "Imagine."

What are some great shows you've seen?

The best show I've never seen is a U2 show. I've never seen four people go at it every night like it might be their last so consistently. The singer's a little over the top, though.

What are some of your favorite songs?

My favorite song of all time is "Amazing Grace."

List up to ten things that could be helpful to someone breaking into the business.

- You are as good as the arguments you get.
- Only move house on a live album—Chinese rugs have ruined more musicians' careers than Chinese rocks (drugs).
- Realize that if you don't die on a cross at thirty-three, some people will want their money back.

- Do not judge your audience by the ones you meet.
- If more than a few times a week everyone at your table is in your employ, leave the restaurant or change jobs.
- Art may be better than commerce, but that doesn't mean artists are better than business people. Far from it; we're egomaniacal, selfish, trouble-making parasites of the human condition. There are people in your record label who are great—try to find them. In Universal, I found gentlemen in Doug Morris, Lucian Grange, Paul Kremen, and Steve Matthews. At the top of the list for me would be Sheila Roche and Keryn Kaplan who run Principle Management, as well as Jimmy Iovine who runs Interscope Records and has become, over years and years, a great friend and bodyguard. He has a very rare thing in the music business, an ear and a nose for what's right.
- Don't forget the stage is a platform shoe.

B Real

CYPRESS HILL

Did you have a mentor or someone who inspired you? If so, what have you learned from that person?

I would say that I was influenced the most by KRS-One and Chuck D. What I learned from KRS-One was to be a versatile MC, to constantly perfect my craft and to maintain professionalism. From Chuck D I learned how much influence you have on people through music and how you can enlighten people through it.

What was your very first job in the music industry, and how did you get it?

I never worked in the industry previous to our first records, but I can say that once we signed it was a crash-course education on how things work. When you're an artist making your first record, all you can think about is recording, but the time you take to learn the biz is beneficial later.

What was your first big break? The first great thing that ever happened to you . . .

Our first break was writing songs for an artist called Mellow Man Ace off of Capitol Records. That's when I began writing seriously. I guess the greatest moment came when we inked our first deal with Sony. It was only the beginning, but at the time, it felt like the greatest moment.

What elements of your job make you want to go to work every day?

The ability to create something timeless that gives people hope, knowledge, and a good time as well. Being able to motivate people through music is a high like no other.

What qualities most helped you get to where you are today?

It's mostly work ethic, besides our so-called talent. You have to work hard to be on top, and once you get to the top you have to work harder to stay there. With success comes more responsibility, and you have to keep your head straight and stay on the grind. There's too much competition these days to be lagging.

If you knew everything at the beginning of your career that you know now, what would you have done differently?

As far as my time with Cypress goes, I wouldn't change a thing. Sure, some songs I might have approached differently in the aspect of cameos and side projects, but other than that the good and the bad are learning experiences. Just never make the same mistake twice.

What is your greatest lesson learned?

Stay in touch with your fans, and the times, and never sell yourself short even if you have to compromise a little.

What are some of your favorite albums?

Criminal Minded, Boogie Down Productions
License to Ill, the Beastie Boys
It Takes a Nation of Millions to Hold Us Back, Public Enemy
Only Built for Cuban Linx, Raekwon
Don Killuminati: The 7 Day Theory, Makeveli (Tupac)
Death Certificate, Ice Cube
Liquid Swords, GZA/Genius
The Eminem Show, Eminem
The Blueprint, Jay-Z
Iron Man
Get Rich or Die Tryin', 50 Cent
Kings of Rock, Run-D.M.C.
Born to Die, Grand Funk Railroad
Follow the Leader, Eric B. & Rakim

What are some great shows you've seen?

The *Raisin' Hell* tour was the first great show I saw, before we broke into the biz.

Others are: KRS-One, the Beastie Boys, Digital Underground, Leaders of the New School, Busta Rhymes, A Tribe Called Quest, Naughty by Nature.

What are some of your favorite songs?

"The Moment I Feared"
"Bird in the Hand"
"Criminal Minded"
"Paul Revere"
"Deep Cover"
"Hail Mary"
"Night of the Living Bassheads"
"Paid in Full"
"Fuck the Police"
"Straight Outta Compton"
"Raw R.A.W."

List up to ten things that could be helpful to someone breaking into the business.

- Know the direction you want to go with your music.
- Write constantly to be on top of your game. The more you write, the better you'll become at it.
- Rehearse your songs once you have them together because the live show is one of the most important tools in promoting an album. The show has to be tight and most of all, entertaining.

- Try to be involved as much as you can in every aspect of your career, from recording to everything else. We all need knowledge of whatever game we play.
- Just be yourself and be good to your fans, no matter how things are going for you, whether you're up or down.

James Brown

Did you have a mentor or someone who inspired you? If so, what have you learned from that person?

Louis Jordan inspired me. He was a mentor to a lot of people. When I saw him, something in my soul made me want to be like him. He made everybody happy. He sang, he wrote, he played, and he danced. He was unbelievable. You don't have anyone like that these days. I would be the closest to Louis Jordan, over anybody. I talk to his wife every so often.

In terms of the business, it was Mr. Bart and Mr. Brando. Mr. Brando was black and Mr. Bart was white. I had both sides. Without learning the business, I would have stayed in the ghetto. Most people have never been exposed to anything, but it can help a black man so much to be black and proud—to be proud of what they are.

What was your very first job in the music industry, and how did you get it?

My advice to kids is to get an education first. But remember there's that whole other line of things that an education won't help you with. You need to explore. You need to be exposed. That's the one thing that fools the *system*—it ain't got no street sense. See, the street has another thing going on all the time. The government wants them to do this, another group wants them to do that, but they're right on the border, making their own rules. The street thing is like Canada, the United States, and Russia. The street thing comes between them all, and you can't fight it. It's like "um-bop-bing"—and you don't know where it's coming from.

What was your first break? The first great thing that ever happened to you . . .

I came up with that half-rhythm that puts it all in another place. People didn't know where it came from. First they thought it was African, but then it wasn't from there either. It wasn't just drums, it was something I put together, one-of-a-kind. God always makes one-of-a-kind, and I thank God for it, whatever it is. I don't know where it comes from. I've looked everywhere, but you have to look inside. There are parts of me everywhere. It's like Moses—he's got parts of himself everywhere. I've got Oriental bloodlines, American Apache Indian, Aztec. . . . My mother is Indian, black, and Oriental. She's a little woman, gets up every morning and does her yoga. I look at her and I say, aha, that's a whole other thing. The Aztec and Apache come from my dad. We've all got it all inside. Nobody controls the universe . . . we all have our places.

If you knew everything at the beginning of your career that you know now, what would you have done differently?

I had a lot of choices, but I am happy what I chose. I was a great athlete, an unbelievable athlete. Baseball—I could catch the ball behind the back and do the splits. Any of that stuff. At football I could catch the ball and pass it behind my back. They can't play like that anymore. They have no idea. Athletics can be a show. The pitcher is a showman. The quarterback is a showman. Back in the day, I'd get that ball, and I saw so many choices. I could do anything. I got all the moves, and that's where it's happening.

What are some of your favorite albums?

I love music.

I can always listen to Jimmy Reed or the Rolling Stones.

Some other great rock bands are Redbone; Blood, Sweat & Tears; Chicago.

They all had *it*. Chicago was so slick you didn't know if it was jazz or funk, or rock, but it was good! Those guys need to come back. I want to see some good acts. I'd go to them all. . . .

What are some great shows you've seen?

Thinking about showmen in the music business, Louis Jordan was one of the best. He had style and showed the manhood. I liked Sinatra, for his mannerisms. He was one of a kind, and he practiced what he preached. I loved Elvis a lot, but they wouldn't let him stretch out into what he really wanted to be. Elvis was what everybody loved, and that was a no-no. James Taylor. Billy J. Kramer. Otis Redding.

Michael Jackson always impressed me. I remember he used to stand there and just watch my feet.

List up to ten things that could be helpful to someone breaking into the business.

- You can't get paid unless you got something to sell. Then you got to get somebody to record it so it can become massive, and people have to want to buy it. You have to be original, down to your clothes. You won't find mine anywhere, because they're my own design. You have to be original. In the beginning, I didn't try to sell it. I gave it away, so that more people saw it. People started talking about James Brown. These days everything is for sale. The cops are even for sale. But you need people to want to buy it.
- You have to clear all the negatives out of the way, look at yourself, and ask, "Can I do this?"
- I pray that I stay healthy and can keep performing. Because the people that I perform for now are the people I was fighting for years ago. They're people who can make a difference.
- You should have emotion, you should have high spirits, but you have to control it too. Use it wisely, but don't lock it away.

Ali Campbell

UB40

Did you have a mentor or someone who inspired you? If so, what have you learned from that person?

Bob Marley and Stevie Wonder, their music inspired me.

What was your very first job in the music industry, and how did you get it?

Lead singer and guitarist (rhythm) with UB40. I decided with Jimmy and Earl to start a jazz/dub/reggae band.

What was your first big break? The first great thing that ever happened to you . . .

Chrissie Hynde saw us play the Rock Gardens and invited us on her British tour.

What elements of your job make you want to go to work every day?

The fact that I don't have to go to work every day.

What qualities most helped you get to where you are today?

Arrogance, determination, good fortune, and a love of reggae music.

If you knew everything at the beginning of your career that you know now, what would you have done differently?

I'd have compromised with the music less . . . and looked after our money more!

What is your greatest lesson learned?

Every day above ground is a good day! Live the life you love, love the live you live.

What are some of your favorite albums?

Natty Dread, Bob Marley and the Wailers
African Herbsman, *Burnin'*, and *Catch a Fire*, the Wailers
Talking Book and *Where I'm Coming From*, Stevie Wonder

Maybe Tomorrow, the Jackson 5
Reggae Gi'Dem Dub, Big Youth
Black Ark in Dub, Lee Perry
Chill Out and *Red*, Black Uhuru

Did you have any posters on your bedroom walls as a kid? Of whom?

George Best (football player for Manchester United and Northern Ireland).

What are some great shows you've seen?

Monster Shack, Scare Dem, Lady Saw, and Ninja Man, Jamaica

Bob Marley and the Wailers, the Odeon, Birmingham, England

The Jackson 5 at the Odeon, Birmingham, England

Stevie Wonder (anywhere!)

Seeed, Germany

What are some of your favorite songs?

"You and I," Stevie Wonder

"Got to Be There," Michael Jackson

"Talkin' Blues," Bob Marley and the Wailers

"Strive," Shine Head

"Small Axe," Bob Marley and the Wailers

"Try a Little Tenderness," Otis Redding

"My Girl," Michael Jackson

"Wherever I Lay My Hat," Marvin Gaye

"Are We a Warrior," Ijahman

"Lord Give Me Strength," Luciano

List up to ten things that could be helpful to someone breaking into the business.

Who am I to give advice?

Mariah Carey

Did you have a mentor or someone who inspired you? If so, what have you learned from that person?

My mother was an opera singer. When I was a baby she sang with the New York City Opera, and she also sang jazz and hung with a lot of jazz musicians as I was growing up. By the time I was five, I would sit in with them and sing songs like "Lullaby of Birdland" and "I Can't Give You Anything But Love." She taught me to really believe in myself as a singer; she taught me never to doubt my ability to succeed.

What was your very first job in the music business, and how did you get it?

When I was thirteen I got a session as a background singer on an R&B song through a friend of the family. I don't remember the name of the song, but I do remember it was the first time I got paid to sing. I remember walking home from the session feeling my first true sense of accomplishment in the music business.

What was your first big break? The first great thing that ever happened to you . . .

When I was seventeen, some musician friends of mine recommended me for a job singing background for Brenda K. Starr. I had already been writing songs and working on a demo tape which she loved . . . she was always trying to get people to listen to it. Eventually she brought me to a party to introduce me to Jerry Greenberg. Tommy Mottola ended up grabbing the tape out of his hands. Tommy put the tape on in his limo as he was leaving the party, and turned around and came back to find me after he heard the first few lines of "Alone in Love," a song I wrote when I was fifteen. That song ultimately ended up on my first album.

What elements of your job make you want to go to work every day?

The satisfaction I feel when I create a new song, or the energy and the love I feel when I perform onstage in front of my fans. That's what keeps me going.

What qualities most helped you get to where you are today?

My intense love of music, my ridiculous work ethic, and my faith.

If you knew everything at the beginning of your career that you know now, what would you have done differently?

I wouldn't have allowed myself to be creatively stifled, and I would have stuck up for myself a lot earlier in my career with regard to artistic and personal freedom.

What is your greatest lesson learned?

Don't run yourself into the ground for this business, or any business for that matter. Life is too short.

What are some of your favorite albums?

Songs in the Key of Life, Stevie Wonder
Off the Wall, Michael Jackson
Perfect Angel, Minnie Ripperton
Ready to Die, the Notorious B.I.G.
Sparkle, Aretha Franklin
Finally, Karen Clark

Reasonable Doubt, Jay-Z
Purple Rain, Prince
The Infamous, Mobb Deep
Low End Theory, A Tribe Called Quest
All Eyez on Me, 2Pac
The list goes on for days . . .

Did you have any posters on your bedroom walls as a kid? Of whom?

Just one: Marilyn Monroe.

What are some great shows you've seen?

About three years ago, I saw Prince play at some club . . . he was still killing it at five in the morning. Chaka was on stage with him . . . it was amazing.

What are some of your favorite songs?

"Outstanding," the Gap Band
"That Girl," Stevie Wonder
"Brooklyn's Finest," Jay-Z/Notorious B.I.G.
"Ante Up" Remix, M.O.P.
"You Brought the Sunshine,"
    the Clark Sisters

"All Night Long," Mary Jane Girls
"As We Lay," Shirley Murdoch
"Forever My Lady," Jodeci
"Just Be Good to Me," S.O.S. Band

List up to ten things that could be helpful to someone breaking into the business.

- Be careful of everyone you meet.
- Never sign anything without someone really explaining it to you.
- Don't worry about feeling stupid if you don't understand what a lawyer, manager, or a record company is saying. Make them explain things to you in terms you understand.
- Try your hardest to listen to their monotonous dialogue even though you'll most likely want to die of boredom during every conversation.

Ray Charles

Did you have a mentor or someone who inspired you? If so, what have you learned from that person?

A guy named Wiley Pitman owned a café in the neighborhood, nicknamed Jellyroll, near where I grew up; he's the first person to take an interest in me and expose me to the piano. He was a good piano player, and he lit a spark in me that was ready to be ignited. The experience changed my life.

What was your very first job in the music industry, and how did you get it?

Playing clubs, as early as 1946, in Jacksonville, Florida, and later Seattle, Washington, where I met my lifelong friend, Quincy Jones, and made my first album.

What was your first big break? The first great thing that ever happened to you . . .

When I moved to Seattle in the late forties, things really started to happen. That's when I became "Ray Charles" and by 1950 I had landed in L.A. and was recording songs. My first bona fide hit, "I Got a Woman," came in 1954, when I was signed with the Atlantic label, where I enjoyed many great years with my friend, Ahmet Ertegun.

What elements of your job make you want to go to work every day?

Music's in my blood, it's like breathing. I need it every day.

What qualities most helped you get to where you are today?

Passion, the love of what I'm doing. And I was determined to be a success, as I wanted to be independent despite my sight loss, which came at an early age from what I believe was glaucoma.

If you knew everything at the beginning of your career that you know now, what would you have done differently?

Not too much. I think overall things turned out pretty well, although early in my career I tried to imitate people I admired, like Nat King Cole, and that wasn't very successful. When I started singing like Ray Charles, things began to evolve.

What is your greatest lesson learned?

Be true to yourself and your own style and be in control of your work, and you'll always know where you're going. A lot of cats in the business didn't pay enough attention to the business side of things, and they paid for it later on.

What are some of your favorite albums?

Of course, some of my early Atlantic recordings and later the country stuff, which put my career on a whole new track and gave me an even bigger and broader audience. Some of my best friends in the business are country musicians, like Willie Nelson. We did some great stuff at ABC, too, and now I'm having fun recording on my own label, Crossover.

Did you have any posters on your bedroom walls as a kid? Of whom?

No. We lived in very poor circumstances, but my mother, who died when I was quite young, taught all the lessons I needed to get through life. We're building a theater in her name and honor in my hometown of Albany, Georgia.

What are some great shows you've seen?

I just did my ten thousandth concert last summer in L.A. We've played about every type of show you can imagine, everywhere in the world, so that's a tough one—I love the jazz festivals where you get to gig and visit with friends.

What are some of your favorite songs?

"I Got a Woman"   "I Can't Stop Loving You"
"What'd I Say"   "Georgia"

I love so many songs—I've always said that there are two types of music: good and bad.

List up to ten things that could be helpful to someone breaking into the business.

- Believe in yourself.
- Take your time developing a style.
- Don't worry about success, let it come naturally.
- Do it every day.
- Trust your own counsel.

Chuck D
PUBLIC ENEMY

Did you have a mentor or someone who inspired you? If so, what have you learned from that person?

I didn't have an actual mentor. Me and Hank Shocklee kind of found our way through the business of music. As college students, myself, Bill Stephney, Hank Shocklee, Harry Allen and Andre Brown, along with Tyrone Kelsey, were just mastering the dialogue, and trying to figure it out from a college viewpoint. We did have mentors who we looked at from afar. One was a college professor by the name of Andre Strobert. He was inspirational in terms of explaining some of the ins and outs of music theory and the spiritual aspect of music, from an African perspective. He was a direct influence.The engineer of our college radio station, John Schmidt, was an influence as well from the technological standpoint.

As far as my heroes, from the outside looking in, I would name James Brown, Sly Stone, and on down—the legacy.

What was your very first job in the music industry, and how did you get it?

My very first job in the business was as an artist. Unofficially in the music business, Hank Shocklee and I did everything from college radio, promoting rap music, playing gigs, doing flyers for artists, promoting clubs, and running clubs. There was a whole lot of stuff on the periphery that gave us experience and showed us how we could handle it as artists. We saw rap music and hip-hop as being a very unorganized pasture. We came in with some organization and structure and did things that were ahead of our time.

The music business isn't organized or structured toward artists; therefore they need a manager. Managers leapfrog into it from one genre and get what they got to get, and then they jump out of it. Same for record companies, same for many artists. Somebody might start out as a rapper, and then go into a more organized area of being a movie star. To me, that's a slap in the face of musicianship, which I think rap is a part of. It's all right to diversify, but people use it as a ladder or stepping-stone into more organized ventures. I think the reason they don't stick around in rap music or hip-hop, like a Dylan would stay in folk, or like a Johnny Cash would stay in country, is because rap, hip-hop, and urban music are so disorganized.

What was your first big break? The first great thing that ever happened to you . . .

My first break was when I hooked up with Hank Shocklee as part of a mobile deejay unit in 1979. Our first break together was when we decided to get with Rick Rubin and be Public Enemy with Def Jam. I was twenty-six, but you have to understand recording records was not a goal of ours. Doing radio was our goal, and recording records was a way to compensate for the lack of hip-hop on commercial radio.

What elements of your job make you want to go to work every day?

Rap was being scrutinized and wasn't being considered official music. It was the fight of the underdog from the underclass that kept me going. They didn't call it real music. Hank Shocklee and I had a goal to destroy all concepts of what organized music is.

What qualities most helped you get to where you are today?

My parents raised me as an independent thinker, so I really didn't have to rely on my peer group for acceptance. I think that's important in raising a child—you want to grow them as independent thinkers and beings, but still with the understanding that there's a world that they have to exist and coexist in. A lot of times, especially in this country, people are trained to follow instead of lead.

If you knew everything at the beginning of your career that you know now, what would you have done differently?

It's impossible to avoid the hypocrisy of lawyers. Lawyers jump sides: they're on the record company's side, then the artist's side, usually on the same day. I've never heard of a lawyer who actually lost money. They just talk about losing time. To me, lawyers are one of the downfalls of the industry. They help make the industry, but they create so many cracks and loopholes and trap doors that it's almost as impossible to deal with them as it is to deal without them.

We took careful steps in the beginning, and we dealt with what we were offered, which wasn't much. We weren't offered a serious album, or a situation that might make us a decent living. At that time, we did our best to try and get the best that we could get, as brand new artists. It's all changed now, but at the same time, I look at everything now with a keen sense of— where were you when we needed you, like at day one? The proper lawyers and accountants all come after you're worth something, or your value is higher.

What is your greatest lesson learned?

Before you get into anything, you should know about what you are getting into. Always be open to learning. You're not going to learn everything before you get in—you're going to learn as you go along, and continue to do your dues, and lead yourself along. I've never really liked it when

I've seen lawyers go from being lawyers to assuming executive positions within the music business, getting salaries and monies that artists can only hope to achieve. To me, I've always thought there was something wrong with that. I understand it is the music business, but there've been a lot of people who have come to the table that have turned the music business into the business of music.

What are some of your favorite albums?

Raisin' Hell, Run-D.M.C.
All Stetsasonic, and lots of Atlantic and Motown for sure . . .

Did you have any posters on your bedroom walls as a kid? Of whom?

Up to seventeen years old, I had athletes on my walls—basketball players, football players, baseball players. No musicians. I listened to radio and music casually. I liked music, but I wasn't a fan of music. When I was bored I listened to music from the AM pop radio when I was growing up—James Brown, Steely Dan, Led Zeppelin.

What are some great shows you've seen?

I've been on forty-nine tours in fifteen years. There's a lot of things I've seen.
Stetsasonic, Amsterdam, 1988
Run-D.M.C., Houston, 1988
James Brown, Atlanta, 2003. In performance, there is no one close, which actually makes me kind of jaded, because if I see anyone else, it's like, okay, but James Brown has the crowd going crazy. You really can't explain what you're seeing, it's like you're seven years old.

What are some of your favorite songs?

"Funky Beat," Whodini

"Black and Proud," James Brown

"Heard It Through the Grapevine,"
    Gladys Knight and the Pips

"A Change Is Gonna Come," Sam Cooke

"They Call Me Muddy Waters," Muddy Waters

Any Sly & the Family Stone

List up to ten things that could be helpful to someone breaking into the business.

■ The best thing that one can do is to go in with a team of organized people—accountants, lawyers, the artists—and try to go into the music business as a team, a self-contained team of people. When somebody has an organized team to come in and make a difference, they're less subject to being thrown for a loop by not being in the business. You know your team won't make choices just because they're more lucrative for them. That's a hard thing to ask for. Even still, there are potholes you might fall in the middle of, or maybe become victimized by collusion. There's a collusion of people in the business that stand together in whatever they've got going on.

Sean "Puffy" Combs

Did you have a mentor or someone who inspired you? If so, what have you learned from that person?

I'd have to say that I had five mentors. During the time that I was coming up, I was blessed to have some older men that wanted to teach me and pass on the legacy. I was taught a lot by Andre Harrell, Russell Simmons, Berry Gordy, Quincy Jones, and Clarence Avant. I can't say that they took me under their wing—I just showed up under their wing one day and wouldn't leave. I was very persistent, and I admired these men so much. I just kept going to them, begging for the knowledge. They all have had lengthy conversations, hours and days of teaching me, and being supportive of me, and helping me become the music man that I am today.

From them, I learned about work ethic and love of music. Right now, we have a music industry where there's not a lot of "music men," people that know the formulas of music, the formulas of a hit record, the formulas of a hit song. It's always about the song and the melody first. They all consistently taught me that. Even in this era of new marketing and new technology, at the end of the day, it's about the song. Everybody that blows up, from 50 Cent to Eminem to Celine Dion and anyone else, it's in the song. You could do all the gimmicks in the world, but if it's a hit record or a hit song, that will always overcome and stand the test of time.

What was your very first job in the music industry, and how did you get it?

I was an intern at Uptown Records. I came about it just by picking up the phone. They were my favorite label, and I would call them every day and pester them, asking for a chance to work for them for free. No one believed me at the time—this was before there were really any interns. I was in college, studying to be a doctor, and everyone was doing internships. I figured they had the same thing in the music industry. But when I called asking about internships, they really didn't know what I was talking about. So I was probably one of the first "interns," and I take pride in that.

What was your first big break? The first great thing that ever happened to you . . .

My first break was when Mary J. Blige's *What's the 411* album finished. I was in my car in New York when I heard it the first time on the radio, and I'd never heard the radio sound so good. It was the first record I had produced, and then the first remix I produced, and it sold two million records. I was like, "Whoa! Oh my God, I don't understand what just happened." I wasn't a producer, and now Jodeci's coming to talk to me. I was a little bit nervous; I had no idea how to act.

What elements of your job make you want to go to work every day?

I'm a fool in love with the industry of music. I'm a fool in love with making people dance and enjoy themselves. I provide for that—I'm obsessed with people enjoying the records that I'm involved with. I have to have that reaction; I'm addicted to people saying they like the record, that they love the record, that it makes them want to dance. Their bodies gyrating, and their bodies giving out sounds when the needle just drops on the record. That right there, I'm addicted to that. That turns me on.

What qualities most helped you get to where you are today?

I don't play any instruments. I'm the consumer. I'm the kid on the dance floor. That's how I produce, that's how I make my music, conscious of the consumer, to please the consumer, because I am one, too. I don't make it to please the critics, or my peers. I make it for people to have a good time and enjoy the song. I want to evoke some emotion, to make you dance, cry, laugh, get angry—I want something to come out of you.

If you knew everything at the beginning of your career that you know now, what would you have done differently?

There's a couple of times when I went with the business, the industry, or a couple of other executives, and didn't go with my gut and with what my body was telling me musically, in terms of how it made me feel on the dance floor. Whenever I didn't go with emotions, every time I went with the "promo" people, or the crossover staff, I lost. So now I go with my gut, and at least I feel better, whether I win or lose. It's all about your gut and your feelings.

Whenever you put the business in it, no matter what, it fucks it up. They say you have to be cost-conscious, but whenever you make decisions based on money when it comes to music, the spiritual contract gets fucked up. Music is a gift from God.

If you break down the response to music in slow motion, you'll see it's uncontrollable. They can't control their hands, their bodies, their voices. If you break it down to the slowest of slow motion, it's the craziest shit you've ever seen.

What is your greatest lesson learned?

You get out of it what you put into it. It's a once-in-a-lifetime chance. If you ever get the chance to be in it, you have to give it your all. If you strip yourself down and feel vulnerable—you're actually not vulnerable; it's you.

Whoever it is, whether it's 50 Cent, or Bruce Springsteen, or Frank Sinatra, if you go from your heart and you give it your all, you're gonna get it back. If you try to pimp the game, if you try to make money off of it, it's gonna break you. If you try to pimp it, it's gonna eventually pimp you.

What are some of your favorite albums?

> *What's Going On,* Marvin Gaye
> *America's Most Wanted,* Ice Cube

Did you have any posters on your bedroom walls as a kid? Of whom?

> Michael Jackson. That was it.

What are some great shows you've seen?

> James Brown, at the Apollo, when I was four and a half years old
> Seeing Biggie perform and rip down a stadium
> Run-D.M.C.—I saw them at Madison Square Garden at the *Fresh Fest* when I was eleven years old. When Run made everybody hold up their sneakers, all thirty thousand people, I thought, one day I want to do that.

> Ten years later, I sold out Madison Square Garden four times. I remember coming out after my intro and looking out over the audience, to the rafters, where I sat when I saw Run. I remember exactly where I'd been sitting. I almost started to cry—I didn't cry because I had to go out and perform, but it was definitely one of the deepest emotional moments for me. I had sat there, ten years before, saying I wanted to do it, and then I sold the place out four times.

List up to ten things that could be helpful to someone breaking into the business.

■ All that glitters is not gold. I am blessed to be able to do what I do; at the same time, it's a lot of hard work. It's not as easy as people think. It's emotionally draining, hugely stressful, and you have to sacrifice a lot. You have to give up a lot of yourself for this. So it depends on how much you love it. Nothing comes without a price. We can see that with everybody who becomes successful in music—so you have to make that decision, whatever price it comes with. And if you're not into it all the way, you're not going to love it. If it won't become a part of your body, your mind, your spirit—you're in the wrong game. That's the only way it relates back to you.

■ No matter all this bullshit I'm talking about right now, that sounds good, and psychologically fly, intellectually deep, and all that shit, at the end of the day, it's all about the hit record. It's always about the song. That's the most important thing for anyone to know. Everything else— all the marketing, all of the philosophy, all the points of view, all the meetings, and everything else I've said before doesn't mean shit if you don't have a hit record with a good melody.

Alice Cooper

Did you have a mentor or someone who inspired you? If so, what have you learned from that person?

Everyone in rock 'n' roll has to give credit to the Beatles. Any band, then or now, needs to sit down and dissect Beatles songs to learn how to write. You can take it in any direction after that, but the basics are the basics. Combine that with Salvador Dalí, horror movies, countless hours of mindless television, and you get an American Frankenstein named Alice Cooper.

What was your very first job in the music industry, and how did you get it?

I've been in a band since I was sixteen. It's the only job I've ever had . . . it's the only job I've ever wanted. We worked our way up from high school talent show to backyard parties to the Hollywood Bowl . . . and everything in between.

What was your first big break? The first great thing that ever happened to you . . .

Frank Zappa took a chance on us when nobody else would. He loved our absurdity, but I don't think he ever saw our commercial potential.

What elements of your job make you want to go to work every day?

I work when I want to and when I do, I'm very disciplined in it. I believe that, bottom line, you should always be a stone-cold professional. I can write about anything that I want to, and I have the freedom to be a genius or a total moron.

What qualities most helped you get to where you are today?

I never take the audience for granted, and I never take myself too seriously. I think the audience deserves every ounce of energy I have. They get my best two hours every night that I'm onstage.

If you knew everything at the beginning of your career that you know now, what would you have done differently?

I might not have drank the ocean of beer and the river of whiskey before figuring out that it was killing me. Then again, I learned a lot about myself during my alcohol days. I don't recommend it, though.

What is your greatest lesson learned?

I truly enjoy it when another artist entertains me. I can appreciate the amount of work that goes into their creations, and if it all comes together and actually works, what a miracle! It doesn't happen a lot, but I've learned that when it does, it's magic.

What are some of your favorite albums?

Strange Days, the Doors
OST, West Side Story
Fun House, Iggy and the Stooges
Having a Rave-Up, the Yardbirds
Hellbilly Deluxe, Rob Zombie

Did you have any posters on your bedroom walls as a kid? Of whom?

I had pinups of Ursula Andress, Julie Christie, and Barbarella.

What are some great shows you've seen?

Rolling Stones in 1964 on their first U.S. tour!
McCartney at the MGM Grand in 2002
Jimi Hendrix opening for the Young Rascals
John Lennon and the Doors headlining a show
    in Toronto (with Alice Cooper on the
    bill) in 1969
The Producers on Broadway
Cirque du Soleil

What are some of your favorite songs?

"Got Caught Stealing," Jane's Addiction
"My Generation," the Who
"My Sharona," the Knack
"Train Kept a Rollin'," the Yardbirds
"Help," the Beatles

List up to ten things that could be helpful to someone breaking into the business.

- Again, always be professional.
- Try and get someone with as much integrity as Shep Gordon to manage you.
- Always know where your money is.
- Never mix up politics and rock 'n' roll.
- Treat the guy who moves the amps the same way that you treat the lead guitar player.
- The minute it stops being fun, realize that you are probably in the wrong business.

Sheryl Crow

Did you have a mentor or someone who inspired you? If so, what have you learned from that person?

I had several mentors but one comes to mind. There was a man in St. Louis, when I was teaching, who picked me out of a bar band to do session work on local commercial jingles. His name was Jay Oliver, and he spent immense amounts of time working with me on working the mic, ways to train my voice to sound like other singers.

What was your very first job in the music industry, and how did you get it?

My first job in the music business was as a sometime session singer on records and jingles. Shortly after moving to L.A., I landed a job as a backup singer on the Michael Jackson *Bad* tour.

What was your first big break? The first great thing that ever happened to you . . .

I would have to say that my first real break was singing on a St. Louis local McDonald's spot that went national. The Michael Jackson tour was a huge break and singing on the Don Henley *End of the Innocence* album opened a lot of doors.

What elements of your job make you want to go to work every day?

The element of my work that motivates me to come in as often as I do is the possibility of coming up with something great. I am always inspired by the desire to write the perfect song. I also love playing!

What qualities most helped you get to where you are today?

The qualities most helpful in achieving success have been the love of learning and the desire to improve. I also love playing music and writing.

If you knew everything at the beginning of your career that you know now, what would you have done differently?

There is nothing I would do differently in my career because I believe all things are perfect.

What is your greatest lesson learned?

My greatest lesson learned in life is to not lose sight of what's important. A career does not make a life. Love is where it's at.

What are some of your favorite albums?

Let It Bleed, the Rolling Stones
Freewheelin', Bob Dylan
Kind of Blue, Miles David
Only the Lonely, Frank Sinatra
Rubber Soul, the Beatles

Sign O' the Times, Prince
All Things Must Pass, George Harrison
Saturday Night Fever
Axis: Bold as Love, Jimi Hendrix Experience

Did you have any posters on your bedroom walls as a kid? Of whom?

Frampton Comes Alive, Boston, Linda Ronstadt (wearing cutoffs, looking in fridge), and Fleetwood Mac's *Rumours.*

What are some great shows you've seen?

Stevie and Joe Walsh, 1980
Frampton, 1975 (mainly because I was thirteen)

What are some of your favorite songs?

"Yesterday," the Beatles
"Tempted," Squeeze
"Don't Think Twice, It's All Right,"
   Bob Dylan
"Old Man," Neil Young
"Gimme Shelter" and "Wild Horses,"
   the Rolling Stones

"Good Morning Heartache"
   and "God Bless the Child,"
   Billie Holiday
"Into Temptation," Crowded House

List up to ten things that could be helpful to someone breaking into the business.

- Be diligent. Do not let rejection set you back.
- Be disciplined—work on your craft a little every day. (This may not be helpful to breaking into the business directly, but in the long run it will help everything indirectly.)
- Don't limit yourself to just what you think you're good at.
- Get a vocabulary—influences can shape a voice.
- Stick to your guns.
- Tell yourself there's no one doing anything more important than you—eventually you will believe it.

- Find one person to run interference for you that you trust (usually a manager or lawyer). Trust is crucial!
- Read—read—read!! (But not trade papers or mags.)
- Be a rock star! No one will believe you if you don't.
- Get the best choreographer money can buy! (Kidding!)

Jonathan Davis

KORN

Did you have a mentor or someone who inspired you? If so, what have you learned from that person?

I remember watching the Doors movies a lot when I was a kid, and actually, funny enough, Andrew Lloyd Webber. Watching *Jesus Christ Superstar* made me realize I wanted to make music. It's funny, they're such extremes, but that musical is such a rocking musical. I loved all of his shit so that was the first thing that inspired me to be in music, and then the rock star aspect of it was watching the Doors and Led Zeppelin back in the day when rock 'n' roll was so thick and so cool.

What was your very first job in the music industry, and how did you get it?

It was with the band. Well, that's in the recording industry. My dad owned a music store, so that started when I was a kid. My first music gig was playing with my dad and his band back when I was five. I started playing drums when I was three years old, and I could actually make beats and shit, so by the time I was five I was kicking ass. He'd have me come up and play in the bars, and the bars would be cool with it. So I'd come in and play a couple songs with him and didn't want to leave 'cuz I got to hang out with Pops. After all the gigs had stopped he opened up the music store, and I learned to play a gazillion instruments 'cuz he had a music school there. Learned the guitar, bass, took some drum lessons, bagpipes, fucked around with all the other instruments like the violin, clarinet, saxophone. It was really about whatever I wanted that day because we had the music school with twenty teachers so there were lessons going on all the time.

What was your first big break? The first great thing that ever happened to you . . .

Our big, big break was when we played down in San Diego at a music conference in Ocean Beach and the surrounding areas. That's when Paul Pontius came out to see us. He'd been watching us for a while. He came out and introduced himself to us, and that's what started the whole thing toward getting a deal. Another defining moment was when we sold out the Whiskey. That was before we got signed, in '93. We just thought we were the shit, selling the Whiskey out.

Our first show as Korn we played at a tittie bar in Anaheim called California Dreams. We played to like fifteen people, but that was awesome. It was our first show. There's nothing like the early days when you're first on the road. I remember when we finally went up to the studio and realized "this is real." Signing that contract . . . I puked. We were at our lawyer's office, and I threw up when we signed the record contract. That was fucking funny.

What elements of your job make you want to go to work every day?

I love just being able to do what I love and get paid for it. I love being able to go out and see the world, and play music. A lot of opportunities have opened up for me, too, to do things like orchestral scoring for movies. I just love entertainment, the whole ball of wax. I love it all.

What qualities most helped you get to where you are today?

Never letting anyone get me down and believing that what we were doing was something special. Forcing it down people's throats even if they didn't accept it. I think that when we were coming up, no one was playing our kind of music. No one had ever heard the kind of music we were doing. The only other band out there like us was the Deftones, and that was it. Us being the harder of the two at the time, it was really, really difficult, and people were like, "Hell no, we'd never fucking sign this. This music is satanic." It was just us being persistent and just going out there and hitting the streets and proving to people that this was the shit and that people liked it.

If you knew everything at the beginning of your career that you know now, what would you have done differently?

Nothing, really. I think looking back everything that happened to us happened for a reason, which propelled us to the next level. Honestly. It's fun, looking back on that and everything we've accomplished when turning the whole music genre around, and helping create a whole new kind of music genre. It's pretty incredible. I trip out when I think about it.

What is your greatest lesson learned?

I think the greatest lesson I learned is, don't ever think you're untouchable, that you're always going to be the shit. Don't stop working. Don't think that it's always going to be this way, and that you don't have to work as hard to keep it. You've always gotta be on your shit and always work hard 'cuz it's not always going to happen the way you want it to.

What are some of your favorite albums?

I really don't listen that much. I'm not really a huge music fan. I play it, and I create it ten hours of the day and after, I get to hear silence.

Rio, *Duran Duran*

2LiveCrew Is What We Are, 2 Live Crew—It changed my life the first time I heard it. They were so fucking nasty and vulgar it was just awesome.

Vulgar Display of Power, Pantera—That made me want to get into heavy music.

Albums by Adam Ant, Flock of Seagulls, Human League, Led Zeppelin

Did you have any posters on your bedroom walls as a kid? Of whom?

Mötley Crüe, the Cult, Christian Death. A bunch of fucking witchcraft posters. I was getting all into black magic and shit. It was really difficult because at that time I was living with my father and he became really religious. They all had to come down because I was listening to the music of the devil.

What are some great shows you've seen?

Rage Against the Machine, Ozzie, Metallica

What are some of your favorite songs?

There are no songs that really stick out in my head. I love the eighties and some nineties stuff.

List up to ten things that could be helpful to someone breaking into the business.

- Get your band together.
- Spread everything equally. Don't try to have one favorite, 'cuz that always ends up with jealousy and that'll make your band break up.
- Get together and write and make sure you have good music. If you're really good, then people will come and see it, and it will sell. It's not that hard. If it sucks, then that's not gonna happen. I see lots of bands out there that are just totally fucking horrible and they keep going and keep going, and it's just not there. You know when you've got something that's fucking the shit. I remember when we started Korn I thought, "This is gonna go somewhere." I never believed in my wildest fantasy that it would go, like, this big, but I knew we had something. It was just about being persistent and playing and playing and playing and passing out handbills and flyering and stickering shit and just tons of self promotion. We created interest in ourselves, 'cuz that would spark people to go, "Who the hell is Korn?" I remember we had stickers everywhere, all over California. Our rehearsal studio had a screen-printing business in the back of the studio, so we'd just pull stickers all night. We'd stay up partying and pull stickers. And then we'd go out and slap them on signposts and stuff. Anywhere our sticker could go, we did it. It created a buzz about us, and people were saying, "Who the fuck is this Korn band?" And then we started putting flyers on every car, I mean we shamelessly self-promoted ourselves like a motherfucker. And after every show we'd go out and hand out samplers, and we'd just be everywhere. So that's really the biggest thing. Self-promote and do everything possible.

■ If you want it bad enough you can make anything happen. Just work work work work, and that's what we did. It's weird, just getting signed in the beginning, once we got in and we went back on the road we were out in vans, and then we moved on to a 1945 Eagle bus. And we just played show after show after show after show and did not stop. We kept going for two years straight and did, like, 320 shows in a year. We just played, played played played played, whatever we could get. We were on tours and we would do one-offs, we'd go to radio stations, and we'd do whatever we could possibly do to make it work. And all that hard work paid off. It was a bitch. Seriously a bitch when you're getting fucked up, too.

Mike Diamond
THE BEASTIE BOYS

Did you have a mentor or someone who inspired you? If so, what have you learned from that person?

I'm still looking for one. We had the good luck and good fortune of having a succession of different people that helped us out in different ways and taught us things. From David Parsons, who put out our first record on Rat Cage, to Rick Rubin and Russell and so many others. As inspirations, I'd mention my older brothers, New York City and its music and culture, and close friends who came to include my future bandmates.

What was your very first job in the music industry, and how did you get it?

I had other shitty jobs to support myself outside of playing music, but my very first job in the music industry was playing in the Beastie Boys. I came about it from just being friends with Adam Yauck and John Berry, from hanging out and going to shows, and then wanting to start our own band.

What was your first big break? The first great thing that ever happened to you . . .

Our first break was basically at our first show ever. It was at Adam Yauck's sixteenth or seventeenth birthday at this loft on the Upper West Side. Dave Parsons had a punk-rock record store at the time in downtown Manhattan called Rat Cage. Dave was at the party, and he came up to us afterwards and said, "Hey, if you guys want to record a record, I'll put it out." That was our first gig ever, and our first break. We'd been making music together for two or three days.

What elements of your job make you want to go to work every day?

I feel very fortunate and very grateful to be in the position of working with two really good friends and my collaborators. I feel grateful that every day I come to work and collaborate with my best friends, and we have a platform to do what we do and have a lot of fun doing it, and at the same time, we can comment on things that are going on in our lives, whether they're personal things or at a worldwide kind of level.

What qualities most helped you get to where you are today?

Having an eye for detail. But basically there has to be nothing else you could possibly do. Otherwise, it's just too hard, it's not worth it. It's too hard a path to take unless you believe that it's completely what you were meant to be doing. I'm not a good example of this, though, because our commitment to music in the beginning was like fans. We were playing for enjoyment, and fairly quickly it got to the point where we were not only doing it for enjoyment but also to support ourselves. I look at us as such a rare exception. I have so many friends who both tried and tried and tried and never succeeded, and tried and tried and tried and did succeed. Either way, they had to be completely beyond committed, and had complete commitment and focus in their actions toward making music.

If you knew everything at the beginning of your career that you know now, what would you have done differently?

First off, I am a real believer in that whatever actions or mistakes we may have made were necessary ones to get to the point where we're at now. That being said, my main advice, what the three of us try to do, is to try to be really open with each other as a band and to put each other first, ahead of all other business influences. I think that's a policy that has served and continues to serve us well, but it took a minute for us to arrive at that as the number-one rule.

What is your greatest lesson learned?

My greatest lesson learned as a musician is to always try to treat people well, whoever they are and whatever they're doing, at whatever level they might be. It doesn't matter where they are, but you have to treat people well.

What are some of your favorite albums?

Cut, the Slits

Attitude: The ROIR Sessions, Bad Brains

There's a Riot Going On,
   Sly & the Family Stone

Run-D.M.C., Run-D.M.C.

Talking Book, Stevie Wonder

Did you have any posters on your bedroom walls as a kid? Of whom?

Isaac Hayes and the Beatles (from the *White Album*).

What are some great shows you've seen?

The Commodores, Bob Marley and the Wailers, and Kurtis Blow, Madison Square Garden, New
   York City, 1979
The Clash, the Palladium, New York City
Bad Brains, CBGB, New York City

What are some of your favorite songs?

"Forever Young," Bob Dylan

"Across the Universe" or "It's All
Too Much," the Beatles

"Bring the Noise," Public Enemy

"10 Zillion Light Years," Stevie Wonder

"Get Up, Stand Up," Bob Marley

List up to ten things that could be helpful to someone breaking into the business.

- Be kind and compassionate (why dis when you can be nice?).
- Think of others before you think of yourself. Though this may seem the antithesis of getting ahead in business, this works in business and life alike.
- Don't wait for someone else to tell you what to do. Be motivated at every moment to do whatever it is that needs doing.
- If someone—your boss, senior, supervisor, whatever—asks you to do something, don't ever fail in getting the task done. If you do, that's fine—but you need to let them know. Remember, these people consider something to be done after they asked once.
- Be honest. Lies only tend to more lies and then to distrust, etc.
- Be on time. Believe me. I am still working on this one. Being late is disrespectful to anyone else you are meeting. When you don't show up on time you're basically telling the other person that your time is more important than theirs.
- Focus. It is very easy to be overwhelmed. Break things down and focus intensely on one thing at a time.
- Treat all beings well and equally because (a) this is the right thing to do, and (b) the people that are today's messengers, waiters, assistants, etc., are tomorrow's stars, CEOs, managers, etc.

Celine Dion

Did you have a mentor or someone who inspired you? If so, what have you learned from that person?

My mother has been my mentor. She continues to inspire me in everything I do. Raising fourteen children with very little money and in a happy household is something that everyone can look up to. When we were growing up in Quebec, both my mother and father devoted every single moment of their lives to make sure that our household was filled with joy, sharing, and love.

What was your first job in the music industry, and how did you get it?

My one and only job in the music industry has been as a singer. I had been singing since I was five years old, mostly with my brothers and sisters at family gatherings and parties. Music was always a big part of our family . . . everyone sang or played an instrument, so it was quite an amazing time when we all got together to entertain each other. We also used to perform at my mom and dad's restaurant, which was a lot of fun, and the customers enjoyed this.

What was your first big break? The first great thing that ever happened to you . . .

I've had so many lucky breaks throughout my career. Perhaps the one that's the easiest to identify was when I had the chance to sing "Beauty and the Beast" with Peabo Bryson. The film was big, I had a chance to work with Disney, and it was my first opportunity to appear on the Academy Awards. After this, I guess you could say that singing at the Opening Celebrations at the 1996 Olympics in Atlanta was a huge break, because the whole world was watching!   This was a huge thrill . . . one that I will never forget.

What elements of your job make you want to go to work every day?

I love to sing, to be onstage and to touch people with my music. I realize that this is a tremendous gift that I have received, and I never lose touch with this. I'm also very fortunate to be surrounded with a great team of people who really care about doing the best that they can for me and for themselves, and this motivates me to give everything I've got to my work. These are the things that make me want to go to work every day.

What qualities most helped you get to where you are today?

Hard work and discipline are the two most important elements that got me where I am today. I know it's not just about having talent, although this is a big part of it. I have to keep my voice in shape, which means a lot of sacrifices along the way. Also, to have faith and belief in what you are doing is something that I've found to be very important in going on with your dreams. None of what we've accomplished would have happened if we didn't believe in ourselves, no matter how many people doubt you along the way.

If you knew everything at the beginning of your career that you know now, what would you have done differently?

I wouldn't have changed a thing, and I don't mean to sound pretentious by this. I'm very happy with the way my career has unfolded. I never dreamed that things would have turned out the way they did. All I wanted to do was to be able have the chance to sing for as many people as possible. I didn't have specific career goals . . . just to be able to sing—that's all. I think most singers feel this way. I feel very fortunate with what's happened to me . . . .and I'm very grateful for this.

What is your greatest lesson learned?

To give the best of yourself at all times. Whether this is singing, or playing sports, or having a meeting, or being a parent. Give everything you've got, and just by doing this, you are succeeding.

List up to ten things that could be helpful to someone breaking into the business.

- Follow your dreams.
- Believe in yourself.
- Keep your voice in shape.
- Surround yourself with the best people.
- Respect everyone's opinion, but do what's best for your heart as well.

Kenneth "Babyface" Edmonds

Did you have a mentor or someone who inspired you? If so, what have you learned from that person?

I started off really into Stevie Wonder and the Jackson 5. Also, my older brother, Melvin, was in a band. That's what kind of started it. There wasn't really a person who guided me throughout my career.

What was your very first job in the music industry, and how did you get it?

In sixth grade, I sang onstage with my brother in his band. They were going to play Top 40 at the mixer, and they needed someone to sing the Michael Jackson parts. At the time, my voice was high and similar to Michael's, so I got that part, and that's what got me started. But then the real bite came when the Jackson 5 visited Indianapolis. They were filming the *Going Back to Indiana* special, and I saw the concert standing backstage . . . that was it!

What was your first big break? The first great thing that ever happened to you . . .

There have been a series of things over the years. You get little breaks and little things open up. I got my first record deal back in 1978 with a group called Manchild, which was a regional group. We were signed to Carl Davis's Chi-Sound records in Chicago. We did a couple of albums on the label, which didn't quite happen and ultimately fell apart. That break didn't ultimately lead to anything, but nevertheless it was the first break.

Looking back, a break is also when you get into a good Top 40 band and are able to learn your trade. Before Manchild I had a band in high school. After Manchild I started another little group that didn't work. I ended up joining a group called the Crowd Pleasers, which was pure Top 40. That was perfect for me because I was doing a lot of writing then: The best way to learn to write a hit song is to play everybody else's stuff. So I was up in Michigan playing Top 40 in different cities.

The next break came when I ended up going to Cincinnati, Ohio, to help Midnight Star record a song that I had written—a song called "Slow Jam." That was another break because in doing that, I was able to meet Antonio "L.A." Reid and the rest of the guys on The Deele. I reintroduced myself to them, and I ended up working with them—helping them write songs and getting a demo together for their group. After I finished doing the demos, and they worked to get a deal, they asked me to join the group, although I wasn't a part of the package when they originally got the deal. So that was another break. Breaks come in all shapes and sizes. Many times there's not one big break. For my career, it's been a series of breaks.

What elements of your job make you want to go to work every day?

I love doing what I do . . . writing music. And I love working with artists and creating music. So that makes it really easy. What makes me not want to work is when I run into the hassles that can come with it, and the politics that come with being on a label as an artist and also being the writer, producer, and businessman. It can be difficult, but ultimately the love of music seems to override it all.

What qualities most helped you get to where you are today?

Persistence. Not giving in, even when things are bad. I just keep going, keep believing that it is going to work out. But the other side is ego—being careful of your ego. Be honest with yourself and honest with your music. If people aren't liking something that you're doing, then try to figure out what it is that they don't like about it, and don't necessarily think that because *you* think it's great, that it is great. Try to figure out what you can do to make it better.

If you knew everything at the beginning of your career that you know now, what would you have done differently?

It's been such a long road that it's hard to say, because everything had something to do with the next thing. It's not like one particular door took me to another door. I could say I would do this differently, but if I had, maybe I wouldn't be standing here today. The only thing I can say is that at the very beginning, I wish I had studied a little more and had been better prepared musically. I wish I had paid a little more attention to music theory in school. I can read a little bit, but I'm not totally on it. I wish sometimes that I'd gone to school and studied classical, so I'd be more prepared for things like scoring. These are things a person can always pick up, but I think ultimately, if I'd studied piano early on, it would have been invaluable. I know a lot of amazing players where I say to myself, "Boy, if I could play like you I would be unstoppable." On the other hand, I think part of the gift is not being able to play like them—I'm able to hear more clearly because of that.

What is your greatest lesson learned?

Have patience. We all get anxious, and we all want things to happen, but sometimes it takes a while. I've been in the business since 1978. Things didn't happen for me till I was almost thirty. Be patient . . . and persistent. It worked for me. It doesn't mean it's going to work for everybody, no matter how great you are. It's hard to hook up with that *right* person who is going to make all the difference.

What are some of your favorite albums?

Fulfillingness' First Finale and *Talking Book,* Stevie Wonder
Thriller, Michael Jackson
White Album, the Beatles

Did you have any posters on your bedroom walls as a kid? Of whom?

Jackson 5.

What are some great shows you've seen?

The Jackson 5 when they performed in Indianapolis. I've seen a lot of people, and I've appreciated a lot of shows in my life, but I think that was the best one, because that was the first concert I'd even been to.

What are some of your favorite songs?

I listen to so many things. I appreciate great artists and melody. I'm as much of a Frank Sinatra fan as I am an Elvis fan or a Stevie Wonder fan, or a fan of Nat King Cole!

I also love the Glenn Miller Orchestra, Duke Ellington, and Count Basie.

There is also great country music—Conway Twitty tunes or Willie Nelson tunes. It's hard for me to name the ultimate songs. You just know if it's good and it touches you.

List up to ten things that could be helpful to someone breaking into the business.

- The reality today, as difficult as it may seem, is that it's actually easier now to break into the business because of where music is and because of technology.
- The biggest problem musicians used to have was finding a studio. That was it. No studio . . . nowhere to make your demo. Now, with computers, it is changing drastically. My advice would be to learn them and take advantage of them.

Missy Elliott

Did you have a mentor or someone who inspired you? If so, what have you learned from that person?

Mary J. Blige was the one who inspired me. From her I learned to never be like someone else, to always be creative, and to stand my ground. When you're a true artist, no one can tell you your vision but yourself.

What was your very first job in the music business, and how did you get it?

My very first job in the music industry was becoming a writer. The first record that I wrote was for Aaliyah, a job that I got through Craig Kallman at Atlantic. He heard some music I had done previously before coming out as Missy Elliott, and he decided to give me a shot at doing one record with Aaliyah, which led to eight records.

What was your first big break? The first great thing that ever happened to you . . .

My first break was when Sean "Puffy" Combs (Puff Daddy at the time) asked me to do a rhyme on a Jenna Thompson album he produced.

The first great thing that ever happened was when I was able to buy my mother a nice brick house. That was the greatest thing that ever happened to me.

What elements of your job make you want to go to work every day?

The love of music. The people I am surrounded by who give me positive energy to keep doing what I do. When I get the chance to win awards, and see that my work isn't in vain—those are the things that make me want to continue to get up and go to the studio.

What qualities most helped you get to where you are today?

My humbleness, because no matter how high I've gotten, or what goals I've achieved, I still know that you can go back to being broke, you can go back to nobody remembering what you did or who you are. I try to stay humble and help people in any way I can. I think that has helped me, and will continue to help me get to further heights.

If you knew everything in the beginning of your career that you know now, what would you have done differently?

I wouldn't have done anything differently because I feel that all the things I did helped me get here. Whether it was good or bad I learned something. When you go through bad situations you learn how to deal with them next time, so I wouldn't change anything in my career.

What is your greatest lesson learned?

Make sure that you know about your contracts, the business side of it. It's fine and dandy to have people love you and scream your name, but when you're out there working hard it's so important that your contracts are right so you can get out of situations and get paid for what you're doing. A lot of time you're so happy that you got a deal that you don't think about the contracts until later, when you've blown up as an artist. Then you go ask—where's this at, and what happened to that? All of those things should come in the beginning, before the signing.

What are some of your favorite albums?

Michael Jackson, Janet Jackson, Prince, Hall and Oates, Madonna, Beyoncé, Chaka Khan, Al Green

Did you have any posters on your bedroom walls as a kid? Of whom?

A lot of New Edition, Salt-N-Pepa, Michael Jackson, MC Lyte, Eric B. & Rakim, a lot of rappers . . .

What are some great shows you've seen?

Janet Jackson   Madonna   Cher

What are some of your favorite songs?

"Work It," Missy Elliott; "Saving All My Love," Whitney Houston; "Goodbye," Guy; "Wanna Be Startin' Somethin'," Michael Jackson (and all Michael Jackson records); "Like a Virgin," Madonna; "Me, Myself, and I," Beyoncé

List up to ten things that could be helpful to someone breaking into the business.

- Anybody who wants to break into the business should know if it's what they really want to do. This business is a lot harder than what you might see on TV. If you want to be a successful artist, music is probably 95 percent work, and only 5 percent play.
- Once you get in the business, you have to have a great attitude because you come across the same people again and again.
- Pay respect to the people who were in this game before you.
- Once again, you have to make sure that your contracts are right. Know all about your royalties.
- Get very familiar with the people who are handling your projects so you can let them know your vision—but have control over your projects.
- Try to stay as far out of trouble as you can because you can lose a lot of fans that way.
- Be yourself—that's how you last in this business.
- Stay creative—let there be no boundaries holding you back from something you want to do.

Gloria Estefan

Did you have a mentor or someone who inspired you? If so, what have you learned from that person?

I would have to say that one of the people that I most admire is my grandmother. She has passed from this life but continues to inspire me on a daily basis. She was ahead of her time, strong, spiritual, loving, and a human dynamo. Although she was born in Cuba in 1905 her dream was to one day become a lawyer. When she had to leave school at a very young age in order to help her mother raise her twelve brothers and sisters, she taught herself how to read and write. She arrived in this country in her late fifties and with her incredible culinary skills began a catering business that would make her financially independent and allowed her to buy her own home and help countless people along the way. She always told me that regardless of how I might try to avoid getting into the music business because I was a painfully shy performer, I would somehow end up doing this as my life's work because it was a gift, and my calling was to share it with the world. I guess she was right after all.

What was your very first job in the music business, and how did you get it?

My first (and only) job in the music industry happened by chance or destiny, depending on your point of view. I was invited to be a part of a band (for one night only) by a friend that attended the brother school to my (all-girl) Catholic high school. His father worked with a man who had created the band, Miami Latin Boys, which had been together for over a year and was playing successfully all around Miami. He asked this man, Emilio Estefan, to come to our rehearsal and give us some pointers. Emilio gave us his thoughts and left. We played our gig and went on to our various activities; mine was working at Miami International Airport as an interpreter as part of my college work-study program. A few months later I attended a wedding where Emilio's band was playing. He remembered me and asked me to sit in with the band for a couple of songs. He asked me to join the band that night, but I told him I didn't think that was possible due to my job and full load at school. He tracked me down a couple of weeks later and asked me again, emphasizing that this would only entail weekends and a couple of nights of rehearsal a week. I joined the band purely for fun and the love of music. One year later we changed the name to Miami Sound Machine because we weren't the "Latin Boys" any longer.

What was your first big break? The first great thing that ever happened to you . . .

Since I was in the band purely for fun everything that happened to me was wonderful! But as time went on and our popularity grew, Emilio asked me to write some original material because he was thinking of cutting a record. He was ready to finance it himself, but a small local label became interested and signed us to a record deal. We cut our first album in 1976. Although it was bilingual, the first hit was in Spanish. It became very popular in the Spanish markets in the United States, taking us from being a local "gig band" to doing concerts in fifty-thousand-seat stadiums all over Latin America. Our big break in English came seven years later when we recorded the song "Dr. Beat" and put it on our seventh album, which was out on the CBS record label. We made our own twelve-inch remix and took it to all the clubs and record pools ourselves. Somehow it got exported and before we knew it, we had a number-one single all over Europe, and the album was at the top of the charts as well.

What elements of your job make you want to go to work every day?

My favorite thing about this career is that, through my music, I have the ability to touch the hearts and minds of people that I will probably never meet. Also, when I perform for my fans I have the opportunity to make them forget their troubles for a while and can inspire them in a positive way. It makes me very happy to know that songs that I've created and sung will be a part of the sound track to someone's life.

What qualities most helped you get to where you are today?

I believe that the qualities that were useful in achieving our dream were perseverance, integrity, patience, believing in ourselves, and making every decision while thinking of our long-term goals and for the love of what we do instead of simply for a short-term gain.

If you knew everything at the beginning of your career that you know now, what would you have done differently?

I can truly say that based on what we know now we would do absolutely nothing differently.

What is your greatest lesson learned?

I believe my greatest lesson learned is to enjoy every moment along the way, even when you're doing things that may not be your favorite thing to do, and be as expressive as possible whenever the opportunity arises.

What are some of your favorite albums?

I guess the past had a very strong impact on me:

Tapestry, Carole King

Innervisions, Stevie Wonder

Catch Bull at Four, Cat Stevens

Goodbye Yellow Brick Road, Elton John

Pretty much anything by the Beatles

Did you have any posters on your bedroom walls as a kid? Of whom?

I never had any posters of anyone up in my room. To me the "stars" have always been the songs themselves. Music has been cathartic in my life and has helped me through many difficult situations. I'm very eclectic in my musical taste and love listening to many artists but have never really idolized anyone.

What are some great shows you've seen?

I love seeing people perform live wherever they may be performing. I will always stop to watch, even street performers if they are really into what they are doing. My first concert was Earth, Wind & Fire. They were incredible, and I had a truly multisensory experience at their show. I once saw Paul Anka, and he was so personable and down-to-earth that I was blown away. I left his show *feeling* something for him rather than just being entertained.

What are some of your favorite songs?

It's impossible to have favorite songs when I love music so much and it makes me feel so many emotions, but I can share some highlights. The first song that made me cry was "El Ruiseñor" by a child singer-actor from Spain named Joselito. He was also my first crush. I was three years old. I remember getting goose bumps while listening to "Ferry Cross the Mersey" by Gerry & the Pacemakers when I was six. My mom and I were pulling into a Laundromat and the song came on the radio. To this day, when I hear that song I smell that dry, clean smell of a Laundromat. "Hold Me, Thrill Me, Kiss Me" by Mel Carter also did something to my heart when I heard it, as did "Summer Breeze" by Seals & Crofts. I also love "It's Over" by Level 42, "Man in the Mirror" by Michael Jackson, "Wonderful World" by Louis Armstrong, "Hot Fun in the Summertime" by Sly & the Family Stone—the list is endless.

List up to ten things that could be helpful to someone breaking into the business.

- Whatever you do, do it for the love of the music.
- Sharpen your tools and prepare as best you can by taking lessons.

- Don't listen to anyone who tells you that something you want to do "will never work."
- Study an alternate career that would also make you happy if you couldn't make a living with music.
- An artist will create whether he's financially successful or not, so never stop creating.

Melissa Etheridge

Did you have a mentor or someone who inspired you? If so, what have you learned from that person?

Well, I grew up in Kansas, so there wasn't a lot of music business around. The one person who really helped me in my life, and in the way I conduct myself in my business, would be my father. As I went into the entertainment world when I was very young, even though he was not in the business, he would always say to me, "Always respect your audience, always be grateful that they have come to hear you because they don't have to come to hear you." He always instilled in me a gratefulness to those I work with and those who actually pay the money to come see me.

A couple people helped me out a lot in the business. One was my manager, Bill Leopold, who's been my manager for twenty years. He's not an artist, but creatively he let me do what I do, which is great. He really mentored me and guided me in my business.

The other would be Chris Blackwell, who finally signed me. He helped me as an artist—to believe in myself, to believe in my work, to believe in what I was doing my whole career, not to worry about whether my music can be played on the radio, to let radio come to me. He was just awesome. He was the man in charge of my records, and the kind of guy you'd want behind you.

What was your very first job in the music industry, and how did you get it?

First time I got paid was when I got up and sang with a country band in Leavenworth, Kansas. It was at the Knights of Columbus. It was a Parents Without Partners dance and I got up in their first set and sang a couple of the Redland Tammy Wynette songs. They paid me ten bucks. I was about twelve or thirteen, so it was like *"whoo-hoo,* this is the way to go!"

I had been in a talent show that became a variety show that would play around town for money. They had played with some other artists, and heard me and said, "We do these gigs, why don't you come sing with us." So I went up and sang, my dad came with me, and that was the beginning of my record career.

What was your first big break? The first great thing that ever happened to you . . .

It's funny because I never had the big, huge break. Everything took so long. Now I look back on it, and I'm glad because it's given me a long career. First I got a break as a songwriter. I got signed to a publishing deal, as a songwriter. I would go work at A&M. Lance Freed at A&M signed me, but A&M Records wasn't interested in me. I was halfway to where I wanted to be. And then I got signed finally, after five years, to a record deal, after being turned down by everyone in town. And then it took me a year to make the record, and then once you make it, does it come out? It's just this road that I was always on. I think I stopped and finally went "Whoa! I did it!" in about 1994 when I was doing my *Unplugged* and Bruce Springsteen came out and sang a song with me.

What elements of your job make you want to go to work every day?

It is such a changing business atmosphere. Nothing is for sure, nothing is forever. It's just like a big ride, and you gotta hang in there 'cuz you love it. I can't do anything else. I love it. . . . I'd be sitting in a bar still playing if none of the wonderful stuff had happened.

What qualities most helped you get to where you are today?

My father's telling me to appreciate it all, to really know that people don't have to come see you, people don't have to listen to you. Be grateful, always be grateful, whether there's five people or five hundred in the audience. I've always appreciated other people's talents that have worked with me. I think my father giving me that sense of gratitude has really helped me ride the ups and downs of this business.

If you knew everything at the beginning of your career that you know now, what would you have done differently?

I only have one small choice that I regret. It has to do with Springsteen. He and I sang "Thunder Road" on *Unplugged.* Afterwards his people asked me if they could include that on the flip side of the single "Secret Garden." And there was a feud between his record company and my record company, and my record company asked me to say no. And I did, and I regret that. Of course, none of those people exist anymore in my record company—it was for no reason other than the ego of my record company. That is the one choice that I made that I regret because I really would have loved that. He's my hero, but I let the business overshadow the music.

What is your greatest lesson learned?

To do it because you love it. And if you can do it and never make a dime and never have recognition, then you're doing it for the right reason. Then, there's the chance that the truth in your work might appeal to someone, anyone, masses, parts of masses.

What are some of your favorite albums?

Born to Run, Bruce Springsteen

Tapestry, Carole King

Tommy, The London Symphony Orchestra. It was a two-album set, it was wicked. I used to listen to that every day . . . they thought I was stunted.

Pirates, Rickie Lee Jones

Did you have any posters on your bedroom walls as a kid? Of whom?

I was *so* not the pin-up girl. . . . It was more like, Why don't I like the Bee Gees? Why don't I like
Leif, you know, all those people . . . and why am I so attracted to Lindsay Wagner?

I did have black-light posters on my wall. I had those wicked, fuzzy posters you get at WalMart
that had all the different colors under the black light. I wasn't even smoking anything, I was
just looking at the posters.

I never had an idol. I wanted so badly to be in that world that it would be painful to put it up on
my wall. I would listen to *Born to Run,* to Bruce Springsteen, but I didn't have pictures of him.
I wanted to be him.

What are some great shows you've seen?

We didn't get to see many in Kansas. . . .

I saw the Eagles touring right before *Hotel California,* and that was just so amazing. It was
when Randy Meisner was with them, and Joe had just joined them. I was spellbound.

Also, Peter Frampton's *Frampton Comes Alive.*

What are some of your favorite songs?

"Jungleland," Bruce Springsteen

"In Your Eyes," Peter Gabriel

"Behind Blue Eyes," the Who

"Piece of My Heart," Janis Joplin

List up to ten things that could be helpful to someone breaking into the business.

I believe the best thing an artist can do is play for everyone, all the time, anytime, anywhere.
You always learn something every single time you get up in front of people to play. There is
nothing like that. You could sit in your room, and you could be in your head, or on your computer, and create all the music and do all that, but until you present it live, real, in front of
people, you'll always be the artist in your bedroom. In this world, the only thing they can't sell
on the Internet is your Self, your being. You want people to want to come see you. So it's maintaining your individuality and not just being a recording. Be an artist and a person.

Eve

Did you have a mentor or someone who inspired you? If so, what have you learned from that person?

My inspiration was the attention I got being a girl and rapping in high school. Of course, I had people that I loved, like Queen Latifah, MC Lyte, and Salt-N-Pepa. I looked at those girls and realized I wanted to be doing the same thing. I started listening to them when I was eleven or twelve. I had a young aunt that lived with me, and she would play them—L.L., Fresh Prince, etc.—so I grew up with them.

What was your very first job in the music industry, and how did you get it?

When I turned fourteen or fifteen I had my first partner, and we did an album together. That was our dream—we completed an album and we had a manager. That was my first job in the local music industry.

Dre was my first deal. I did a demo for him, and he put one of my songs on the *Bulworth* sound track. I was excited about that, I guess that was my first thing.

What was your first big break? The first great thing that ever happened to you . . .

When I went to Ruff Ryder's and did some songs with DMX and the whole family. That's when people started to notice me.

When my first song was on the radio, and I had my first video out—if I walked down the street people would yell, "You're that girl! You're that girl!" When people start coming up to you, that is the craziest thing. It's a great feeling, though, especially when people really start liking your music. You feel like, I'm doing what I want to do, but at the same time, a lot of people like my music—not just me!

What elements of your job make you want to go to work every day?

You've got to love what you do. There's a lot of political stuff involved beyond being an artist. There's just so much to make you want to give up, but if you love it, you just can't stop. For me, this is my first love. I just love the process of making songs. I love going into the studio with the producer and talking about an idea, hearing the first drum pattern, and then hearing the music, sitting and writing lyrics, going in the booth, putting the lyrics to the song, and then having a song. The experience of building a song is the best thing ever.

What qualities most helped you get to where you are today?

I am very determined and ambitious. Those are two words that I use all the time. I always set goals for myself—I don't write them down, though; I know what I want, and I know what I feel like I need to have in my life.

If you knew everything at the beginning of your career that you know now, what would you have done differently?

I don't regret anything. Sometimes the things you don't know, help you. You have to go through it yourself.

Everything is a learning experience. Everything that I went through, I went through to get to where I am now. So many things in my life were complete lessons, and no matter what mistakes I made, I think I made them to get to this point.

What is your greatest lesson learned?

There's always another person around you, whether it be a manager, or the producer, or the head of the record company—but you have to trust your instincts. Be you. Being an artist is really hard. A lot of people don't get it. A lot of people are corporate, and they don't get it at all, so you have to be true to yourself.

What are some of your favorite albums?

Any Tupac album
The Miseducation of Lauryn Hill, Lauryn Hill
Get Rich or Die Tryin', 50 Cent

Did you have any posters on your bedroom walls as a kid? Of whom?

I had Michael Jordan. I loved Michael Jordan, still to this day. He was the only person on my wall.

What are some great shows you've seen?

When I was younger I didn't go to a lot of concerts—I always felt that I should be the one onstage. I swear I did. I think the only concert I saw when I was younger was Shabba Ranks, because I love reggae. Other than that, I didn't want to go. I still don't go, unless it's somebody that I really love.

New Edition was popping.

I went to see Alicia Keys in Chicago—her show was really good. She's really good.

What are some of your favorite songs?

I go through different songs. I go through spurts. Right now, I'm listening to 50 Cent, R. Kelly, Tupac. When I was thirteen to fifteen, it was Jodeci and Biggie. I loved Biggie when I was fifteen!

List up to ten things that could be helpful to someone breaking into the business.

I think the one thing for women, since this is such a male-dominated business, is that you have to demand your own. You have to demand your respect. Let people know that you're about your business. Let people know you are here to do a job just like them.

Everlast

Did you have a mentor or someone who inspired you? If so, what have you learned from that person?

Divine Styler was the biggest influence on me in music. He was the first person to tell me I could really do this music thing. He played me all the first hip-hop mixes that inspire me to this day.

What was your very first job in the music industry, and how did you get it?

Deejaying with a high school buddy for Nel Carter's Christmas party. I was fifteen, I drank like seven vodka tonics and vomited everywhere. Needless to say he never took me on another gig.

What was your first big break? The first great thing that ever happened to you . . .

Probably Ice-T hearing my first demos and signing me to his label.

What elements of your job make you want to go to work every day?

The amazing feeling of making something out of nothing and hopefully making others feel it. That's the shit.

What qualities most helped you get to where you are today?

Being too stubborn to listen when people tell me what can't be done and being too stupid to care.

If you knew everything at the beginning of your career that you know now, what would you have done differently?

I would have started my own label when I was seventeen.

What is your greatest lesson learned?

Anger is a gift and a curse. It can fuel creativity, and it can burn a lot of bridges.

What are some of your favorite albums?

Harvest, Neil Young

*It Takes a Nation of Millions to Hold
Us Back,* Public Enemy

Grace, Jeff Buckley

King of Rock, Run-D.M.C.

Mama's Gun, Erykah Badu

Electric Ladyland, Jimi Hendrix

Cypress Hill, Cypress Hill

Paranoid, Black Sabbath

Tea for the Tillerman, Cat Stevens

Did you have any posters on your bedroom walls as a kid? Of whom?

KISS, Star Wars, Bruce Lee, bikini chicks, i.e., Farrah Fawcett or any Charlie's Angel.

What are some great shows you've seen?

Murphy's Law, Fishbone, and the Beastie
Boys, Hollywood Palladium, 1984

KRS-One, the Palace, 1989

Rage Against the Machine and House
of Pain, 1993. They rocked!

Tom Waits, the Beacon, New York, 2000

Sade, Hollywood Bowl, 2002

What are some of your favorite songs?

"Long Time Coming," the Otis
Redding version

"Out on the Weekend," Neil Young

"Girl from the North Country,"
Johnny Cash and Bob Dylan

"Hand on the Pump," Cypress Hill

"Don't Believe the Hype," Public Enemy

List up to ten things that could be helpful to someone breaking into the business.

- Do it yourself.
- Trust no man.

- Read what you sign.
- Do it for the love.

Perry Farrell

JANE'S ADDICTION, PORNO FOR PYROS

Did you have a mentor or someone who inspired you? If so, what have you learned from that person?

The person I most admired in the music business was Bill Graham. He was the greatest promoter of all time. Bill was focused and intense. His passion was putting on parties that were very fun and freaky, and he worked very hard. When you went to one of his events, one could feel that the person who was putting on the show loved music and loved musicians. His back stages were notorious. His events changed the world. He was the man responsible for such groundbreaking tours as the Grateful Dead, the Rolling Stones, as well as Led Zeppelin. At one point in his life Bill quit promotion because he was disgusted with the hustle of the music business; but he returned to produce *Live Aid, Farm Aid, Amnesty International,* and the *"US" Festivals.*

What was your first big break? The first great thing that ever happened to you . . .

My first break in entertainment was a white lightning lie. I was for a brief moment in time a liquor distributor. One afternoon, I was making a delivery to a club in Newport Beach. I sat by the bar and watched a video of a fashion show the club had done the previous Saturday night while waiting for the sexy female manager to sign off on the order. The manager came back with the order and sat down at the bar. She asked me if I had any experience modeling. Well, I began to create, "I happen to be a triple threat. I can do it all—model, sing, dance." "Well," she says to me, "come back tomorrow, and I will see if we can get you into the next weekend's performance." In three weeks' time I was starring.

What elements of your job make you want to go to work every day?

What excites me most about going to work is the thought of blowing people's minds and maybe becoming a matchmaker. Maybe two young, hot, and sexy people will have such a good time at my festival that they will fall in love, eventually get married, and have a jazzy family.

What qualities most helped you get to where you are today?

The quality that carries me furthest in life is mischief. I like going down slopes with no previous tracks. Sometimes I see a treasure; sometimes there is a reason no one goes down there. . . . But having something that is rare is having something that people are likely to pay for.

If you knew everything at the beginning of your career that you know now, what would you have done differently?

If I have any regrets it would be twofold: first that I was kicked out of Hebrew school for feeling up girls and fighting, and secondly that I did not retain the language the first time I was taught it. When I was bar mitzvahed at thirteen, I was a lot more interested in girls and sports and thought of Hebrew as a requirement to get attention and money, and I would get to throw a big dance party. It was my first concert. The depth and perfection of the language of Hebrew is something I would realize later to be a pillar in my life. Crucial to maintaining balance and structure.

What is your greatest lesson learned?

The greatest lesson I have learned about the music industry is to be patient while applying firm pressure. The old guard in the industry have a way of waiting people out. They fight a war of attrition. You can expect things to go slowly and be decided at the last minute. However, these execs should be avoided. Time is the most precious commodity we have. I look to work with those who are decisive in their actions and take calculated risk every year. I never exclude old methods, but this year's innovation is next year's success.

What are some great shows you've seen?

Live music has always been where it's at for me. The recording industry will rise and sag, but you can bet every Friday night people will be out looking for peace and pleasure. The Chili Peppers doing handstands in '84 on a Sunday afternoon. The Minutemen were punk legends growing up. They played the docks of San Pedro and the deserts of Joshua Tree. I learned how to put on shows by building stages and designing flyers for the L.A. underground who couldn't put on shows in the "usual" venues.

Some great shows I have seen were:
Led Zeppelin's last tour—outdoors while it poured on us in northern Florida
The Stones, Emotional Rescue tour—with girl on shoulders
The Who and the Clash on tour together!
Of course Jane's Addiction's first tour was with the Ramones, pairing up and destroying every
    club that was trashy enough to have us. Our next tour was with my idol Iggy Pop.
      Out came that cock of his in Detroit, "It feels great to be back home," he told the crowd.
Burning Man; riding on the back of a customized motor carriage racing naked kiteboarders

Rage Against the Machine opening for us up at Castaic Lake. We got ready in a trailer filled to
the rim with topless women.
Meeting Kurt Cobain in the basement of the Palace in a pair of rubber boots I had taken from
their broom closet
Henry Rollins jumping into the crowd at the Cathey DeGrand and riding people like horses
Losing my shoe and my car when Bowie came to Los Angeles
Singing "Don't Call Me Nigger, Whitey" with Ice-T onstage at Lollapalooza

List up to ten things that could be helpful to someone breaking into the business.

Things I would tell my son about the industry are:

- The music drives everything—without great music to work with, you will live your life in fear.
- Work with people who love music or you'll always be trying to explain yourself—and your time is too precious.
- Do sit-ups and push-ups and get fresh air.
- Always be ready to record.
- Buy the latest technology.
- Leave people with the feeling that they are smart and sexy.
- Go to bed whenever you want, but get up early.
- Be good company, and learn to relate to all ages and walks of life.
- You can learn a lot in five minutes.

Fatboy Slim

Did you have a mentor or someone who inspired you? If so, what have you learned from that person?

Paul Heaton (Housemartins singer and school friend) badgered me into quitting my job and turning pro. He bullied me into believing I could do this. . . .

What was your very first job in the music industry, and how did you get it?

Bass player in the Housemartins.

What was your first big break? The first great thing that ever happened to you . . .

Joining the Housemartins just as they got signed. Six months later we were all over the radio. Eight months later, on the main stage at Glastonbury!

What elements of your job make you want to go to work every day?

A simple love of music, whether playing other people's or making my own.

What qualities most helped you get to where you are today?

Not taking myself too seriously and refusal to give up.

If you knew everything at the beginning of your career that you know now, what would you have done differently?

Je ne regrette rien.

What is your greatest lesson learned?

You can't make an omelette without breaking a few eggs.

What are some of your favorite albums?

Abbey Road, the Beatles
Innervisions, Stevie Wonder
Duck Rock, Malcolm McLaren

Did you have any posters on your bedroom walls as a kid? Of whom?

The Clash.

What are some great shows you've seen?

The Clash, twelve times
Prince
Chemical Brothers, Red Rocks

What are some of your favorite songs?

"Paranoid Android," Radiohead
"What's Going On," Marvin Gaye

List up to ten things that could be helpful to someone breaking into the business.

- Don't give up.
- Don't give up.
- Don't give up.

Flea

Did you have a mentor or someone who inspired you? If so, what have you learned from that person?

Every musician I ever listened to, including the ones I played with: some are Hillel Slovak, Anthony Kiedis, Jack Irons, Dizzy Gillespie, my stepfather Walter Urban, Miles Davis, Jimi Hendrix, Black Flag, the Germs, Led Zeppelin, Stevie Wonder, Funkadelic, Aphex Twins, Public Enemy, Brian Eno, Fela Kuti, Can, John Frusciante, John Coltrane, Talking Heads, Lightnin' Hopkins, Billie Holiday, Erik Satie, and my music teacher at Bancroft Junior High School, Mr. Charles Abe.

What was your very first job in the music industry, and how did you get it?

I attended L.A. public schools and was a trumpet player in the Bancroft Junior High School Band.

What was your first big break? The first great thing that ever happened to you . . .

In my senior year (ninth grade) at Bancroft Junior High, I was given a solo. I sat in the first trumpet chair and conducted the junior orchestra in a blue polyester suit. It was an incredible night in my life. I also won a scholarship for one hundred dollars for private lessons.

What elements of your job make you want to go to work every day?

I love music. The depth of feeling and knowledge to reach for is infinite.

What qualities most helped you get to where you are today?

Caring about doing my job well.

If you knew everything at the beginning of your career that you know now, what would you have done differently?

I would have not done drugs (except maybe weed), taken a spiritual path—developed a spiritual practice—earlier in life, and I would have continued my academic study of music, which I abandoned during high school.

What is your greatest lesson learned?

Pay attention.
What goes around comes around.
Love no matter what.

What are some of your favorite albums?

Catch a Fire, Bob Marley
G.I., the Germs
Olé Coltrane, John Coltrane
Kind of Blue, Miles Davis
Group Sex, Circle Jerks
Expensive Shit, Fela Kuti
Una Mas, Kenny Dorham
Ege Bamyasi, Can
Sandinista! and *London Calling*, the Clash
A Love Supreme, John Coltrane
Trout Mask Replica, Captain Beefheart

Are You Experienced?, Jimi Hendrix Experience
One Nation Under a Groove, Funkadelic
Blue, Joni Mitchell
After the Gold Rush, Neil Young
Songs in the Key of Life, Stevie Wonder
Horses, Patti Smith
Heaven Up Here, Echo and the Bunnymen
13 Songs, Fugazi
Mingus Ah Um, Charles Mingus

Did you have any posters on your bedroom walls as a kid? Of whom?

Farrah Fawcett.

What are some great shows you've seen?

Nusrat Fateh Ali Khan, Universal Amphitheatre
Black Flag (Dez Cadena Singing Era), the Starwood
The Meat Puppets, Club Lingerie

The Butthole Surfers, somewhere downtown
Ahmad Jamal, Catalina's Bar and Grill
Jane's Addiction, Father's Rights Benefit, at the Palace

What are some of your favorite songs?

"Ramble On," Led Zeppelin
"Washington Bullets," the Clash
"Lady," Fela Kuti

"Bemsha Swing," as performed by Ornette Coleman or Don Cherry

List up to ten things that could be helpful to someone breaking into the business.

■ Work hard and always tell the truth.
■ Be yourself.
■ Meditate.

Mick Fleetwood

Did you have a mentor or someone who inspired you? If so, what have you learned from that person?

My mentor in this line of business was Peter Green. Not only was I inspired by the pure genius of his playing, it was Peter who taught me to be motivated by being inspired and driven just for the music. That type of motivation enabled me to persevere and make my dream come true in terms of being a drummer. And then it was a question of just growing up and maturing. In fact, I can't remember any time in Fleetwood Mac history where we haven't been there for the music and have not been totally into what we were doing. I don't think any of us ever really approached it as a huge business. We've always been people that had a strong sense of loving what we were doing. So I guess that precedent set by Peter Green was and has remained an incredible guide in my career for me to live by, and I will always be thankful and respectful of him for teaching me that.

What was your very first job in the music industry, and how did you get it?

I left my mom and dad in northern England, which was Gloucestershire, went to London on the train, with a drum kit literally wrapped up in blanket. I got off the train and went to my sister Sally's flat in London in Knotting Hill Gate where I lived in the attic. I put the drums in the garage where I practiced. Lo and behold, the next-door neighbor, a chap by the name of Peter Bardens, a great keyboard player, knocked on the door. He had heard me practicing and said, "Do you want a gig?" And there you have it . . . my first job. A few weeks later I was playing underaged in a really rundown seedy club in London called the Mandrake Club, and that was the beginning of my drumming career . . . all from a knock on the door. Sadly, Peter passed away last year, but he and I remained friends till the end.

What was your first big break? The first great thing that ever happened to you . . .

Looking back, I'd say that outside of getting a job to begin with, my first break was getting my first recording contract with a band called the Cheynes. You probably never heard of us, we never made it, but we were on EMI in London. I remember there was a radio station in Luxembourg, Radio Luxembourg, that played our record, and the biggest thrill in my early career was actually hearing myself being played on the radio. That's always a good memory for me.

What elements of your job make you want to go to work every day?

Not that I do it every day of my life, but when we work, it is really a reconnecting with what I started out doing when I was about eleven years old, which was to play drums. I had a major dream to become a drummer. I always remember that and respect how lucky I am to basically do what I love to do, and I would wish that for anyone and everyone. I am fully aware that that's not always the case with people who do various things in this life. I am very lucky to be doing something that I love to do, so going to work is a pleasure. I always remember where it started. It was a dream I had and it has come true, and so I respect it a lot.

What qualities most helped you get to where you are today?

One thing I believe helped me was my ability to actually visualize myself becoming a success-ful drummer. When I say successful I don't necessarily mean being rich or famous, but rather knowing that people would hear my music, that they would enjoy it, and that I would always have a forum to play it. Anytime in my whole life that I wanted anything badly I didn't just think about it or just physically try to do it . . . I literally, over and over again, pictured myself doing it. I am fortunate enough to say that I have done that with all things in my life and I have been able to make a majority of them come true. Another thing that helped me, not to be too senti-mental, but in reality was the way I was brought up. My parents were quite open-minded and completely supported everything their children wanted for themselves, especially when it came to the artistic side of doing things. Both my sisters ended up in the arts as well . . . and all with the blessing of our parents. Let's face it, for my parents to allow me to quit school as a teenager and move to London because I told them I wanted to be a drummer is pretty incredi-ble. I suppose they knew that I would find a way to do it anyway, so why not encourage my idea and hope that I worked hard enough to make it come true. Sadly, my father passed away over twenty-five years ago, but my mother is still alive, and she shows the same type of support to all of her grandchildren and great-grandchildren. I really admire her for that because I've re-alized that when a young person has a lightbulb that goes on, it is so important for that to be encouraged and nurtured. I think that is really why I have such respect for the whole journey and why I am still here, because I was allowed to do something that meant a lot to me.

If you knew everything at the beginning of your career that you know now, what would you have done differently?

My career really speaks for itself, and I wouldn't change anything. There are certain elements that came along while building my career I might have done differently. I wouldn't have been drinking so much, and I would have spent more time with my daughters Amy and Lucy, but my career is something that took a very natural flow, and I don't have any complaints.

What is your greatest lesson learned?

Well, I'm still learning lessons. I suppose the biggest lesson to date is a sense that you can have a career, and you can also have a home life, and that took me a long time to learn. I am blessed with having a lovely wife that I have been with for almost fifteen years, and she and I have beautiful twin daughters just a little over two years old who I enjoy to the fullest. I am now totally connected to my two older daughters and my grandson and I crave their presence as much as I do a drum kit. The reality is, first time around my career came first over family and I have fortunately learned to balance that out. To be blessed with a family that loves me and to have the incredible career that I do, how stupid would I be if I didn't figure out how to keep them both alive at the same time.

What are some of your favorite albums?

Live at The Regal, B.B. King

Cloud Nine, George Harrison

Imagine, John Lennon

Abbey Road, the Beatles

Between the Buttons, the Rolling Stones

Any Marvin Gaye record

Any Howling Wolf, John Lee Hooker,
  or Buddy Guy

Did you have any posters on your bedroom walls as a kid? Of whom?

Cliff Richards and the Shadows, an English pop star, who is still alive, and still very popular. Basically, he was England's Elvis Presley and has a lot to do with my early influences. Believe it or not, I got to know Elvis Presley through Cliff Richards. There was a connection there for me, and I actually had posters of Cliff Richards and the Shadows in my bedroom.

What are some great shows you've seen?

I have been a big fan of Pavarotti for many years and Lynn, my wife, and I went to Las Vegas, of all places, to see him live for the first time. He was unbelievable. His presence alone was inspiring, but to hear that voice come from only a few feet in front of me was pretty amazing. I'm very happy to have been able to see that before he retires, which there have been rumors of. I have seen numerous Rolling Stones shows and there are two that stand out in my mind. I think one of the greatest shows I ever saw, a moving show, was the Rolling Stones at Hyde Park, when Brian Jones had passed away. They released hundreds of thousands of white butterflies to pay tribute to Brian. That was the first time I believe Mick Taylor played with them, who I knew from John Mayall's Bluesbreakers. That was an incredible concert, probably my favorite concert. Last year I saw the Stones in L.A. It was an incredibly intimate setting to see a rock band, and Lynn and I were blown away. They all looked great, sounded better than ever, and after all these years still appeared to be having as much fun as they did when they first started. That to me was pretty cool and I just sat there and said "alright."

What are some of your favorite songs?

> "Jealous Guy" and "Imagine," John Lennon. "Imagine" is just a classic song.
>
> "All Things Must Pass," George Harrison. It is a beautiful song from George.
>
> "Blowin' in the Wind," Bob Dylan—really any number of Bob Dylan songs. "Blowin' in the Wind" is a classic song, it's always apropos, it's apropos right now, and that guy is a genius.

List up to ten things that could be helpful to someone breaking into the business.

- Listen to your heart, and believe the first message you get. At least that way you know that you have done what your own heart has told you to. There is nothing worse than not doing that. You may not "make it," but you'll be doing what you are supposed to be doing (at least) for a period of time, and you should allow yourself.

- Don't doubt yourself. If you see something, go for it. I think a lot of people that have made it in this business have listened to themselves or at the very least have been encouraged by people that believed in them. When you get a sense of either of those things, listen to what's being said—whether it's within you or from without, from other people. I think that is a tremendous help to get started and give you the spirit.

- Learn to appreciate what you have achieved and stay as grounded as you can. Success can be measured in different ways.

- Believe in your music.

- I think another part of learning how to make it and getting your first break is learning to listen to people. I think you are really blessed if you can. Try to remind yourself to be open to listening to people, getting feedback and becoming objective about who you are and what you do as soon as possible so you don't have an inflated understanding or an incorrect understanding of what you really are either as a musician, a singer, a writer. I don't mean to be a killjoy, but having an objective standpoint is really useful. It can put you in the right place at the right time. Know that you can hold your own, and listening to people is a major part of learning about what I call health compromise—you cannot exist in this business in my opinion unless you are a complete asshole. You need to listen to other people and learn to work with other people and that is probably one of the biggest benefits to a person starting out in this business.

Peter Frampton

Did you have a mentor or someone who inspired you? If so, what have you learned from that person?

I didn't really have a mentor, but Hank Marvin, the guitarist from the Shadows, was who I wanted to be. He had a huge influence on me. He's still vital and making music. Whether you have a song on the charts or you don't, you can still play music.

What was your very first job in the music industry, and how did you get it?

I had a weekend job in a music shop selling strings, guitars, etc. I got the job from contacts of mine whom I met through playing music.

What was your first big break? The first great thing that ever happened to you . . .

I was asked to fill in as the guitarist for a very popular local band, the Conrads, which David Bowie had been a part of. I was fourteen at the time, and it was my first real break.

What elements of your job make you want to go to work every day?

The beauty of it is, the elements of my work are the elements of my all-consuming hobby, music. It just happens to be my job, so I get to do what I love.

What qualities most helped you get to where you are today?

Number one: Stubbornness! I've never really given up. You just have to keep fighting and believe what you do is good. I enjoy what I do. Tenacity would be another quality I attribute to myself.

If you knew everything at the beginning of your career that you know now, what would you have done differently?

I would have gotten the business manager that I have now! I would have sought him out much earlier in my career. Musically, I don't think I would have made any other choices as to what I did. I think that has been an unfolding series of events. I would have paid more attention to the business side of things. I really didn't care about that as I never really cared about the money. Until it's gone!

What is your greatest lesson learned?

The greatest lesson I have learned is to watch my finances more closely. Usually creative people don't use the mathematical side of their brain, but you must.

What are some of your favorite albums?

Kind of Blue, Miles Davis

*The Unauthorized Biography of
   Reinhold Messner,* Ben Folds Five

Sgt. Pepper's Lonely Hearts Club Band,
   the Beatles

Quintet of the Hot Club of France,
   Django Reinhardt

The Shadows

Wired, Jeff Beck

Rattle and Hum, U2

Did you have any posters on your bedroom walls as a kid? Of whom?

Some Spanish bullfighter.

What are some great shows you've seen?

Paul McCartney, Peter Gabriel, ZZ Top, Aerosmith, and U2.

What are some of your favorite songs?

"Nuages," Django Reinhardt

"Pride (In the Name of Love)," U2

"Brick," Ben Folds Five

"I'm Not in Love," 10cc

List up to ten things that could be helpful to someone breaking into the business.

It's very difficult when you're starting out in the business to get a good deal. The object as you progress is to own your own material. That's the name of the game.

And, get a business degree before you form the band!

John Frusciante

Did you have a mentor or someone who inspired you? If so, what have you learned from that person?

My stepfather, Larry, was a really good guy to have around when I was growing up. At school, every day was a new argument—with kids, with teachers. With kids, it would be because they made fun of things I liked that they'd never heard of, like King Crimson. With teachers, it was like when they wouldn't let me do a book report on *The Anti-Christ* by Nietzsche. Larry and I would always discuss these things when I came home, and he always made me feel like I was right. I felt in him that I had somebody who believed in me. It means a lot to you when you're a kid to have an adult who really does believe in you and sees something in you.

I remember a teacher named Mr. Hughes at my junior high school. It was his responsibility to hold the detention class, and kids either loved him or hated him. He was very funny but also very strict. Once you knew him, you also came to realize how funny even his strictness was. When I was in eighth grade he asked the prettiest girl in class to come get me out of another class to come to him—usually when he did that, you knew you were in trouble. When I got to his office, he said, "John, I want you to sit down and write a letter explaining what you think about me as a teacher, and to sign it, so when you're famous I can show it to my students." It made me feel good. I always knew that I was going to be a musician for a living, but nobody else believed me. Maybe other kids did, once they started to hear me play, but not at that point for sure. Mr. Hughes was saying it based on nothing but my attitude toward music and what he saw in my eyes. I really appreciated that.

When I was a teenager, I devoted myself to learning Frank Zappa's music. I thought of him as the perfect human being who could do and say no wrong. I knew I wanted to be the best guitarist I could be, and I would learn very difficult music that he had written. I would imagine him standing in front of me with his baton, and I would play at the technical level I imagined he demanded from his musicians. He calmed something in me when I was fifteen or sixteen, which was when I practiced more than at any other time. If you're in a certain amount of pain or confusion when you're growing up, it's nice to have someone who always makes you laugh or smile. When you don't have somebody like that, you're left with your own sadness or pain. I've always had people like that. A few years ago it was Martin Gore and Dave Gahan. Right now, it's

Peter Hammill from Van Der Graaf Generator. When I think about him, it fills me with good feelings. I often think about what the world would be like if we didn't have these images that correspond to our own subconscious pain and cancel it out. These images have kept me happy in times that otherwise would have been very bleak.

What was your very first job in the music industry, and how did you get it?

I was eighteen years old when I joined the band. I had been living on my own for about a year, and my dad was paying something like four hundred dollars a month for me to go to some kind of music classes. I did that for a while, then I pretended to do that, and he cut me off. And then I joined the Chili Peppers.

What was your first big break? The first great thing that ever happened to you . . .

Joining what was, at that time, my favorite band. I feel very fortunate to have gotten into the business the way that I did, which was just by making a friend who played bass in a band that was already moderately successful. I didn't expect that I could ever be more popular than what the Chili Peppers were at the time, selling seventy thousand records or so. Playing at the Palace or the Roxy seemed like the height of fame.

When we first became highly successful, it was actually more of a letdown to me. The last time that I saw the Chili Peppers before joining the band (at Hillel's last show at the Palace), my girl-friend at the time, Sarah, asked me whether I would still like the Chili Peppers if they played the Forum. I didn't think that could ever happen. To me, if they did, they wouldn't be the same band. They wouldn't have any of the things I liked about them. At that time, the thought of the Chili Peppers sounding anything like we sound now would have seemed far-fetched. It would have seemed very unlikely for the band to have the kind of sound that really does translate well in an arena.

I had an image of what the band meant to me, and at the time of *Blood Sugar*, I felt like we were overstepping that image by becoming as popular as we started to become. I was mad about making the transition from playing clubs to theaters; it wasn't even arenas yet, just four- or five-thousand-seat venues. In retrospect, I hadn't yet realized that I am what people think of me. I still wanted people to think I was what I thought I was. Letting go of that was very important. You and your music can be so many different things to so many different people, and in some way, each one of them is right. Their perception of you is the real thing for them, so why should you be the one to control it? I realized that at various times in my life, my images of people were all that made me happy. Those images were more important than who they actually were. When you meet a person, it can kind of blow it. Your image of them is much more elastic and much more magical. I'm very proud to be able to mean a lot of things to different people.

What elements of your job make you want to go to work every day?

I feel that there is still more territory to cover musically. I feel like we're getting better. I see Flea growing as a musician; I see Anthony growing as a singer and songwriter. I feel like there's a lot more to do within the context of this group that is of interest to me. If that wasn't there, if I felt like we were past our prime, I wouldn't want to do this anymore. I'd rather continue in a direction that interested me, whether or not it was commercially viable. Luckily right now, the thing that interests me is also the thing that makes me a good living.

What qualities most helped you get to where you are today?

The fact that I am doing this out of a total love for music. Music has saved my life so many times. Since I was a little kid, it's been a best friend. It's been the one thing I can depend on and what makes life seem infinite. Since I was seven years old, music has made me see clearly that everything is infinite; that space is everything while at the same time, it is nothing. This was clear to me just by listening to KISS.

When I was twelve, we moved to the Valley. When you're a kid, the Valley seems like this boring place with a bunch of geeks, where everybody's kind of square and nobody knows what's going on. I had developed this total devotion to music, and I wanted to make it my life. I needed to make sure I was good at it, so I became very disciplined. At that point, all I could play was punk rock. But I knew it was going to be at least five years until I got out of the Valley, so I figured I might as well practice as much as I could so that by the time I got out of there I would be a good guitarist. I gradually went from practicing a couple hours a day to practicing as much as fifteen hours a day. That's why at seventeen I was confident I was going to be able to make a living making music.

There's a certain feeling that runs through my brain, through the music I listen to and through my life. I knew that feeling was going to be the essence of my music, and that certain people were going to gravitate toward it. I can't take credit for the feeling—it's something that's been there since I was a little kid. I never had any doubt that I was going to succeed. Most importantly, I knew that I was making music for the right reasons.

If you knew everything at the beginning of your career that you know now, what would you have done differently?

I'm very happy and proud to be who I am, and whatever mistakes I've made only helped me become this person.

What is your greatest lesson learned?

Music is not something that you are in control of. It comes from somewhere else. If you're that middleman between the cosmos and the real world on earth that the music comes through, you are very lucky. When you record music, it's not your job to try to control anything. It's more about being in the right place and flowing with the energies that are in the air around you and with the people that you are making the music with. The second that someone thinks music comes from themselves, and that they are the ones responsible for it, is when they go off track. The most important thing you could realize is that you are the least important part of the whole process. Music is going to be made whether any one artist is here or not. If John Lennon or Jimi Hendrix had disappeared, music still would have gone on, changed, grown, and been the beautiful thing that it is. You take away the music, all you have are the individuals, and they don't mean anything. The individual is nothing—it's the music that's in the air all the time that's important, and you have to be humble in the face of that.

What are some of your favorite albums?

I'm naming ones I love, but I can name five hundred others that I love equally. Especially with bands like the Velvet Underground or the Mothers, I love a lot of their albums equally. I'm just trying to pick one per band.

(GI), the Germs
Trout Mask Replica, Captain Beefheart
    and the Magic Band
Low, David Bowie
The Least We Can Do Is Wave to Each
    Other, Van Der Graaf Generator
The Velvet Underground, the Velvet
    Underground
Not Available, the Residents
Cut, the Slits
The *Ekkehard Ehlers Plays* series,
    Ekkehard Ehlers
Raw Power, the Stooges
Hark! The Village Wait, Steeleye Span
Closer, Joy Division
The Idiot, Iggy Pop
Adolescents, the Adolescents
What Makes a Man Start Fires, Minutemen
I Say, I Say, I Say, Erasure
Penthouse and Pavement, Heaven 17
Fireside Favorites, Fat Gadget
Burning from the Inside, Bauhaus
Over the Edge, the Wipers
The Slider, T. Rex

Remain in Light, Talking Heads
Burnt Weeny Sandwich, Frank Zappa
    and the Mothers of Invention
Travelogue, the Human League
Desert Shore, Nico
Slayed?, Slade
Funkadelic, Funkadelic
Red Medicine, Fugazi
Barrett, Syd Barrett
Here Come the Warm Jets, Brian Eno
Black Celebration, Depeche Mode
Red, King Crimson
Trilogy, Emerson, Lake & Palmer
Close to the Edge, Yes
'75, Neu!
Flammende Herzen, Michael Rother
Get Out, Pita
Plus Forty Seven Degrees 56' 37" Minus
    Sixteen Degrees 51' 08", Fennesz
Liege and Lief, Fairport Convention
Led Zeppelin IV, Led Zeppelin
The New York Dolls, the New York Dolls
The Ramones, the Ramones

Did you have any posters on your bedroom walls as a kid? Of whom?

Depends on what age. . . .

When I was seven, it was Sylvester Stallone, John Travolta, and KISS. When I was ten, I had a garage where I had ads for punk-rock shows, like X, the Germs, and Black Flag.When I was thirteen, I had a nice Ziggy Stardust poster, but it was mostly pictures cut out of magazines. I separated them into sections—Frank Zappa, David Bowie, Jimi Hendrix, Jeff Beck, Jimmy Page, and the various people section.

When I was seventeen and moved to Hollywood to live on my own, I started buying eight-by-ten photographs from the memorabilia stores on Hollywood Boulevard. My room was covered in eight-by-tens of Divine (I was deep into John Waters), Nina Hagen, Jayne Mansfield, Marilyn Monroe, the New York Dolls, and David Bowie.

What are some great shows you've seen?

The Butthole Surfers at UCLA in 1989 was an amazing show. I also saw them in New York, which was equally amazing.

Jane's Addiction, in 1989–91. I saw them a lot, and they were incredible. It was hard for me to imagine a band being more powerful. Eric Avery was such a great presence, and Perry gave it everything he had. It was beyond inspiring.

In the last five years, I've had the good fortune of seeing Fugazi a lot of times. I'd seen them as early as 1990, but in the last few years I've probably seen them twenty times. Every one of those shows was equally wonderful and exciting and fresh. Every performance they give is completely different from the next. They don't use a set list. They know every one of their songs, and just go from song to song, barely pausing in between. To me, they are exactly what a band should be—the perfect show for my taste.

What are some of your favorite songs?

"Lady Grinning Soul," David Bowie
"The Musical Box," Genesis
"Forensic Scene," Fugazi
"The Trees They Do Grow High," Joan Baez
"Holiday," the Bee Gees
"Ride into the Sun," Lou Reed
"Drugs," Talking Heads
"Black Angel's Death Song," the Velvet Underground
"Wonderful Woman," the Smiths

"White Queen," Queen
"Epitaph," King Crimson
"Frankenstein," the New York Dolls
"Today Your Love, Tomorrow the World," the Ramones
"Free Money," Patti Smith
"Girl," T. Rex
"Remember (Walking in the Sand)," the Shangri-Las
"Duke of Earl," Gene Chandler

"Snow Blind," Black Sabbath

"Police Story," Black Flag

"Presence of a Brain," Parliament

"Maybe," the Chantels

"Be My Baby," the Ronettes

"I Feel Love," Donna Summer

"You're So Fine," the Falcons

List up to ten things that could be helpful to someone breaking into the business.

- Give it everything you have in your performances.
- Practice as much as you can. A band like the Mars Volta practices, like, ten hours a day, and that just seems right on to me. They're people really trying as hard as they can to be the best they can be. To me, these are the things that guarantee a person a place in the music industry.

I feel like people who are in it for the wrong reasons might get lucky and be successful; people who are doing it for the right reasons might not reach that millionaire level of success, but they will always achieve a kind of success in their own hearts which will fulfill them for their whole lives. If they make music that's good, they should be able to at least make enough money to live by playing. If the type of music they play is so abstract that they can't make enough money to live, I believe they can still feel a kind of success that's as deep as any. Music is that fulfilling.

A lot of the music that I am excited by now is made by people who have jobs. It's made by people whose direction isn't determined by trying to satisfy a public, or trying to be successful in the music business. Too much music these days is contaminated by the desire to be successful. What was great about punk rock to me as a kid in 1979 was that they were making music because they had to; it was a pure form of expression. They weren't making music because they were trying to get anywhere with it, or be on the radio. There was no chance of punk being on the radio. To me you make music because you're interested in music. You follow the direction that your interests dictate, not what is dictated by the public or the record business. I love listening to music by people like Fugazi, the Black Eyes, the Mars Volta, electronic people like Pita, Fennesz, Ekkehard Ehlers. These people are making the music that interests them with no expectation of it being successful in the music business. This music is relaxing to me because there's purity to it that a lot of people in the music business, or people who are constantly chasing success, don't have.

Nelly Furtado

Did you have a mentor or someone who inspired you? If so, what have you learned from that person?

My grandmother, who as a widow emigrated from Portugal to Canada in her late fifties. She is now approaching ninety years of age. She still lives alone, in a small house, baking and gardening every day with passion. She has taught me to live for the moment.

What was your very first job in the music industry, and how did you get it?

Singing backup vocals for an independent hip-hop group out of Toronto at the age of sixteen.

What was your first big break? The first great thing that ever happened to you . . .

I sang a duet with my mother at the age of four at a church festival. It was in Portuguese and the crowd loved it—they loved me! I knew then that performing in front of thousands one day was definitely in my crystal ball. I saw it.

What elements of your job make you want to go to work every day?

I love the craft. Writing songs, working on production, or rehearsing a show—it is truly satisfying and challenging.

What qualities most helped you get to where you are today?

A sheer belief that my dream would come true.
A lust for music and culture.
A burning desire to connect with others in a universal way.
Work ethic.

If you knew everything at the beginning of your career that you know now, what would you have done differently?

I would have gotten less caught up in the petty business details, and focused more on being an artist and living to document life. Never get so busy that you lose your passion for writing songs. It is a delicate balance.

What is your greatest lesson learned?

You have got to fend for yourself in this life. The world is tough, so you have to make things happen, because no one will do it for you. I have also learned about love—it is a self-fulfilling prophecy.

What are some of your favorite albums?

Definitely Maybe, Oasis

My Life, Mary J. Blige

Grace, Jeff Buckley

When I Was Born for the 7th Time, Cornershop

O Paraíso, Madredeus

Did you have any posters on your bedroom walls as a kid? Of whom?

Urban early-nineties stars such as Kriss Kross, Salt-N-Pepa, TLC, LL Cool J, Ice-T, High 5, Mary J. Blige, Boys II Men, Chi Ali, Supercat.

What are some great shows you've seen?

Radiohead, *OK Computer* tour

Beck, *Odelay* tour

Caetano Veloso, *Noites de Norte* tour

Concerts by Cesaria Evora, the Roots, Outkast

What are some of your favorite songs?

"Power Fantastic," Prince

"Terra," Caetano Veloso

"Not a Pretty Girl," Ani DiFranco

List up to ten things that could be helpful to someone breaking into the business.

- Great songs
- Guts
- Love/hate appeal
- Good manager
- Good business manager
- Good lawyer
- Passion
- Intensity
- Drive
- Body double

Dave Gahan

DEPECHE MODE

Did you have a mentor or someone who inspired you? If so, what have you learned from that person?

David Bowie showed me it was okay to feel and be different. Also the Clash still inspire me to want to reach further and that my best is not enough. Anything is possible.

What was your very first job in the music industry, and how did you get it?

I've never had a job in the music industry!

What was your first big break? The first great thing that ever happened to you . . .

Supporting Fad Gadget at the Bridgehouse Pub in Canning Town, East London. Daniel Miller (White Records) was mixing his sound. Daniel is one of a kind—he adopted us and helped us make a single. It's all we wanted to do.

What elements of your job make you want to go to work every day?

Wanting to make a difference, to inspire as I was (and still am) when I needed it most.

What qualities most helped you get to where you are today?

Not giving up, keep trying.

If you knew everything at the beginning of your career that you know now, what would you have done differently?

Not sweat the small stuff, think about the big picture, get off the cross!!

What is your greatest lesson learned?

Listen, but follow your heart, not your head.

What are some of your favorite albums?

Ziggy Stardust, David Bowie

Led Zeppelin I, Led Zeppelin

Beggars Banquet, the Rolling Stones

London Calling, the Clash

Ágætis Byrjun and *( ),* Sigur Rós

Did you have any posters on your bedroom walls as a kid? Of whom?

Bowie, T. Rex, the Damned (I was in the fan club), pictures of choppers and drag cars.

What are some great shows you've seen?

The Clash, Hyde Park

Jane's Addiction, last show, first *Lollapalooza* tour, Irvine Meadows

Sigur Rós, Beacon Theatre, New York

What are some of your favorite songs?

"Moonage Daydream," "Heroes,"
   and "Rock 'n' Roll Suicide," David Bowie

"Brown Sugar" and "Sympathy for
   the Devil," the Rolling Stones

"Three Days," Jane's Addiction

"London Calling," the Clash

"Black Dog" and "Rock and Roll,"
   Led Zeppelin

"Back in Black," AC/DC

"The Colour of Spring," Talk Talk

"Imagine," John Lennon

"What's Going On," Marvin Gaye

"Voodoo Chile" and "Angel," Jimi Hendrix

"Lust for Life," Iggy Pop

"Venus in Furs," Velvet Underground

I could go on and on, the list is too long . . .

List up to ten things that could be helpful to someone breaking into the business.

- Be willing to work with and as a team.
- Don't compromise your dream.
- Read every piece of paper you sign, and if you don't understand, find someone who does!
- Keep trying.
- It's never gonna be perfect, so don't waste your time thinking that's the answer.
- Enjoy the ride.
- Do it with love and heart.
- Go easy on the beers!!

Noel Gallagher

OASIS

Did you have a mentor or someone who inspired you? If so, what have you learned from that person?

The people from the city of Liverpool.

What was your very first job in the music industry, and how did you get it?

My first job was as a roadie. I believe they're called technicians these days. I got the job purely through a chance meeting with the guitarist from a band called Inspiral Carpets. We were at a Stone Roses gig, got talking, and the rest is a blur.

What was your first big break? The first great thing that ever happened to you . . .

The first great thing that happened was I wrote a song called "Live Forever."

What elements of your job make you want to go to work every day?

I don't want to go to work any day, let alone every day!

What qualities most helped you get to where you are today?

My songwriting (apparently!).

If you knew everything at the beginning of your career that you know now, what would you have done differently?

Taken a two-year break after the *Morning Glory* world tour.

What is your greatest lesson learned?

English.

Did you have any posters on your bedroom walls as a kid? Of whom?

Yes. The Smiths, the Beatles, the Stones, the Stone Roses, Bob Marley, and the Jam.

What are some great shows you've seen?

U2, G Mex Centre, Manchester, 1990

Neil Young, Apollo Hammersmith, 2003

Paul Weller, Glastonbury, 1994

The Who, Shepherds Bush Empire, 2000

Coldplay, T in the Park, 2001

Radiohead, Glastonbury, 2003

List up to ten things that could be helpful to someone breaking into the business.

There are no tips, no magic rules. Just enjoy yourself as much as is humanly possible.

Barry Gibb

THE BEE GEES

Did you have a mentor or someone who inspired you? If so, what have you learned from that person?

Yes, there were two. Robert Stigwood and Arif Mardin: Robert taught me about life itself, and Arif allowed me to fall in love with making records. I love them both dearly.

What was your very first job in the music industry, and how did you get it?

About 1958 we did some demos with Bill Gates, a Brisbane, Australia, deejay. He heard us singing at a racetrack in Redcliffe, Australia (he was one of the race drivers) and helped us create the name Bee Gees.

What was your first big break? The first great thing that ever happened to you . . .

Meeting Robert Stigwood.

What elements of your job make you want to go to work every day?

Listening, being part of a team, creating a song and making it something you love. It certainly isn't work. It is in reality a labor of love.

What qualities most helped you get to where you are today?

Believing in myself more than anyone believes in me and being open to change.

If you knew everything at the beginning of your career that you know now, what would you have done differently?

Listened more and spoken less.

What is your greatest lesson learned?

That your children, your wife, and your family are the core of your world and everything emanates from that center.

What are some of your favorite albums?

Modern Sounds in Country and Western Music, Ray Charles

Twenty Greatest Hits, Frank Sinatra

Harvest, Neil Young

Sgt. Pepper's Lonely Hearts Club Band, the Beatles

Thriller, Michael Jackson

Songs in the Key of Life, Stevie Wonder

Did you have any posters on your bedroom walls as a kid? Of whom?

What bedroom?

What are some great shows you've seen?

Michael Jackson, Wembley Stadium

Dame Edna on Broadway

Nelson Mandela, Wembley Stadium

Harry James at Ronnie Scott's club

What are some of your favorite songs?

"Crying," Roy Orbison

"It Keeps Right on A-Hurtin'"

"The Days of Wine and Roses"

"Wee Small Hours"

List up to ten things that could be helpful to someone breaking into the business.

- Listen to your own opinion. It will always be important. To be controlled by anyone is wrong.
- Have your own independent advice.
- Don't believe anything you read about yourself.
- Your power lies in loyalty, and no artist ever made it alone.

Josh Groban

Did you have a mentor or someone who inspired you? If so, what have you learned from that person?

I've been so fortunate to have so many loving, supportive people in my life. As far as true mentors go, besides my parents I would have to say that David Foster was the first guy in the music business to really say to me, "You can do it and I'm going to help you." He gave me real-world confidence and acted as a great teacher of the industry.

What was your very first job in the music industry, and how did you get it?

I had lots of jobs as a singer but never for pay. They were mostly charity concerts, and I was doing them in high school, so I was just happy to sing and be heard. The first time I ever sang "professionally" was at the inauguration concert for Governor Gray Davis in 1998 when I was seventeen. I got it because David Foster knew my voice teacher and said, "Quick . . . who do you have that can sing 'All I Ask of You' from *Phantom of the Opera*?" I was a theater student at the time and knew the song perfectly. I sent over a tape of myself singing it and I was rehearsing for the event the next week. The first time I ever made money as a singer was when I signed my record deal two years later and received an advance.

What was your first big break? The first great thing that ever happened to you . . .

I feel like the lead up to my record deal was a series of breaks. I guess the biggest happened a couple months after the Governor's concert. David Foster called me back and said he needed me to fill in for Andrea Bocelli with Celine Dion at the Grammy rehearsals because Andrea was doing a concert in Germany and wouldn't be there until the night of the show. I was still seventeen and it scared the crap out of me, not to mention the fact that I had no concept of "big break" at the time. I just wanted to be able to do a good job and I was afraid I wouldn't, so I said no. He called back an hour later and said that he wasn't asking me, he was telling me what time to be there. He believed in me, and it was a day that changed my life.

What elements of your job make you want to go to work every day?

Constantly having the opportunity to express myself in my truest form. Singing brings something out in me that can't be matched by anything else I do in my life. It's my most honest form of communication and so it is a joy to be able to get that out of my system every day. It's also fun because of the love for music I've had since I was a kid. It's a dream to be able to be right in the middle of the creative process. Since I'm new to this, every day is a learning experience, and the feeling of constantly having to be on the ball makes the work more exhilarating even if it's mixed in with all the anxiety.

What qualities most helped you get to where you are today?

Whoever said that luck meeting preparation equaled success was pretty right on. I was so blessed to have been in great situations, but they were all trial by fire and I always had to be ready for anything to get through it. I think I have the ability to excel under pressure and that's been the most important thing for me. I also think that I've been able to focus on what's most important and prioritize. I never lost track of who I am and what I set out to do, despite a world of distraction.

If you knew everything at the beginning of your career that you know now, what would you have done differently?

I don't really have a good answer to this one because of how new this is to me and how happy I am with what has happened in my career so far. I'm more experienced now when it comes to performing and handling the stress. I would go back and tell that scared kid to relax a little bit and not let the demons get to him.

What is your greatest lesson learned?

Patience. That, and not being sarcastic to print press . . . they can't hear you joking around in black and white!!

What are some of your favorite albums?

The first album I ever bought was Paul Simon's *Graceland* and it's a favorite to this day. I love artists that bend boundaries and get people to think outside a genre and explore new ground. Bjork's *Debut,* Peter Gabriel's *So,* Stevie Wonder's *Songs in the Key of Life,* anything recorded by Luciano Pavarotti.

Did you have any posters on your bedroom walls as a kid? Of whom?

I wasn't a poster guy. I think I had one of Batman when I was young but that was it. I bought lots of posters with good intentions but never put them up. When I have kids I'm giving them Scotch tape for Christmas.

What are some great shows you've seen?

My parents were so cool in taking me to see great show when I was a kid. I loved theater and they made sure I was exposed to as much as possible. I love Stephen Sondheim, so my favorites were *Sunday in the Park with George* and *Sweeney Todd.* As far as concerts go, Elton John at the Hollywood Bowl and Bela Fleck and the Flecktones at the Wiltern Theater stand out as favorites, but there are really too many to mention.

What are some of your favorite songs?

It's so hard to say. Any song off of the answers to the "Favorite Albums" question. I was able to record one of my favorite songs from a Cirque du Soleil show. It's called "Let Me Fall" and it's about not being afraid to take risks and getting back up after failure.

List up to ten things that could be helpful to someone breaking into the business.

- Be ready for anything.
- If you want to be a singer, I can tell you from experience, you will have to sing *all the time*. Get used to hearing "Hey, let's go over to the piano and do that song" in uncomfortable situations.
- Also, be nice and keep a good attitude. It sounds silly, but I've seen so many talented people lose it because of bad people skills.
- I guess most of all, just work as hard as you can when you feel your moment has arrived. David Foster used to say to me, "Your golden microphone is in front of you right now and you have to use it or it will be passed on."

MC Hammer

Did you have a mentor or someone who inspired you? If so, what have you learned from that person?

My mentor was Nick "Baby Love" Salerno. He taught me everything about the business from setting up and running a record label to independent promotion, and billing and collecting from distributors.

What was your very first job in the music industry, and how did you get it?

My first job was as an artist. I had to learn the art of producing. I had to learn the art of recording. The art of song structure. The art of melody, harmony, and choruses and finally the art of performing.

What was your first big break? The first great thing that ever happened to you . . .

My first break was at a nightclub called Silks in Oakland. I danced and rapped and performed there for thousands of hours.

What elements of your job make you want to go to work every day?

The smile that comes across the faces when my music and life touch others and make them happy.

What qualities most helped you get to where you are today?

Hard work!! Rehearse and rehearse some more!! And never quit believing in my vision.

If you knew everything at the beginning of your career that you know now, what would you have done differently?

I would have applied myself and paid more attention to the accounting and financial management of MC Hammer, Inc.

What is your greatest lesson learned?

Never ever allow others to sign the checks and manage my money!!

What are some of your favorite albums?

Thriller and *Off the Wall,* Michael Jackson

Purple Rain, Prince

Bigger and Deffer, LL Cool J

Anything by James Brown

Did you have any posters on your bedroom walls as a kid? Of whom?

I had Jackson 5, James Brown, and Ohio Player posters.

What are some great shows you've seen?

James Brown, Prince, Madonna, Michael Jackson, Janet Jackson, and yours truly.

What are some of your favorite songs?

"Baby Be Mine," Michael Jackson

"Just Shopping," the Dramatics

"Never Too Much," Luther Vandross

"Latest, Greatest Inspiration,"
   Teddy Pendergrass

"Ecstasy," Barry White

List up to ten things that could be helpful to someone breaking into the business.

- Learn to write songs.
- Hire a connected manager. One that has other hot veteran acts.
- Retain a music and entertainment attorney.
- Hire a music business accountant.
- Hire a bookkeeper. (To watch all other accountants.)
- Use a Web-based management system to keep track of all your business personally.
- Do not sign with a tour agency. Keep all options open.
- Diversify and create multiple revenue streams for yourself outside of the music industry. Movies, television, retail, etc.
- Find a wife or husband and be content with your family.
- Find God and commit your life to him.

Isaac Hayes

Did you have a mentor or someone who inspired you? If so, what have you learned from that person?

My high school music teachers, guidance counselor, and jazz musician Lucious Coleman. They taught me to work hard, get an education, and always strive to be the best you can be.

What was your very first job in the music industry, and how did you get it?

Singing with a blues band, Calvin Valentine and the Swing Cats. I was recommended by Lucious Coleman.

What was your first big break? The first great thing that ever happened to you . . .

Winning a talent show in high school.

What elements of your job make you want to go to work every day?

Creating, just creating.

What qualities most helped you get to where you are today?

Tenacity and vision.

If you knew everything at the beginning of your career that you know now, what would you have done differently?

I would change the route by which I made it.

What is your greatest lesson learned?

Don't be too serious. Stay in touch with reality.

What are some of your favorite albums?

Songs in the Key of Life, Stevie Wonder
Hot Buttered Soul
Shaft

Did you have any posters on your bedroom walls as a kid? Of whom?

We didn't have posters back then.

What are some great shows you've seen?

Motown show with Michael Jackson.

What are some of your favorite songs?

"The Windows of the World"
"By the Time I Get to Phoenix"

List up to ten things that could be helpful to someone breaking into the business.

- Be honest with yourself and know you have talent.
- Don't go only on what your mama says.
- Work hard and hone your skill.
- Don't step on anyone on the way up the mountain. Give them your hand, not your shoe sole.

Whitney Houston

Did you have a mentor or someone who inspired you? If so, what have you learned from that person?

My mother, Cissy Houston, is the person who inspired me. She taught me to be a strong woman in this industry.

What was your very first job in the music industry, and how did you get it?

My first industry job was recording background vocals with my mother and Luther Vandross for Chaka Khan. I also sang with my mother on some of her nightclub appearances. As a matter of fact, that's where Clive Davis first heard me—at a club called Sweetwater's in New York City.

What was your first big break? The first great thing that ever happened to you . . .

The first great thing I can remember was singing a solo in church. The song was "Guide Me Oh Thou Great Jehovah."

What elements of your job make you want to go to work every day?

I love performing for a live audience.

What qualities most helped you get to where you are today?

The love of God and a strong family foundation.

If you knew everything at the beginning of your career that you know now, what would you have done differently?

That's a tough question. The music business has changed so much since I first got signed. I would say learn all you can about the business.

What is your greatest lesson learned?

The greatest lesson that I learned was from my mother, which is "to thy own self be true."

What are some of your favorite albums?

Most of the albums I listen to are gospel—Fred Hammond, Kim Burrell, John P. Kee. I love the Sweet Inspirations, anything by Stevie Wonder or Chaka Khan—but mostly gospel.

Did you have any posters on your bedroom walls as a kid? Of whom?

I had Chaka Khan and Aretha Franklin posters in my room.

What are some great shows you've seen?

I've seen great shows by Luther Vandross, Anita Baker, John P. Kee.

What are some of your favorite songs?

There are many . . . but a few are:

"Amazing Grace"
"Let Brotherly Love," Daniel Winans
"We are Blessed," Fred Hammond

List up to ten things that could be helpful to someone breaking into the business.

My best piece of advice for someone starting out would be to remember that the music business is a business and learn all you can about the business side of things.

Liam Howlett
THE PRODIGY

Did you have a mentor or someone who inspired you? If so, what have you learned from that person?

It wasn't so much a mentor or one particular person. It was the feeling I got from seeing people who didn't have any musical background writing amazing records. A whole music scene that was born out of people saying "fuck it, if they can do it, I can do it better!" Do you get me?

What was your very first job in the music industry, and how did you get it?

Fuck the music industry, that's for record companies and managers. That's not my department.

What was your first big break? The first great thing that ever happened to you . . .

The first thing that happened to me that I saw as important was when I had entered a mix competition to do a three-minute mix under one name. A week later I thought what I had done was shite, so I did another under a different name, and subsequently came in first and third. It wasn't like a big break, but it made me feel ten feet tall.

What elements of your job make you want to go to work every day?

Writing music is just something I have to do, if it stays in my head then I'm fucked. The studio is like a rubbish dump—some ideas good, some bad, but just get it the fuck out of my head.

What qualities most helped you get to where you are today?

One of my best qualities is the ability to be excited about the smallest detail or sound—like a whole track can be born just because I buzzed off a cymbal. If I hear something when I'm out coming out of a radio in a shop or whatever, I'll go to extreme measures to know what it is. Ideas can come from anywhere, so everything is important.

If you knew everything at the beginning of your career that you know now, what would you have done differently?

Nothing, you have to learn still.

What is your greatest lesson learned?

Learn from your mistakes.

What are some of your favorite albums?

Oh, fuck. That's hard 'cuz it always changes, and it's boring.

Did you have any posters on your bedroom walls as a kid? Of whom?

I only ever had one hero when I was young and that was Bruce Lee. I only have one picture in my house now, and that is a twelve-foot-tall Bruce Lee print . . . in my toilet.

What are some great shows you've seen?

The last time I can remember genuinely being blown away was when I saw the White Stripes play.

What are some of your favorite songs?

Listen to my mix album. There are some on there.

List up to ten things that could be helpful to someone breaking into the business.

The only thing for me is you have to be selfish and write music so you are happy. If you are, whatever happens after that, your integrity will be intact. Yeah.

Ice-T

Did you have a mentor or someone who inspired you? If so, what have you learned from that person?

I think my only mentors in the business have been Russell Simmons and Don King. They both became very successful, but they kind of kept themselves. Don King did it with his hair combed in the air, which basically meant "kiss my ass." He came out of prison and worked around, and he managed to make himself wealthy. And there are people who hate him. I think for me to have a mentor it's got to be somebody who's always been hated, too; still, he's managed to keep himself successful.

Russell Simmons is still the same guy he was twenty years ago, and he did it with his hat turned backwards. For my mentors, I'd have to pick somebody who was able to do it but maintain themselves.

What was your very first job in the music industry, and how did you get it?

I've never had a real job in the industry, so I guess making my first record. I was rapping in a beauty parlor, Good Freds in South Central Los Angeles, just to entertain some people. I had a crowd of people, and this guy walked up to me and asked if I would like to make a record. Of course I said yes, and he took me to the studio. He had a track that was already there, and he had girls singing on it. The actual track was made by Jimmy Jam and Terry Lewis. It just so happened that he asked me. I just actually said all the lyrics I had in my head, and made a record called "The Coldest Rap."

That was my first thing. I learned early . . . I signed contracts I didn't read . . . I made maybe five hundred dollars off that record.

What was your first big break? The first great thing that ever happened to you . . .

The answer above was my introduction into actually making money for records. Up to that point I had just been rapping. I truly didn't take it serious as an income. That was like in 1982, so no one had ever really bought a car with rap. It wasn't really a feasible way to get paid, it was just something to do. I think that that kind of purity of form, knowing I wasn't really planning on making money with it, made it that raw. If you think you're gonna get on television, you may not tell dirty jokes. But I didn't ever think it was going to be able to be sold, so that's where the Ice-T style came from—the street.

I think the first great thing, when I really knew the shit was big, was long after my first album had come out. It was when I went out on the *Dope Jam* tour and I did "Colors." Up to that point I had done live dates and I had a gold record, but I hadn't seen the true power. I opened for a group of New York acts who really didn't know who I was. We went to San Antonio, Texas, and when the bass line of "Colors" came on, I saw like ten thousand people go nuts. I was like, "Oh, this shit is big." And then I went to Tennessee, and I was like "Whoa!" People like KRS-One weren't getting as much love as I was. That's when I really came to understand national and regional music.

What elements of your job make you want to go to work every day?

I have a recurring dream of being broke. I have a recurring dream of working at Jack in the Box with some guy yelling, "More fries!" And I have a recurring reality of me going broke. So I, like, have a lot of money and then my manager, Jorge, will call me and go, "You know, you gotta stop spending." So I get up and go to work every morning because I need the money. I'm not going to lie. I haven't hit that cushion of success that allows me to take a year vacation. I spend too much. I mean, I could make a million dollars tomorrow, but I'm gonna go out and buy that fucking F50, I'm gonna go buy the McClaren, and I'll be broke again. It's how I live. It's easy to spend. I tend to want a lot of shit, so I live at the broke level. I do have some things though.

What qualities most helped you get to where you are today?

I think it's just early hustling qualities that were put into me on the streets. No matter what you're gonna do, you're not gonna get it unless you're willing to break a sweat. Nobody can sit back on their ass and have money just drop in their lap. It seems like it to the people that don't work, but the cats that work, no matter at what level they are, are working continuously. A drug dealer is handling phones all day, he's got two pagers, he's leaving, he can't stay. No matter what you do you got to bust your ass. I don't care if you're an athlete, I don't care who you are. I mean, why is Kobe Bryant Kobe Bryant? Like he says, 'cuz he works for it. I think you just gotta be willing to work hard at whatever you do.

If you knew everything at the beginning of your career that you know now, what would you have done differently?

I would have done everything differently. If I knew what I know today, I probably would have lived yesterday differently. It's like a paradox, there's no way out of that. But then at the end of the day, I'm happy where I'm at. I'm truly happy. I've made quite a few mistakes, but that's just part of life.

What is your greatest lesson learned?

The biggest lesson in music is that the game board is continuously changing under your feet. So no matter how great you are today, the game board changes so greatness doesn't really stand on solid ground. It's like what you're on is a lava flow. What is a hot record today, when you listen to it ten years from now you're, like, "I liked that shit?" You could make an album, and it could be hot, but if you don't put it out that month, it'll be dead. Everything just moves around under you, so you gotta move with it. It's not like you build a building and it'll be there tomorrow. It's like fashion, everything is changing, the vibes are changing. It's a real unstable playing field. That's why people who do entertainment try to own businesses, something that's a little bit more stable.

What are some of your favorite albums?

Black Sabbath's first album, which I used a lot on my records

Are You Experienced?, Jimi Hendrix Experience

Paid in Full, Eric B. & Rakim

Yo! Bum Rush the Show, Public Enemy

Albums by Sade and the Delfonics

Did you have any posters on your bedroom walls as a kid? Of whom?

I can't remember if I had anything up on the walls. Probably car pictures. I've always been into cars—fancy cars, low riders, exotic custom cars. I didn't really get into high-end stuff like Bentleys and all that until I knew what they were. But I've always been into slick cars and sports cars.

No record or movie posters though. I think the first group that I really, truly got into as a fan would be Parliament. I knew their shit.

What are some great shows you've seen?

Slayer, Anthrax, and Megadeth in Anaheim. They fucking freaked my mind out with upside-down crosses. I thought I went to hell. I was turned out.

Parliament—I went to see George Clinton. I saw him land the Mother Ship. That's like a religious experience, seeing the fucking mother ship come down out of the Earth and seeing him come out in a big fur coat, saying, "Yo, the bigger the headache, the bigger the pill. They call me the Big Pill."

Run-D.M.C.—I was rapping then, but I truly didn't understand the magnitude of rap. I went to a concert and saw Run and saw the Adidas walk across the stage with lasers, and I saw Jam Master Jay come out on a riser, and I thought, "This shit is rock 'n' roll; this shit is big." And then he scratched the record, and it went through the speakers, and I was like, "Oh my God, I could be on the stage, just like that." Until then, I thought it was always going to be club music.

What are some of your favorite songs?

The craziest record I ever heard in a club was Public Enemy's "Rebel Without a Pause." Not knowing the record before, just standing in a club and hearing that thing come on. It was like, "What the fuck is this!" It just shook me. I was in New York City at a club called Latin Quarter.

"For My Dogs," DMX

"Angel of Death," Slayer

List up to ten things that could be helpful to someone breaking into the business.

The trick to breaking in is knowing that it's not easy and knowing that it is a really, really hard game to win. Look at Madonna, look at any of these celebrities—this is not an easy task! Only one thing harder than being the Mack is staying the Mack. That came out of the movie *The Mack,* and you can't say it any better than that. I tell new artists—have humility and have the understanding that you want a million dollars, but if it was that easy to get a million dollars, there wouldn't be so many Hyundais. Okay? What you're asking for is damn-near impossible, so be ready to put out supernatural efforts.

Billy Idol

Did you have a mentor or someone who inspired you? If so, what have you learned from that person?

From John Lennon and Lou Reed, I learned you have to risk to create and you have to look for a certain level of quality in your results, your songs.

What was your very first job in the music industry, and how did you get it?

In 1975, in my punk band Chelsea with Tony James and Gene October, which turned into Generation X in 1976. I played guitar and wrote the songs (with T. James).

What was your first big break? The first great thing that ever happened to you . . .

Being at the heart of the mid-seventies English punk movement gave me many avenues because it involved not only music but art and fashion.

What elements of your job make you want to go to work every day?

I decide when I want to work!

What qualities most helped you get to where you are today?

A love of music. Single-mindedness. Not taking no for an answer. Not letting my limitations put me off—in fact I made the most of them. I found I could trust my instincts, so I stuck to them through thick and thin.

If you knew everything at the beginning of your career that you know now, what would you have done differently?

For all the being prepared, events always spin off—so nothing.

What is your greatest lesson learned?

Believe like the audience does and keep your dreams in play. The only real reward in rock 'n' roll is the loyalty of your audience.

What are some of your favorite albums?

Raw Power, Iggy and the Stooges

To Be a Lover, George Faith and Lee "Scratch" Perry

Hunky Dory, David Bowie

Best of Tim Hardin, Tim Hardin

Who's Next, the Who

Suicide (first album), *Suicide*

Plastic Ono Band, John Lennon

Did you have any posters on your bedroom walls as a kid? Of whom?

Velvet Underground.

What are some great shows you've seen?

Captain Beefheart, Rainbow Theatre in London, 1970

Sex Pistols at the 100 Club

Suicide at the Peppermint Lounge in New York, 1981

Marc Bolan at the Wheelie Festival in England

MC5 at the Phun City Festival in Worthing, England

What are some of your favorite songs?

"Dream Baby Dream," Suicide

"Radio On," Jonathan Richman

"New Kinda Trick," the Cramps

"Israelites," Desmond Dekker

List up to ten things that could be helpful to someone breaking into the business.

- You have to watch, read, learn, live, everything you can about music (or the biz) from every angle. (Even if that's just reading about it.)
- Always be ready for action—to go onstage.
- Never think it's not gonna happen and never think it's over.
- Learn to find a special sense of place in your songs and find what can bring that out!
- If you can, laugh your way through!
- Try and go at the music biz from a new angle they don't expect. However far out it might seem, you're probably right!

India.Arie

Did you have a mentor or someone who inspired you? If so, what have you learned from that person?

My mother was my mentor. She taught me everything I know about singing just by being a singer herself. She sang around the house a lot, but she also made a go at being a professional singer when she was in her late teens and early twenties. Motown wanted to sign her—she didn't want to sign without her band, though, so she said no.

In kindergarten, when it was time for me to learn the days of the week, she wrote a song to help me learn which we would sing every day on the way to school. Singing was always there. One day when I was older, she realized I had a voice—not just a singing voice but a voice as a writer. She stopped me in the kitchen and said, "Do you want to be like me and your aunt and sing in the kitchen and at church, or do you want to be a singer?" I didn't know the answer then, but she urged me to take a shot at being a singer. She thought I had something that people would like to hear. Three months later, I started writing songs and playing guitar.

I started playing at coffee shops. I had three songs, and I really liked it, but I also felt like I had found something that I was *meant* to do. I went away to school and kept writing songs. Eventually, I asked her if I could leave school and focus on singing. She said no at first, until she heard my songs and realized how serious I was about it. After that, she told me I could live with her for two years, that I wouldn't have to pay any rent; basically, that she would support me until I got things off the ground and I could feed myself. She did that for me then, but even as a child, she had always told me I could be anything I wanted. I didn't have to be a singer; I didn't have to be a doctor. It was whatever I wanted, which really helped me feel free.

I have also always admired Stevie Wonder a great deal. I love him.

What was your very first job in the music industry, and how did you get it?

It was in September, three months after I started writing songs and playing guitar. I had played wind instruments before, like trumpet and saxophone. I was in the recorder ensemble, playing alto soprano recorder. But when I first picked up the guitar, I felt like I had found what I needed to take that next step as a singer/songwriter. So I practiced, literally, twenty hours a day, because I had never had to use my hands that way before. Someone told me about this open mic in Atlanta, which I decided to go to. I played, and I got a standing ovation. They invited me to come back the next month, only this time they paid for everything—they flew me in, paid for my hotel. They also paid me three hundred dollars, which was a lot of money to me then. From then on, I got paid almost every time I played. I think it was mostly because people just liked me, and they appreciated that I was so earnest about what I was doing.

What was your first big break? The first great thing that ever happened to you . . .

Every moment seems to have a corresponding other moment. The first thing that comes to mind was the moment I picked up the guitar and wrote my first song. It opened up this whole other thing I didn't know I had inside. It was an inspirational love song, and I had no idea that if I wrote, inspirational songs would just come out. I didn't know I could sing and play guitar at the same time. So that started it all, because once I started writing my own songs, I respected myself as a musician. I was twenty-one then. . . .

The corresponding moment was after the release of *Acoustic Soul* when I got to be on "Oprah Winfrey." That show is known for being empowering to women. When I was first writing the songs in the beginning of what has now become my career, I didn't realize I was writing songs that spoke so loudly and so clearly to women. I was only speaking from my perspective, but I guess as a black woman it's only natural that it might speak to women and black women. When I was on "Oprah," it was just me and my guitar.

Watching the women in the audience sing along and cry was an "aha" moment—I realized why I am doing this.

The first time I went out of state was when I played on the b-stage with *Lilith Fair*. It was so encouraging to get feedback from people like Bonnie Raitt or N'Dea Davenport or just from the audience—nobody knew me, but they liked me there too. It was a great moment, because I knew I was spoiled in Atlanta where everybody knew me.

Another great moment was when Master P wanted to start a music label called Harmony. His attorney had heard of me, so they flew me to Louisiana, and I sang my inspirational song called "India's Song." I was in a room with all these dudes with gold teeth, everyone had a gun in their pocket, and they were singing with me. I'd never been in that kind of environment, so it struck me (no matter how clichéd it is) that music really does transcend. I loved it.

My first job was when I sold the very first song I wrote called "Sweet Essence" to a girl group named Divine. I co-produced it and produced the vocal. It was like "Oh!—*This* is producing!"

What elements of your job make you want to go to work every day?

I love singing songs that I wrote. I am expressing myself every time I do that. I am very detailed about how I feel in my songs. I am telling the perfect truth for myself, and it feels and sounds good to me. I feel free. Even with time, songs still ring true because they take on new meaning. There's a song called "Strength, Courage & Wisdom" on *Acoustic Soul* that always means something different to me depending on the moment. If I'm having a hard show, or have to perform on live-feed TV, or if something is really bothering me, when I sing that song, it all goes away. When I wrote that song it wasn't even for me, or about me, but it's my favorite right now.

What qualities most helped you get to where you are today?

Number one—I really, really, really, really love music. I make it because I love music itself. I like to listen to it; I like to play it; I like to read about it; I like to write it—everything. Because of the prominent role music has always had in my life, I feel I was born with this love for it. It's almost a character trait. I feel music at different places in my body. When I listen to John Mayer, I feel it down my neck and in my stomach. With Stevie Wonder, I feel it in my whole body.

I'm also a hard worker. I've never worked as hard for anything as I have for my music.

As the years have gone by, and I see the effects my music has on people, that has kept me going as well. When I'm writing, it's all about me. It's actually a very selfish exercise, but then when I see how people respond, and identify, with the lyrics and the songs it becomes something totally different. Like Roberta Flack said, "When you release a song it belongs to the universe."

If you knew everything at the beginning of your career that you know now, what would you have done differently?

I would have put out a few more independent albums. I touched on it, but I would have *done* it. I think it empowers the artist. It teaches you about how you look, how to perform so you're not cold on MTV. If you've never done it, how can you really be good at it? I think doing more independent work would have been good because of the kind of artist I am. The big music industry thing is okay—it lets me do a lot of things and go a lot of places—but I think that I am a grassroots person and a grassroots artist. The success that I feel like I would have found as an independent artist not only would have empowered me, I think it would have been satisfying too. I don't know if I had to do it this big just yet. That first year was hard because I had to grow into this thing that I wasn't necessarily ready for. One thing I tell everybody is that if you can record yourself and have who you are musically cross over well to a recording, the grassroots thing is valuable in so many ways.

What is your greatest lesson learned?

To pay attention to my business. I haven't necessarily been duped out of anything, but knowledge is power. I feel like I could have had more in a lot of different areas—monetarily, opportunities, space—if I had been more aware all along. I don't regret it, because I wasn't ready to be "the CEO." But that *is* what happens. I have nineteen employees, and I'm the leader, but I didn't realize that for a while. Once I did, I became aware of how much time I had let go by ignoring things I should have been paying attention to.

What are some of your favorite albums?

I'm more of a singer person, but I love Stevie Wonder's *Songs in the Key of Life* and *Journey Through the Secret Life of Plants.* I'm a singer person first, songs second, albums third. I love Bill Withers, Stephen Bishop, Luther Vandross, Stevie Nicks, Cyndi Lauper, Collin Ray, the Eagles, Trisha Yearwood, Michael Jackson, Vince Gill, Oleta Adams, Lahla Hathaway.

Did you have any posters on your bedroom walls as a kid? Of whom?

I didn't have any. I was a very serious kid, especially about music. I remember hearing Sade and thinking I didn't like her because she sang off-key. When I told my mom that, she said, "Well, she's out there doing it and you're not." She would say things like that to me all the time, but I didn't know what she meant until I recorded my first album. After I finished recording *Acoustic Soul,* the first album I bought was *Lovers Rock,* and I ended up playing it all day. I would leave my house and it would still be on. I had to have it with me when I rode on airplanes. It got to the point where I had to have it everywhere. I grew to really love and respect Sade, so I had to go out and buy every album, and then the boxed set, and try to figure out why I was so late, why I had been so judgmental. When I was younger, if it wasn't Stevie Wonder, it wasn't good enough, so I definitely didn't have posters. I was way too critical and shy—God forbid anyone would know I had a crush on El DeBarge or Ronnie from New Edition. If I did have posters, it would have been them and George Michael and (remember) Jermaine Stewart. I loved him and 5 Star.

When Sade called me and asked me to go on tour, I had learned my lesson. At that point, I wanted to be like her.

What are some great shows you've seen?

When I had become a performer I had only seen Michael Jackson during the *Thriller* tour. I got to go backstage, which was really cool even though I didn't see Michael. I feel like I should be into things that are more "classic," but often I am not.

One of my favorite performances was actually Paula Cole. She made me understand what it means to be "free" onstage. She came to Atlanta and did a show at a small theater called the Roxy. She hit the piano with her feet, danced around with her underwear showing sometimes. Nothing mattered, though, because she was free. She beatboxed, and talked about Dolly Parton, and her hair wasn't curled or styled, she wore no makeup, but it was like she was saying "This is me, this is what I like." She had three encores.

I saw the *Africa Fete,* which was a tour of African pop stars that went around the states in 1999. It was Baaba Maal, Taj Mahal and his African Cora Orchestra, and Oliver Mtukudzi. That show really shaped the way I looked at the art of performing. Oliver went first and I couldn't believe that it could get any more exciting than that—and he was just the opening act! No one on the stage was invisible, the background singers each had a percussion instrument, and at the end he and a male singer did this dance together. He was the leader of the show, but they were all stars. Taj Mahal successfully blended American guitar with African string instruments, and I really *felt* it. It really worked, if you know what I'm saying. I was inspired to explore my African roots through music. Taj told me not to be afraid. I think his background singer was an African priest—it was like he glowed when he walked across the stage. I have never seen that before or since. Then Baaba Maal came out and his show was *exciting.* It was like African Michael Jackson! He sang and danced and did them both very well and naturally. The people in the front kept putting their kids onstage, and there were these boys—they looked about twelve years old—and they danced. Do you hear me, they didn't dance, they *danced.* The crowd was throwing money, everybody was singing and playing instruments—it was very electrifying. When I was really just at what I thought was the height of excitement, everybody left the stage and Baaba Maal and his background singer—who is blind and his best friend from childhood—did an acoustic set. Baaba played guitar, and they sang the most moving two-part harmony. It made me feel so good inside. That show taught me a lot. It's okay to let everyone shine, that sometimes less is more but dynamics are the best, that experimentation and exploration can work. Both Paula Cole and *Africa Fete* made me want to be free onstage. Because of them, my show is different every day.

What are some of your favorite songs?

"Summertime"

"Isn't She Lovely?"

"Visions"

"Lonesome Road"

"Grandma's Hands" and "Ain't No Sunshine," Bill Withers

"I'm Coming Back," Lalah Hathaway

"True Colors," Cyndi Lauper

"Night Shift," the Whispers

"You Bring Me Joy," Anita Baker

"I Can't Make You Love Me," Bonnie Raitt

"Nothing Comes to Sleepers" and "Outstanding," Gap Band

"You've Got a Friend" and "Don't Let Me Be Lonely," James Taylor

"Song for You," both Donny Hathaway's and the Carpenters' versions

"On & On," Stephen Bishop—I used to sing it everyday when I was a little girl

"What You Won't Do for Love," Bobby Caldwell

List up to ten things that could be helpful to someone breaking into the business.

- ■ I appreciate when someone is good and unique. Stevie Wonder is that. Cyndi Lauper is that. Erykah Badu is that. It's a combination of being technically sound but also unique in some form or fashion. It can be the way you look, or what you do with your voice, whatever. I think that's important because it gives you your own mark.

- ■ I think it's important to have a strong sense of self, because a picture goes a long way. If you don't know how you want to look, people could start taking pictures and you could end up being portrayed as anything all the way in Germany. Then that's what people think you are, because people don't have any contact with you except your videos, pictures, and whatever other images are out there. If you have a strong sense of self, it will help with your imaging, and of course, will cross over to your music, how you build your business, how you deal with people. When you know what you want out of yourself, out of your pictures, out of your life, out of your clothes—it makes the ride more fulfilling, and I think people appreciate that. It also helps the next generation of musicians, which is what we want to do, so music just keeps getting better. I want to see a combination female Stevie Wonder/Stevie Nicks/Sarah Vaughn/Stevie Ray Vaughan. I would love to see that someday—that would be a strong lady!

Michael Jackson

Did you have a mentor or someone who inspired you? If so, what have you learned from that person?

Berry Gordy, Diana Ross, Thomas Edison, Walt Disney, James Brown, Jackie Wilson. I learned a lot from them— how to be a visionary, how to be creative, how to be persistent, how to be determined, how to have a will of iron and to never give up no matter what.

What was your very first job in the music business, and how did you get it?

I don't remember back that far, but I think I was around six years old. My father would know how we got the job, but we performed at a club called Mr. Lucky's.

What was your first big break? The first great thing that ever happened to you . . .

The real big break was when Motown signed us. We had auditioned in Detroit, and then Berry Gordy invited us to play at a private party in this small town in Indiana. All of our favorite stars as kids were there—Diana Ross, Smokey Robinson, the Miracles, the Temptations, Stevie Wonder. We performed next to an indoor pool at this huge mansion with marble everywhere around us. We performed, and they just went crazy. They loved it. I remember to this day when Berry walked up to us after and said, "Boys, you're signed."

What elements of your job make you want to go to work every day?

I want to work every day. I just love the idea of creating worlds. It's like taking an empty canvas, or a clean slate, and all the paint you want. I love the idea that you can just color and paint and create worlds, create anything at all. And these worlds can last forever. People can see them years later and still be awe-inspired. It's amazing.

What qualities most helped you get to where you are today?

Faith, determination, and practice.

If you knew everything at the beginning of your career that you know now, what would you have done differently?

I would have practiced more.

What is your greatest lesson learned?

Not to trust everybody in the industry. There are a lot of sharks, and record companies steal. They cheat. You have to audit them. It's time for artists to take a stand against them, because they totally take advantage of artists. They forget that it's the artists who make the company, not the company who makes the artists. Without the talent, the company would be nothing but just hardware. And it takes a real good talent that the public wants to see.

I think God plants seeds through people on the earth, to bring some bliss and escapism, some joy and some magic. Without entertainment, what would the world really be like? It would be a totally different world for me. I love entertainment. And my favorite of all is film. It's the greatest, and the most expressive of all the art forms. The power and magic of movies and music touch the soul. It's almost like religion—you get so involved, so caught up. You go in the theater a different person than you come out. You live it. You're a part of it. You forget you're sitting in a seat. That's powerful, and I love that.

What are some of your favorite albums?

These days, most albums have one or two good songs and the rest stink. I love the great show-tune writers very much. I love Rogers and Hammerstein, and I love Holland-Dozier-Holland, from Motown. They were geniuses. I also love Stevie Wonder's *Songs in the Key of Life* and *Talking Book*. He is a genius. Hearing his music made me say to myself, "*I* can do this, and I think I can do this on an international level."

Another moment was when the Bee Gees came out in the seventies. I cried listening to their music. I knew every note, every instrument. When they did *Saturday Night Fever,* that did it for me. I said to myself, "I gotta do this! I know I can do this!" So I started working on *Thriller*. It was fun. I just started writing songs. I wrote "Billie Jean." I wrote "Beat It" and "Startin' Something."

Some other favorite albums are . . .

Nutcracker Suite, Tchaikovsky | *The Sound of Music*
What's Going On, Marvin Gaye | All Sly & the Family Stone albums
Live at the Apollo, James Brown

Did you have any posters on your bedroom walls as a kid? Of whom?

I had Brooke Shields posters everywhere. My sisters would get jealous and tear them off the wall.

What are some great shows you've seen?

I like the real entertainers, the ones who make you get goose bumps watching them under that one spotlight. James Brown, Jackie Wilson, the Delphonics, the Temptations, Frank Sinatra, Sammy Davis. I saw James Brown a lot when I was young because we used to have to go onstage after him for Amateur Hour at the Apollo. I'd be in the wings studying every step, every move. . . .

Seeing James Brown and Jackie Wilson at the Apollo made me cry. I'd never seen anything like that. That kind of emotion, that kind of fever and feeling in the room, it was like another higher, spiritual plane they were on. It was like they were in a trance, and they had the audience in the palm of their hand. I loved how they could control the audience like that, with that kind of power. And they would get so into their singing they'd have tears running down their face. I can't tell you how incredible it was. It's magic . . . real magic.

What are some of your favorite songs?

There are so many great songs, just like there are so many great movies. But if I had to name a few, I think the sixties had some of the best melodies of all time. I think the simple ones are the best. Peter, Paul and Mary, the Mamas and the Papas, the Supremes, any Motown, they were all wonderful. The Drifters go a little further back, but I love "On Broadway." It's genius. I love "Alfie," and I love Burt Bacharach very much. The Beatles, like "Eleanor Rigby," "Yesterday."

I also like Debussy's "Claire de Lune," "Arabesque," and "Prelude to the Afternoon of a Faun."

List up to ten things that could be helpful to someone breaking into the business.

- Study the greats and become greater.
- Be a scientist. Dissect everything.
- Believe in yourself. No matter what, I don't care if the whole world is against you, or teasing you, or saying you're not gonna make it . . . believe in yourself, no matter what. Some of the greatest men that have made a mark on this world were treated like that, you know, "You're not gonna do it, you're not gonna get anywhere." They laughed at the Wright Brothers. They laughed at Thomas Edison. They laughed at Walt Disney. They made jokes at Henry Ford. They said he was ignorant. He didn't have a college degree, because he dropped out of school. Disney dropped out of school. They even took Ford to court to prove his intelligence. That's how far they went. But these are men that shaped and changed our culture, our customs, they way we live, the way we do things.

Jewel

Did you have a mentor or someone who inspired you? If so, what have you learned from that person?

I did have a mentor, and he taught me to never trust anyone. I've been inspired by people like Nina Simone, Charles Bukowski, Paul Westerberg, Madonna, and other artists who have an irreverent approach to their art, which I think is important. I don't think anything is sacred.

What was your very first job in the music industry, and how did you get it?

My parents were performers. They did shows in hotels for tourists, and I grew up singing with them starting at age six. My dad and I became a duet after my parents got divorced when I was eight.

What was your first big break? The first great thing that ever happened to you . . .

Sleeping in my car and singing in that coffee shop seems liked a really blessed time. I didn't think I would ever get signed to a label, but somehow I got a really big following going. I started with zero fans and ended up doing two shows a night. It was really awesome. I did five-hour shows, told the audience stories, and they'd tell me stories. Then labels started showing up, and it was suddenly really surreal. It was like being Cinderella.

I had always thought I'd be able to make a living at it, but I never thought I'd be God's gift to records. I grew up singing every night and every weekend. I had been performing and gigging my whole life. As early as age twelve there was always some rich schmuck around who wanted to make a record for me. Of course, something always fell through. When I was sixteen, there was this shady, playboy-type character who probably could have gotten me a deal, but now I know that would have been disastrous. I was still in school, and I know now how mentally unformed my brain was. It ended up working out a few years later. By the time I was ready, it was a very different story. Really big labels were in bidding wars over me, and it was a totally different scene than being in Homer, Alaska, and having some rich fisherman tell me he was going to make me a record.

What elements of your job make you want to go to work every day?

Bukowski said that if you take the writers away from their typewriters, all you'll have is the sickness that made them type in the beginning. I should never quit writing.

What qualities most helped you get to where you are today?

I'm tenacious. I'm a quick learner. I practice really hard. I've always been very dogged about practicing every day. My dad and I used to practice five hours a day, and then doing gigs at night on top of that. I've always been very professional and very hardworking. I've always taken it very seriously and have never been a flake who didn't show up on time. I've always been the kind of kid who would save a dollar instead of spend one. I've always loved words.

Also, my parents were divorced, and my dad and I really didn't get along. He liked horses and he liked performing, so I took a lot of time to get good at those things so that we'd have some common ground. I think a lot of that plays into it, as well as being an overachiever.

If you knew everything at the beginning of your career that you know now, what would you have done differently?

One of the best things I did was to try and build a contract that supported longevity as much as possible. I took really high mechanical royalty rates over a big advance. I could have gotten a huge advance, and with me sleeping in a car, you'd think I would have thought that a couple million dollars would set me for life. But for some reason, I was really interested in my songwriting, and I didn't take that much money up front. You repay them for all of that anyway, through your record sales, so it's not really yours. Unless of course you don't sell any records, then you won the gamble and the label lost. But that's not a gamble you want to win, because you're not selling records, which means it's the only money you'll ever make.

I turned down a big advance and took one of the highest mechanical royalty rates. As long as I sold a million records, the mechanical royalty rate would go up by a designated amount of points with each record. It ended up working out a lot better for me, but it meant, as an eighteen-year-old kid who built that contract, that if I was successful I would have won, but that if I wasn't, I should have taken the couple million. It was a gamble, and I bet on myself.

You can always think of a million things you could have done differently, but there's no way to avoid a lot of mistakes. I tried to build a career that would give me the chance to be a writer for a long period of time and not just sensational. You have to make a decision every day whether you are going to support fame or support art. Both are fine, but you have to know which you are choosing so you don't end up with a career that isn't the one you intended to have twenty years down the road. I've turned down a lot of things that would have made me more famous because I didn't feel they were the right things to support me as an artist or writer.

What is your greatest lesson learned?

Almost any artist is neurotic for many reasons. In general, they're very gifted, sensitive people who have been hurt, or gifted, sensitive people who want to try and help, who want to feel better. Those things don't go away when you become famous. Whatever ghosts haunt you become magnified fiftyfold with fame. Fame doesn't usually change anyone for the better. It doesn't make you feel more secure about yourself. It doesn't make you feel more talented, or more beautiful. Generally, if you have those concerns or worries, it makes you feel like you're living a lie because you're not talented, or you're not beautiful, or whatever. One of the things I've learned most about getting famous is that it is a magnifying glass that will make you a worse person, especially because there are so many people around who are willing to let you be a brat, and willing to let you be a bad person. You have to work a lot harder to discipline yourself emotionally. There are a lot more distractions, and things just move faster. There are a million things that will validate all of your neuroses. You can avoid dealing with yourself for a long time, but that is why it often ends up in a crash, like some rock 'n' roll cliché on VH1's *Behind the Music.*

I think writing, in and of itself, lays you bare. I'm amazed by how much my writing is like my subconscious trying to speak to itself. Writing has always been a pretty revealing process for me. My boyfriend, Ty, is such a grounded, level person who can help me see clearly. It's good to have someone like that around who doesn't just see the hype. Who you surround yourself with becomes terribly important.

What are some of your favorite albums?

Ella Fitzgerald Sings the Cole Porter Songbook. They were made for each other. She's such a smart singer, not only technically, but intellectually. He's such a smart lyricist, but he's also facetious. He'll juxtapose very sweet melodies with kind-of naughty lyrics. As a smart singer, she allowed the listener to catch his ironies and subtleties, which you otherwise may not have picked up on.

Let It Be, the Replacements
Achtung Baby, U2
Albums by Bruce Springsteen and Edith Piaf

Did you have any posters on your bedroom walls as a kid? Of whom?

Oddly enough, I had a Leif Garrett poster, which is funny because there is no way I knew who he was. But other than that, I always shared a room in the cabin with my brothers, and there was uncovered insulation on the walls so we couldn't really hang anything up.

What are some great shows you've seen?

Not a lot made it to Alaska, and I really haven't seen that many shows since I've been famous. I am on the road all the time.

My first concert was Bon Jovi when I was in Hawaii in eighth grade. It was a spectacle.

I saw Springsteen shows in England and Jersey that were awesome. I don't use stage lights or set lists. I come from a very old-school entertainer background, where if you kick ass you don't need anything to distract you from kicking ass or to distract the fans from the fact that you can't sing. I don't like rehearsed shows, where the singer drops to their knee at the same lyric of the same song of every show. That's why I liked Springsteen—it was just white lights and an empty stage.

What are some of your favorite songs?

Nina Simone covered a song called "The Other Woman." It's really well-crafted.
"Miss Otis Regrets," Cole Porter
"Love for Sale," Cole Porter

List up to ten things that could be helpful to someone breaking into the business.

- Know before you start whether you're going for fame or artistry. Somebody may want you to go onstage and be half-naked, and you might do it if you want to be famous, and you might not do it if you want to have longevity. You can always get undressed later.
- A lot of artists have a fear that if you understand business it will make you a bad artist. The opposite is true. I think the more you know about contracts, about what is expected of you, about what is going to put pressure on the label and what's going to put pressure on you, the more freedom you will have as an artist. You should have your lawyer go though every paragraph of contracts with you, and you should know what the alternatives and options are.
- I encourage everybody to trust nothing but their own intelligence. This business is based on artists, but the artists make the least amount of money. No other business runs like this, where other people take such big cuts. There have been a lot of stoned or high musicians signing a lot of contracts and setting really bad standards. Many musicians felt lucky to get free coke and have the chance to play gigs.
- Staying on top of your business is important. It's so shady—you give really sensitive, semibrilliant savants who have been broke their whole life millions of dollars and expect them to know what to do with it. It's a car crash pretty much every time. I think managers should make artists take business classes as soon as they start getting famous.

■ I believe in music, and I believe in art. There are very few people in this business who do. But if you're into music because you love music, there are some people out there who will help you for the right reasons. I think if you're trying to get signed, sending out your tape to every A&R guy out there makes you a bit common. A&Rs generally have no ears. There are still a few people out there with ears like John Kolodner, Mo Ostin, Arif Mardin, and Ahmet Ertegun, but in general they're all young schmucks who are looking for something to copy—whatever is big. They're looking for the next Britney Spears, or the next Jewel, or whatever. They don't really have much foresight. So when you send your tape around, and it starts to get on everybody's desk, even if it is good, it just becomes common. It's a weird psychology. The best thing you can do is to kick ass, be the best at what you do, and worry about nothing else. That's what worked for me—I attracted a huge following, people started hearing about me from other people, and then the radio stations started playing me locally. I think when you're talented, and you let that talent show, people start to notice, and the rest takes care of itself. Otherwise, you get really good at learning how to sell and market yourself until your talent matures, and that seems like a backwards way to go.

■ I see too many bands worrying about their hair cuts rather than their songwriting. I hate it when artists don't work hard. I opened for Deep Blue Something right before I was about to break. They sang that "Breakfast at Tiffany's" song. We played small clubs—five hundred people or so. I remember them getting onstage and putting their feet up, acting like they were Metallica. Then they'd go backstage and talk and talk about how they were going to play stadiums. I'm sorry if they're reading this book, but you just knew they were going nowhere. You knew they were a one-hit wonder. They were shitting their money. I hate it. They were wimps, they were sissies, and they wanted everything handed to them. It makes me sick. Working hard, touring hard, and building your fan base are the only ways to build longevity beyond someone being intrigued by one song. The more you keep your head down, the more humble you stay, the more you realize you have to work for everything you get.

Elton John

Did you have a mentor or someone who inspired you? If so, what have you learned from that person?

Any great piano players—Winifred Atwell, Jerry Lee Lewis, Little Richard, Floyd Cramer.

What was your very first job in the music industry, and how did you get it?

Tea boy at Mills Music, Denmark Street, London.

What was your first big break? The first great thing that ever happened to you . . .

Backing Patti LaBelle and the Belles.

What elements of your job make you want to go to work every day?

You never know what's in store or what you might create.

What qualities most helped you get to where you are today?

Persistence and love of what I do.

If you knew everything at the beginning of your career that you know now, what would you have done differently?

Never sign a management contract!

What is your greatest lesson learned?

Never sign a management contract and *never* sell your publishing.

What are some of your favorite albums?

Exile on Main Street, the Rolling Stones
Grace, Jeff Buckley
Heartbreaker, Ryan Adams

After the Gold Rush, Neil Young
And thousands more . . .

Did you have any posters on your bedroom walls as a kid? Of whom?

Dusty Springfield.

What are some great shows you've seen?

> The Band, Royal Albert Hall
> Jimi Hendrix, the Marquee
> Derek and the Dominos, Auditorium Theatre, Chicago
> Keith Jarrett, Washington, D.C.

What are some of your favorite songs?

> "Don't Give Up," Peter Gabriel
> "I Put a Spell on You"
> "Going Back"

List up to ten things that could be helpful to someone breaking into the business.

- Always get a second opinion.
- If you get turned down once, keep going.
- Respect your peers.
- Play *live*.
- Listen to new acts and older classics.
- Try to appreciate all types of music.
- Don't dish anyone in public. I've done this, and it's not a good idea.
- Never listen to reviewers/critics.
- Videos aren't going to expand your shelf life—play live.
- Save some money (I can't believe I said that).

Steve Jones

THE SEX PISTOLS

Did you have a mentor or someone who inspired you? If so, what have you learned from that person?

The Faces and the New York Dolls. They were very inspirational to me. Watching them I learned how to get out of living in Shepherd's Bush. It's a dump. Seeing the New York Dolls made me want to play music more in a band manner. I had listened to their record for a long time because Malcolm McLaren had it in his shop, and I used to listen to it with him, to their first album. No one showed us the ropes, though.

What was your very first job in the music industry, and how did you get it?

My first job in the music business was stealing equipment. I had no idea what to do with it, but it was my only connection to the music business. I used to be a thief anyway, so when I decided I wanted to be in music, I started stealing equipment. I had all kinds of stuff—fucking trombones, fucking electric guitars. The stupidest thing was one of those big things you sit down and blow—a French horn.

What was your first big break? The first great thing that ever happened to you . . .

After we had done the Bill Grundy show, when I swore on TV. The next day it was out of control as far as the press went. Before that we were kind of getting a name for ourselves in the music press, but after the Bill Grundy show, we were a household name overnight. It seemed like it was happening. Little did I know, it was the beginning of the end.

What elements of your job make you want to go to work every day?

Insecurity. I hated rehearsing. I couldn't stand rehearsing, I still don't like it. But I wanted to be famous, I guess.

The other guys liked to rehearse. It's a pain in the ass to me, but I did it anyway because I wanted to be famous. But I'm not one of those people who sits in his bedroom for hours on end. I didn't like going to work. I just wanted to be famous without doing anything, basically.

What qualities most helped you get to where you are today?

Being honest and being naive. If I hadn't been naive I would have written songs like every fucking idiot who writes songs—verse, chorus, verse, chorus, whatever. Because I couldn't really play music well, we just kind of came up with our own structures. Obviously you've got to be talented too—you don't just make it on timing.

If you knew everything at the beginning of your career that you know now, what would you have done differently?

I would have made friends with Bill Gates when he was in his garage.

What is your greatest lesson learned?

Don't trust no one. There's so much bullshit out there. I got disappointed so many times when you open up to someone and trust them a bit. I got disappointed a lot.

What are some of your favorite albums?

Every Picture Tells a Story, Rod Stewart
Too Much Too Soon, the New York Dolls
Raw Power, Iggy Pop
Legend, Bob Marley
Ziggy Stardust, David Bowie. One of our big influences, and Mick Ronson was probably my favorite guitar player. I really appreciate him now for how good he was and how underrated he was.
Roxy Music and *For Your Pleasure,* Roxy Music

Did you have any posters on your bedroom walls as a kid? Of whom?

The Faces, Black Sabbath (I don't know why, I didn't really like them that much), and a picture of Pete Osgood, a soccer player for Chelsea.

What are some great shows you've seen?

Roxy Music, Greek Theater, 2002. One of the best shows I've ever seen.
The Faces (with the New York Dolls opening), Wembley, 1972
Terence Trent D'Arby, the Roxy, 1987. He was really good.
Mott the Hoople, Hammersmith Odeon, around 1971
Ziggy Stardust and the Spiders from Mars, Hammersmith Odeon

What are some of your favorite songs?

"Rock and Roll," Led Zeppelin

"Purple Haze," Jimi Hendrix

"My Jealous Mind," Alvin Stardust

"Maggie May," Rod Stewart

An old reggae version of "Young, Gifted and Black"

List up to ten things that could be helpful to someone breaking into the business.

I don't care about anyone else, really. I had to learn my way, and I did all right. I think when you get too much information, you fuck things up. Follow your heart. Follow your instincts. It's just street smarts. . . .

R. Kelly

Did you have a mentor or someone who inspired you? If so, what have you learned from that person?

My mom and Lina McLin. My mom taught me never to give up. Ms. McLin taught me about music and life and how to transform my music and communicate it into all different areas. "Don't let them label you," she told me. "Perform and appreciate the art and the gift of music in all its forms." Opera, dance, classical—there really aren't any barriers.

What was your very first job in the music industry, and how did you get it?

I did a Jules commercial in Chicago. The line was "When you look at Jules, you're looking at a friend." Of course I never got paid. I got the job through a guy named Steve Robinson who came to my high school looking for a teacher to recommend people who could sing, and the next thing I knew, I was doing it.

What was your first big break? The first great thing that ever happened to you . . .

My first big break was when I started street performing and singing in the subways. It was not the traditional way to perform, and it helped me get rid of my shyness. Singing to strangers strengthened my voice. I had to sing loud enough so I could be heard over the "el." With my voice stronger I felt more prepared, and learning how to perform for different kinds of people gave me my confidence.

What elements of your job make you want to go to work every day?

I'm in love with my job. Music flows through me all the time. You could say I'm impregnated with music, but the baby never gets born. Instead I just keep having these dizzy spells. I'm always at work; my work is a vacation.

What qualities most helped you get to where you are today?

My zeal, my inner strength, my ability to get over adversity—whatever form the adversity used to take and now takes. I never take "No, you can't" as an answer. My mother said, "Keep going, even if you're down by fifteen points, you can always come back." I'm stubborn and don't believe in "just in case" scenarios, the safe way out. I'm going for it.

If you knew everything at the beginning of your career that you know now, what would you have done differently?

Careerwise, nothing, because I believe in destiny. Every career triumph and career setback I've experienced has made me able to do what I do now and to endure what I have to endure now.

What is your greatest lesson learned?

Trust yourself before anyone else. Only you know your limits.

What are some of your favorite albums?

Songs in the Key of Life, Stevie Wonder   *12 Play,* R. Kelly

Rapture of Love, Anita Baker   *Brian McKnight,* Brian McKnight

What are some great shows you've seen?

Bobby Brown, back in the days . . .   The Winans

Stevie Wonder   Luther Vandross

What are some of your favorite songs?

"We Are the World"   "Ribbon in the Sky"

"I Believe I Can Fly"   "What's Going On"

List up to ten things that could be helpful to someone breaking into the business.

■ Don't spend money on professional portfolios and demos—if the tracks are wrong, you lose because the track is the first thing anyone hears. You got ten seconds tops to reach anybody and the best you could do is sing a cappella and let the listener hear what you can do with your voice.

■ If what you do is tracks, just don't go get any singer. Just present your tracks so the listener isn't distracted by something other than what you're trying to present.

■ Think about the lessons you've heard that I and others like me have told you about.

Alicia Keys

Did you have a mentor or someone who inspired you? If so, what have you learned from that person?

I have to say that I had a number of mentors. Some were very real and personal. Some mentors I learned so much from by watching from a distance. My "up close" mentors were people like my mother, who showed me independence, tolerance, strength, the importance of keeping appointments I'd made (whether I wanted to go once the time came or not), determination, and love. My Nana, who helped show me the love of reading, which led to my love of writing. My Auntie, who showed me that you may not always get what you want, but you damn sure better not stop trying! My Fafa, who showed me what it's like to be treated like a princess, and now I just can't seem to accept anything less.

I've also been truly inspired by wonderful people like Marvin Gaye, Quincy Jones, Mary J. Blige, Maya Angelou, Assata Shakur, Langston Hughes, James Baldwin, Marian McPartland, Oscar Peterson, Satie, Beethoven, and Chopin. All these people are my mentors as they have taught me, inspired me, and shown me that nothing great comes without a fight, struggle, sacrifice, and love for the cause. Nothing wonderful comes without going out on a limb, and nothing timeless comes without breaking the mold.

What was your very first job in the music industry, and how did you get it?

Well, I was too young to work in the music industry, but I definitely worked in music on my own, and those experiences prepared me for the industry work later. As a person who just loved being around music, always needing a little extra dough for subway rides to get to the music, I worked as a teacher's aide, teaching theory. When I was only fifteen, I taught grades seven through eleven theory concepts, composition, sight-reading, some history, and anything else that would keep the class interested for that two-hour session.

I also worked with kids after school and practiced with them and taught them piano. This was a nice way to keep my skills up and a great way to make some extra cash to pay for the train rides I would take to the Bronx, to write a song with anybody that had tracks (this was before I put two and two together and started to write my own stuff on the piano) or to any club I could sneak into that played music in any form!

What was your first big break? The first great thing that ever happened to you . . .

Well, I was in a group. We were friends who all went to school together. We sang everywhere, in the hall on the way to class, on the train, a cappella at little functions, anywhere! We'd go to my house or anywhere someone was involved in music and just write and sing for hours. It came before everything else. Who knows what in the world we were writing, but we loved it. One day one of the girls in the group said her cousin had some people he knew in "the business" who wanted to hear us sing. Oh my goodness, we were *soooooo* excited and *soo* nervous that when we sang for this man, we probably sang sharp, flat, and everything in between!!! But, he must've seen something in us because not long after, he started to work with us. We went to the PAL (something like a community center) on 124th Street in Harlem every day after school and practiced this one song for hours. In between we would try to throw in some of the things we had been writing and working on, but he wasn't interested in that, he just wanted us to learn one popular song that was already out so that he could showcase the fact that we had the potential to be commercial. So we grinned and bore it 'cause, shit, we were singing!

After about nine months of singing this same one song, the guy told us that we had an appointment to sing for Russell Simmons. Oh my goodness, we couldn't believe it!!! We got all prepared and went downtown to this huge twelve-floor building of which three *entire* floors belonged to Mr. Simmons. Since we all came from little apartments, we never saw anything like that before! It was almost more oppressive for us than impressive, 'cause the tension was rising and the nerves were kicking in. We waited a good hour, and you know how your mind works overtime when you have to wait. Nonetheless, the time finally came for us to sing, and we were so excited and nervous we probably sang sharp, flat, and everything in between . . . and as it turned out, Mr. Simmons didn't call back (although he was kind and told us we did well and that we were pretty before we left that day). I don't even think he knows to this day that I was one of those four nervous girls who sang for him years ago.

That experience led me to meet some of the wonderful people that I know today, including my present manager, Jeff Robinson. Without them, I'd probably still be singing that same one song.

What elements of your job make you want to go to work every day?

The people that I work with are creative and kind, and we are a family. Another reason I love my job is that I can express my heart, be it anger, joy, love, hate, anything at all—I can say it. Sometimes it comes out as a great song, sometimes it doesn't, but at least I get it off my chest.

The challenges and hectic schedules always test my character and constantly make me reevaluate myself, what I stand for, how I'm changing, etc. I love what I do, and it's quite an interesting day at the office.

What qualities most helped you get to where you are today?

Patience, not needing much sleep, tenacity, determination to get where and what I want out of myself, practice, kindness, humility, and love.

If you knew everything at the beginning of your career that you know now, what would you have done differently?

Nothing, and I really mean that. There are things I would have rather not done, but I'd have never known that had I not screwed up. So sometimes a screwup can put you on the right track.

What is your greatest lesson learned?

My greatest lesson learned so far is that it's *very* important to love yourself in this life! Everyone has opinions and more opinions and judgments and a million things to say. If you don't love yourself and hold on to the true people who really love you in all stages of your life, then you can get lost in a sea of misdirection. You can lose yourself and your original ideas, your morals, and the reasons why. It can darken your heart. So it's important not to get caught up in things that don't really mean anything or to give attention to things and people that don't really care about you. I take everything at face value and stay close to my core.

That's the biggest lesson that I've learned so far, and I stick by it to stay connected to myself.

What are some of your favorite albums?

Some Kind of Blue, Billie Holliday
What's Going On, Marvin Gaye
The Stranger, Billy Joel
Miseducation of Lauryn Hill, Lauryn Hill
Everything Is Everything, Donny Hathaway
Ready to Die, the Notorious B.I.G.

Don Killuminati: The 7 Day Theory,
  Makaveli (Tupac)
Jagged Little Pill, Alanis Morissette
Nevermind, Nirvana
Anything by Nina Simone, and the list
  goes on and on and on . . .

Did you have any posters on your bedroom walls as a kid? Of whom?

All the posters I had in my room as a kid are all too embarrassing to mention in this publication!

What are some great shows you've seen?

One of the *best* shows I've ever seen in my life was Prince at Madison Square Garden, with Chaka Khan, Dougie Fresh, Larry Graham, and some others. It was incredible. It was true heart and soul, talent, and showmanship. I stood up the entire time mesmerized and screaming. He made you feel, made you dance, made you think. It was a true experience. I went home exhausted because of all the energy I expended at that show (and I didn't even perform)! I watched it like a hawk, and I vowed that when it was my time to hit the stage I would make people feel something!

I also remember seeing Michael Jackson when I was about six years old. We sat *soooooo* far up in the balcony, it was more like watching a tiny spot, but I remember being taken with all the energy that I felt in the arena. I also remember asking why there were so many ambulances around. Who was sick? I remember a lot of people fainting.

What are some of your favorite songs?

"'Round Midnight"
"Melancholy Mood"
"Adore," Prince
"Flying High in a Friendly Sky," Marvin Gaye
"One More for the Road," Frank Sinatra
"You're All I Need to Get By," Marvin Gaye
   and Tammi Terrell & Mary J. Blige
   and Method Man

"Smells Like Teen Spirit," Nirvana
"If I Was Your Girlfriend," Prince
"Gymnopédies," Erik Satie

List up to ten things that could be helpful to someone breaking into the business.

■ Know your business. Don't be passive or you will get taken advantage of.

■ Keep doing what you love to do. If it's singing, always be somewhere singing. If it's playing keys or guitar, take every opportunity to do that.

■ Keep performing, no matter what. It's good for your spirit, it keeps your chops up, and you never know who you're gonna meet or who's gonna see you that one night.

■ When someone says "you'll never . . ." or "you won't . . ." or "you can't . . . ," cut them off as soon as possible or keep them at a distance. Don't believe that shit!

■ Mostly, as hard as it is at times, believe in yourself no matter what. You gotta be your biggest fan, 'cause people will always take your lead. If you feel like you hold the greatest secret, people will feel it and believe it, too.

■ My personal favorite—don't try to be like anyone else. Be you!!! It's so much more interesting.

Anthony Kiedis

Did you have a mentor or someone who inspired you? If so, what have you learned from that person?

As a kid, I was a cocky little bastard who thought he didn't need a mentor. Eventually I realized I idolized my father and came to accept him as my mentor. He showed me the joy of nonconformity, the freedom of antiestablishmentarianism and turned me on to Roxy Music and Ernest Hemingway. He also got me into the dictionary.

I was also influenced by Woody Allen, gravity, the Marx Brothers, teenage girls of the seventies, David Bowie, Grandmaster Flash and the Furious Five, P-Funk, Magic Johnson, James Brown, and, as an ongoing inspiration, Darby Crash.

What was your very first job in the music industry, and how did you get it?

My first job in the music world was introducing à la MC style my friend's band called Anthym. I would do these elaborate and comically theatrical intros to their little club shows—another art I learned from my father. I didn't get paid, but I loved the rush. Previous to that, I had performed in the chorus line of musical productions at Fairfax High.

What was your first big break? The first great thing that ever happened to you . . .

I'm not so sure I agree with the idea of "breaks." I feel like you create your own "breaks" or opportunities by putting yourself in creative situations and working hard at what you love to do. The first great thing that happened didn't happen to me. It happened with me and my best friends when we were asked to put together a one-time-only band performance to open a show.

What elements of your job make you want to go to work every day?

I don't want to go to work every day. Some days I'm filled with the light of musical ecstasy and I can't wait to go to be a part of creation, and some days I just don't feel it. On the days when I am feeling it, it's the sense of making something out of thin air. Where there was once a blank page, there is now a poem, a song. I also feel blessed to have my work revolve around friendship and love.

What qualities most helped you get to where you are today?

Being able to recognize the beauty in life.

If you knew everything at the beginning of your career that you know now, what would you have done differently?

It all happened perfectly, even the pain and loss. It had to be as it was. The mistakes are what made it sweet when it found its rhythm.

I wasn't very organized about the approach to "my career." I didn't look at it like this thing that needed to be carefully molded and perfectly manicured. My band had a life of its own, and when I put some good food and energy into it, it grew beautiful fruit. When I put poison in it, and starved it of love and care, it grew shit sandwiches.

What is your greatest lesson learned?

An untamed ego will destroy the party. Never give up hope on anything or anybody. Let people know you love them before they die. Clean your emotional house and trust your intuition. Don't take yourself too seriously.

What are some of your favorite albums?

I am not a favorites person, nor am I a list person. A few of my favorite albums are:

Double Nickels on the Dime, Minutemen   *Kid A,* Radiohead
Science Fiction, Ornette Coleman   *Santa Monica '72,* David Bowie
Hardcore Jollies, Funkadelic

Did you have any posters on your bedroom walls as a kid? Of whom?

I only had one poster on my wall, Andy Warhol's *Chelsea Girls*.

What are some great shows you've seen?

Nirvana, Brazil   Art Blakey and the Jazz Messengers, 1980
Public Enemy, Greek   Jane's Addiction, Lollapalooza
PJ Harvey, Viper Room   Mad Society, Starwood
Chris Rock, Comedy Cellar   45 Grave, Al's Bar
DIL, Olympic   Talking Heads, Palladium
Fela, Olympic Auditorium   The Clash, Palladium
Iggy Pop, The Whiskey, 1975ish

What are some of your favorite songs?

I like some Beatles songs, some Funkadelic songs, some Fela songs, some Lou Reed songs, some T. Rex songs. Songs that remind me of heavy childhood times mean a lot to me.

"Family Affair," Sly & the Family Stone   "Redemption Song," Bob Marley

"School," Nirvana   "Win," David Bowie

"Wonderful World," Louis Armstrong

List up to ten things that could be helpful to someone breaking into the business.

- Don't read lists.
- Be in love with everything.
- Suit up and show up.
- Surround yourself with intelligent and loving people who share your enthusiasm for sound.
- Don't confine yourself to the pre-existing blueprint for anything.

Lenny Kravitz

Did you have a mentor or someone who inspired you? If so, what have you learned from that person?

Nobody I knew personally. I was inspired by all the great musicians I listened to growing up.

What was your very first job in the music industry, and how did you get it?

I was a staff writer for Almo Irving Music. I was discovered by the great writer and singer David Lasley. At the time, I was living on the street, and he heard my music and took me into the publishing company. I was seventeen and had nothing, so I spent the entire five thousand dollars on clothes.

What was your first big break? The first great thing that ever happened to you . . .

Getting signed. I was told for so many years that I could not make the kind of music that I was making and finally someone accepted me the way that I was.

What elements of your job make you want to go to work every day?

My love for music. I cannot live without it.

What qualities most helped you get to where you are today?

Determination and focus.

If you knew everything at the beginning of your career that you know now, what would you have done differently?

My first record deal would have been better. At the time, I didn't know as much as I know now. I could have owned my masters because when I got signed I arrived with them. C'est la vie.

What is your greatest lesson learned?

God bless the child that's got his own. And not compromising.

What are some of your favorite albums?

Innervisions, Stevie Wonder

What's Going On, Marvin Gaye

Rastaman Vibration, Bob Marley

Electric Ladyland, Jimi Hendrix

Kind of Blue, Miles Davis

Fresh, Sly & the Family Stone

Plastic Ono Band, John Lennon

Third Album, the Jackson 5

Led Zeppelin IV, Led Zeppelin

Did you have any posters on your bedroom walls as a kid? Of whom?

Jimi Hendrix, Led Zeppelin, and KISS.

What are some great shows you've seen?

James Brown, Apollo Theater

The Jackson 5, Madison Square Garden,
    New York City

KISS, the Forum, Los Angeles

Pink Floyd, Superdome, New Orleans

Duke Ellington, Rainbow Room

Miles Davis, Playboy Jazz Festival

What are some of your favorite songs?

"You Are the Sunshine of My Life,"
    Stevie Wonder

"Have You Ever Been (to Electric Ladyland)"
    Jimi Hendrix

"Darling Dear," the Jackson 5

"My Life in the Sunshine," Roy Ayers

"That's the Way of the World," Earth,
    Wind & Fire

"Angie," the Rolling Stones

List up to ten things that could be helpful to someone breaking into the business.

- Do not compromise your art.
- Learn the business.

Avril Lavigne

Did you have a mentor or someone who inspired you? If so, what have you learned from that person?

My parents are the ones who pushed me and got me to where I am today. They saw something inside of me and knew it was their job to help me get it out. They have encouraged me since I was a little girl to fulfill this dream of mine.

What was your very first job in the music industry, and how did you get it?

I actually used to work as a janitor for Arista Records. . . . I'm just kidding. I guess right now, what I am doing, this is my first job in the music industry, just being an artist.

What was your first big break? The first great thing that ever happened to you . . .

My first break was taking a trip to New York City to work with a producer named Peter Zizzo. He had believed so deeply in me and was determined to work with me. One of the first great things that happened to me was getting my musical ideas out and recorded and the magical moment of sitting back and listening to what I had just made.

What elements of your job make you want to go to work every day?

When I am on tour I know I get to play a show every night, and the satisfaction of reaching a whole audience is one of the things that makes me love what I do. I love how every day is a different day because I am always in a different place, with different people, and new atmospheres, and there is always something exciting taking place. There is never a regular routine. It is always fucked, and that's why I like it!

What qualities most helped you get to where you are today?

It was a risky time for me to dive into the music industry because of all the bullshit pop that was around. I could easily have been pushed into becoming one of those acts because that's what was selling at the time, but I stayed true to myself and to my music and I didn't allow people to tell me what to do. Honesty, staying strong, being real, and believing in myself are the qualities that helped me get where I am today.

If you knew everything at the beginning of your career that you know now, what would you have done differently?

It is still a learning process right now because this is still very new. I am always learning something every day.

What is your greatest lesson learned?

When you are in the public eye you have to be careful with what you say, so I have learned sometimes not to say too much.

What are some of your favorite albums?

Jagged Little Pill, Alanis Morissette
Beautiful Midnight, the Matthew Good Band
Nevermind, Nirvana
Dookie, Green Day
Sing Sing Death House, the Distillers

Any Beach Boys, Creedence Clearwater Revival, or the Beatles
Celebrity Skin and *Live Through This,* Hole
Dizzy Up the Girl, the Goo Goo Dolls

Did you have any posters on your bedroom walls as a kid? Of whom?

I was never allowed to put posters up on my wall because my mom did not want me to ruin the paint.

What are some great shows you've seen?

Alanis Morissette, Coldplay, Dillinger Four, the Matthew Good Band, and Oasis.

What are some of your favorite songs?

"Right Through You," Alanis Morissette
"Wonderwall," Oasis
"Iris," the Goo Goo Dolls
"Basket Case," Green Day
"I'm Just a Girl," No Doubt
"Bad Moon Rising," Creedence
  Clearwater Revival

"I Get Around," the Beach Boys
"Knockin' on Heaven's Door," Bob Dylan
"Imagine," John Lennon
"Strawberry Fields Forever," the Beatles

List up to ten things that could be helpful to someone breaking into the business.

- Be yourself.
- Always stay strong.
- Never give up.
- Be confident.
- Be happy with your sound.

- Be involved with the business aspects of your career.
- Believe.
- Watch who you trust.

Simon LeBon

DURAN DURAN

Did you have a mentor or someone who inspired you? If so, what have you learned from that person?

Yes, my beloved mum, Ann Marie LeBon, who taught me to believe in myself.

What was your very first job in the music industry, and how did you get it?

My first job was as front man with Duran Duran. I'd heard from my ex that there was this arty sort of pop group rehearsing and working (the tables, the kitchen, and the deejay booth) in a nightclub, the Rum Runner, and more importantly that they were after a lead vocalist. So I bowled up one day wearing my finest, now famous, pink leotards, clutching an accounts book full of lyrics and surreal poetry. A day later we'd completed our first song together, "Sound of Thunder," and surreal surprise—I got the job.

What was your first big break? The first great thing that ever happened to you . . .

The only breaks we ever had were the ones that we made for ourselves. Truly the greatest thing that ever happened to me was listening to a passage of music in my cot and realizing that I knew where it was going to go next.

What elements of your job make you want to go to work every day?

Nick Rhodes.

What qualities most helped you get to where you are today?

Imagination, sheer determination, the ability to swallow your ego at times, the will to succeed, and a robust liver.

If you knew everything at the beginning of your career that you know now, what would you have done differently?

I would have taken more interest in the legal work at the beginning—things like the kind of deals we made and signed. You are on such a high because someone wants your music that you have worked so hard to make that you don't pay much attention to the legal and contractual obligations that you sign to. I wish I would have paid more attention then.

What is your greatest lesson learned?

Expect nothing, be ready for anything; never complain, never explain; never say would've, should've, or could've; always judge a book by its cover and always mix yer drinks.

What are some of your favorite albums?

L.A. Woman, the Doors

Dummy, Portishead

Let It Bleed, the Rolling Stones

London Calling, the Clash

Transformer, Lou Reed

Sign O' the Times, Prince

Second Toughest in the Infants, Underworld

In the Jungle Groove, James Brown

Nevermind, Nirvana

Did you have any posters on your bedroom walls as a kid? Of whom?

Just the one of Sophia Loren.

What are some great shows you've seen?

U2, *Zoo TV*

James Brown, Chicago Park West, 1982

Delaguarda, London, 1999

The Red Hot Chili Peppers, the Astoria, London, mid-nineties

David Bowie, *Serious Moonlight* tour, Frejus, France, 1983

Talking Heads

What are some of your favorite songs?

"Samba Y Amor," particularly Bebel Gilberto's version

"Three Little Birds," Bob Marley

"Pretty Vacant," the Sex Pistols

"#9 Dream," John Lennon (*Ah bowakawa pousse pousse*)

"Take Me to the River" and "Love and Happiness," Al Green

And so many more, but you know that already

List up to ten things that could be helpful to someone breaking into the business.

A heavy blunt instrument and a prominent bosom. Failing either of those, a sense of humor will always come in handy.

Mark McGrath

SUGAR RAY

Did you have a mentor or someone who inspired you? If so, what have you learned from that person?

John Lydon inspired me by proving that commitment was as valuable as talent. Brian Wilson and Paul McCartney inspired me to attempt songwriting.

What was your very first job in the music industry, and how did you get it?

My first job was as a signed artist to Atlantic Records in January of '94. We basically hustled and knocked on doors to make it happen.

What was your first big break? The first great thing that ever happened to you . . .

Our first big break was hooking up with management in New York. We were able to do this by selling the farm and making a video with McG on 35mm film, which was rare for a demo.

What elements of your job make you want to go to work every day?

I think the key words here are every day. Being a musician allows you not to have to resign to contemporary restraints, i.e., the nine-to-five lifestyle. It allows you to work in a timeless vacuum where any waking moment may spawn creativity.

What qualities most helped you get to where you are today?

Being able to take risks and rebound from failure. When you are offering art for public consumption you must be resilient. Also, be nice! You would be surprised how far common courtesy will carry you.

If you knew everything at the beginning of your career that you know now, what would you have done differently?

If I knew then what I know now, I wouldn't be here. Our complete naïveté gave us the freedom to do anything. We wouldn't take no for an answer because we didn't even understand the question.

What is your greatest lesson learned?

That it is called show *business*. If you care about your art so much and you sign a contract, take the time to read it, even if you can't understand it.

What are some of your favorite albums?

Never Mind the Bollocks, the Sex Pistols

Love, the Cult

Pet Sounds, the Beach Boys

License to Ill, the Beastie Boys

Appetite for Destruction, Guns 'N Roses

Legend, Bob Marley

Night Nurse, Gregory Isaacs

Did you have any posters on your bedroom walls as a kid? Of whom?

The Who, the Sex Pistols, Tony Alva, Larry Bertlemann, Mark Richards, the Damned Specimen, Bauhaus.

What are some great shows you've seen?

U2, *Joshua Tree,* L.A. Sports Arena, 1985

Steel Pulse, Irvine Meadows, 1989

Iron Maiden, Irvine Meadows, 1985

Rage Against the Machine, Santa Monica Civic Auditorium, 1993

Korn, Club Lingerie, 1994

What are some of your favorite songs?

"God Only Knows," the Beach Boys

"Not King James Version," "Ravers," and "Your House," Steel Pulse

"(White Man) In Hammersmith Palais," the Clash

"Relax," Frankie Goes to Hollywood

"One Love" and "No Woman No Cry," Bob Marley

"The Way You Look Tonight" and "Summer Wind," Frank Sinatra

"Rock Box" and "It's Tricky," Run-D.M.C.

"Lucky Man," the Verve

"It's a Mistake," Men at Work

List up to ten things that could be helpful to someone breaking into the business.

■ Network—Find out the key people and where they hang. (See Guy Oseary.)

■ Read the trades, be informed. Information is a huge commodity.

■ Don't kid yourself. If you can't visualize your goal, don't bother.

■ Assume you know nothing. Ask questions, 'cuz people love to talk about themselves.

■ If it is a group situation, make sure you are compatible with all elements. (After fifteen years, our band has all of its original members, and we still kinda like each other!)

■ Get a good lawyer. Even if you are just thinking about the music industry.

- Never take no for an answer.
- Don't be afraid to break the rules.
- Don't hear the word "unsolicited."
- May you be as lucky as I am.

Sarah McLachlan

Did you have a mentor or someone who inspired you? If so, what have you learned from that person?

Early on in life (ages four through thirteen or so) I learned I loved the sound of beautiful voices and harmonies of Joan Baez, Simon & Garfunkel, and Billie Holiday. They inspired me to sing and to learn to play the guitar. Later on in my teens, Kate Bush was there to show me that my voice was an instrument and soon after, Peter Gabriel appeared to blow my mind. It was his music that made me realize what I so wanted to do—write and perform music that moves others in the same way his music moved me.

What was your very first job in the music industry, and how did you get it?

Some guys I knew started a band called the October Game when I was in high school in Halifax. I started out as a keyboard player, but when they realized I could sing, I was quickly promoted.

What was your first big break? The first great thing that ever happened to you . . .

Both the first break and great thing happened at the same time. The band aforementioned got our first gig opening up for a Vancouver act called Moev—they were on a small indie label called Nettwerk. Mark Jowett, who is now head of A&R there, was the guitar player in the band and, after hearing me sing, asked me to join them. My mother, as you can imagine, had a fit at the thought of me quitting school at seventeen and moving to the west coast to join a band, so that didn't happen. But, we kept in touch, and two years later they offered me a record deal.

What elements of your job make you want to go to work every day?

My love and passion for music, and the desire and need to create.

What qualities most helped you get to where you are today?

A strong sense of self and of what is right, compassion, drive, and a healthy dose of pig-headedness.

If you knew everything at the beginning of your career that you know now, what would you have done differently?

Nothing . . . I feel very blessed, even though there have been bumps in the road, there is always something to be learned from so-called mistakes.

What is your greatest lesson learned?

To remember to always stay true to yourself and what you believe in, and to take the time to understand what that truly means. You can't be good to anyone if you're not first good to yourself.

What are some of your favorite albums?

Spirit of Eden and *Laughing Stock*, Talk Talk
Closing Time, Tom Waits
Blue, Joni Mitchell
Pieces in a Modern Style, William Orbit
Thursday Afternoon, Brian Eno
So, Security, and *Passion*, Peter Gabriel
Lamb Lies Down on Broadway, Genesis
All That You Can't Leave Behind, U2

Stardust, Willie Nelson
Universal Mother, Sinéad O'Connor
Acadie, Daniel Lanois
Wrecking Ball, Emmylou Harris
Pink Moon, Nick Drake
Diva, Annie Lennox
The Kick Inside, Kate Bush
A Rush of Blood to the Head, Coldplay

Did you have any posters on your bedroom walls as a kid? Of whom?

Oh yeah, *Tiger Beat* was the big thing. . . .
Leif Garrett, Shawn and David Cassidy, Farrah Fawcett, Wonder Woman. I'm sure there were others but I can't remember.

What are some great shows you've seen?

U2, Peter Gabriel, Sinéad O'Connor, Emmylou Harris.

What are some of your favorite songs?

"Mercy Street," "In Your Eyes," "Don't Give Up," "Family Snapshot," and "Solsbury Hill," Peter Gabriel
"Ol' 55," Tom Waits
"River," Joni Mitchell
"Beautiful Day" and "One," U2
"Unchained Melody," Willie Nelson
"Wild Horses," the Rolling Stones

List up to ten things that could be helpful to someone breaking into the business.

- Talent
- Stay true to yourself and your goals.
- Find people you can trust to help you who are in it for the right reasons.
- Understand the business enough to be able to forget about it.
- Get a good lawyer.
- Try as best as you can to ignore criticism, as it is generally useless and negative.
- Be prepared to work your ass off, and don't bother if you're not willing to give it 110 percent.

Madonna

Did you have a mentor or someone who inspired you? If so, what have you learned from that person?

My Russian history teacher—Mrs. Fellows
My English literature teacher—Mrs. Boyle
My art teacher—Blossom Coho
My ballet teacher—Christopher Flynn

All during my high school years they encouraged me to:

believe in my dreams,
think outside the box,
take the road less traveled by.

What was your very first job in the music industry, and how did you get it?

My first job was playing drums for a band called the Breakfast Club. We did a show at CBGB's. I got it because my boyfriend at the time was the lead singer and guitarist in the band and the drummer got sick. Since I had been practicing secretly on my own for months, I got the gig.

What was your first big break? The first great thing that ever happened to you . . .

My first big break was getting my demo to a deejay named Mark Konin at Danceteria. He gave it to Michael Rosenblatt, an A&R guy at Sire Records who gave it to Seymour Stein, the president, and that's how I got signed.

What elements of your job make you want to go to work every day?

Having clever and ingenious people to collaborate with and knowing that my talent is a gift from God. I don't own it, I'm just a channel.

What qualities most helped you get to where you are today?

Being incredibly disciplined and focused.
Having a strong will.
Being grateful.

If you knew everything at the beginning of your career that you know now, what would you have done differently?

Not taken anything personally.

What is your greatest lesson learned?

That everything in the physical world is an illusion and that life is the opposite of what you think it is. That the only way to get in life is to give.

What are some of your favorite albums?

I don't have a favorite album.

Did you have any posters on your bedroom walls as a kid? Of whom?

None. I was not allowed to have posters in my bedroom.

What are some great shows you've seen?

David Bowie at Cobo Arena in Detroit in the mid-seventies when I was in high school.
Bob Marley at University of Michigan in the late seventies.

What are some of your favorite songs?

I don't have a favorite song.

List up to ten things that could be helpful to someone breaking into the business.

- The only thing that lasts is soul consciousness so that is the number-one thing to work on. Everything else is ephemeral and does not last.
- When you leave this world, it will not matter how popular you were or how many number-one records you had but rather what you gave the world—How much Light and Love you shared.
- Do not take shortcuts.
- Have certainty that everything that happens to you is ultimately a blessing.
- There is no point in asking for everything and having it all unless you intend to share it with other people.

Natalie Maines

THE DIXIE CHICKS

Did you have a mentor or someone who inspired you? If so, what have you learned from that person?

Lots of people inspired me, but the person who taught me the most was my dad, Lloyd Maines. I learned a lot about music, studio work, and producing from him. He also told me how important it is to stay true to who you are in a business that pulls you in a lot of different directions.

What was your very first job in the music industry, and how did you get it?

I sang a few jingles for local commercials. I also sang backup on a few records that my dad was producing.

What was your first big break? The first great thing that ever happened to you . . .

It was the Dixie Chicks. I always knew that I would be in the music business. I also always had the feeling that it would happen when it was supposed to happen. I was never beating down doors making people listen to me sing.

What elements of your job make you want to go to work every day?

There are so many things that I love about my job. I love the variety of things that we get to do. Be it making records, tours, photo shoots, videos, or TV. I love seeing the world and meeting all kinds of different people.

What qualities most helped you get to where you are today?

Honesty, integrity, passion, talent, knowing when to compromise, and when to stay strong.

If you knew everything at the beginning of your career that you know now, what would you have done differently?

Nothing. I believe everything happens the way it is supposed to happen. I know I don't want to be pregnant on tour again.

What is your greatest lesson learned?

To know your business inside and out.

What are some of your favorite albums?

Flaming Red, Patty Griffin

Smokin' the Dummy, Terry Allen

Globe Sessions, Sheryl Crow

Thriller, Michael Jackson

Forget About It, Alison Krauss

Let Love Rule, Lenny Kravitz

Live, James Taylor

Miseducation of Lauryn Hill, Lauryn Hill

Purple Rain, Prince

Did you have any posters on your bedroom walls as a kid? Of whom?

I had my room wallpapered with pictures of Bon Jovi, Sebastian Bach, and Guns N' Roses.

What are some great shows you've seen?

James Taylor, Ricky Scaggs, the Rolling Stones, and Lyle Lovett.

What are some of your favorite songs?

"Imagine," John Lennon

"Secret of Life," James Taylor

"Mary," Patti Griffin

List up to ten things that could be helpful to someone breaking into the business.

- Talent
- Courage
- Energy
- Self-respect

Marilyn Manson

Did you have a mentor or someone who inspired you? If so, what have you learned from that person?

Anton Lavey, Alexandro Jadorowsky, Gottfried Helnwein, and a guy named Paul who ran the first real magazine I wrote for when I was twenty. None of them are musicians, but each of them taught me about persona, conception, manipulation, and the manifestation of what is in your head into a tangible art form. Music ended up being the centerpiece.

What was your very first job in the music industry, and how did you get it?

I was paid two hundred fifty dollars to write Yngwie Malmsteen's bio for his record label. I lied about my experience and no one bothered to check, so I was a godforsaken journalist.

What was your first big break? The first great thing that ever happened to you . . .

I was able to open for a series of bands that probably regret, in retrospect, having to perform after me.

What elements of your job make you want to go to work every day?

I can't live without creating, and since I am a creation incarnate, I will die for what I do. I am what I do.

What qualities most helped you get to where you are today?

Willpower. Perfection. Reckless disregard. My big nose.

If you knew everything at the beginning of your career that you know now, what would you have done differently?

I've realized that Marilyn Manson is ten years old, so I behave that way and create that way. I am a brat with scars and I haven't hit puberty yet.

I have no regrets. Just enemies, lawsuits, and a trail of urban legends.

What are some of your favorite albums?

Ziggy Stardust and *Hunky Dory*, David Bowie   *Abbey Road*, the Beatles

Bring You My Love, PJ Harvey   *The Wall*, Pink Floyd

OK Computer, Radiohead   *Raw Power*, Iggy and the Stooges

Did you have any posters on your bedroom walls as a kid? Of whom?

KISS, Iron Maiden, and *Playboy* centerfolds.

What are some great shows you've seen?

The first Jane's Addiction tour   Peaches

Radiohead   Love and Rockets

What are some of your favorite songs?

"Quicksand," David Bowie

"Smack My Bitch Up," the Prodigy

"Happiness Is a Warm Gun," the Beatles

List up to ten things that could be helpful to someone breaking into the business.

Stay out of my way.

Shirley Manson
GARBAGE

Did you have a mentor or someone who inspired you? If so, what have you learned from that person?

I've been inspired by far too many artists to mention here. Suffice it to say, had it not been for their profound influence and pioneering spirit, I'd not be making records or touring the world today.

What was your very first job in the music industry, and how did you get it?

Simon Potts of Capitol Records signed my band Goodbye Mr. Mackenzie (in which I was a backing vocalist and keyboard player) to an album deal after seeing us play an utterly appalling show in London. I was nineteen years old.

What was your first big break? The first great thing that ever happened to you . . .

Goodbye Mr. Mackenzie landed a UK tour opening up for Blondie, and their manager, Gary Kurfirst, who at the time was running Radioactive Records, happened to suggest that I should call upon him if I ever decided to strike out and do something musical on my own. Years later I did indeed call and true to his word, he offered me a record deal to which I am still signed today.

What elements of your job make you want to go to work every day?

The male groupies.

What qualities most helped you get to where you are today?

Tenacity and vulgarity.

If you knew everything at the beginning of your career that you know now, what would you have done differently?

I regret nothing. Except perhaps some of the god-awful hairstyles I sported in the late eighties.

What is your greatest lesson learned?

That it's never a great idea to eat too much pizza shortly before going onstage.

What are some of your favorite albums?

The Scream, Siouxsie and the Banshees   *To Bring You My Love,* PJ Harvey
White Album, the Beatles   *The Bends,* Radiohead
Aladdin Sane, David Bowie   *The Capitol Years,* Frank Sinatra

Did you have any posters on your bedroom walls as a kid? Of whom?

Starsky (Paul Michael Glaser) of the detective series *Starsky and Hutch.*

What are some great shows you've seen?

Siouxsie and the Banshees, Edinburgh   Nine Inch Nails, Madison, Wisconsin
Nick Cave and the Bad Seeds, Berlin   Radiohead, Chicago
The Pixies, Barcelona   U2, New York City

What are some of your favorite songs?

"Somewhere over the Rainbow,"   "The Drugs Don't Work," the Verve
    Judy Garland   "I Got It Bad and That Ain't Good,"
"Crazy," Willie Nelson   Nina Simone
"Let Me Try," MC5   "Smells Like Teen Spirit," Nirvana

List up to ten things that could be helpful to someone breaking into the business.

Nurture a complete lack of pride, integrity, and good taste. Indeed, the complete lack of a brain entirely might help your case. Then go buy yourself a gun, hire a great lawyer, and sleep with your accountant.

Maxwell

Did you have a mentor or someone who inspired you? If so, what have you learned from that person?

Without a doubt, Hod David and Stuart Matthewman have been the most instrumental in my musical development. Not only because of the music we have made together, but mainly because of their unflinching support and belief in me. It's been my saving grace in many a time of doubt.

The other great mentor of sorts was having no choice but to choose music as my great escape from the reality of my world. With music I could enhance the reality of my living and hopefully help or give someone something to get them through the funky-funky we live through at times. I just had to do this.

What was your very first job in the music business, and how did you get it?

I've worked at a fast-food place, in a movie theater, and in restaurants. I have never worked one minute when I did anything related to music. Music is play, not work.

What was your first big break? The first great thing that ever happened to you . . .

I wrote my first melody on the J train when I was riding back home one afternoon. I couldn't believe it. It wasn't great but the idea that no one ever heard it or made it before I did was an unexpected rush. I was hooked and needed more.

What elements of your job make you want to go to work every day?

Once again, I don't consider what I do as work. The only work I do primarily is promotional. I guess, fighting off the need to keep my sacred space and fostering a positive outlook when people and opinions lean on the judgmental and cruel. That's work! Suffice to say, I haven't had it that bad. It's all been a huge blessing of a life.

What qualities most helped you get to where you are today?

I'm still building and refining. The journey is always happening. Keeping fame in perspective; seeing your ability and who you are as separate keeps the precious balance and keeps me grounded.

If you knew everything at the beginning of your career that you know now, what would you have done differently?

I know what I know now because of what I didn't know then. Regret, however tempting it is, is not productive. I'm no saint. I work on this, and it is hard work.

What is your greatest lesson learned?

The one I'm learning now and the one I hope to learn tomorrow. I don't mean to sound so Zen, but it's true. There's always something around the corner.

What are some of your favorite albums?

Too many to say; I have an eclectic assortment of music I listen to. I get a lot of recommendations from Stuart and Hod, but I pretty much love soul music. It speaks to me like no other.

Did you have any posters on your bedroom walls as a kid? Of whom?

Sports Illustrated swimsuit issues turned into Bob Marley and Martin Luther King's pictures and quotes. I can't front though, I wasn't mad at Janet Jackson and Sade back then. *Wheeeww!*

What are some great shows you've seen?

Radiohead, The Roots, Prince, Björk, Sade (I've only seen her on tape though; I'm still living that down.)

List up to ten things that could be helpful to someone breaking into the business.

I'm no expert, but if you love the craft, the rest will follow. The process is the most important part of it all. Accolades are nice and all but they bring great responsibility. When it's nothing but the music and nothing but the art, you know your worth, even if it takes a while for others to catch on.

Melanie C

THE SPICE GIRLS

Did you have a mentor or someone who inspired you? If so, what have you learned from that person?

My mum is a singer, and when I was growing up I was very proud and wanted to be just like her. I also fell in love with Madonna in the early eighties, and she is my biggest inspiration to this day. From both of them I have learned the power of individuality and personal expression.

What was your very first job in the music industry, and how did you get it?

I recorded some backing vocals for a theatrical show. It was my first experience of a recording studio, and I was hooked. My next gig was the Spice Girls!

What was your first big break? The first great thing that ever happened to you . . .

I have been really lucky. I was unemployed for a year after leaving college, trying to break into the music industry. I auditioned for a girl band that eventually became the Spice Girls. It was a big break!

What elements of your job make you want to go to work every day?

Performing is my love. I have the freedom to express myself and entertain people. I couldn't wish for a better job. Some days are tough but you have to keep things in perspective.

What qualities most helped you get to where you are today?

I believe there has been a huge amount of luck, but I'm very determined, hardworking, and very ambitious. It all helps.

If you knew everything at the beginning of your career that you know now, what would you have done differently?

I really wouldn't change a thing. I truly believe I have been blessed. I just hope I can continue to be successful in music. I will never stop trying.

What is your greatest lesson learned?

Never take anything for granted. I will always be grateful and work hard. It's so important to be true to yourself too.

What are some of your favorite albums?

Songs in the Key of Life, Stevie Wonder

Revolver, the Beatles

Ray of Light, Madonna

Californication, the Red Hot Chili Peppers

Did you have any posters on your bedroom walls as a kid? Of whom?

I had posters of Madonna—she had the monopoly on my bedroom walls.

What are some great shows you've seen?

I saw Madonna's *Girlie Show* and *Drowned World* tours. They were amazing. No one puts on a show like Madonna.

I also saw the Chili Peppers at Reading Festival, Oasis at Earls Court, and Blur at the Mayan in L.A. They're three gigs which stick in my mind.

What are some of your favorite songs?

"Sir Duke," Stevie Wonder

"Eleanor Rigby," the Beatles

"Song 2," Blur

"Supersonic," Oasis

"Secret," Madonna

List up to ten things that could be helpful to someone breaking into the business.

- A dream
- Faith
- Determination
- A thick skin!
- Luck
- Strength
- Support
- Diplomacy
- A good work ethic
- Oh yeah . . . and talent—that helps!!

John Mellencamp

Did you have a mentor or someone who inspired you? If so, what have you learned from that person?

My grandfather used to say if you're going to hit a cocksucker, kill him. Meaning never start anything that you do not intend to finish.

What was your very first job in the music industry, and how did you get it?

I have been playing in bands since I was eleven. My first paying job was at that age. We played at a basement party for five dollars.

What was your first big break? The first great thing that ever happened to you . . .

I played at a student convocation and received a standing ovation when I was in my early teens. I played a song by Donovan, "Universal Soldier." That incident encouraged me to continue in music.

What elements of your job make you want to go to work every day?

The creative process. Being able to take an idea and turn it into something by the end of the day.

What qualities most helped you get to where you are today?

Tenacity.

If you knew everything at the beginning of your career that you know now, what would you have done differently?

I sold my publishing one afternoon in London for a very small amount of money. I didn't even know what I was selling. I had no idea what publishing was. I still do not own some of my biggest hits and probably never will.

What is your greatest lesson learned?

Never stop being yourself. Never alter who you are to please anyone. Not a record company or manager. And never, ever, change your name to Johnny Cougar.

What are some of your favorite albums?

Highway 61 Revisited, Bob Dylan

Blue, Joni Mitchell

Exile on Main Street, the Rolling Stones

Carney, Leon Russell

Gasoline Alley, Rod Stewart

Anything by Robert Johnson

Did you have any posters on your bedroom walls as a kid? Of whom?

Bob Dylan and Donovan.

What are some great shows you've seen?

Lou Reed performing "Rock N Roll Animal"

Iggy Pop performing "Search and Destroy"

Bob Dylan

James Brown, 1966

Jethro Tull performing "Aqualung"

What are some of your favorite songs?

"Like a Rolling Stone," Bob Dylan

"Gimme Shelter," the Rolling Stones

List up to ten things that could be helpful to someone breaking into the business.

Always be honest and never kiss ass.

Moby

Did you have a mentor or someone who inspired you? If so, what have you learned from that person?

It's hard to answer the first question in the negative, but no, I've never had a mentor.

I've been inspired by countless people, but usually the inspiration has come from people whom I haven't actually known.

What was your very first job in the music industry, and how did you get it?

My first job was working as a deejay in a nightclub called the Beat in Port Chester, New York.

I would work Monday nights from ten P.M. to four A.M. and I was paid four dollars an hour (but the ginger ale was free).

What was your first big break? The first great thing that ever happened to you . . .

As odd as it might sound, my first break was probably getting the aforementioned job at the Beat. As grim as the work was (playing records to three or four drunks at four A.M. on a Monday night), I was just amazed that I was getting paid to listen to music.

What elements of your job make you want to go to work every day?

As trite and clichéd as this might sound, what inspires me to work on music every day is simply the joy and satisfaction that I get from working on music every day.

What qualities most helped you get to where you are today?

A deep and comprehensive love of music.
A complete inability to do anything else.

If you knew everything at the beginning of your career that you know now, what would you have done differently?

I wouldn't have done as many side projects. Side projects can be fun, but more often than not they can be distracting, and they can even serve as a lazy substitute for real work.

What is your greatest lesson learned?

Find what you love and work as hard as you can at it.

What are some of your favorite albums?

Goat's Head Soup, the Rolling Stones

Protection, Massive Attack

Floating into the Night, Julee Cruise

Roxy Music, Roxy Music

Rhapsody in Blue, George Gershwin

Closer, Joy Division

The Clash, the Clash

My Life in the Bush of Ghosts,
   Brian Eno and David Byrne

Marquee Moon, Television

Man Machine, Kraftwerk

*It Takes a Nation of Millions to Hold
   Us Back,* Public Enemy

The Great Southern Trendkill, Pantera

Purple Rain, Prince

Déjà Vu, Crosby, Stills, Nash & Young

What's Going On, Marvin Gaye

London Calling, the Clash

Bryter Layter, Nick Drake

Low, David Bowie

Freedom of Choice, Devo

Heaven Up Here, Echo and the Bunnymen

and so on, and so on . . .

Did you have any posters on your bedroom walls as a kid? Of whom?

So many . . . Adam and the Ants, Black Flag, the Dead Kennedys, Minor Threat, Joy Division, Gary Numan, etc., etc.

What are some great shows you've seen?

Any GWAR show. I love GWAR.

Mission of Burma, Pogos, Bridgeport,
   Connecticut, 1982

The Sex Pistols, Roskilde, Denmark, 1997

Roxy Music, Greek Theater,
   Los Angeles, 2001

David Bowie, Area 2 at the Gorge,
   Summer 2002

John Fogerty, Hammerstein Ballroom, 1998

Black Flag, the Ritz, Summer 1983

U2, Slane Castle, Ireland, 2001

What are some of your favorite songs?

"I Only Have Eyes for You," the Flamingos

"One," U2

"Mysteries of Love," Julee Cruise

"Mother of Pearl," Roxy Music

"The Message," Grandmaster Flash

"Purple Rain," Prince

"Black Hole Sun," Soundgarden

"Philadelphia," Bruce Springsteen

"Shipbuilding," Robert Wyatt

"All Apologies," Nirvana

"Firestarter," Prodigy

"Is This It," the Strokes

"I Wanna Be Your Dog," the Stooges

"Are Everything," Buzzcocks

"Fascist Groove Thing," Heaven 17

"Atmosphere," Joy Division

"Don't Leave Me This Way," Harold Melvin
and the Bluenotes

"Right Back Where We Started From,"
Maxine Nightingale

"Angie," the Rolling Stones

"Heroes," David Bowie

"Anytime," Brian McKnight

"Blueberry Hill," Fats Domino

"(White Man) in Hammersmith Palais,"
the Clash

List up to ten things that could be helpful to someone breaking into the business.

- Work hard.
- Keep your priorities straight and don't start wars over things that are essentially unimportant (i.e., size of dressing room, office with windows, size of limo, name on guest list, etc.).
- Avoid drugs.
- Don't be knowingly cruel towards anyone, no matter what they've done to you.
- Always remember that 10 percent of popular music has the potential to be sublime and that the other 90 percent is mercenary, distasteful trash.
- Be persistent.
- Work harder.
- Be more persistent. Again.
- Avoid people who just want to make you feel bad about yourself.
- Even more importantly, avoid people who just want to make you feel good about yourself. They're called sycophants, and they're the most dangerous people that any musician can be surrounded by.
- Don't cheat on your significant other.
- Don't cheat with someone else's significant other.
- Be wise with your money. When you make money you should save it, and invest in your career. Don't buy stupid things like expensive cars and fur coats. The earning curve for most musicians is quite short, so when you make money you should save it and invest it. And the best investment is in yourself and in your music. Instead of buying a car and a fur coat and a trip to Tahiti you should build a recording studio for yourself and put whatever money is left over into some nice, safe, and diverse investment vehicles.
- Don't give jobs to friends or family members.
- Don't loan money to friends or family members. If you wanna buy your mom a house, fine. But don't give your Uncle Pete seventy-five thousand dollars for his real estate deal in the Everglades. If you loan money to someone you should always assume that it's never coming back to you.
- Don't play with people's emotions.

- Always be nice to everyone, especially the people who make the effort to listen to your music. A musician who is rude to a fan is a musician who has seriously lost the plot.
- Never cancel a show.
- Never say no to an interview unless you are so well established that you can afford to.
- Never pay a commission on gross income.
- Never give your publishing to a record company.
- The shorter the term of the record deal, the better it is for you. A long record deal only benefits the record company. *Unless* you can get guaranteed releases for each record. Then you're set. So when new artist Joe Schmoe brags about getting a *ten-album deal,* you should just shake your head in pity for them. A "ten-album deal" just means that if the record company wants to they can release your next ten records. If they don't want to release your records they don't have to. And you just sit around with no deal and no way of doing a new deal with a new label.
- Don't insult other musicians.
- Never turn your back on new technologies or new styles of music. Music snobs just end up in on-line chatrooms complaining about musicians who are open-minded and successful.
- Always remember that almost everyone else with whom you work actually works harder than you.

Tom Morello

RAGE AGAINST THE MACHINE, AUDIOSLAVE

Did you have a mentor or someone who inspired you? If so, what have you learned from that person?

While I've had many sources of inspiration, I would have to say that my early development as a person and a musician were funneled through one person: Mary Morello, my mother. She helped instill in me a political fire to fight the power and confront injustice, and she was also completely open-minded to my decision to pursue music. From hosting my unlistenable punk-rock band in her basement, to supporting my decision to move to a squat in Hollywood to seek the heavy metal Holy Grail with a Harvard diploma in my back pocket, seemingly gone to waste, she was always supportive. So from her, I've learned courage, tolerance, and open-mindedness, all of which influence me on a daily basis.

What was your very first job in the music business, and how did you get it?

I was a wandering minstrel at a renaissance fair for five summers. I got the gig because I was able to improvise a pirate chantey or two, and I looked really great in tights.

What was your first big break? The first great thing that ever happened to you . . .

My first break was on a hot Hollywood summer night, when my friend Adam Jones (who would later surface as guitarist for the band Tool) knocked on my apartment door and demanded that I accompany him to Al's Bar in downtown L.A. At the time, I was working as the scheduling secretary for U.S. senator Alan Cranston and had to get up very early in the morning. I hemmed and hawed, but Adam was persistent and succeeded in dragging my ass out of bed. At Al's Bar that night, we stumbled upon a band that would become my favorite local band, a group called Lock-Up. It turned out that my band at the time shared a rehearsal space with Lock-Up, and when Lock-Up kicked out their guitar player, I got the gig. We were soon signed to Geffen Records, subsequently dropped, and Rage Against the Machine rose like a phoenix from those rock ashes.

What elements of your job make you want to go to work every day?

I am very grateful to be able to play music for a living and explore my creativity as a guitarist, songwriter, and band member while at the same time making use of the platform that it provides to reach a large audience with a political message.

What qualities most helped you get to where you are today?

An obsessive-compulsive nature would have to be top of the list. Whether it was practicing scales eight hours a day or spending an equal amount of time trying to drum up a gig for my band. You can say what you want about me, but you can't say I'm not stubborn. While I was attending Harvard University, I would practice four hours a day, and that did not mean three hours and fifty-eight minutes a day. There were times where I had a fever of 102, an exam at eight in the morning and began practicing at one A.M. after finishing my studies, and as the sun was rising my fingers were flying in a frenzy across the strings until five A.M. and not a second before. P.S. I don't recommend this.

If you knew everything at the beginning of your career that you know now, what would you have done differently?

I don't think I would have admitted to wearing tights at the renaissance fair.

What is your greatest lesson learned?

For many years, I was very careerist in my musical goals. The goal was to get a record deal or produce a hit song to have "success." When I played in Lock-Up on Geffen Records, every music-industry nightmare cliché that could have happened did happen. When we were dropped and the band broke up, I vowed to never again play a note that did not come from the heart. Soon thereafter, Rage Against the Machine was formed, and I believe it was the absolutely uncompromising musical and political nature of the band which was the reason that it earned a large following. The lesson is simple; as a creative person, your creativity must come first.

What are some of your favorite albums?

The self-titled Clash album may be the greatest expression of rock 'n' roll power and angst ever captured on tape. Public Enemy's *It Takes a Nation of Millions to Hold Us Back* holds the same place in the world of hip-hop. Bruce Springsteen's *Nebraska* is a tremendous record with great lyrics that tap into the dark heart of America. Jane's Addiction's *Nothing's Shocking* combined the power of heavy metal riffage with underground artistry to make an absolutely unique and wonderful blend.

Did you have any posters on your bedroom walls as a kid? Of whom?

KISS, KISS, and more KISS. Tin-foil KISS posters, wall-sized KISS posters, KISS lunch boxes propped up against the wall. Anything with Gene Simmons's bloody tongue on it got my dollar. Oh yeah, and Led Zeppelin too.

What are some great shows you've seen?

The Clash at the Aragon Ballroom in Chicago was life-changing. It made me realize that even with no money for expensive gear and little technical ability on the guitar, that I too could make powerful music if I just played my heart out and told the truth.

Tool—at a tiny club called Raji's in Hollywood on a summer's night in 1991—was the greatest band in the world at that moment. Do not doubt it.

Black Sabbath at the L.A. Forum on their first reunion tour. I went to this concert to see one of the favorite bands of my youth for a nostalgic kick, and they absolutely destroyed the place. They put on one of the greatest and heaviest shows I've ever seen.

Bruce Springsteen in Santa Barbara on his solo acoustic tour in support of the *Ghost of Tom Joad* album. It was astounding to see the immense power and artistry that came across with just one man and an acoustic guitar. Politics and personal redemption never sounded so good.

What are some of your favorite songs?

"Biko" by Peter Gabriel is as good a song as anyone ever recorded. There is such great power and inspiration in the melding of music and lyrics on that lasting tribute to the great South African activist Steven Biko.

"Maggie's Farm" is the great "fuck the boss" anthem for all time and rings as true today as it did when it was written.

"Fight the Power" by Public Enemy is an anthem for the ages, and I'm certain it will inspire restless youth and continue to fan the flames of discontent well into the future. It still riles me up when I hear it and makes me want to go smash the state.

List up to ten things that could be helpful to someone breaking into the business.

- The music industry is filled with jackasses and posers. So beware.
- For those individuals who aspire to create music with honesty and integrity, you must keep focused on your creativity, who you are as an artist; who you are as a person, and what you want to say. But at the same time, you must be vigilant and keep your jackass armor securely in place.

Morrissey

Did you have a mentor or someone who inspired you? If so, what have you learned from that person?

I was never gripped by one single person—always a mish-mish of various influences. I was generally moved only by people who had suffered a great personal tragedy in their lives. A battle with self-destruction always helped—it saved so much time later on.

What was your very first job in the music industry, and how did you get it?

Both Johnny Marr and I signed to Rough Trade Records as the Smiths twenty years ago. EMI had previously put us in the studio to do some demos, but they didn't like the songs, so they wouldn't sign us. When we signed to Rough Trade those very same songs became hugely successful.

What was your first big break? The first great thing that ever happened to you . . .

I never had one. Everything I've achieved I've had to crawl through fire and brimstone to reach.

What elements of your job make you want to go to work every day?

None. Singing is a vacation, and not a job—unless you're Broccoli Spears.

What qualities most helped you get to where you are today?

Unemployment, chiefly.

People always tell me I could go much further if I would only learn to be more tolerant. But I can't. I can't stand polite conversation, and I find it impossible to endure crashing bores. I can't pretend to like anybody so I'm not remotely cute or clever when it comes to "getting on." So, you see, I probably have no qualities to speak of.

If you knew everything at the beginning of your career that you know now, what would you have done differently?

I know less now than I did then.

What is your greatest lesson learned?

Fame = money = lawsuits.

What are some of your favorite albums?

The New York Dolls,
the New York Dolls

Horses, Patti Smith

Chelsea Girl, Nico

Did you have any posters on your bedroom walls as a kid? Of whom?

The New York Dolls, Anne Sexton, Vita Sackville-West, Bruce Wayne and his youthful Dick Grayson, the entire cast of *Bonanza,* and Oscar Wilde.

What are some great shows you've seen?

T. Rex, 1972

David Bowie, 1972

Roxy Music, 1972

Lou Reed, 1972

Mott the Hoople, 1972

The Sex Pistols, 1976

The Ramones, 1977

Patti Smith, 1977

What are some of your favorite songs?

"Hey Ma," Mayeus LaFleur

"Lilac Wine," Nina Simone

"There Are Bad Times Just Around
the Corner," Noel Coward

"So Little Time," Diana Dors

"Your Pretty Face Is Going to Hell,"
Iggy & the Stooges

"Some Say I Got Devil," Melanie Safka

"My Country 'Tis of Thy People You're Dying,"
Buffy Sainte-Marie

"Death," Klaus Nomi

"Moon Over Kentucky," Sparks

List up to ten things that could be helpful to someone breaking into the business.

■ Whatever you do, don't form a limited company. It will not offer protection, and it will simply make it easier for your own accountants to sue you—which they will, in time.

■ As soon as you become famous, someone will sue you. When you go to court you should remember that lawyers lie and barristers lie, and very few people in the legal profession actually have any interest at all in upholding the law. Similarly, if a judge does not like your face then that judge can ignore the facts and ignore the law and ignore the truth and rule against you. Judges are above the law and answerable only to God. This is because if judges were actually quizzed on their behavior they wouldn't know what to say.

■ Your accountant will get you into trouble with the tax authorities—and then will offer to get you out of that trouble . . . for a price.

■ In the midst of all these inevitabilities, remember to make as much music as possible—time has a habit of passing.

■ And try not to be too cynical. (Just kidding.)

Nelly

Did you have a mentor or someone who inspired you? If so, what have you learned from that person?

Musically, I was inspired by LL Cool J and, personally, by my mom. I learned that hard work is the key—you just have to keep working hard!

What was your very first job in the music industry, and how did you get it?

I started rappin' with my friends, and together we just did whatever it took. We performed in front of all kinds of people until we found the right people that could make it happen.

What was your first big break? The first great thing that ever happened to you . . .

Getting played on the radio—Magic 108—that was the first break, and it felt great!

What elements of your job make you want to go to work every day?

The fans are a big part of this whole gig. I am also very driven. I'm driven to be the best, driven to provide for my family—just driven.

What qualities most helped you get to where you are today?

Competitiveness takes you where you want to go!

If you knew everything at the beginning of your career that you know now, what would you have done differently?

Read the whole contract!

What is your greatest lesson learned?

Sign your own contract!

What are some of your favorite albums?

Big Boi and Dre Present . . . Outkast, Stankonia, and *ATLliens,* Outkast
Inconceivable, Hippycrickets

Shinin' & Bigtymin, T-Mac & P-Squad
Biggie Smalls

Did you have any posters on your bedroom walls as a kid? Of whom?

Michael Jordan and Run-D.M.C.

What are some great shows you've seen?

Puffy, Bad Boy, 1998
Smoking Groove

What are some of your favorite songs?

"Jesabel," R. Kelly
"California Love" and "Dear Mama," 2Pac
"What's My Name," Snoop Dogg

List up to ten things that could be helpful to someone breaking into the business.

- Stay hungry.
- Learn the business as much as you can.
- Read all of your contract.
- Most importantly, work hard.
- When you think you're working your hardest—pump it up and work harder!

Willie Nelson

Did you have a mentor or someone who inspired you? If so, what have you learned from that person?

I grew up in a small town in Texas where I started music early. I started when I was five or six years old, learning to play the guitar. My grandparents were music teachers, so they taught my sister and me how to play. We would listen to the radio, to all different kinds of music, so my heroes were guys like Ernest Tubb, Roy Acuff, Hank Williams, and Bob Wills. Bob Wills was a great bandleader; he always played great music, and people traveled for miles to hear his bands.

I learned that you are only as good as the musicians around you. If you have a few good guys around you that you can depend on when you walk out there and know that you're covered, that's the important thing to look for. You need people you can live with comfortably because they're going to be like family. I would much rather take a musician who was easy to live with, but maybe not quite as good as the guy who was not easy to live with.

What was your very first job in the music industry, and how did you get it?

My first job was with a Bohemian polka band, and I was about nine years old. There was a guy named John Raycjeck who had a blacksmith's shop in the town of Abbott where I grew up. My grandfather also had a blacksmith's shop, so I would go down and hang out with John and some of his kids who were my age. He had twenty-one kids. He also had a band, made up of his family, and they would play dances in the town of West, which was about six miles from Abbott. He wanted me to come down and play rhythm guitar in his band, and he paid me eight dollars. It was a nonelectric rhythm guitar, so there was no way they could have heard me (which was probably a good thing), but I learned a lot just by starting out with professionals like that who let me play, make my mistakes, and learn.

What was your first big break? The first great thing that ever happened to you . . .

The first time that I made eight dollars (like I mentioned above) because I had been making about fifteen cents an hour picking cotton and bailing hay, so this was a big boost. I hit the big time.

The next thing you know I was playing a couple nights a week, going to school. It continued with those guys for a while, and then I put my own band together with my brother-in-law (well, he would become my brother-in-law—at the time, he was just going with my sister). So we had a little family band—my football coach played the trombone, my dad played rhythm guitar and fiddle, and we played in two or three little beer joints in West. From there, we ventured out into Waco, and then to Fort Worth, and Dallas. I just kept doing it. I had a fan club in Hillsboro, Texas, when I was sixteen.

What elements of your job make you want to go to work every day?

I enjoy playing music. I enjoy the band that I have. It's what I would be doing, hopefully, regardless of where I came from. The fame is fine, but I think I'd still be in some beer joint playing two nights a week.

What qualities most helped you get to where you are today?

The fact that I worked in all those places (like beer joints) and didn't mind that kind of work. When you work in those places, continually for a long time, and then move on to other things that are easier, like tours, it's a piece of cake. You've already learned all of the hard stuff, you've already learned everything you'll ever need to know back in those other places.

If I had to name three things I learned, it would be patience—one, two, and three.

If you knew everything at the beginning of your career that you know now, what would you have done differently?

I wouldn't want to change many things, because I think the things that were set up for me, the hand that I was dealt, is the hand that I played and continue to play. I wouldn't want to change dealers; it feels like it's working out the way it was supposed to.

What is your greatest lesson learned?

I always laugh while I'm playing music and jamming with the guys. Some of my best licks have occurred because I made a horrible mistake and had to pull myself out of it. I think some of those things are so funny that if you can get into them, you will learn a lot from your mistakes; you'll learn that all notes are leading somewhere, and you just have to stick with it until you get where you need them to be.

What are some of your favorite albums?

I like Ray Charles's first country album, *Modern Sounds in Country and Western Music,* where he took all the traditional country standards and sang them his way, with a great orchestra and arrangements. I think he did more for country music with that one record than any of us have ever done.

Anything by George Jones, Bob Wills, or Hank Williams—these are the guys I grew up with and learned from.

I like Frank Sinatra, Bing Crosby, Perry Como, Louis Armstong—it would be hard to mention albums, because I don't really think about them that way.

Did you have any posters on your bedroom walls as a kid? Of whom?

I wanted posters.

What are some great shows you've seen?

The first time I saw Leon Russell was the greatest live show I've ever seen.

What are some of your favorite songs?

"Stardust"   "San Antonio Rose"
"Your Cheatin' Heart"   "Moonlight in Vermont"
"He Stopped Loving Her Today"

Krist Novoselic

NIRVANA

Did you have a mentor or someone who inspired you? If so, what have you learned from that person?

Like countless others before and since, it was reading books like *The Dharma Bums* and *On the Road* that first jolted me into adopting a certain alternative perspective. Playing music was—and is—just one manifestation of that perspective. Buzz Osborne from the Melvins turned me on to punk rock. He lent me his albums—Thanks, Buzz. It was after my third listening to Flipper's *Generic* album . . . everything just sort of clicked. It was the first time I remember consciously thinking of punk rock as the great art form that it is—as heavy and transcendental as any of the greatest music ever made. All that from a Flipper record.

Flipper was and still is a blip on the screen of conventional musicological thought. To me, this conundrum presents irrefutable proof that "conventional musicological thought" is quite often a crock. Don't get stuck!

What was your very first job in the music industry, and how did you get it?

My first job was the first time I got some small sum of money for playing in a small place for a small number of people. The lesson? It's not where you *start* the race. . . .

What was your first big break? The first great thing that ever happened to you . . .

Looking back, I have to say it was in high school when Kurt Cobain asked me to start a band with him. He was a great artist. Music, painting, poetry, drawing, sculpture . . . Regardless of the medium, he had a beautiful and unique way of expression. The biggest thing in my life was being part of Nirvana.

What elements of your job make you want to go to work every day?

I have always been driven by compulsion. The success of Nirvana has given me the luxury of not having a "day job." I don't suppose this comes as a great shock to anyone.

Before Nirvana (and while we were getting started), I was an industrial painter. Aircraft factories, paper mills . . . you name it, I painted it. I liked my coworkers and the sense of completing a project with a group of people . . . but mostly remember it feeling like a chore. I've always been driven by compulsion. Cleaning a cat box is a chore. Traveling around in a crappy van with your two best friends playing music for anyone who lets you is a compulsion. Any action driven by compulsion is ripe for success. If music compels you—go for it. If it's a chore, it could be time to think about something else.

What qualities most helped you get to where you are today?

Nirvana was driven by the desire to make and play great music. Early on, we would be disappointed if we had lame rehearsals. We knew when we were plugged into the great rock spirit and when we were not.

We played as often as possible . . . rehearsals or shows. If you're going to be a musician, that ethos can do you nothing but good. Play in every club in your town, like we did. Play parties, like we did. Play in towns a few hours' drive, like we did. Drive farther and stay the night, like we did. Play for a handful of people, like we did. Just *play*.

Remember to have as much fun as possible. Beware of the aforementioned "chore factor." If you don't love every part of it (from playing onstage all the way to sleeping in between a kick drum and a bass amp in the back of a van), get out of the way and make room for someone who does.

If you knew everything at the beginning of your career that you know now, what would you have done differently?

Like most musicians, I suppose I would have spent more time focusing on the machinery of the business . . . developing a "business savvy."

That said, I think the "alternative perspective" provided by people like Jack Kerouac made me a less than ideal candidate for business school.

What is your greatest lesson learned?

Don't compromise on music. If it doesn't feel right, don't give in.

Did you have any posters on your bedroom walls as a kid? Of whom?

I had a poster of Gene Simmons that I cut out of the *KISS Alive* booklet in my junior high school locker.

What are some great shows you've seen?

Jane's Addiction, Seattle, 1988

Many, many Sonic Youth shows

Screaming Jay Hawkins, live in a hotel bar, Paris, 1993

The Rolling Stones, MTV Video Music Awards, 1994

Soundgarden, in a park, downtown Olympia, 1987

Butthole Surfers, Olympia, 1984

Pearl Jam, Sand Point, Seattle, 1992

Foo Fighters, House of Blues,
   Los Angeles, 2000

The Who, the Gorge, Washington, 2001

Black Flag, in a community center in
   Walla Walla, Washington, 1984

Mudhoney, Satyricon, Portland, 1988

The Red Hot Chili Peppers, Rio de Janeiro, 1993

What are some of your favorite songs?

"Wasn't Born to Follow," the Byrds

List up to ten things that could be helpful to someone breaking into the business.

- Have as much fun as possible.
- Be here now.
- Love yourself and others.
- Make love not war.
- Neither feast nor famine—all things in moderation (including moderation).
- Give peace a chance.
- Have a nice day.
- Six of one, half dozen of the other.
- A chicken in every pot, two garages for every car.
- Power to the people.

Paul Oakenfold

Did you have a mentor or someone who inspired you? If so, what have you learned from that person?

My father inspired me. He was a musician. I remember when I was a kid, he was always playing Elvis and Beatles records. I learned from him to be original, work hard, and if you believe in what you're doing, to never give up. Perseverance.

What was your very first job in the music industry, and how did you get it?

A&R for Champion Records in London. I was nosing around the industry trying to find a job, and through a contact, the owner of the label gave me a chance. My first two signings were Will Smith and Salt-N-Pepa.

What was your first big break? The first great thing that ever happened to you . . .

That was it. I signed Will Smith, then remixed his first record, "Girls Ain't Nothin But Trouble." It went right to the Top 10 on the pop charts.

What elements of your job make you want to go to work every day?

It's still hard to think of it as a job—I'd do it for free. It changes every day. I wear many different hats . . . perform, remix, produce, and run a record label. I don't know any other job like that.

What qualities most helped you get to where you are today?

I understand how music is constructed. I know how to work a crowd. And I understand and pay attention to the business aspect.

If you knew everything in the beginning of your career that you know now, what would you have done differently?

I may have timed things differently. When you are dealing with new genres of music, it's not always best to be first on the scene. An example is when I released a record called "Bullet in the Gun." At first, it only went to 38 on the pop charts and stalled. A year later, radio got a hold of it and started giving it a lot of play. We re-released it, and then it went into the Top 5. I was lucky I was able to re-release it because in America you can't do that.

What is your greatest lesson learned?

It's very important in the record business to listen to people's experiences and learn from them, same as it is generally in life.

What are some of your favorite albums?

Joshua Tree, U2
What's Going On, Marvin Gaye
Blade Runner (soundtrack), Vangelis
License to Ill, the Beastie Boys
Nevermind, Nirvana
When all of those records came out, they were pinnacle points in their musical genres. They all have withstood the test of time—they can all be played now, and their lyrical content is relevant today. I love playing them, either deejaying them out, or at home.

Did you have any posters on your bedroom walls as a kid? Of whom?

I wouldn't have had a picture of Donny Osmond on the wall. I was a football fan, and I wasn't into a lot of pop acts. I had the Chelsea Football (soccer) club up. I'm a huge fan of "The Blues," as they're called.

What are some great shows you've seen?

Pink Floyd, *Delicate Sound of Thunder* tour, Wembley Stadium
Prince, *Purple Rain* tour
Run-D.M.C., *Raisin' Hell* tour
U2, *Zooropa*

What are some of your favorite songs?

"Lose Yourself," Eminem
"Walk This Way," Run-D.M.C.
"Come As You Are," Nirvana
"Off Ramp," Pat Metheny
"What's Going On," Marvin Gaye
"Beautiful Day," U2
Various Beatles
Various Elvis

List up to ten things that could be helpful to someone breaking into the business.

■ Persevere! Don't give up.
■ Determination
■ Originality

Ric Ocasek

THE CARS

Did you have a mentor or someone who inspired you? If so, what have you learned from that person?

Buddy Holly inspired me to get a guitar.

Bob Dylan inspired me to write lyrics and not worry about my voice.

The Velvet Underground showed me that chaos and art can be part of music.

John Lennon showed me it's all in the song.

What was your very first job in the music industry, and how did you get it?

I drove a truck for a music distributor in Cleveland, delivering records to stores. The second day on the job I got robbed at gunpoint and handed over three boxes of Frank Sinatra records to the thieves.

What was your first big break? The first great thing that ever happened to you . . .

Getting radio play on WBCN in Boston, on our first demo of the Cars.

What elements of your job make you want to go to work every day?

I don't have a job, but I work on music whenever I feel compelled, which is often. I like going from a blank page to a song.

If you knew everything at the beginning of your career that you know now, what would you have done differently?

I wouldn't change a thing because all failures and successes are part of the whole picture. I regret nothing, and live for nexterday.

What is your greatest lesson learned?

No deal is a deal, until it's a deal.

All people don't care about music.

A lot of bad music becomes hits.

There's a difference between artful music and showmanship.

What are some of your favorite albums?

Greatest Hits, Buddy Holly
The Velvet Underground and Nico, the Velvet Underground
Seventies folk music: Phil Ochs, Eric Anderson, Joni Mitchell, etc.
Albums by the Beatles, Bob Dylan

Did you have any posters on your bedroom walls as a kid? Of whom?

Never hung a poster.

Never idolized anyone.

Never had a hero.

Never had a hobby.

What are some great shows you've seen?

The Velvet Underground, Max's Kansas City   T. Rex, Boston
MC5, Ann Arbor   Ministry, New York City
Bad Brains, Irving Plaza, New York City

What are some of your favorite songs?

"That'll Be the Day," Buddy Holly
"I'm Waiting for the Man," Lou Reed

List up to ten things that could be helpful to someone breaking into the business.

- Don't give up.
- Do original material.
- Love music.
- Be a fool wise in your own folly.
- Don't fake it.
- Don't believe or live on your press.

Dolores O'Riordan

THE CRANBERRIES

Did you have a mentor or someone who inspired you? If so, what have you learned from that person?

There are many artists who inspired me: Elvis, John Lennon, and my favorite female artist, Sinéad O'Connor. When I saw Sinéad rise to fame I knew I could also do that.

What was your very first job in the music industry, and how did you get it?

I never really worked in the industry. I signed a six-album, six-figure deal when I was in school, sixteen years old.

What was your first big break? The first great thing that ever happened to you . . .

A gig we did in Limerick where twenty to thirty record companies reps flew into Shannon on the same flight. It became a bidding war.

What elements of your job make you want to go to work every day?

I love it genuinely. If I get tired of doing the same thing, I change it, i.e., touring, writing, promotion tours, videos, selecting photography, etc.

What qualities most helped you get to where you are today?

Determination, hard work, no social life for about seven years, living with a bunch of relatively strange people of the opposite sex on a bus, having patience with pissy toilet seats, smelly socks, etc.

If you knew everything at the beginning of your career that you know now, what would you have done differently?

I wouldn't have been so ultrasensitive to other people's problems. I wouldn't have taken fame so seriously. I wouldn't have cared what people thought of me.

What is your greatest lesson learned?

If you don't like it, change it. Only you can control your own situations in life. Don't waste it being unhappy.

What are some of your favorite albums?

The Smiths

The Cure

John Lennon

Marvin Gaye

hundreds and thousands more . . .

Did you have any posters on your bedroom walls as a kid? Of whom?

Simon LeBon, Nick Kershaw, Morrissey, and Depeche Mode.

What are some great shows you've seen?

My first was the Waterboys in Limerick in 1996. I have only been to about three gigs in my life. I don't go to concerts at all.

What are some of your favorite songs?

"Yellow Submarine" and "Watership Down" remind me of being a kid.

"Woman" or "Imagine," John Lennon

"November Rain," Guns N' Roses

"Whiskey in the Jar," Thin Lizzy

List up to ten things that could be helpful to someone breaking into the business.

- Don't let anybody tell you what to do.
- Open up a can of whup-ass on them if they do.
- Don't take it seriously, it's just a game.
- Go easy on the substances, the consequences suck.
- Peelin' em off is the easy cheezy way for women, but it helps if you're crap.

Ozzy Osbourne

Did you have a mentor or someone who inspired you? If so, what have you learned from that person?

Yes, the Beatles. I learned melody from them.

What was your very first job in the music industry, and how did you get it?

Tuning car horns at Lucas's factory in Birmingham . . . my mother got me the job there because she worked there as well.

What was your first big break? The first great thing that ever happened to you . . .

Forming Black Sabbath.

What elements of your job make you want to go to work every day?

To avoid the dog shit in my house!

What qualities most helped you get to where you are today?

Determination and self-belief.

If you knew everything at the beginning of your career that you know now, what would you have done differently?

Not a damn thing!

What is your greatest lesson learned?

Never push your grandma when she's shaving.

What are some of your favorite albums?

Revolver, the Beatles
Sgt. Pepper's Lonely Hearts Club Band, the Beatles
Led Zeppelin I, II, and *III,* Led Zeppelin

Did you have any posters on your bedroom walls as a kid? Of whom?

Completely covered by the Beatles!

What are some great shows you've seen?

I saw Paul McCartney this year, and it blew me away!

What are some of your favorite songs?

"The Long and Winding Road," the Beatles   "When the Children Cry," White Lion

"Whole Lotta Love," Led Zeppelin   "Sister Christian," Night Ranger

List up to ten things that could be helpful to someone breaking into the business.

- If you play an instrument: practice, practice, practice.
- Be confident, have charisma . . . and sing, don't talk!

Luciano Pavarotti

Did you have a mentor or someone who inspired you? If so, what have you learned from that person?

My parents were big fans of opera and, from the very beginning, my inspiration in opera was them and what I heard around me: broadcasts of the great opera singers of the time on my parents' radio. From a very young age, I wanted to be a tenor, like my father, Fernando, who had a beautiful voice until he died at age ninety. I also had fantastic teachers—my first teacher was Maestro Arrigo Pola, a tenor himself, who taught me my technique and grounding. I then studied with Ettore Campogalliani, another wonderful teacher. Another huge influence was the wonderful soprano Joan Sutherland. She and her husband, Maestro Richard Bonynge, took me under their wings when I was young. She was my true mentor and Maestro Bonynge is an expert on the voice and gave advice on roles. After that, I learned from other colleagues and all the conductors I worked with, particularly the great Maestro Karajan.

What was your very first job in the music industry, and how did you get it?

In 1961, I won the Achille Peri prize and part of the prize was to sing my first true recital at the theater in Reggio Emilia. This was a big success for me and, from there, I began to be noticed by the music "business."

What was your first big break? The first great thing that ever happened to you . . .

In 1963, the great tenor, and one of my heroes, Giuseppe di Stefano became ill and I substituted for him in *La Bohème,* at Covent Garden in London. I also filled in for him on the television show *Sunday Night at the Palladium* before a TV audience of around fifteen million. It was a huge, huge success. I met Joan Sutherland and Richard Bonynge at the time, and, from that moment, I did not look back.

What elements of your job make you want to go to work every day?

I am one of the biggest fans of the tenor voice who ever lived. I also love being around all different kinds of people. So, to be able to make my profession sharing the tenor voice with audiences around the world is the best job that ever existed as far as I am concerned.

What qualities most helped you get to where you are today?

The best thing I ever got was a great singing education. As I said, I had very fine teachers and received the best advice. My voice, I know, is very distinctive, but the best thing I was taught was my technique. I spent many years studying technique—one year I spent practically on one exercise! It is this technique which has allowed the longevity of my voice.

If you knew everything at the beginning of your career that you know now, what would you have done differently?

I am not a person of regrets, particularly in my career, and it is always important to look forward, not back. I am an optimist and have regretted very few decisions I have taken in my career. I would possibly have sung a couple more particular roles which I just didn't get around to performing and recording.

What is your greatest lesson learned?

It is not only important to greet the right opportunities with open arms but it is also important to know when to say no—in my case, when a role has not been right, not to sing for long periods without a break. The worst thing a singer can do is take on the wrong roles and roles that their voices are not quite ready for. For a long career which enables the voice to maximize its potential, it is important to take this advice.

What are some of your favorite albums?

I adore listening to any recordings of great tenors like Jussi Björling, di Stefano, Kraus, Domingo, Carreras and sopranos such as the great Maria Callas and Joan Sutherland.

I also adore listening to operas which are not suitable for my voice, so which I would never perform—the operas of Michael Tippet, for example. I think two of the best recordings I made were *Madama Butterfly* and *La Bohème* with Maestro Karajan.

Did you have any posters on your bedroom walls as a kid? Of whom?

Growing up, I loved the great tenors, such as Caruso, Corelli, and Gigli.

What are some great shows you've seen?

I have been in and seen many great operas, but a modern musical production I recently enjoyed was *Rent*. It took the immortal story of *La Bohème* and set it in a contemporary world. The music is very moving. Nicoletta loved it so much that she produced the show in Italy.

What are some of your favorite songs?

I love a wide range of music but it always has to come back to opera and Neapolitan songs—any music which loves the tenor voice.

My favorite operas are *Un ballo in maschera, La Bohème,* and *L'elisir d'amore.*

List up to ten things that could be helpful to someone breaking into the business.

For a singer:

- Find a good teacher who understands your voice.
- Take advice from and respect those with experience.
- Work hard—you need to study, study, study.
- You need to develop your technique and never stop working on it.
- Don't take on roles too early in your career.
- Don't take on too much work in a concentrated period of time—you need to pace yourself and protect your voice.
- You need to be resilient—a lot of people will be pulling you in all directions.
- Learn when to say no.
- Learn from your colleagues.
- Don't get carried away with the celebrity lifestyle—it is right for some people, but not others. Be yourself and spend time with family and friends who mean most to you.

Johnny Ramone

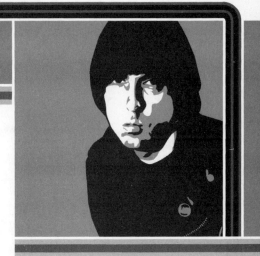

Did you have a mentor or someone who inspired you? If so, what have you learned from that person?

No, I never had a mentor. I guess a person is very fortunate if they do have one. I try to be a mentor to other people now, but I wasn't lucky enough to have one. It would have made things a little easier, and things a little faster as far as the learning process. When you have to learn for yourself, it's a little slower going.

What was your very first job in the music industry, and how did you get it?

Being in the Ramones. Before that I was just a construction worker. I got laid off from my job at twenty-five. I bought a guitar, and we started the Ramones. Tommy, our drummer, kept talking to me and Dee Dee about starting a band. I kept saying no, I didn't want to do that. And then I got a guitar, we rehearsed for six months, played our first show, and then had a record deal about a year later.

What was your first big break? The first great thing that ever happened to you . . .

Losing my job was probably my first break.

In August of 1974 we played our first show at CBGB . . . by the summer of '75 I think we knew it was happening then. There was a *Rolling Stone* article; a page covered the CBGB rock festival, and we got most of the pages written about us. And I think at that point we started to feel we were really good. We were pretty confident right from the start.

What elements of your job make you want to go to work every day?

Knowing that I felt we were the best at what we did. I felt no matter what, no matter how much we weren't getting along, or not talking to each other, I was still in the best band there was for that period of time. I didn't see anyone out there who could top us, so that was enough to keep me going.

What qualities most helped you get to where you are today?

A lot of luck, because you have to find other people who you're on the same wavelength with. And watching a lot of concerts and listening to music all my life I think I had a lot of knowledge about visually what it took to be good. I would always review every concert that I went to in my mind, even though I wasn't in a band—what they were doing right and what they were doing wrong and making mental notes of it so that when I started to do it I tried to apply all that. It's hard just listening to the music . . . I mean, I would know what's good but until you start having to write songs the visual component hadn't factored in yet.

If you knew everything at the beginning of your career that you know now, what would you have done differently?

Yeah, but it probably wouldn't have made things better. I would have taken it a little more seriously, in terms of recording and spending the time. I never spent any time, it was always, just call me and I'll do one take. I felt like I could just walk on. I guess it came too easy. You know, you just buy a guitar, and all of a sudden you're in a band, and all of a sudden everything's gelling and you got a record deal—it was all so easy for me.

What is your greatest lesson learned?

That it's not very important. . . . I'm just an entertainer. Everything I owe I owe to the fans. Also, try not to compromise.

What are some of your favorite albums?

All the early Beatles albums, probably *Beatles for Sale* might be my favorite.
Elvis's Sun Sessions, or any greatest-hits album, especially fifties greatest hits
Gary Glitter, Slade, Early Bowie, T. Rex were really good.
Early Rolling Stones, while Brian Jones was still in the band. Sixties Rolling Stones, I can't listen to anything after that.
The Doors

Did you have any posters on your bedroom walls as a kid? Of whom?

I wasn't allowed to put posters up, and I really didn't care. Now, my house is full of posters. I have movie posters, different rooms, different themes, thirties, forties, Universal horror, sci-fi, Elvis posters, I have a rock 'n' roll poster section, and Disney. As a kid, I never cared. I was always into being orderly, and I guess to me if you put stuff up it always looked messy. You have to get stuff with the right frames and the right spacing. I'm a little crazy with this stuff.

What are some great shows you've seen?

The Who, saw them ten times, all with Keith . . . nothing after Keith. The Who wouldn't be worth seeing without Keith.

I saw the Doors and the Who in '68 or '69, and the Doors managed to upstage the Who even though the Who is the best live band. Jim Morrison managed to do it.

From our era, the Clash was the best band I'd seen from 1975 on. It was best the second-album tour.

Funny bands, I mean you could see something like Grand Funk Railroad in their prime and they were great live.

Slade, I saw them right before we started. That was one of the things that really inspired me. I saw the New York Dolls, and I thought "Oh, I could do this as good as them," and then I saw Slade and I realized these guys were tremendous. And that inspired me to do it.

List up to ten things that could be helpful to someone breaking into the business.

- Learn all your roots. Learn all the rock 'n' roll stuff you can from the time rock 'n' roll started till now.
- Listen to all the great bands.
- Know what it takes to be good.
- Try to watch as many old film clips and video stuff of these bands, and see what they're doing.
- If you were in a band in 2003, all you grew up with were bands from 1998, 1999, then you've never seen anything great. And if you don't see things that are great you're not going to know what it takes. But if you go back and study all the stuff that came before you, in the fifties, sixties, early seventies, you see what they're doing. The Beatles are in a class to themselves— they're on another planet. Who you should watch depends on what the band is like. I have a friend who's into pop music, so I'll show him bands that I feel are the better of the pop bands, you know, the Small Faces, Slade, things like that.

Nick Rhodes

DURAN DURAN

Did you have a mentor or someone who inspired you? If so, what have you learned from that person?

I have always been attracted to people who create the new and influence the next generation. I constantly find inspiration through painters, poets, writers, film directors, photographers, fashion designers, and, of course, musicians.

What was your very first job in the music industry, and how did you get it?

At sixteen years old, I formed Duran Duran with John Taylor. Never did make it to art school.

What was your first big break? The first great thing that ever happened to you . . .

Seeing punk bands perform live and realizing that they were only a few years older than me and that I knew all of the same chords on the guitar. After that, I discovered synthesizers and quickly realized that they were the future of modern music.

What elements of your job make you want to go to work every day?

The desire to create something better than the day before.

What qualities most helped you get to where you are today?

Self-belief, tenacity, patience, attention to detail, and a relentless sense of humor.

If you knew everything at the beginning of your career that you know now, what would you have done differently?

I would have certainly learned more about the business mechanism of the industry, then hopefully this would have resulted in my refusal to sign such foolish contracts. Most musicians find out the real value of their songs and master recordings far too late in their careers.

What is your greatest lesson learned?

Take good, professional advice but beware the greed of others.

What are some of your favorite albums?

Andy Warhol's Velvet Underground,
   the Velvet Underground
White Album, the Beatles
Roxy Music, Roxy Music
TransEurope Express, Kraftwerk
Remain in the Light, Talking Heads
Imagine, John Lennon

Fresh, Sly & the Family Stone
Odelay, Beck
Dummy, Portishead
Felt Mountain, Goldfrapp
2001 (Instrumental), Dr. Dre
All of David Bowie in the seventies

Did you have any posters on your bedroom walls as a kid? Of whom?

Glam rock and pop art.

What are some great shows you've seen?

Iggy Pop with David Bowie playing
   keyboards
The Velvet Underground reunion shows in
   Paris
Queen in the seventies

The Clash in the late seventies
Peter Gabriel in the eighties
David Bowie, *Thin White Duke* show, 1976
And many operas at Bregenz and the English
   National Opera in London

What are some of your favorite songs?

"Jealous Guy," John Lennon
"All Tomorrow's Parties,"
   the Velvet Underground
"If You Want Me to Stay," Sly & the
   Family Stone
"Pretty Bacon," the Sex Pistols
"I Am the Walrus," the Beatles
"Groove Is in the Heart," Deee-Lite

"I Feel Love," Donna Summer
"You Can't Put Your Arms Around a Memory,"
   Johnny Thunders
"Warm Leatherette," the Normal
"Another Girl, Another Planet,"
   the Only Ones
"Showroom Dummies," Kraftwerk

List up to ten things that could be helpful to someone breaking into the business.

- Write great songs.
- Play live shows.
- Think different. Be fearless.
- Take care of the details.
- Timing is everything.

- Remember, style matters.
- Protect your sense of humor (you'll need it).
- Build the story.
- Know where you are going.
- Don't give up.

Keith Richards

Did you have a mentor or someone who inspired you? If so, what have you learned from that person?

As a musician, I can name a thousand influences. My mother played a lot of jazz when I was growing up—Sarah Vaughn, Ella Fitzgerald, Billy Eckstein—a lot of the late forties, early fifties stuff. I grew up with that kind of music in the background. We were also kind of limited in our choices at that time in England, because we didn't have a record player. It was only BBC, so I was brought up on a very strict BBC diet. If you sorted through it, you'd probably find half an hour here or there of some interesting stuff. There was also a lot of classical music, because of the BBC. At the time I hated it (because it was forced upon you), but in later years, I realized those guys did have something going for them.

As I got into music, I would have to say Presley's "Heartbreak Hotel" or Little Richard's "Long Tall Sally" were like a bolt of lightning and a streak of heat. They came when I was at the age when the music being played in the middle fifties, especially on the BBC, was like, "I am the pink toothbrush, you are the blue toothbrush, how much is that doggie in the window?" Rock 'n' roll hit me when I was about thirteen. It started coming over the airwaves, and suddenly you felt like you were connected to the world. I used to talk to John Lennon about this, and we both came up with the same metaphor—suddenly the world became Technicolor; before that, it was black and white. In a way, for people of my generation it was the end of the war. We lived with the war, and in the ruins of it. We were still on rationing until well into the fifties. Especially with cane sugar—that was the last thing to come off rationing, which is probably why a lot of us are still skinny.

What was your very first job in the music industry, and how did you get it?

It was at a school gym around Christmas, when I was fifteen. I can still remember actually feeling the first time I was paid, because I got paid in coins—it wasn't even enough for paper. It was half a crown, which was two shillings and sixpence in English old money, which is probably about ten pence now. I wouldn't spend it for anything, even though I was still broke. Eventually I did, out of necessity. It was amazing, because suddenly it was like, "Wow, I'm a pro."

There was something special about getting the money, especially when the money isn't really why we were doing it. We were just doing it because we wanted to try it out, and see what would happen if we got up onstage. I wanted to play with a bunch of guys. I was together with a couple other bunches before the Stones, really ramshackle groups, but we got laid.

What was your first big break? The first great thing that ever happened to you . . .

As far as breaks go, it was kind of a weird thing with the Stones. We were virtually anti-pop at the time, without realizing there was about to be a sea change. We were very snobbish in our own stupid, little way—"we're not a rock 'n' roll band, we're a rhythm and blues band." There was a weird clique of people who were really interested in blues, known as purists. They were idealistic about their blues. Muddy Waters was actually buzzed off when he came onstage with an electric guitar. The same thing happened to Dylan a few years later.

We just grew up with this feeling that something was happening. With the Stones, our only aim was to get a couple of regular club gigs and, if possible, to make a record. There was a burning desire to get into the studio, which at that time was like going to heaven and staying alive at the same time. We wanted to get into the studio and see what it came back like, and see what we could do with it. Play it back and see how we could improve it. We wanted to learn hands on. Even though the technology back then was caveman compared to now, it was still changing all the time. Throughout my whole career, I realized I was on the cutting edge of all this electronic stuff—two tracks, four tracks, eight tracks, sixteen. We were always living with the latest possibilities that the military allowed us.

Ian Stewart was the first to get us into the studio to make some demos. As far as I am concerned, it's his band. Andrew Oldham came on board after he had left the Beatles, and suddenly we were making a record deal with Decca. It was really insane. It was suddenly a big business. One minute we were looking for something to keep the fire going, and the next we're in the head office of Decca Records with these drooling old men, telling them, "If you want us, you're gonna pay!" It was pretty heavy stuff.

What elements of your job make you want to go to work every day?

Growing along with it has been the realization that songwriting is something you can actually do. It becomes the most important part of you, because it takes you over, like writing of any kind. You see everything through the filter of "that's a song" or "that's a story." That became fascinating to me, so it was suddenly that I wasn't just a guitar player, I became much more intimately involved in the making of music, putting it all together, which had never occurred to me before. With the pressure of the game, Andrew Oldham boxed Mick and me in a kitchen and said, "Come out with a song." I said, "Well, we've got some food, so I guess we can last for a while." Eventually, we did come out of the kitchen, with "As Tears Go By," which within six weeks was in the Top 10 by Marianne Faithfull. Before that I thought of songwriting as a totally separate job—like there's the blacksmith, and there's the stonemason, and you did this, and I did that. So at that point I integrated that I was not only a guitar player, but that I could write what I was going to play, instead of just revamping all the time. It was an eye-opener.

What qualities most helped you get to where you are today?

It's not that difficult, quite honestly. I'd probably be playing guitar at home even if I'd become a plumber. To me, it's the blessing that the thing I love to do turned out to be my work and my living. When your hobby becomes your living, you've got to give your thanks and praise. If there is such a thing as luck, I'd be the first to say there is. I've always felt incredibly lucky because I was given the chance to find out what I could do, and grow, and let me see the world.

If you knew everything at the beginning of your career that you know now, what would you have done differently?

Of course, I would have kept the piano down on one track here or there, and I wish I hadn't stayed up for nine days because it broke my nose in the process. But on a musical level, I look upon it all as an adventure that I'm on. It goes so fast that it's impossible to get off, but I am also curious to see where it's headed. I've been given this unique perspective on life, and I am wondering when I'm going to have to pay it back. Hopefully, I can defer it.

What is your greatest lesson learned?

I was always impressed with a tombstone of a nameless musician I once saw. All it said was MUSICIAN—HE PASSED IT ON. It's the "passing it on" more than any other thing that you pass on. The people that I learned from and inspired me, one wonders, who passed it on to them? And then you realize you're in this long, long line that goes back thousands of years to the troubadours and the bards, and you're a part of this ancestral line. It's pretty hyped up these days, but then musicians always used to wear little bells on their toes. I feel part of a long tradition of wandering minstrels, with half my life spent on the road playing music to people, getting to know them, and trying to keep them happy.

When I started listening to Chuck Berry, I wanted to know who he listened to, and where he picked it up, and then you learn about Muddy Waters and Robert Johnson, and you follow it back. Then a little further, there's classical music, and you see how Mozart came out of Bach, and how Bach came out of Corelli. I could easily take you back a few hundred years. There's the incredible spine of roots music, folk music, and country music, which runs throughout the ages. The big sea change in the history of music, and why we're so lucky, is that you can record it now. Up until that point, you had to read it off the page or just learn it by ear. With records and playback, this whole other area began, which we're still reverberating from. I don't know what I'd do without a playback.

What are some of your favorite albums?

Best of Muddy Waters, Muddy Waters
Rockin' at the Hops, Chuck Berry
The Best of . . . The Everly Brothers, Buddy Holly, T-Bone Walker, Robert Johnson, Little Walter, Little Richard, Fats Domino. The greats are the greats. Tomorrow I'm doing an overdub
for Jerry Lee Lewis. We just keep passing it on.

Did you have any posters on your bedroom walls as a kid? Of whom?

We didn't have posters when I was a kid. This was the late forties, early fifties, after the war,
and they weren't on rationing! I used to draw on the wall. . . .

What are some great shows you've seen?

Speaking about our own performances, the amazing thing to me is that no matter where we
are playing—Istanbul, Sydney, Bombay, New Jersey, London—once we're in that room, and
we've got our thing going, you could be anywhere. I used to be more critical when I was
younger, but now I just see this beautiful, straight line going up—every show is great, and the
next one is better than the one before. There aren't any dips and highs. It just gets higher and
higher.

At the Paramount Theater in 1964 I saw Joe Tex, the Shirelles, Curtis Mayfield, and the Im-
pressions all in one afternoon. I've seen plenty of great stuff, but that one sticks. Just to be in
the audience and see that incredible lineup, one after the other. Mick and I were about the only
white guys in the audience, just drooling.

James Brown at the Apollo in 1964. I remember going back to the dressing room and James
said, "Oh, yeah, you're those kids from London, England." It was always "London, England." At
that time, the Famous Flames were performing with him, and I was amazed because he had one
of the Flames there taking his shoes off, and another rushing off to get him some food. Suddenly they'd become slaves, and I was there, watching this thing go down, saying "Whoa! He
don't call himself the 'King of Soul' for nothing!"

What are some of your favorite songs?

"Nearness of You," Hoagy Carmichael—I've always had a fixation on it.
"Too Much Monkey Business" and "Jo Jo Gunne," Chuck Berry
"Stop in the Name of Love," Holland-Dozier-Holland

I know what I don't like, but this list could go on and on. . . . Pick up some Bach and some
Mozart. Get some John Lee Hooker. Quincy Jones. Django Reinhart and Oscar Alemán were
both great guitar players. The Ronettes, Tina Turner, Etta James, Big Maybelle, Bessie Smith,
Billie Holiday—let's not forget the ladies.

List up to ten things that could be helpful to someone breaking into the business.

- First get your head examined.
- Don't be discouraged at the beginning. The whole music thing is chaotic right now. There are so many different ways it might go right now, and so many different ways to enter. It's not the same as when I started, when there were just a few monoliths that you had to attack. You have so many different potentials now.
- The music business is basically like an ocean, and there are a lot of sharks. If you're a small fish, don't get too close to the big fish all at once. You want to attract their attention but not enough to eat you.
- Be humble when you make it.

Lionel Richie

Did you have a mentor or someone who inspired you? If so, what have you learned from that person?

From the business standpoint, one great example would be Berry Gordy. He didn't teach school; you couldn't get him in a university. I actually saw Berry Gordy on the job. I was a college student at the time, an economics major and accounting minor at Tuskegee Institute in Alabama. You didn't have access to successful multimillionaires, especially black, so this was my first opportunity, when I joined Motown. I had the chance to actually see, up close and personal, a hands-on mogul at work. It was absolutely fascinating. He was a tyrant. Not only was he creative, and a songwriter, he was also a very shrewd businessman. I got a chance to see both sides of the coin. I saw how he dealt with artists and how he dealt with the business. It was invaluable just to watch this, but then I had access to him too. I could go and ask him questions, and it was just a fabulous beginning.

What was your very first job in the music industry, and how did you get it?

I was the biggest fan of the business. I would hang out at every backstage thing. Anything that came through town, I was the big fan of the day. We probably all did the same thing, going from big fan and enthusiast to getting a piece of the business in some way. My entrée into the business was joining the Commodores.

The biggest break for "Lionel Richie" was when I brought my saxophone to college to learn how to play it. The Commodores didn't ask me if I knew how to play it . . . they just asked me if I had a horn. And I didn't volunteer the information that I could only play it by ear. So it wasn't until three or four years with the Commodores that I told them I couldn't read the music. That was when I realized I could play by ear—at that point I thought there must be a logical reason why you know what you know.

My actual first job in the music industry was the signing of the Motown contract. Up until that, the Commodores were just a band. We traveled all over, everywhere, but the first time that we actually plugged into the music business was Motown Records.

What was your first big break? The first great thing that ever happened to you . . .

We were actually the opening act for the Jackson 5 for two and a half years at the beginning of their career. I got a chance to see Michael from the time he was seven to right now. We didn't get the Motown contract until after we had played the North American tour with the Jackson 5. It was absolutely amazing, watching these five little kids go onstage and act like grown professionals, only to come off stage and turn back into little boys.

The first "great thing" was very late in my career—I didn't really get it at the beginning because I was so busy trying to make the band work. When you're in a band, you're trying to make sure that you're doing enough to pull your own weight. And if anybody was going to be kicked out of the band I figured the guy who couldn't read music would be the guy thrown out first—especially when we signed the Motown contract and the first thing they said to us was, "Who are the writers, and who are the lead singers of the band?" I couldn't raise my hand to either one of them so I knew I was gone. It wasn't really until "Easy" or "Three Times a Lady" that I ever felt fully like, "Oh my God, I think I can do this. . . ." Up until that point I was in sheer terror that at any moment I was going to get a notice saying, "Okay, Rich, we're gonna cut back on the budget. You're gone."

What elements of your job make you want to go to work every day?

I started out as a fan. Even to this day I can still make the statement that if I could just make sure that the bills were paid, and I could still travel like I'm doing, and everything else was paid for, I would still do this. It's still a hobby. It's not something that I dread. It's still not a job, and the day it becomes a job is the day I quit.

It's fascinating. What I like about it most is right when you think you're a pro at what you're doing, the business changes, and you have to learn something new. What makes me get up every morning is that I'm extremely nosy—I want to know what's next. I think that's one of the secrets for all of us in this business—right when you think you've got your finger on the button, it goes left a little bit. Funk comes in, funk goes out. Disco comes in, disco goes out. Acid rock comes in, punk rock goes out. And by the time you finish, you've been around the circle and someone says, "Wow, you've been in the business twenty-five years!" And you say, "I have?! I thought this just happened yesterday." Your name changes from "Yo, Rich!" to "Mr. Richie" and I wonder to myself, "When did I become 'Mr. Richie' . . . Shit!"

But it's so amazing. You're always chasing that inevitable end, but it never ends. That's the part that makes me get up in the morning. There is no formula to this crap; it really is fly by the seat of your pants. The only reason to get in this business in the first place is because you actually like it, because otherwise it's painful.

What qualities most helped you get to where you are today?

Passion. The other part is that if you hang around long enough, you get a sense of who you are. It's the best psychoanalysis you'll ever do in your life. It's the only business where you'll keep asking yourself, "Why am I doing this, and what do I do now?" As time goes on, they start interviewing you . . . "Why did you leave the Commodores?" I don't know. It was just what happened at the time.

They're looking for logic in a business that's not logical. So you're constantly trying to answer these logical questions. "Why did you write the song?" I don't know. It was there at the time. "But you must have a logical answer? Were you depressed that day, Mr. Richie?" I don't know!

Now that I look back on it, I see it was basically a diary of my life. Since I didn't keep a diary every day, just go back and listen to the Commodores *Blue* album, or "Sail On" or "I'm Easy Like Sunday Morning" . . . that's exactly what I was thinking at the time, which gives me a lot of insight into what I was about at that time. Now it's the window to my life—it was just writing that window.

If you knew everything at the beginning of your career that you know now, what would you have done differently?

Of course there are the things I would have cleaned up better. I would have dealt with the leaving of the Commodores better. I would have had that final tour together. I would have dealt with my marriages and my divorces in different ways, my relationships in a different way. I think what made it all so exciting and "fly by the seat of your pants" was that you didn't know the answers to the test. What made it quite enjoyable, if you want to know the truth about it, is that you didn't know whether the outcome was going to be good or bad. You just believed in it.

I think of the artists of today and I go, "God, why would you want to get in the business today? It's more screwed up than ever." Then I realize—no, it's not. It's the first time they've ever done it. This is their adventure now. I look back on the time that I started, and I think I was so much more logical. Then I realize I wasn't—we were the gangsters in 1975 and 1985. I remember looking at the establishment at that time. I remember being at the Grammys with Henry Mancini looking over at me and thinking, "Who let this thug into the Grammys, with his long hair." Now I look at everyone and say, "Okay, now it's your turn." Now I look like the establishment. We can't use logic to figure it out . . . everybody has their time.

What is your greatest lesson learned?

The first thing you have to understand is we're not a business of talent. We're a business of relationships, and if you establish relationships along the way, you'll grab a hold of some friends who'll carry on your career forever for you. But if you don't make relationships, then your career will end at a certain point, because there will be no one that wants to be around you.

There are two relationships. One is with your fans, which you should never break away from. Always let them know where you are. And secondly, there's the relationship with the industry. The guy who was the mail boy last week is president of a record company this week, and the same guy who you said "go screw yourself" to . . . Do not go there. The phrase to try never to use in your entire career is "fuck you." Because it normally means just that. Fuck you means fuck you. That phrase will come back to haunt you every time. In and out of the industry, but more so in the industry. That's a phrase no one seems to forget.

What are some of your favorite albums?

Anything that Marvin Gaye did in life. I'm a Marvin Gaye fanatic.
P-Funk, George Clinton
Madman Across the Water, Elton John
White Album and *Sgt. Pepper's Lonely Hearts Club Band,* the Beatles
Otis Redding—I knew the Bar-Kays so that made it even more special.
Led Zeppelin I, Led Zeppelin

Did you have any posters on your bedroom walls as a kid? Of whom?

I was the odd couple. I was in the middle of the civil rights movement with a Jimi Hendrix poster on one wall and an "I want you for the U.S. Army" poster on the other. I was your basic militant at heart. I also had Buddy Miles and Jimi Hendrix, the Temptations, and Led Zeppelin. Those were my three all-time prime ones. I think I still have them.

What are some great shows you've seen?

The Temptations when they were all together. I saw them first in Birmingham, Alabama, and again in Chicago.
James Brown on the campus of Tuskegee Institute
Led Zeppelin, Montreal
Bob Marley (who ironically, at the end of his career, did his last show with the Commodores at Madison Square Garden as the opening act . . . what was that turn? Where'd that come from?)
Sly & the Family Stone, Apollo Theater . . . it was just ridiculous.
Sammy Davis Jr., Frank Sinatra, Dean Martin
And, of course, Michael Jackson

What are some of your favorite songs?

"Yesterday," Paul McCartney　　　　"Hey Jude," the Beatles
"What's Going On," Marvin Gaye　　　"My Girl," the Temptations

List up to ten things that could be helpful to someone breaking into the business.

- Find someone who's in the business. If you want to get into the retail business, find a record shop. If you want to get into the music part of it, then you have to hang around a studio. Hang around a producer. Hang around somebody who's in the studio, even if you have to just take coffee to the guy. Work for free for the first few months. If you want to be a songwriter, you have to hang around other songwriters. You gotta be around someone just to hang out. Because the more you can see, the more you can hear, the more you will understand how they put it together. It helps tremendously to watch a pro at work. You can go to school, but you have to get around somebody who is doing it.

- Learn the word "free." You may not be able to do it now, but when you're eighteen, free can work pretty well. After that, you know, the pressures of life get on you, but while you're at your mom's house (I love that phrase), while mom and dad are still paying the bills, between fifteen and eighteen, is the time you really start. I think most of us got in around that time, when someone else was paying the bills. I had college tuition going on when I was with the Commodores.

- There's gotta be a starting point, and the closer you can get to somebody who is doing what you want to do, the better it is. But you have to hang around and just live it. And while the pressure is not on you, you get to watch somebody else with the pressure, and it teaches you how to deal with it. The worst thing in the world to do is what's happening a lot now, where the kids work for four years on their first album, which becomes a number-one album, and then the label needs the next record in six months. But they'll never have it, because the artists don't know how to do it in six months—they know how to do it in four years. And that's a problem, because they don't have another four years to wait. So if you actually saw how someone handled the next record and the next record and the next record, you'd be better off. Once the green light turns on, it's all about give me the next record. They don't want to hear about you going away to get your thoughts together. . . . What? Next!!

Sonny Sandoval
P.O.D.

Did you have a mentor or someone who inspired you? If so, what have you learned from that person?

There are several people who have passed down their love of music to me. I grew up in a young, rock 'n' roll family that was always listening and playing music. My uncle Noah played drums in a few different rock bands. Bands like AC/DC, Black Sabbath, Led Zeppelin, Cheap Trick, etc. My uncle Damaja Lee taught me the roots of reggae music. And the streets taught me about hip-hop. My appreciation for all these types of music put me in this position.

What was your very first job in the music industry, and how did you get it?

I've never worked for the industry. I've been involved with music ever since I was a teenager. We were playing music in the underground for seven years until one day an A&R rep for Atlantic Records said he wanted to sign us. So I guess my first job in the music industry started the day we wrote our first album for Atlantic Records.

What was your first big break? The first great thing that ever happened to you . . .

Our first break happened at a club in Walled Lake, Michigan. An A&R rep by the name of John Rubeli came to see us play. There were about seven hundred kids on a school night that came to see us play. The kids went off, the show was tight, and we got signed.

What elements of your job make you want to go to work every day?

I have the best job in the world for the simple fact that I get to be a kid all the time. Not to say that it's not hard work at times, but I get to make music with people I love and take that music around the world for anyone to hear. I just want to continue to get better at what I do and go even further than we have gone.

What qualities most helped you get to where you are today?

Passion and love for the music we make. Hard work and dedication in making sure people hear that music. Intelligent business decisions when dealing with the industry. Humility and appreciation for life in order to stay balanced in this business.

If you knew everything at the beginning of your career that you know now, what would you have done differently?

I honestly believe this is the beginning of our career. We have always taken the staircase to success and never the elevator. This way you learn with every step.

What is your greatest lesson learned?

Love and respect! Don't ever burn your bridges.

What are some of your favorite albums?

Joshua Tree, U2

Uprising, Bob Marley and the Wailers

Reggatta de Blanc, the Police

Slip, Quicksand

Raisin' Hell, Run-D.M.C.

Tear It Up (live), Black Uhuru

Quickness, Bad Brains

Pennywise, Pennywise

Love and Hate, Dennis Brown

Back in Black, AC/DC

Make Yourself, Incubus

Adrenaline, the Deftones

Too many to list . . .

Did you have any posters on your bedroom walls as a kid? Of whom?

Bad Brains, the Beastie Boys, Bob Marley, Peter Tosh, and Bones Brigade.

What are some great shows you've seen?

Run-D.M.C., the Police, Deftones and Quicksand, Bad Brains and Deftones, Santana, Gypsy Kings, Michael Rose, H.R.

What are some of your favorite songs?

"Walking on the Moon," the Police

"I Used to Love Her," Common Sense

"Heathen," Bob Marley

"Here I Come," Dennis Brown

"Samba Pa Ti," Santana

"Fools Gold," H.R.

"Where the Streets Have No Name," U2

"Sabotage," the Beastie Boys

"Eyes of a Stranger," the Payolas

"Between the Sheets," the Isley Brothers

"My Philosophy," Boogie Down Productions . . .

etc., etc.

List up to ten things that could be helpful to someone breaking into the business.

It's as simple as this . . .

- Hard work, passion, dedication, love, respect, self-respect, earn respect, integrity, hard work
- "It's not what you know, but who you know."
- Be at the right place at the right time.
- Sell out and do everything the industry tells you.

Seal

Did you have a mentor or someone who inspired you? If so, what have you learned from that person?

My first mentor was named Mr. Wren. He was a teacher in my elementary school. He'd been a singer himself, but when that didn't work out, he went into teaching, which is a much more admirable profession anyway. I had a detached relationship with my father and mother at home, so there wasn't a lot of communication going on in my house. Mr. Wren opened up the concept of communicating through music to me. He realized that I had this voice, and he would inspire me at every available opportunity. He would constantly tell me I should get up and sing.

The first time I sang publicly was when he convinced me to sing at a PTA meeting. I sang Johnny Nash's "I Can See Clearly Now." I was eleven, and that was the first inkling I got that music was my vocation.

What was your very first job in the music industry, and how did you get it?

I must have been around nineteen when I did a session for a guy named Pete Heins. He was a keyboard player in an English band called Light of the World. He had heard that I sang through his wife, Pauline, who was a customer in the shop I worked in. I would sing in the basement, and I guess she heard me at some point. They gave me my first session in the studio, demo-ing a track for them.

What was your first big break? The first great thing that ever happened to you . . .

The chart success of a track called "The Killer" that I did with Adamski (aka Adam Tinnley), who was a very popular keyboard wizard on the back of the acid house explosion in 1988–89 in Europe. He was signed, but when his record company released the track, they didn't really promote it. However, it was so strong that it became a Pan-European number-one. I got a deal after that because I had cowritten and sung the song.

What elements of your job make you want to go to work every day?

I *have* to. There's not a choice. If I don't sing, if I don't make music, I become sick, physically and emotionally.

What qualities most helped you get to where you are today?

I am a survivor, which was instilled in me from my rocky childhood. Being a survivor teaches you resilience.

I learned a strong work ethic from my father. He said, "What's worth doing is worth doing well." I've always strove for excellence. I've lived a pretty ideal existence, and I've never wanted to settle for second or second-best.

I'm also an optimist. I always think it can be better. I always believe the day can be brighter.

If you knew everything at the beginning of your career that you know now, what would you have done differently?

I've been very fortunate—I've had and continue to have a great career. I just wish I had realized that those were really fantastic times, even though they seemed arduous. I would have enjoyed the whole process a lot more. I took things way too seriously. I applied too much importance to areas that actually didn't require that much attention, and less to some that did.

What is your greatest lesson learned?

Music is a great communicator. It has the ability to transcend all barriers—language, national, or anything else. We're talking about a very powerful and seductive medium, and I think those of us who have the gift of manipulating that medium need to adhere to a responsibility. One must be careful with the message that one proliferates. The greatest lessons I have learned actually sound like contradictions. On the one hand, I've learned that there is a great responsibility that comes along with having this gift of communicating and reaching millions of people. And on the other, I've learned that it is only music. I'm not a neurosurgeon, or a plastic surgeon, restoring faces of burn victims or performing an operation to remove a cancerous tumor. That's hard-core pressure, and a different level of serving the world. This is only music, and therefore, one isn't to take all the trappings that come along with fame or the benefits that are the fruits of your labor too seriously.

What are some of your favorite albums?

Innervisions is my all-time favorite album. It's the most perfect album of all time.
The Hissing of Summer Lawns, Joni Mitchell. It's perfect and beautiful.
What's Going On, Marvin Gaye
Axis: Bold as Love, Jimi Hendrix Experience
Fresh, Sly & the Family Stone
Crosby, Stills & Nash, Crosby, Stills & Nash
Joshua Tree, U2

Did you have any posters on your bedroom walls as a kid? Of whom?

I wasn't really a poster guy, but I did have one of Bob Marley.

What are some great shows you've seen?

Prince, *Purple Rain,* London. No matter what you say about Prince, you have to remember, he was *that* guy who was insanely talented. He was a musician's musician.

U2, *Achtung Baby,* Anaheim Stadium. Fantastic.

What are some of your favorite songs?

"Imagine," John Lennon

"Ne Me Quitte Pas," Jacques Brel. One of the most beautiful love songs ever written.

"Corcovado," Stan Getz, Astrud Gilberto, and João Gilberto. The lyrics are just beautiful, and the live version is breathtaking.

"What's Going On," Marvin Gaye—a masterpiece

"Where the Streets Have No Name," U2—a masterpiece

"Bridge Over Troubled Water," Simon and Garfunkel

I could go on all day. . . .

List up to ten things that could be helpful to someone breaking into the business.

I have two big pieces of advice, if I'm even qualified to give advice.

- The first is that you can't make it happen by applying pressure and force. You have to *let* it happen by believing that it actually already is. That doesn't mean you lessen your work ethic, but it means that you are conscious of where you are exerting the energy. If you try to will or force it to happen, you may end up pushing it further and further away. You have to live and believe as though it is. Everybody is a star—it's just believing that you are. Let it come, without being lazy.
- The other thing is to be open. Some songs sound so contrived. They may be carefully and masterfully constructed, but the thing that really determines whether a song has longevity, whether a song resonates with people in that inexplicable way, is if the artist was open at the time it was made. If they were coming from that divine place. If the music was coming from a divine place and was able to flow through the artist in an unadulterated manner. Do whatever you can to make yourself open. That's why it took me so long to make this damn album! I wasn't open. Sometimes you need to go through some kind of adversity in order to open you up. I'm not saying that's an excuse and you need to do that to yourself every time. For me, this time, I needed to go through something.

Gene Simmons

KISS

Did you have a mentor or someone who inspired you? If so, what have you learned from that person?

I was born and continue to be an only child. The most influential person in my life was and continues to be my mother. I don't say this for effect. It's certainly not intended to be a sound bite. The reality is, despite the fact that my mother, a German Nazi concentration camp survivor, didn't travel the world, never had a proper education, and isn't "sophisticated" in the least, she continues to spout wisdom the likes of which I haven't heard from our wisest sages.

Her wisdom is practical. Something I can and do use every day. "Reach for the stars," she would say. Or, when I would come home with a $10 million check in my hand, she would say, "Very nice. *Now* what are you going to do?"

What was your very first job in the music industry, and how did you get it?

My first job in music, almost by definition, was the first time anyone paid me for playing music. That would have to be as a member of one of my first groups, The Long Island Sounds in 1965. Here I was slaving away at two newspaper routes every day after school, just so I could collect about fifty dollars at the end of the week, and just by playing onstage with the Sounds for two nights, I would come home with *three times that amount* . . . and get more girls, too!!! Now, that's a job I like.

What was your first big break? The first great thing that ever happened to you . . .

My first break (professionally) was when, quite by accident, the band I was in, Wicked Lester, got some free time at Electric Lady Studios to do some demos. Lester recorded an album for Epic, but we disbanded the band and reformed as KISS. The first break led to KISS becoming the number-one American Group Gold Record Champions . . . of all time, I might add!!! (RIAA Group Category). Humble be damned.

What elements of your job make you want to go to work every day?

I'm usually up by 6:30 to 7:00 every day. I'm not a bird, and I don't really care for worms, but early birds *do* get to eat the worms. I meet people every day who complain about their jobs.

And how much they hate the work the job entails. I don't really have a job, but I love to work. Maybe it's not really about the job. Maybe it's about the love of doing the work. The harder I work, the luckier I get.

What qualities most helped you get to where you are today?

I don't really have the right qualities to be a rock star. For one thing, I refuse to say "wassup" and have never said "dude." I don't get high and never have. I don't drink and have never been drunk. I don't smoke and never have. So, that doesn't make me the best guy to have around when the other guys want to get blitzed. I also refuse to associate with losers. So, that only leaves the girls. That part, I like. I've been described (to my face and behind it) as: arrogant (I am), self-absorbed (of course, if I'm not interested in me, who's going to be?), demanding (absolutely, lazy people should not have access to power—they should be waiting behind a turnstile somewhere in Middle America, and politely ask you if you want fries with that).

My qualities for success in life, in love, and in all things is a take-no-prisoners attitude. It has served me well.

What is your greatest lesson learned?

Lessons I have learned might include: Love, contrary to what we've been taught, is *not* the most powerful force in the world. *Money* is. The simple proof may be as simple as going to a bus stop and telling the bus driver you'd like a ride (on the bus ride of life, if you will) . . . and try telling him you don't have money. Tell him you love him. See if he lets you on. . . . Or, you might be a mother with her starving child on the deserts of the Kalahari. There's a caravan passing by. You're both near death. The fastest way to buy your child life (and yourself as well) is with money. Money is the currency of love. Money is the *expression* of love. With money, you can buy the operation your mother needs. With money, you can give to charity and feed the poor. With money, hell, you can even (supposedly) buy God. Even He/She/It gets the hat passed around at the end of the sermon. Sorry to dispel everyone's romantic notions. But life makes its own demands, despite our *preferred* fairy-tale version of it.

What are some of your favorite albums?

Favorite albums might be a potpourri of box sets: Patsy Cline, Dave Clark Five (yes, my beloved Dave Clark Five), Tony Bennett, Nat King Cole, Jimi Hendrix, Elvis, Frank Sinatra, Phil Spector And . . . KISS

Did you have any posters on your bedroom walls as a kid? Of whom?

Posters in my bedroom usually consisted of the classic horror movies I grew up loving. *Frankenstein, King Kong, The Hunchback of Notre Dame.* I adored those movies, and both *King*

Kong and *Hunchback* made me cry hopelessly at the end. They still have that effect on me. In *Kong*, "'Twas beauty killed the beast" and "Why was I not made of stone?" absolutely leave me in tears. I related to these characters. They were all feared because they were different. I felt the same way. I came from Israel, and I was always the biggest one in my class. But I never picked on anyone. In point of fact, I've never had a fight in my life. I have cracked a skull or two, but it's never been a fight. I was never the bully. Nonetheless, because I look the way I look, I was mostly feared during my teenage years, so I related much more to King Kong than to rock stars. Besides, Kong was bigger. And he was a King.

What are some great shows you've seen?

Great shows were not always rock shows. Most bands bore me. "Here's my new song" . . . *yawn*!!! I always preferred acts that gave me bang for the buck . . . like KISS . . . like the Crazy World of Arthur Brown . . . like the Tubes . . . like Marilyn Manson in his heyday. . . . I've enjoyed bands, but I've also enjoyed Liberace, the Radio City Rockettes (I love them) . . . and, of course strip clubs. They're my favorite shows.

List up to ten things that could be helpful to someone breaking into the business.

Ten Rules to Break into the Music Business (or any business) is a sucker's game. Anyone who tells you there are ten steps to this or that is giving you the easy way out. And, that doesn't usually work. The truth is, most successful people in music aren't by any stretch of the imagination the most qualified. Let's be honest here. Rock stars can't even read or write music!!! That includes me. It's true we write and sing our own songs, but we do it in our own way. None of us went to school. None of us knows or understands music theory. Qualified??? I don't think so.

The same things apply to real estate tycoons, shmatte tycoons (if you don't know what *shmatte* is . . . too bad), and most areas that do not demand technology, mathematics, and quantum physics . . . which includes most of the jobs in the world.

So forget the ten-step deal . . . it's a fraud.

The only thing you've got is (get ready for this one) . . . *you*. Yep. That's the tool that will get you the farthest in life. You need people skills. They won't and can't teach you that in life . . . or in school. You have to be so sure of what you believe in (no matter what it is) that you should be able to (without much thought) sell ice cubes to Eskimos. What that means is that most of the stuff we buy, including music, isn't necessary. Food is. Music is not. So everything in music involves someone convincing you that you really need this. You really want this. You have to have it. To be cool, especially. If you can do that . . . maybe you've got a place waiting for you in the music business. Make that MAYBE with all capitals.

And don't forget good luck.

Joseph Simmons

RUN-D.M.C.

Did you have a mentor or someone who inspired you? If so, what have you learned from that person?

My dad and my big brother. When I was a kid, you know, eight, nine, ten, Russell had all the right moves. He had the right gold, the right jewelry, the hairdo, the sneakers. I looked up to my dad as the real role model, but to my brother, Russell, as the cool guy, somebody I was trying to be.

What was your very first job in the music industry, and how did you get it?

It was not a job. I was the son of Curtis Blow. I was a rapper, I used to deejay for Curtis Blow, and they called me DJ Run, the Son of Curtis Blow. And we did shows, and then we put out the records and did more shows. Then I took a leave of absence and then came back as Run-D.M.C. It happened that quick.

What was your first big break? The first great thing that ever happened to you . . .

I think the first time I thought it was really happening was when I was with Curtis Blow. We did roller-skating rinks, and they were packed. We'd be doing Christmas rapping on the rinks. I was, like, "This is big." I was getting fifty dollars a show, it was great. Here I am, fourteen, thirteen years old and performing in front of people, and it was happening. So it was big then, but then it got bigger with Run-D.M.C. I had a head start. Before I put out my group, I was down with Curtis Blow, and he had records out. That was 1979.

What elements of your job make you want to go to work every day?

What makes me want to go to work is family unity. I'm the president of Phat Farm Footwear. It's just a pleasure working with my brother at the office. I still do side rhymes and mini-projects as Reverend Run. I made a record with Jagged Edge a year or two ago. If you call me for a rhyme I might do one. But not as Run-D.M.C. I retired that group.

What qualities most helped you get to where you are today?

Don't be the guru of your crew. I always liked to have somebody to look up to. I don't want to be the highest. I don't want to be in charge all the way. I want to have somebody who's higher than I am.

If you knew everything at the beginning of your career that you know now, what would you have done differently?

I'm happy with the way my life's turned out. You know, as a child you do childish things. The Bible says as you get older you put those things away. I've made little mistakes, but I think overall my guidance has been God and he's been good to me.

What is your greatest lesson learned?

I'm always learning. So the greatest lesson learned is hard to say, when I look back. Always have a mentor. Always have someone to look up to.

What are some of your favorite albums?

Greatest Hits, Run-D.M.C.   *The Best of Anita Baker,* Anita Baker
Reasonable Doubt, Jay-Z   *The Best of Sade,* Sade

Did you have any posters on your bedroom walls as a kid? Of whom?

Dr. Jay (Julius Irving) and Earl Monroe.

What are some great shows you've seen?

U2, Florida
George Clinton, the *Mothership* tour, New York City
Run-D.M.C., Raisin' Hell

What are some of your favorite songs?

"Giving You the Best That I Got," Anita Baker
"Together Forever," Run-D.M.C.
Sade—all songs on the greatest-hits record

List up to ten things that could be helpful to someone breaking into the business.

- Go be an intern.
- Go carry travel cases for Jay-Z.
- Go work for free in the place that you love.
- In order to make something great happen, you gotta love the thing you do.

Robert Smith
THE CURE

Did you have a mentor or someone who inspired you? If so, what have you learned from that person?

Hearing/seeing Jimi Hendrix and the Beatles: I dreamed. . . . Hearing/seeing David Bowie and the Rolling Stones: I wished. . . . Hearing/seeing the sensational Alex Harvey Band and Thin Lizzy: I knew. . . . And I have been inspired by a huge number of artists ever since—the three things I think they have all had in common: individuality, vision, and creative conviction.

As far as learning goes . . . Whenever I feel I am "going wrong" I listen to the song "Pink Moon" by Nick Drake—it never fails to remind me that if as a musical artist you believe in every word, every note, and every breath, then there is no "going wrong."

What was your very first job in the music industry, and how did you get it?

I was lucky in that I was able to give myself my first job—as guitarist, singer, and songwriter in a "school version" of the Cure!

What was your first big break? The first great thing that ever happened to you . . .

When I was still at school the (Easy) Cure won a national UK "battle of the bands" type competition and as a result signed to a German pop label. . . . We were given a thousand pounds (a fortune!) which we spent on equipment, and a few days in a recording studio—however, the label in question rejected all our songs (most of which later featured on our first album *Three Imaginary Boys*) and insisted we record a selection of cover versions. . . . We refused, and after a six-month stalemate the label dropped us. . . . We walked away happily unscathed, having had a valuable insight into the crass machinations of "the music business," and at the same time having passed our first "integrity test." . . . All this and we had a van full of new gear too!

What elements of your job make you want to go to work every day?

I get to choose my hours, my workmates, and my workplace—to play and listen to music whenever I want—and to (occasionally) get wasted on the job without fear of getting fired!

What qualities most helped you get to where you are today?

Perseverance, perfectionism, and a sense of perspective.

If you knew everything at the beginning of your career that you know now, what would you have done differently?

Not too much as I have no real regrets . . . If pushed I would say that even though I knew from the beginning the "independent" label "Fiction" the Cure was signed to (and indeed all the majors we released through) valued commerce over art, I lived with it as I figured that it was "better the devil you know." . . . Had I known how shabbily we would be treated from 1996 on, I think I would have negotiated a way out sooner. . . .

What is your greatest lesson learned?

Failure on your own terms is worth more than success on someone else's.

What are some of your favorite albums?

Twenty that spring to mind . . .

Magical Mystery Tour, the Beatles

Are You Experienced?, Jimi Hendrix Experience

Five Leaves Left, Nick Drake

Trout Mask Replica, Captain Beefheart and His Magic Band

Tapestry, Carole King

Led Zeppelin II, Led Zeppelin

Astral Weeks, Van Morrison

Next, the Sensational Alex Harvey Band

Ziggy Stardust, David Bowie

One World, John Martyn

This Year's Model, Elvis Costello

Treasure, Cocteau Twins

Asylum Years, Tom Waits

Doolittle, the Pixies

The Hounds of Love, Kate Bush

Nevermind, Nirvana

Loveless, My Bloody Valentine

Maya, Banco De Gaia

Mellon Collie and the Infinite Sadness, the Smashing Pumpkins

Come On Die Young, Mogwai

Did you have any posters on your bedroom walls as a kid? Of whom?

Jimi Hendrix, David Bowie, Rodney Marsh (footballer), the 1966 England World Cup winning football team, Catwoman, Kirk Douglas as Spartacus!

What are some great shows you've seen?

In the '70s: David Bowie, Thin Lizzy, S.A.H.B., the Rolling Stones, Hall and Oates, Nils Lofgren, the Mahavishnu Orchestra, the Clash, the Stranglers, Siouxsie & the Banshees, Wire, Rory Gallagher, Joan Armatrading, Iggy Pop, Be Bop Deluxe

In the '80s: The Pixies, Dinosaur Jr., the Psychedelic Furs, 13:13, Echo and the Bunnymen, 10,000 Maniacs

In the '90s: Ride, the Prodigy, the Smashing Pumpkins, David Bowie, Depeche Mode, Supergrass

In the '00s: Mogwai, Cranes, Zwan . . .

What are some of your favorite songs?

Twenty that spring to mind . . .

"America," Simon & Garfunkel

"Pink Moon," Nick Drake

"Are You Experienced?," Jimi Hendrix Experience

"Cyprus Avenue," Van Morrison

"(Looking for) the Heart of Saturday Night," Tom Waits

"You Really Got Me," the Kinks

"The Faith Healer," the Sensational Alex Harvey Band

"Life on Mars," David Bowie

"Couldn't Love You More," John Martyn

"Tea and Sympathy," Janis Ian

"Monkey Gone to Heaven," the Pixies

"Heart Shaped Box," Nirvana

"Vapour Trail," Ride

"Human," the Human League

"The Hounds of Love," Kate Bush

"Walking in My Shoes," Depeche Mode

"Small Blue Thing," Suzanne Vega

"Blown a Wish," My Bloody Valentine

"1979," the Smashing Pumpkins

"My Father My King," Mogwai

List up to ten things that could be helpful to someone breaking into the business.

- If you have initial principles you should not let them go as you will never get them back. . . .
- Always remember: Anyone can be rich—anyone can be famous—but not anyone can make great music.
- You don't usually get to do a lot of it again—so make the most of it all as it happens.
- Never respect anyone who demands respect.
- Choose your heroes carefully. . . .
- Believe that a very high percentage of the people you meet in the music business are not doing what they really want—in fact, believe that a lot of them don't actually like music. . . .
- Always get good legal advice before signing anything.
- If it doesn't feel right . . . it never is!
- Believe in yourself.
- That old thing about 99 percent perspiration is pretty true. . . .

Britney Spears

Did you have a mentor or someone who inspired you? If so, what have you learned from that person?

The person in this business who has been and continues to be my biggest inspiration is Madonna. I've learned from her to not be afraid of who you really are.

What was your very first job in the music industry, and how did you get it?

Joining the cast of the Mickey Mouse Club. It was my first experience with singing, dancing, and acting, but it also gave me a strong work ethic.

What was your first big break? The first great thing that ever happened to you . . .

My first break was performing "I Don't Care" on *Star Search*. I was so excited when I won the first round and got to come back for the semifinals to perform "Love Can Build a Bridge." We were actually going through some of my things in storage a few months ago and I found the black velvet dress with huge poofy sleeves that I wore!

What elements of your job make you want to go to work every day?

Definitely being able to travel all around the world, experiencing different cultures, and meeting so many people that I wouldn't have an opportunity to know otherwise. All the free clothes that are sent to me is a great incentive as well!

What qualities most helped you get to where you are today?

Patience, confidence, passion, and family values.

If you knew everything at the beginning of your career that you know now, what would you have done differently?

I would have made sure to speak up more and stand up for myself right from the beginning.

What are some of your favorite albums?

Acoustic Soul, India.Arie

A Beautiful World, Thicke

Thriller, Off the Wall, and *Bad,* Michael Jackson

Rhythm Nation 1814, Janet Jackson

Like a Prayer, Madonna

Whitney Houston, Whitney Houston

The Dock of the Bay, Otis Redding

Purple Rain, Prince and the Revolution

Sign O' the Times, Prince

CrazySexyCool, TLC

Did you have any posters on your bedroom walls as a kid? Of whom?

Brad Pitt, Brad Pitt, Brad Pitt!

What are some great shows you've seen?

I recently saw *Hairspray* on Broadway in New York City. It was such an amazing show from start to finish. I had so much fun and loved it! I'll probably go see it again.

What are some of your favorite songs?

"Wicked Game," Chris Isaak

"Feeling Love, " Paula Cole

"Billie Jean," Michael Jackson

List up to ten things that could be helpful to someone breaking into the business.

- Believe in yourself.
- Be confident.
- Trust that no matter what happens—what's supposed to be will be.

Serj Tankian

SYSTEM OF A DOWN

Did you have a mentor or someone who inspired you? If so, what have you learned from that person?

Many people and many things have inspired my days.

Life and its many immersing mysteries keep me bedazzled.

What was your very first job in the music industry, and how did you get it?

My gear junky frenzy drove me to work at a musical instruments dealer for two weeks.

What was your first big break? The first great thing that ever happened to you . . .

As far as art, it was the moment I realized that I would not see happiness without melting into the path of music.

As I stepped onto my path, all things became aligned.

What elements of your job make you want to go to work every day?

The creation of music.
Artistic endeavors around the creation of that music.
Good people to work, share, and be inspired with.

What qualities most helped you get to where you are today?

In terms of music . . .
My unbalanced work ethic that I'm trying to resolve.
If I don't know certain things, please teach me.
The gift of losing myself in the moment.

If you knew everything at the beginning of your career that you know now, what would you have done differently?

Nothing. I am living the experience that I need to learn and taste.

What is your greatest lesson learned?

That we are but a spec of light (grace) sitting in an ocean of infinity.

What are some of your favorite albums?

Too many to list. I can't do this one. It's a logistical nightmare.

Did you have any posters on your bedroom walls as a kid? Of whom?

None I can remember, except for one of Bob Marley.

What are some great shows you've seen?

Iron Maiden, Irvine Meadows, 1984
Queensryche, *Operation Mindcrime* tour
Lollapalooza (second year) with Pearl Jam,
   Soundgarden, Ministry, etc.
Tito Puente, Blue Note, New York City

Baaba Maal, downtown Los Angeles,
   around 2000
Slayer—lots of great shows
Faith No More, the Palladium, Los Angeles
Pink Floyd, Rose Bowl, Pasadena, California

What are some of your favorite songs?

Another logistical nightmare, especially since I have a tendency to not remember album or song names (okay, even people's names).

List up to ten things that could be helpful to someone breaking into the business.

- Musically, learn from others, but stay true to your heart and tastes.
- Avoid labels, descriptions of style, flavor, genre, etc.
- Realize that you don't own the music, that you are a conduit of universal thought and sound.
- The bullshit you don't believe from the start, don't start believing later.
- Before cutting any business deals, talk to other artists and business people.
- Concentrate on using success to propel the art, not vice versa (that'll happen automatically).
- While touring, live your life as you would at home (as much as you can).
- Invest in portable recording gear.
- Divide your income by thirty or forty, and spend accordingly. It's not a steady job, you've got to make the funds last.
- Experiment with things without losing your vision or path.

Shania Twain

Did you have a mentor or someone who inspired you? If so, what have you learned from that person?

My mother was always one of my greatest heroes.

What was your very first job in the music industry, and how did you get it?

My first gigs were in local bars. My mother booked me and acted as my manager.

What was your first big break? The first great thing that ever happened to you . . .

I pretty much struggled through my whole career until I got my record deal in Nashville. That was truly my biggest break.

What elements of your job make you want to go to work every day?

Simply the music.

What qualities most helped you get to where you are today?

Passion for music and hardworking nature.

If you knew everything at the beginning of your career that you know now, what would you have done differently?

I really can't think of anything I would change, how could I? It's all turned out so well.

What is your greatest lesson learned?

Pack your own parachute.

What are some of your favorite albums?

Rumours, Fleetwood Mac   *Gold,* Abba
Even in the Quietest Moments, Supertramp   Greatest Hits, the Bee Gees

Did you have any posters on your bedroom walls as a kid? Of whom?

Olivia Newton-John, Nazareth, Rush, and Tony Danza.

What are some great shows you've seen?

Pink Floyd, the Eagles, Van Halen, Ricky Martin.

What are some of your favorite songs?

"Yesterday"   "Everything I Do"

"Love Hurts"   "Roxy Roller"

List up to ten things that could be helpful to someone breaking into the business.

- Be as original as possible.
- Dare to be different.
- Be a good listener, but never compromise your gut feelings.
- Be realistic and hardworking.

Steven Tyler

Did you have a mentor or someone who inspired you? If so, what have you learned from that person?

From seeing people like Janis Joplin and the Beach Boys, I learned that if you're going to leave your house, you better make it worth your while. When people come to see you, you better give them something that is better than what is on a record.

My father was a pianist. He went to Juilliard and played in a band, so his playing was around from the time I was born. I remember him playing his Steinway in a twelve-by-nine room in the Bronx, where I learned all of the fundamentals. He gave me three things . . . a sense of rhythm, the ability to make a melody, and a penis that curves to the left.

What was your very first job in the music industry, and how did you get it?

My grandfather and his brothers came over from Italy. They had cellos, pianos, and fiddles, and played ballroom music in the twenties and thirties. The first band I played with was with my father. I was fifteen, and we played weddings, bar mitzvahs, everything. . . . My father played piano, and I played the drums. My uncle Ernie Tallarico played saxophone, we had a bass player named Stuffy Gregory, and a trumpet player named Charlie Gauss. I made maybe twenty bucks a night, and it was great.

It was either that, or bagging groceries or mowing lawns. Whenever I had a girlfriend I had to buy her chocolates, or we didn't get to "go steady." So I'd go down to the local A&P and just bag groceries. If you stood in the line for six hours, you made ten dollars in quarters.

What was your first big break? The first great thing that ever happened to you . . .

It was before Aerosmith, with a band called Chain Reaction. We were playing the Palisades Amusement Park in things called the *Good Guys Shows*. In New York it was on WMCA. They had a bunch of jocks who were called the Good Guys. We would be set up in the bandstand in Palisades Park and sing a bunch of songs with my Carnegie Street pants, a mink vest, and hair down to my shoulders. It was very hippie, very Sonny and Cher, very those days. The crowds would start to scream. It freaked me out because I was used to playing the Jewish Center and after school at the lunchroom, where you had spitballs, and maybe a girl. It was just different.

Back then, whatever local bands were around could open up for a touring band, unlike today, where you bring them with you. We had a manager who helped us with that, and we went out with the Byrds during their "Mr. Tambourine Man" time. We had a drummer, so I was the lead singer, and I got to dance around with a tambourine and all that shit and the girls would start to scream. We were also playing our own songs, so that coupled with the pandemonium in the audience made me think, "Holy shit, this is what I want."

Consequently, I saw a bunch of bands play live, like Janis Joplin, and saw what kind of insanity the audience was going into. It was really great.

What elements of your job make you want to go to work every day?

Why does a dog lick his balls? Because he can.

It's really the same thing. Why Joe and I do what we do, it's because we can. We don't have to, or want to, but we can. I know we have families, and they may take this the wrong way, but it gives your life a deeper meaning when you start from a teenager with some harebrained idea and then you get it. There were ten thousand bands in the sixties and seventies, maybe hundreds of thousands, that were trying to make it across America, and we got it. The very fact that I look over and still see Joe is incredible. It's the real fucking thing. He's got these leather boots up to his knees and this jacket from hell, which, by the way he doesn't wear when he's offstage. In the early days, they used to all make fun of me, and of course now they're all in their bangles and beads, calling the kettle black.

There's a clarity that comes with experience. There are so many phony people around. So many people trying to save their jobs with their egotistical banter. Who knew that Sony was sitting around fifteen years ago with this Japanese guy talking zeros and ones, talking digital, that that was going to be the downfall of the whole careers of those of us who were around in the sixties and seventies. To take our back catalog and turn it into mush when all along they've been making seventy-five cents and we've only been making a quarter anyway. What the fuck? Who's really behind all of this? You have to sleep with one eye open, and be really careful. One of the elements of my job that makes me want to go to work every day is seeing the beautiful person who is really behind the person, the inner man, when you're capable of seeing it. The guys who have been around for a while are capable of seeing much more than the young people who get taken advantage of.

We can play a song like "Sweet Emotion" and the place roars, just on the bass line alone—that's the shit. And that we have a road crew, a road manager, and a production manager that put up and take down the stage every day. They love what they do to such an extent that if anything gets in the way, including KISS's production, they have a fucking shit fit. It's life or limb to protect their band. It's great.

What qualities most helped you get to where you are today?

My personality. I did this song once called "The Sun," and I sounded like a choir boy. It was all right, it was angelic, but it didn't have the shit. Then I learned how to put *"yack-kak-kouk-wakkow!!!"* into it instead of "it comes once a day . . ." (sung very gently). Learning how to put my personality and my Italian background into the music was a pivotal turning point. It was an epiphany. When you listen to the first whole record, I had to put a little stink on my white boy voice which I didn't like. I loved it when I heard it back. Then Joe's guitar was always off the wall, so when I finally worked with Joe and left those other bands that were taking speed and then practicing, it was just a different type of music that came out. We took speed, but we wouldn't try to practice. I could argue forever and say those guys were polishing a turd, and we were polishing the blues. But really, it was just that perfect mixture of my father's classical, with my love of the Yardbirds and Elvis. I had the Yardbirds, my sister had Elvis and the Everly Brothers, and we all got caught up in *Machine Head* by Deep Purple. That time was the pivotal spot, and since then the band has really been the drug the whole time.

If you knew everything at the beginning of your career that you know now, what would you have done differently?

Where do I start? First of all, I would say if the words "in perpetuity" is in your management contract, in any way, shape, or form, fire your business manager. We didn't even know what that word was, and it was in every contract we ever signed. Why the fuck am I giving someone a piece of my publishing for songs I wrote before he was in puberty. Who knew?

Never argue with your best friend when you're high. That's how every band broke up—over a girl and giving the middle finger.

A lot of that I still hold today. It's a big battle inside for me to try to get the band to go away somewhere and record—to leave their wife and dear ones at home, come out and give me some angst, give me some passion, give me some feeling. Not to bring how comfortable you're used to being now. It works every time, especially if you get a fight first, you know damn well what you're up against. I don't mind fighting still. I set it up, that we'll all go away, and if someone doesn't want to, I'll go and the songs come out without him. Bands always fight, with weird ego things. These are little secrets I happen to know. I'm not saying you won't have breath from hell if you floss your teeth and brush your tongue, but it sure helps. Same thing with going away somewhere and "being a band" again. It's saying I don't think my Ferrari is more important than the band. So I say, give me two weeks and let's go look at some stuff. When you're a band, and you stay together all the time, you kind of burn out on each other's shit. But when you're writing a record, and you have a couple months off, go away and try to evoke some of the old demons. Rent a house. Go to Longview Farms. Get to know each other in a musical capacity and not a performance capacity. Be a human be-ing instead of a human do-ing.

What is your greatest lesson learned?

We are spiritual beings stuck in human bodies. That was a huge lesson. Once I realized that if you're not getting high from the music you make, and are getting high from the drugs that you take, then you're fucked up. When it's "how high are you?" instead of "hi, how are you?", you're in the wrong door.

Music and love can save the world. We've been to China, and Japan, and places where people didn't know a blick of English, but people are singing the songs verbatim and understanding from the music. There's a lot of emotion in music, with minors and fifths and suspensions and words laid over it, it just says it all. You have to play your heart, and if something is evoked, and a baby is there, or suddenly something is breathing, undulating, palpitating, or people are fucking to your music, then it's a good thing. Love, compassion, and forgiveness are all in the music. They're in every Dylan song I've ever heard, if you look through it awhile, or listen with your heart. Music is spirituality. When mommy is humming to her baby, baby doesn't understand shit, but he hears the love. It's incredible.

Another important lesson is to learn the rules, so you know how to break them properly. Everyone is telling you what to do, how to sing, how to play, how to stand onstage, how they're gonna put the ropes up that you're gonna swing on.

What are some of your favorite albums?

Exile on Main Street, the Rolling Stones

Are You Experienced?, Jimi Hendrix Experience

Talking Book, Stevie Wonder

Led Zeppelin I or *II,* Led Zeppelin

Highway 61 Revisited, Bob Dylan

Two Virgins, John Lennon

Smiley Smile, the Beach Boys

Albums by Sly & the Family Stone

Did you have any posters on your bedroom walls as a kid? Of whom?

The Beatles, the Rolling Stones, the Yardbirds, Sonny Terry and Brownie McGhee, Sophia Loren, Laurel and Hardy, Miles Davis, and Gandhi, across the room from Maharishi Mahesh Yogi.

What are some great shows you've seen?

Led Zeppelin at the Tea Party in Boston in 1969. When they went into "Dazed and Confused," it was just fucking unreal. I would have loved it if I didn't have the album, but when you have the album, and you hear them play it even better than the album, that was special. When I was growing up, there were a lot of guys out there who thought the record was one thing, and then hired some other band to play it later, and they all played it six ways to Sunday. It never sounded good. Then you had these bands in the seventies and eighties that played their shit

too fast. What you want to do is hear it the way it is on the record, because that's what you
smoke pot to, and fuck to, and love to. That is the tapestry of your life.

I used to go down to the Fillmore all the time and see Joplin, Country Joe & the Fish, Spirit.
Hendrix—I saw him at Monterey and at the first Woodstock (woke me up that morning).

The Who at Woodstock. It was just a cluster fuck. I was so stoned I don't remember the half of it.

The Beach Boys—When you go see the Beach Boys, and they play every song in the space of
two or three hours, thirty or forty songs, all classic, it's incredible.

U2 at Madison Square Garden in 2002

AC/DC

What are some of your favorite songs?

"No Surprise," Aerosmith

"Just Like a Woman," Bob Dylan

"Stairway to Heaven," Led Zeppelin

"Honky Tonk Women," the Rolling Stones

"Great Balls of Fire," Jerry Lee Lewis

"Think About It," the Yardbirds

"Dance to the Music," Sly & the Family Stone

"Purple Haze," Jimi Hendrix

"Maybe," Alison Krauss

List up to ten things that could be helpful to someone breaking into the business.

- Have two lawyers, and have one lawyer always watching the other lawyer.
- Never give your publishing away.
- Never chew gum when you're on an interview, and they're taping you (as I am now).
- If some manager wants too much of your publishing, always add a sunset clause.
- Never tell a secret and expect it to stay a secret. Look what you're burdening them with.
- Get busy now—if you're going to write songs, start now. Experience is the key to it all.
- Start on the piano and the drums—the rest will come easy. Take piano or drum lessons for
  three years and then you're home free. Especially as a singer—then you know what your gui-
  tar player is trying to do to you, and what you can lay over it for a melody.
- Even when you pass around the chocolates, everyone's not tasting them the same way you are.
  Don't expect people to hear what you're saying the way that you mean it. You may mean it one
  way, and they're hearing it differently.
- Don't ever quit—no matter what anybody says. We played in clubs where we played for beer.
  Nobody would come in, but the guy would still make us play. It wasn't because he loved the
  band, but we were down in the dumps, had no money, and wanted to drink. Hence our addic-
  tions. That's supposed to be funny!
- If you're gonna treat music like a hobby, go fucking work at Starbucks. The songs are everything. There's so much in the songs that's coming out of your head, so keep writing, keep listening, keep learning.
- Be dangerous and take chances. You only learn by fucking up, and knowing it.
- Stay clean—dope is temporary, music is forever.

Lars Ulrich

Did you have a mentor or someone who inspired you? If so, what have you learned from that person?

My father was definitely the main musical inspiration. I grew up in a household in Copenhagen, Denmark, that was very rich musically. Copenhagen in the sixties was sort of a musical hotbed, and a center for jazz music. My father was a professional tennis player, but his passion was music, and he was very involved in the music scene. He wrote about jazz music for a Danish newspaper. There was a lot of music always around when I was growing up, and a lot of musicians hanging around. He played a little himself—the clarinet, saxophone—he was actually in a couple bands that were fairly well known in Denmark in the fifties. So I grew up listening to Charlie Parker to Coltrane to Dexter Gordon to Sonny Rollins. I remember the first time I heard Hendrix and the Doors and the Stones was around my father. So that certainly would be where music originated for me.

I started getting more and more into rock music, up through the seventies. He took me to my first concert, in 1973. Deep Purple was playing in Copenhagen—I was nine years old, and I got dragged along, and it all sort of went from there. I was very impressed with the energy and the spectacle—with Ritchie Blackmore playing guitar with his foot and all that crazy stuff.

The most important thing I learned from my father was openness—trying to be open to anything, continuing to search for new things and never be too stuck in a one-dimensional outlook on music, and culture generally. I grew up in a very open, nonjudgmental household. I could sit down with my dad on any day and listen to Motörhead, and then five minutes later listen to John Coltrane. There was no real separation of these things—there was only music that was very good and had some special qualities to it, and music that was less good and had fewer qualities. It was not limited by genres, and I think I have tried to respect that and support that in my outlook both in and outside of Metallica.

What was your very first job in the music industry, and how did you get it?

I formed a band in 1981 called Metallica, and my first job in the music business was drummer of Metallica. I've never been in another band. Metallica was my first musical experience, really.

I was seventeen, so there wasn't time for any other experiences. I don't have the classic "starting-in-the-mailroom" or being a fucking intern.

I grew up in a very rich household on two fronts—there was sports and there was culture, more specifically music but not limited to music. I kind of had this vain, somewhat ignorant notion that I was going to follow in my father's footsteps and be a professional tennis player. There wasn't really pressure, but tennis was always there. I don't remember ever not playing tennis. It was part of my upbringing. But music was always simmering underneath that, as a passion. Music was the escape. Music was what I threw myself into to get away, especially from the disciplinary sides of tennis.

After I finished school in Denmark, I went to spend some time with Nick Bollettieri, who later coached people like Agassi, Monica Seles, and all those guys. He had a tennis camp in Florida, and really for the first time I got subjected to the disciplinary sides of the sport. It was almost a boarding school kind of environment, and it really fucking freaked me out, being out there practicing serves four or five hours a day. It really turned me off, and I started wanting to have a few beers and smoke some pot, so music became much more interesting.

What was your first big break? The first great thing that ever happened to you . . .

Three different scenarios . . .

First break: My family was spending so much time in America—we didn't really have any commitments in Denmark—so we thought going to L.A. would be a good thing. We moved to L.A. in the fall of 1980, after my stint in Florida at the tennis prison. About a year later, I formed Metallica with Hetfield. We spent the better part of '82 doing our thing on the club circuit in L.A. This was prime Mötley Crüe, Ratt kind of time in L.A. What we were doing—this kind of pseudo-European, metal kind of thing, morphing European metal bands with European punk bands—didn't really sit very well in the L.A. landscape in the year 1982.

In September, we went up for the first time to San Francisco, and it was magical. Up in San Francisco, there was a whole different scene, a whole different kind of awareness of the European metal stuff that we were all gravitating toward. It wasn't so much about what you looked like or any of that. When we went up there, instantly we were so at home. That was really the first time we ever felt any kind of love from anybody. We ended up going to San Francisco once every couple of weeks for the rest of 1982 and then eventually moving up there with Cliff Burton. He joined the band on the one condition we move to San Francisco, which was a decision that took about two seconds to make, and we've been up there for twenty years now.

Number two was in the spring of 1984: *Kill 'Em All* came out in the summer of 1983, and we were kind of doing things around the States. In the spring of 1984 we went to Europe for the first time and opened up for this band called Venom who were big heroes of ours. We played a two-week tour with them in three- to five-thousand-seat halls in Western Europe. On that tour, we were like, "Fuck!" There were people that knew our shit; there were people that were really receptive to it—thousands of them. And most of the stuff we'd done in America at that time was still in the hundreds. I remember walking out onstage in Milan, Italy, and it was like five thousand people who knew what we were doing. They knew every song. It was such a moment. So that two-week tour in 1984 was definitely when it started to feel real. There are people that were into it, and passionate about it.

Number three . . . America was still lagging a bit behind, but in 1986 on the *Master of Puppets* album, we went out and opened up for Ozzy in arenas in America. That was the first time we were really exposed to the American mainstream. We went out and played in front of fifteen thousand Ozzy fans every night for eight months, and after forty-five minutes, a lot of those people were Metallica fans who had never really been turned on to anything we had done before. Those eight months we spent with Ozzy were a pretty big breakthrough.

What elements of your job make you want to go to work every day?

When you strip away the fame, and all the stuff that comes with it—the interviews, the recognition, the meet and greets—and it's just four guys in a room together playing music, or four guys onstage playing together—whether there's five people there or fifty thousand—in the purest of those moments, it is about people connecting through music. It's just magical. Those moments are the reason I still do it.

I'm closer to forty now than I am to thirty. With kids, and with family, it becomes harder to travel, the touring, or going to the studio for eight, ten, twelve hours a day. In the purest moments, when it literally is four guys in a room playing music, every other side of it is so worth it. That's what fuels my fire, especially with these guys. When you're lucky enough to be with someone like James Hetfield, whom I've been with for twenty-two years, and you can still be going, and still be connected, especially after what we went through two years ago, those first meltdowns. We came out on the other side of that feeling closer, more connected. The best part of that whole meltdown period was getting the opportunity to really appreciate everything. Once you start getting to a place where you potentially prep yourself for the end of the road, you have a different level of appreciation than you had before.

That's what fuels me. I also don't know anything else. I'm thirty-nine years old—twenty-two of those years were spent in Metallica, seventeen of those not in Metallica. It's pretty wacky.

What qualities most helped you get to where you are today?

My good looks . . .

It's hard to talk about this with a straight face, but I think my tenacity is key. The word *no* doesn't really exist when something has to be accomplished. It doesn't matter if I'm one guy out of a hundred—if I know something's right for me or for the band, or for something that's going on, the word *no* just doesn't exist. I will make sure that the best thing happens and the right thing happens. I think I've got incredible will. I can push it just a little further than most other guys, in terms of reaching, in terms of tenacious levels, that type of stuff.

I've actually just realized this recently as I've started doing interviews again. I consider myself, in a kind of perverse, subconscious way, to be Metallica's number-one fan. So I have a side of me that makes sure that what Metallica does makes their number-one fan happy. If their number-one fan is happy, then there's a really good chance that number two to whatever number you want will be happy, too. I think I have this ability to remove myself from being in the band, so it's not about commercial elements. Sometimes the guys will sit there and talk about things in musical terms, and I'll sit there and say, "I don't really give a shit if it's difficult to play or easy to play—it's gotta move me!" I think I have the ability to step outside of my role as the drummer, one of four members in Metallica, and critique it in a different way, as the number-one fan. I think that helps people connect to what we're doing. This is all pretty difficult to talk about without sounding full of shit. . . .

If you knew everything at the beginning of your career that you know now, what would you have done differently?

I like to think that the essence of this band is "jumping without knowing where you're going to land." I think that we've always just done, and then afterwards we've thought. Sometimes when you try and make that the way that you do things, you take some hits. I wish that when I got myself involved in all that Napster stuff three years ago that I knew what I was getting myself into because I got completely sideswiped by that one. My therapist tells me that the hardest thing for me to deal with in my personality is being ambushed. But from my perspective, it was like this . . . there was an unfinished version of a song we were still working on in the studio that was showing up on radio stations across the country, and we traced the leak back to some company called Napster. We'd better go and fuck with them and put an end to that. Oops!! I'm not saying that I'm not proud of the fact that we stood up for what we believed in—it was just a very surreal time. I can't be as black and white as to say I wish it had never happened; I just wish I knew more about what the fuck I was getting myself into. There really are very few things I wish never happened. One of those would be the death of Cliff Burton, in a horrible accident. I'm not one of those guys who give into the "everything happens for a reason" thing. I believe that most human beings make decisions based on intuition, instinct, and gut. I think in our most vulnerable moments we kind of jump into things blindfolded, and once in a while you end up in situations you couldn't have anticipated.

Then of course there was my white leather jacket episode, where for three months I only wore a white leather jacket. I also wish that had never happened. . . .

What is your greatest lesson learned?

It's about heart, instinct, soul, gut, balls, and emotions. It's not about ability; it's not about commerce, competition, any of that stuff. If you try to protect all those emotional aspects of it, then it's very difficult to fuck up. What we try to do in Metallica is something I call my curling analogy. In the sport curling, they send this oversized ashtray down the ice, and these guys run in front of it with brushes and try to make the path that the curling ball is on as pure as possible, making sure there are as few obstacles in its way. In terms of Metallica, what we try to do is protect the purity of what we do by making sure that there are as few outside pollutants in the way of our musical instincts that we are so protective of and also making the decision-making process as clean as possible.

If it's about heart and soul, you can never go wrong. You have to look inside yourself. Don't listen to what Lars Ulrich says, don't sit there and listen to what Guy Oseary says, don't sit there and listen to what somebody's written in a fucking book. If you can find your truth, then you've won.

What are some of your favorite albums?

The timeless stuff, in no particular order . . .

Made in Japan, Deep Purple
No Sleep 'Til Hammersmith, Motörhead
Achtung Baby, U2
Let There Be Rock, AC/DC
Lightning to the Nations, Diamond Head
Get Yer Ya-Ya's Out, the Rolling Stones
Ramones, the Ramones

Sabotage, Black Sabbath
Battle of Los Angeles, Rage Against the Machine
Babylon by Bus, Bob Marley
Toxicity, System of a Down
Kind of Blue, Miles Davis
Definitely Maybe, Oasis
Elephant, the White Stripes

Did you have any posters on your bedroom walls as a kid? Of whom?

In 1973–76, it was all about Deep Purple, Status Quo, Uriah Heep, Sweet, Slade, Black Sabbath. In 1976, as with most other twelve-year-olds, it was all about KISS for a couple years, then in 1979–82 it became all about Iron Maiden, Saxon, Tygers of Pan Tang, Angel Witch, Diamond Head, Motörhead. Then the posters got replaced by Metallica.

What are some great shows you've seen?

The first time I went to see Deep Purple in 1973 was pretty awesome. I saw them another two or three times in the next few years after that.

Thin Lizzy (1974–76) used to come to Denmark and blow me away.

First time I saw the Ramones in Copenhagen in '77

The Sex Pistols in Copenhagen in '77

AC/DC, I saw them open up for Rainbow in '77. Then they came back in '78 and did their own show, which was awesome.

Motörhead obviously blew me away; I saw them play at the Country Club on a day off from the Ozzy tour in 1981. That was stunning.

The first time I saw Oasis play at the Fillmore (San Francisco) in February of 1995—I'd never seen anything like that. Noel Gallagher comes out onstage and walks up to the microphone and says, "This is a song about *me*. It's called 'Rock 'n' Roll Star.'" And then they just threw down their fucking arrogance for the next seventy-five minutes. I've always been attracted to bands that truly didn't give a shit. When you never truly knew what was going to happen next. Ritchie Blackmore was the closest to that in those seventies dinosaur rock bands.

People like Bon Scott or Axl Rose or the Gallagher Brothers—these arrogant fucking rock stars where you just don't know what's going to happen next have always appealed to me greatly. Most of the time with Metallica you knew what was going to happen next.

What are some of your favorite songs?

I'm old-school. Most of them were buried in the albums above.

List up to ten things that could be helpful to someone breaking into the business.

- I wish I had spent more time learning the basics of drums, taking more lessons. After we put out our first record I realized I actually didn't know anything about basic, rudimentary drumming. So I went back and spent a year or two learning rudiments like paradiddles and all that kind of shit. So I wish I had been a little more schooled in my instrument before I started the band. It was kind of funny to sit there with one or two records out and still be taking lessons.
- I don't have too many complaints. We've had awesome managers; we've had awesome people around us who've been very straight shooters, very fair. I'm proud of the track record we've had.
- If you treat people fairly, and treat people with respect, a lot of times you'll get that back. If you're an asshole, then people will be an asshole back to you. Of course we've strayed, but most of the time, we've done a pretty clean thing.

Scott Weiland

STONE TEMPLE PILOTS

Did you have a mentor or someone who inspired you? If so, what have you learned from that person?

Ross Hickok, a Huntington Beach punk rocker, was my first role model. I filled in his shoes singing with his brother Corey's punk band.

What was your very first job in the music industry, and how did you get it?

Poor, malnourished starving artist musician. There was no job interview.

What was your first big break? The first great thing that ever happened to you . . .

Opening up for Henry Rollins at the Whiskey with Mighty Joe Young.

What elements of your job make you want to go to work every day?

Writing and producing my own songs.

What qualities most helped you get to where you are today?

I am a loving person. I always believed I would make it. There was never any doubt in my mind.

If you knew everything at the beginning of your career that you know now, what would you have done differently?

I never would have started shooting heroin.

What is your greatest lesson learned?

No matter how strong my belief in my will to succeed, it has never been enough to win the war against my drug addiction.

What are some of your favorite albums?

Abbey Road, the Beatles
White Album, the Beatles

OK Computer, Radiohead
Nevermind, Nirvana

The Soft Bulletin, the Flaming Lips   *Exile on Main Street,* the Rolling Stones

Never Mind the Bollocks, the Sex Pistols   *Nothing's Shocking,* Jane's Addiction

Did you have any posters on your bedroom walls as a kid? Of whom?

KISS, Shaun Cassidy, and Duran Duran.

What are some great shows you've seen?

At the drive-in.

Nirvana, Raji's, *Bleach* tour

Jane's Addiction, John Anson Ford Theatre, 1989

What are some of your favorite songs?

"Waiting for Superman," the Flaming Lips   "Imagine," John Lennon

"The Long and Winding Road," the Beatles   Any Nirvana song ever

List up to ten things that could be helpful to someone breaking into the business.

- Sell your soul.
- Have no morals.
- Don't whine about it later.

Pharrell Williams

Did you have a mentor or someone who inspired you? If so, what have you learned from that person?

All of the musicians that I've ever come across in my life that did different shit. I've always been motivated by them. Everyone from Stevie Wonder, to Steely Dan, to Steppenwolf and Stereolab.

I'm inspired by what is missing in life. I'm inspired by what music I feel is missing.

What was your very first job in the music industry, and how did you get it?

With Teddy Riley, I got discovered at a talent show. I was seventeen or eighteen.

What was your first big break? The first great thing that ever happened to you . . .

I never really focused on it too much. I just work, and try to make great music.

What elements of your job make you want to go to work every day?

The element of discovery. A lot of times it happens in the shower, or on a plane, and you just know you have to do it.

What qualities most helped you get to where you are today?

Again, the element of discovery is it.

If you knew everything at the beginning of your career that you know now, what would you have done differently?

I would have learned more. I went to school, but I would have learned even more. I would never have stopped learning, bookwise.

I still know everything I've learned, and I am still learning, but there's nothing like being taught by a teacher.

What is your greatest lesson learned?

This is too personal for me. It demystifies my character.

What are some of your favorite albums?

I'd rather not name any.

Did you have any posters on your bedroom walls as a kid? Of whom?

I never had any posters when I was a kid. I could never afford any.

What are some great shows you've seen?

A Tribe Called Quest, William & Mary,
 around 1998
The Eminem Show was amazing.

Justin Timberlake's show is dope now.
Limp Bizkit always puts on a good show.

What are some of your favorite songs?

"Celestial Blues," Gary Bartz
"Bonita Applebaum," a Tribe Called Quest
"Protoype," Andre 3000

"Cough Up a Lung," Jay-Z
"Haitian Divorce," Steely Dan

List up to ten things that could be helpful to someone breaking into the business.

- Keep God first. God gives us the inspiration and the push to unlock the doors to different worlds that we want to enter.
- First thing is to educate yourself on your craft. Actually love what you do—do it because you love it, not because you want whatever money you imagine you could make off of it. You should worry about the business side of it—don't corrupt your craft and what you love with selfishness. The bright side of it is that if you do what you're supposed to do, all the other things will come.
- Stay determined. Work hard at it. Work hard at getting it out. Be unafraid of taking different methods when trying to get it out.
- Everything is a numbers game. Just know that the more times you try, the higher the probability that things will work out.

Robbie Williams

Did you have a mentor or someone who inspired you? If so, what have you learned from that person?

No, not really.

What was your very first job in the music industry, and how did you get it?

I auditioned to be in a boy band, and unfortunately I got in.

What was your first big break? The first great thing that ever happened to you . . .

When I realized I could write poetry and sing melodies. Not a break really, but a realization.

What elements of your job make you want to go to work every day?

I don't want to go to work every day. That's why I got into this business in the first place.

What qualities most helped you get to where you are today?

I just keep turning up.

If you knew everything at the beginning of your career that you know now, what would you have done differently?

Absolutely nothing. Hindsight is pointless.

What is your greatest lesson learned?

That I'm all right really.

What are some of your favorite albums?

3 Feet High and Rising, De La Soul   *Hunky Dory*, David Bowie
Looking for a Day in the Night, the Lilac Time   *Behaviour*, the Pet Shop Boys
Dusty in Memphis, Dusty Springfield   *Ready to Die,* the Notorious B.I.G.

Did you have any posters on your bedroom walls as a kid? Of whom?

They were all soccer. My favorite was Oxford United, and all the players had their left testicle out.

What are some great shows you've seen?

U2, Anaheim

Clutch, Camden

Oasis, Glastonbury

Public Enemy, Brixton

Happy Mondays, Manchester

Prince, *Lovesexy,* Earl's Court

What are some of your favorite songs?

"Wichita Linesman," Glen Campbell

"Ode to Billy Joe," Bobbie Gentry

"One," U2

"Mr. Bojangles," Sammy Davis Jr.

"Something in the Way She Moves,"
   James Taylor

List up to ten things that could be helpful to someone breaking into the business.

Just be kind and talented.

Brian Wilson

Did you have a mentor or someone who inspired you? If so, what have you learned from that person?

Over the years, there have been quite a few people who've inspired me. My father. Rosemary Clooney taught me how to sing with love. The Four Freshmen taught me harmony. My brother Dennis really bugged me until I finally wrote a song about surfing. My brother Carl turned me on to Chuck Berry who taught me how to rock 'n' roll. Phil Spector taught me how to use echo and how to combine instruments to make new sounds. Burt Bacharach taught me to compose songs to express emotion. And the Beatles taught me that good enough wasn't good enough. I had to do better to stay ahead of the curve.

What was your very first job in the music industry, and how did you get it?

I never had a job in the music industry. My first "job" was as a member of my group, the Pendletones, which became the Beach Boys.

What was your first big break? The first great thing that ever happened to you . . .

My first "big break" was that my parents loved music and gave me whatever instruments or lessons I wanted. By the time I was sixteen, I had a piano, an organ, and a tape-recorder on which I used to practice recording technique. The first great thing that happened to me was one day I was at this record store. The store was Leshon's. I think it was in Inglewood. Anyway, they used to have these listening booths where you could take in a record and hear it before you bought it. I was in this booth, and I put on a record by the Four Freshmen. Suddenly, it was like I was bathed in a special glow, and that's when I knew what I wanted to do with my life.

What elements of your job make you want to go to work every day?

There is nothing as rewarding as singing background vocals and making a four-part harmony sound that somebody can listen to and feel loved. I also really dig doing concerts and giving all that love to an audience and having them give it back to me.

What qualities most helped you get to where you are today?

Will. My last name is Wilson. I have a really strong will. I will not be denied.

If you knew everything at the beginning of your career that you know now, what would you have done differently?

I probably would have made *Pet Sounds* a solo album and made it clear to the Beach Boys that I needed to make music on my own as well as with them. But that wasn't me at the time.

What is your greatest lesson learned?

Humility.

What are some of your favorite albums?

Rubber Soul, the Beatles
Four Freshmen & 5 Trombones, the Four Freshman
Graceland, Paul Simon
Songs in the Key of Life, Stevie Wonder

What's Going On, Marvin Gaye
Sail Away, Randy Newman
The Phil Spector Christmas Album
Pet Sounds, the Beach Boys

Did you have any posters on your bedroom walls as a kid? Of whom?

No. We had a really tiny bedroom. My brothers and I had barely enough room for our beds and a little dresser. But if I could have had a poster, it would have been of Mickey Mantle. He was my hero.

What are some great shows you've seen?

Paul McCartney. I saw him twice last year. What electricity. Two years ago, I saw Billy Joel and Elton John together at the Forum. That was an incredible concert. I could see them every night. I saw R.E.M. at the Greek Theatre. Dug that a lot. Melinda and I went to see Frank Sinatra a while back. There was nobody like him. I also got to see Rosemary Clooney perform and met her too. I was so thrilled that she knew who I was. And the first show I ever went to see was the Four Freshmen. My father took me, and I got to meet them. That was quite a night.

What are some of your favorite songs?

"Too Much Heaven"
"Let It Be"
"What a Fool Believes"

"Be My Baby"
"California Girls"

List up to ten things that could be helpful to someone breaking into the business.

- Believe in yourself.
- Put love in your music.
- Don't let people tell you what to do or what will sell.
- Follow your heart.
- Don't sign away your publishing.

Stevie Wonder

Did you have a mentor or someone who inspired you? If so, what have you learned from that person?

Probably my greatest mentor has been God. The reason I say that is my mother was predominantly a single parent, but at a very early age I developed this relationship with God, like his being my father. I'm not saying that to say that it was a deep and spiritual thing, I'm just saying that as a little boy, my faith was in the unknown, the unseen, the undone. The faith I had was in the prayers. I believed in the impossible. I believed that through prayer things could really happen.

There were people who I definitely followed musically when I was a little boy—the Staple Singers, the different blues people that I would hear on the streets playing harmonica, Little Willie John, and Neil Sedaka, the Beatles when they came out, and Motown (before I even knew anything about Motown, I'd heard about Berry Gordy). Then there was my curiosity about Africa, the land that people never mentioned. I would hear different sounds—I remember hearing the Zulu, the click sounds, Xhosa. The radio was my eyes and ears to the world. I could sit on the floor for hours and hours listening to different accents—people from England, people from Canada—I would sit there imitating the sounds of people who spoke Italian, Spanish, Arabic. Of course, I didn't understand them—it was just the sounds that I was curious about. I also remember as a little boy hearing (guitarist) Wes Montgomery. I could not see what the sounds were, but they gave me images of what they were. Those textures really invoked a place in me to putting those sounds together.

I became introduced to Motown through Ronnie White, and as I got into music and everyone involved in Motown, I became introduced to other sounds. Obviously all the Motown people, like Marvin Gaye, were mentors—and family—to me. Anyone over thirteen years old (I was eleven when I first came to Motown) was my boss. I couldn't eat candy after a certain hour. I couldn't be up after a certain hour. Everyone loved me and wanted me not to end up in situations like other child stars, like the Jackie Coogan story. I learned about getting a legal guardian, and what that meant, and that my mother could never be in charge of my money. They taught me about drugs and what drugs do to you, and why I shouldn't do it. All of those usual things you hear about. I mention this because the people I met were mentors, and all the experiences I had happened through God bringing them to me in my life.

So it was not just being in the right place, but in the right spirit. Not to say that I didn't have my own experiences, as I still do, and go through different things, but my consistent mentor has been God. Through everything, I find hope, and I find tomorrow. Along the way there are people like Quincy Jones—what a great example. The spectrum of his career when he's done—so many people, musically, so many experiences that he's had in his life. The experience that Quincy Jones has had in his life, I would only compare to Nelson Mandela, to what he's gone through, and what he's done. He was treated less because he was black. He had to eat rats. It's an amazing story. Then the experiences of all those people that he met in his life, I'm sure that they were mentors, too. They were always brought to him by the opportunities that God gave him. And he never gave up. He saw the good in it. I think that's how I feel, and that's why I can love music today as much as I did when I first discovered it. It's still new to me. It's still exciting.

What was your very first job in the music business, and how did you get it?

My first job was Motown. That was the first time I got hired. Again talking about situations and circumstances, there was a rule that my mother had, that I could not go across the street by myself. I knew the neighborhood that we lived in very well. I didn't venture across the street, but I knew the whole block very well, with my eyes closed, but with my ears wide open. One particular day I heard this music coming from a few blocks away. It was loud, coming from speakers. I wanted to go to it. I walked to the drugstore that was on the corner, and a friend of mine walked me to where the music was. I went to the front yard, and there were these two guys, sitting on the porch, playing guitar with an amplifier. They had a microphone that I started singing on and jamming with them. It was that situation, through me meeting both of them (one of them was the cousin of Ronnie White of the Miracles), that started everything. Ronnie was coming home in the next day or so. They invited me to come over again and go over to Ronnie's home. I went, and I sang for him. And through that I met Brian Holland of Holland-Dozier-Holland, and he worked it out for me to have an audition at Motown. I went to Motown, and I sang, played instruments. Midway through, I heard that Berry Gordy was coming down to hear me. He was having dinner, but he came down anyway. That ultimately led to my being signed at Motown.

What was your first big break? The first great thing that ever happened to you . . .

As far as my career moving forward, the first great thing that happened was the fourth song that I had done, "Fingertips." I had actually done the song before on an album called *The Jazz Soul of Little Stevie.* Clarence Paul, who was like a father, brother, director, and producer to me, worked out a little thing with "Fingertips" *live,* and we started doing it on tour when I went out with the *Motown Review.* It was the closing song that we did, and this particular time we did it in Chicago at the Regal Theater. I was on right before Mary Wells, and we closed with "Fingertips." That was when Berry Gordy decided that song should come off the album to be featured as a single, and which became "Fingertips Pt. 2," my first number-one song ever. It was number-one in *Billboard* magazine and number-one in *Cash Box* magazine. It was the first time that a person of my age had a number-one song in all those categories simultaneously.

What elements of your job make you want to go to work every day?

All of the elements of work. The fact that I love music. The fact that I love producing. The fact that I love writing songs. The fact that I like challenging myself and doing something that is unique to me. Understanding influences.

What qualities most helped you get to where you are today?

My love for life. My love for music. God. My desire to inspire.

If you knew everything at the beginning of your career that you know now, what would you have done differently?

More of what I've done better.

What is your greatest lesson learned?

I'm still learning it. There are so many lessons. The greatest thing that I know is to love—to love yourself, to be loved enough to be encouraged and inspired by the love. And doing those things that you do love.

What musicians did you love when you were a kid?

I just love music. The funny, funny thing is that in my neighborhood if someone would be playing a song like "Dream Lover," people would be saying "Oh . . . white boy! White boy!" Or call it a corny song. Then in the predominantly white school that I went to, as a black kid, partially sighted, I'd hear people say, "What is that blues stuff? What are they saying?" Basically people are coming from a place where they don't allow themselves to discover different things, so they couldn't really relate.

What are some of your favorite albums?

There's so much more, but some of my favorite music is:
Sly & the Family Stone
The Beatles
The Staple Singers
Miles Davis
Richard Pryor's humor
Steve Martin's humor
The Five Blind Boys
Stravinsky
Michael Jackson's *Thriller* was a great album.

Songs in the Key of Life was a great album. Objectively, and I'm saying that being a producer. I had to listen objectively—is this making me bored, am I getting tired of this? What I measured with *Songs in the Key of Life* as an example even though it was a double album was *Sgt. Pepper,* which I thought was a good album: even though it was just a one-album situation, and it seemed to go by so fast that I wanted to hear it again. That's what I wanted to do with *Songs in the Key of Life,* even though it was a double-set with four extra songs.

There seemed to be very clear definite harmonies in Take 6's first CD. I'd never heard a group do that before. Those harmonies were—forget about it.

Miles Davis had a few different CDs that were incredible.

The Genius of Ray Charles was great.

There are so many great CDs you can talk about.

I love reggae. I love Bob Marley.

Another great entertainer was Donnie Hathaway. He was an incredible singer, he was one of the world's best singers. He died in 1980 when he was on fire—he lived too short.

What are some of your favorite songs?

I like a lot of different albums, a lot of different people. My favorite categories would be:
Jazz—I've always been inspired by jazz.
Rap—I'm challenged by it lyrically, because I think that there is so much to say that has yet to be said. I think that it can be a way of healing the world.
Gospel—Take 6 is an incredible group. There are other great groups in gospel.
There's a lot of great pop and rock stuff that has come out, and obviously R&B.
Country music I like, because of the simplicity of the lyrics. Simple as it is, there's a lot being said in it. I like that.

What are some great live shows you've been to?

I went to Sly & the Family Stone's show once. I was nineteen when I heard them do "Thank You for Letting Me Be Myself" and the whole of Madison Square Garden was shaking like that, I said, "You know what, someday I want to do that at Madison Square." When I did "Superstition" at Madison Square and the people started going crazy like that, I said, "*Ahhhhh.* Yeah! Thank you, God, for making this happen." It was an incredible moment for me. We had done "Superstition" before, but I think it was the same day we had done the Martin Luther King holiday, and I was just really excited. Forget about it, it was crazy.

Toto
Elton John

Graham Central Station
Take 6
Paul McCartney
The Winans

Bob Marley—at a black music association event. I saw him, and then at the end of it I left with him, and we kind of played together. The first time he was performing with me, we didn't jam together, and then I got into his music more, and what he was trying to do. He was actually supposed to be on tour with me when I did the *Hotter Than July* tour. He got very ill, though, and couldn't travel, unfortunately. I spoke with him the last time when I was on tour; I called him, and he was in Germany. I told him to get well. I didn't really know him—I knew that he was very serious with his Rastafarian beliefs—Haile Selassie and all of that. I didn't know him like that, we didn't have discussions about it. But I knew he was very well read and didn't take any shit—which is a good thing, I can relate to that.

I talked to someone recently, whose father had a studio in Jamaica. Bob Marley had actually done a version of *Visions.* It was very raw.

Prince—saw the *Purple Rain* performance.
Pink Floyd when they did *The Wall.*
John Lennon and I worked together in New York.
Jackie Wilson
B.B. King

List up to ten things that could be helpful to someone breaking into the business.

- Commit yourself. Don't get hung up on what you have done. Be encouraged by what you can do, because there's always more to be done. For someone who's starting to break in, don't say, "Oh man, here we go. I'm in it." Just because you're in it doesn't mean things are going to get easier, that you're not going to have the challenge of working. Give thanks. Be happy. Give God praise for the fact that you have succeeded—show your appreciation by doing the very best that you can do, consistently. Don't get so hung up on the fact that you've done it, that you stop. Don't get so overwhelmed by the fact that you've done it.
- For those who haven't done it yet, prepare yourself to do the very best that you can do. Work on your craft, so that when you do get the opportunity, you really have something that you can offer. Remember what your desires are when you go in. If you should be so fortunate to get in, give it all you have. Don't be afraid of failure.
- In closing, for any person that I've inspired in my life, I greatly appreciate it to the utmost, but I cannot take the credit for it. You have to thank God for it, for being able to be in this, to do whatever it is that he supports me to do.

Rob Zombie

Did you have a mentor or someone who inspired you? If so, what have you learned from that person?

James T. Kirk inspired me as a child. What I learned from him was that even when stranded on a hostile alien planet, such as Beta Antares IV, there will always be an abundant surplus of hot alien babes in silver bikinis ready to party.

What was your very first job in the music industry, and how did you get it?

Singing backup for Musical Youth. Unfortunately, I had pink eye the day they recorded "Pass the Dutchie" and never received the attention I deserved. I got the job through an ad I saw in *Modern Plumber Magazine*.

What was your first break? The first great thing that ever happened to you?

I was lying face down drunk in the gutter when suddenly a limo pulls up. None other than KISS axe master Gene Simmons steps out and trips right over me. Fortunately, he dropped his sizable wallet in the process. The money I stole/borrowed from his wallet would be used to record the first of many worthless demos.

What elements of your job make you want to go to work every day?

Sometimes I think it is the ability to spread musical joy and wonderment to a world desperately in need of a hug, but then I realized it was just the free booze and hookers.

What qualities most helped you get to where you are today?

My mind-blowing ability to memorize complicated Monty Python routines, along with my uncanny laser precision with a rock-hard dodge ball to hit the fat, slow kid square in the nuts at recess.

If you knew everything at the beginning of your career that you know now, what would you have done differently?

I would have ignored the advice of management that "Rap and country music will never hit the Top 10. . . . Satanic monster metal is where it's at, kid."

What is your greatest lesson learned?

That as soon as one of the many "music know it all" folks tells you that "you are going to destroy your career," you are actually about to score your biggest hit yet.

What are some of your favorite albums?

You Gotta Wash Your Ass, Red Foxx

Spook Along With Zacherley, Zacherley

Music to Be Murdered By, Alfred Hitchcock
    and the Jeff Alexander Orchestra

Love Songs from a Cop, Joe E. Ross

Did you have any posters on your bedroom walls as a kid? Of whom?

Abe Vigoda, Norman Fell, Chet Atkins, and Farrah Fawcett-Majors.

What are some great shows you've seen?

Tiny Tim live at the Haverhill, Massachusetts, Rotary Club's Annual Christmas Bingo Jamboree circa 1971

What are some of your favorite songs?

"Where My Bitches At? (The Yo'
    Ho' Mix)," Pat Boone

"Buttercups and Puppies Forever,"
    Slayer

"Cannabalistic Drifter Dance Party,"
    Boxcar Willie

"I Am Not Spock (Unless You Pay Me),"
    Leonard Nimoy

List up to ten things that could be helpful to someone breaking into the business.

- When out to dinner with your A&R guy, always ask, "Is this dinner recoupable against my royalties?"
- If anyone uses the term "lifestyle marketing," get very nervous.
- Don't assume that just because you are signed to a major label that your CDs are actually in stores where you are playing your sold-out show.
- Don't be surprised when you discover that the lowest paid person involved with your band is you.
- Bands acquired in million-dollar major-label bidding wars go directly to the cut-out bin.
- If you have sold under five hundred thousand records, get your unrecouped ass out of that swanky tour bus and get back in the van.
- Everybody you trust at the label will be fired before the release of your first album, so don't bother learning their names.
- If constantly being told that "you fucking suck" hurts your feelings, then I suggest that you quit now.

LEGENDS

Chris Blackwell

FOUNDER OF ISLAND RECORDS

Did you have a mentor or someone who inspired you? If so, what have you learned from that person?

Unquestionably, it would have to be Ahmet Ertegun. He is my hero. Somebody who loves music first and foremost, not just in the music business for the sake of the business. He loves music, he loves artists, and is a fan of talent, which I believe is where you should be.

What I learned from him very early was the value of creating a label identity which was synonymous with good quality and good music. In my early days I used to come up to New York, buy 78s and 45s and take 'em down to Jamaica and sell them at vastly inflated prices. Whenever I'd see an Atlantic record, I'd immediately pick it up. If I played it and I really didn't like it, I would doubt my own opinion. Another thing later on was that Ahmet Ertegun was somebody who so definitely enjoyed himself with what he was doing—he just loved it, you could see he just loved it, you could see how much he enjoyed himself even when things were difficult or frustrating! His sense of humor would prevail. He was basically always a joy to be with, and artists love him.

What was your very first job in the music industry, and how did you get it?

I never really had a job, until I sold Island to Polygram. That's the first time I had a job. My first enterprise was starting Island Records in Jamaica in 1959.

What was your first big break? The first great thing that ever happened to you . . .

My first, big, explosive break was "My Boy Lollipop" by Millie Small. That was a huge international hit.

What elements of your job make you want to go to work every day?

The excitement of being part of the process. The enjoyment of being part of the process. Being involved in creating something, making something happen, seeing something come out, be released, and hopefully become a part of people's lives . . . they will hear something, see something. . . .

At the time you're doing it, you don't necessarily recognize what impact it's going to have, but I enjoy the process of working with people and trying to help them reach where they're wanting to reach, and making things happen. That's really the biggest joy for me—to actually get things to happen.

What qualities most helped you get to where you are today?

I think a little bit what I said earlier about Ahmet. Being a fan of talent and being genuinely interested in helping them achieve their potential. Some things are achieved by doing nothing, not getting in their way. And in other ways, helping and giving them some guidance at times. It varies who you're working with and what the situation is. Sometimes, like let's say in the case of U2, the best thing was just to stay out of the way and give them the support they needed in order to achieve what they wanted to achieve. I don't think I ever gave them one scrap of advice on anything. I think they knew what they wanted to do, they had very good management, and they're very smart guys. In other cases and different people I've helped them find the direction or whatever. . . .

What is your greatest lesson learned?

Patience.

What are some of your favorite albums?

Broken English, Marianne Faithfull   *Joshua Tree,* U2
Haile I Hymn, Ijahman   *Tea for the Tillerman,* Cat Stevens
Exodus, Exodus   *Celebration,* Womack and Womack
Catch a Fire, Bob Marley

What are some great shows you've seen?

Bob Marley at the Lyceum and in Milan
U2—many shows

List up to ten things that could be helpful to someone breaking into the business.

- Make sure that you really love music.
- Have patience.
- The problem is everyone is in such a hurry and the business of music takes over from the music itself. But if you really love the music, if you really enjoy music, then patience is not a problem to have, because you're enjoying the whole process of what is happening; you're not in a big hurry to get on to the next thing.
- Listen to the artists you are working with.
- Be clear in what you say.
- Keep your word.
- Don't listen too much to the radio (what you are hearing was conceived eighteen months earlier).

Dick Clark

Did you have a mentor or someone who inspired you? If so, what have you learned from that person?

From a performance standpoint, I always admired the "television talkers"... Arthur Godfrey, Steve Allen, Gary Moore. From a business standpoint, I've always been inspired by the independent entrepreneurs in entertainment.

What was your very first job in the music industry, and how did you get it?

I first worked in a mailroom of a radio station. I became a disc jockey and eventually became involved in the music business. My involvement there included talent management, record manufacturing and production, distribution, music publishing, and the production of music concerts.

What was your first big break? The first great thing that ever happened to you . . .

My first break was to get a job as a radio announcer in Philadelphia. Subsequently, I was made the host of *American Bandstand*. That was the greatest career event that ever happened to me.

What elements of your job make you want to go to work every day?

The challenge of doing things I've never done before.

What qualities most helped you get to where you are today?

Bulldog determination.

If you knew everything at the beginning of your career that you know now, what would you have done differently?

I would have fought to hold on to my music interests and include them in my television enterprises.

What is your greatest lesson learned?

Be aware that big corporate morality is nothing you can count on.

What are some of your favorite albums?

I've worked with too many people over the years to name a favorite.

Did you have any posters on your bedroom walls as a kid? Of whom?

My brother and I shared a bedroom. We didn't have any posters up, but the ceiling was painted dark blue, and it had luminous stars and planets upon it.

What are some great shows you've seen?

The Beatles, the Convention Center, Atlantic City

Elvis Presley, the Arena, Philadelphia

KISS, the Forum, Los Angeles

Black Sabbath, the Hollywood Bowl, Los Angeles

Gloria Estefan, the Forum, Los Angeles

What are some of your favorite songs?

Again, I've worked with too many people to name a favorite.

List up to ten things that could be helpful to someone breaking into the business.

- Try to focus on your ultimate goal.
- Take whatever jobs necessary to get there.
- Don't give up!

Ahmet Ertegun

FOUNDER OF ATLANTIC RECORDS

Did you have a mentor or someone who inspired you? If so, what have you learned from that person?

I grew up in Europe. My mother, Hayrunisa Rustem, was my first influence. She was very musical. She always bought the popular hits of the day, wherever we were. So I heard all the European hits and the Josephine Baker records when I was little, and Mae West, the Mills Brothers, the Boswell Sisters, as well as the occasional Louis Armstrong record. My next big influence was my brother Nesuhi, who was five years older. He took me to see my first jazz concerts in London when I was around nine years old, and he taught me about art, literature, and music.

I must mention my greatest mentor, my father Mehmet Munir Bev, who taught us ethics and honesty, humility, and pride; as well as my sister Selma, who always exemplified those virtues; my cousin Sadi, who was an inspired poet; and my aunt Yenge, an angel who brought me up and was my role model. Professor Sterling Brown of Howard University was very influential, as was Dr. Thomas Williston, who introduced me to African-American cultural and social life in Washington.

Last but not least was Max Silverman, who ran the Maxie Waxie music shop in the black section of the capital, where I discovered the ingredients that made people buy a particular record.

My later influences were my philosophy teacher Bill Gorman, my coworkers Jerry Wexler and Noreen Woods, and most important, my wife, Mica.

What was your very first job in the music industry, and how did you get it?

I was a graduate student majoring in philosophy, a jazz and blues lover, a collector of rare recordings, and a regular at nightclubs. In other words, as a colleague once pointed out, I was totally unemployable. So, naturally, I decided to go into the record business. I managed to persuade my dentist to invest ten thousand dollars in what many of my friends thought was a harebrained adventure, and in 1947, Herb Abramson and I started a little independent label which we called Atlantic Records. As it turned out, my dentist had made a very good investment.

What was your first big break? The first great thing that ever happened to you . . .

When we had our first hit in 1949 with Stick McGhee's "Drinkin' Wine Spo-Dee-O-Dee."

What elements of your job make you want to go to work every day?

I love my company, I love my work, I love my artists. It is a great life—this life of music. There is still no better feeling than hearing a great new artist or a great new song for the first time. And there is still no greater satisfaction than creating a hit record. I never imagined that I would be able to earn a living from doing something that I really enjoyed so much. When you are doing something you truly love, then no hours are too long, no problem is too complicated, because there really is nothing else you'd rather be doing. When we started Atlantic, I thought we would make records for two or three years, and then I'd have to figure out what to do with the rest of my life. I am very glad I was wrong. Especially since it meant I never had to get a real job.

What qualities most helped you get to where you are today?

Knowing how to make a record, and, most importantly, knowing how to make a record that people will buy . . . Passion, enthusiasm, and love for the music . . . And, above all, the ability to put it all together. If you are working just for the money, then it will be merely work, and you will live a less rewarding life. But if your work is driven by passion and knowledge, then any success you achieve is that much sweeter.

If you knew everything at the beginning of your career that you know now, what would you have done differently?

I would have offered another twenty thousand dollars to beat out RCA for Elvis Presley. And I would have held out for a bigger offer when we sold the label in 1967. But otherwise I wouldn't change a thing. However, if I had had another life to lead, I would love to have been a jazz musician and played in Duke Ellington's or Jelly Roll Morton's band.

What is your greatest lesson learned?

That the truly great artists have not only an innate talent, but very often the clearest vision of what they should be doing with that talent. In my own personal experience, this has been true of everyone from Ray Charles to Aretha Franklin to Buffalo Springfield to Phil Collins to Jewel to Kid Rock, and all of the great jazz musicians from Erroll Garner to John Coltrane. When we are lucky enough to stumble across these gifted artists, it is our job to create the environment where their natural ability can flourish. It's a tricky balance between staying out of the way and standing close enough to be able to give whatever guidance you can. If we believe in an artist, then we must believe that there is an audience for that artist. We are the vehicle which fosters that magical connection between artist and listener, and we can never lose sight of the fact that we are merely a conduit which opens the way for that connection to be made.

What are some of your favorite albums?

This would be a very, very long list. There have been so many great recordings made over the past eighty years, it's impossible for me to pick just a few favorites.

Did you have any posters on your bedroom walls as a kid? Of whom?

Bobby Hackett, Louis Armstrong, Django Reinhardt, Pee Wee Russell, Lester Young, Carole Lombard, Joan Bennett, and Fred Astaire.

What are some great shows you've seen?

I still vividly remember my brother Nesuhi taking me to see Cab Calloway's orchestra at the London Palladium in 1932. Then, a bit later, we went to hear Duke Ellington. It was an incredible experience for me. I had never seen any black people, and, while I had heard jazz on records, the sound of those bands live was unbelievable. Many years later, it was the great rock bands that came closest to generating the same sort of exhilaration. After we signed the Stones in 1971, it got to the point where I would go to their gigs just to hear the introductions to the songs—they would give you such a big kick because you knew what was coming up. The same was true of the Led Zeppelin concerts. It was that kind of excitement, that kind of adrenaline. Over the years, I have been to thousands of shows; I still go to see as many live performances as I can. There is nothing like it in the world.

What are some of your favorite songs?

I would have to give the same answer as I did for the albums.

List up to ten things that could be helpful to someone breaking into the business.

- What works best is what works best *for you.* There is no one right way to make it in this business. Some people take great delight in making sweeping judgments about our business, often pitting one way of working against another. It's all nonsense.
- The most important thing is to find the right people and the right path to help you realize your dream. It's not unlike a good marriage or any good partnership.
- Whether you are striving to be a musician, a songwriter, a producer, a manager, a booking agent, a label executive . . . whatever your goal, choose it because it is something you not only love to do, but you can actually do.
- Some people achieve quick success, and some face roadblocks and initial failure. For those who are struggling, I say persevere, do not give up. Many of the great people in our business, artists and executives alike, have gone through many trials and tribulations before making the grade.
- For those of you who do succeed, now or later, remember that the greatest quality of a winner is humility. You must never lose sight of where you came from.
- And above all, you must never lose the passion that made you want to be in this crazy business in the first place.

Berry Gordy

FOUNDER OF MOTOWN RECORDS

Did you have a mentor or someone who inspired you? If so, what have you learned from that person?

Several, but much of my inspiration and learning came from songs. So you might say the early songwriters were my mentors—the ones who wrote for the Ink Spots, the Mills Brothers, and Nat King Cole. On a personal level, though, it was my father, "Pops," who was a wise, strong, and ethical role model.

What was your very first job in the music industry, and how did you get it?

Writing songs for George Goldner. My writing partner, Roquel Davis, introduced us.

What was your first big break? The first great thing that ever happened to you . . .

Getting to work with Jackie Wilson. He was the consummate performer, interpreter of a song, and Mr. Excitement all in one. He set standards, which made it tough on everyone who came after him.

What elements of your job make you want to go to work every day?

I love working with creative people.

What qualities most helped you get to where you are today?

The joy of helping people reach their potential.

If you knew everything at the beginning of your career that you know now, what would you have done differently?

That's hard to say, because I was so lucky with all my decisions I'm not sure that I would change anything. Even the ones that were wrong turned out to be better in the long run because I learned something and altered my actions.

What is your greatest lesson learned?

Be yourself and find people you can trust.

What are some of your favorite albums?

Depending on my mood, anything from the Ink Spots to Oscar Peterson, from Diana, Stevie, Marvin, or Rick James to Frank Sinatra, from Bacharach/David compositions to Earth, Wind & Fire, from all of Motown to Tupak, P. Diddy, Eminem, and other rappers.

What are some great shows you've seen?

I enjoyed many, but the greatest ones I've seen were performed by Jackie Wilson, Sammy Davis Jr., and Michael Jackson.

What are some of your favorite songs?

Some of those early songs that come to mind are "Paper Doll," "You're Nobody 'Til Somebody Loves You," "Into Each Life Some Rain Must Fall."
Later: "Anyone Who Had a Heart," "I'll Try Something New," "Tracks of My Tears."
Songs by Nick and Valerie, Stevie and Marvin, Whitfield, Strong, Holland-Dozier-Holland, and many other Motown songs.

List up to ten things that could be helpful to someone breaking into the business.

- Plan for success: Start with integrity, end with integrity.
- Try to treat setbacks as opportunities.
- Learn all you can about whatever you want to do. Knowledge is never wasted.
- Stay focused on your goal.
- Be true to yourself and demand truth from others. A foundation built on truth can stand forever.

Quincy Jones

Did you have a mentor or someone who inspired you? If so, what have you learned from that person?

I have several different kinds of inspirations. In the beginning it was local musicians: Buddy Catlett, Clark Terry, Ray Charles (we started together when I was fourteen and he was sixteen), Benny Carter, Duke and Basie, Miles Davis. The business guys also had a big impact on me, including Picasso and Stravinsky. Picasso had twelve lithograph plants. He was an artist who was protecting himself to be independent and the same with Stravinsky.

I got stranded in Europe in 1959. I was twenty-six years old, and there with a big band of thirty people—if that's not a postgraduate course, I don't know what is. We went everywhere—Yugoslavia, all over Sweden, Finland. Just dragging this band around with no management, no agency, or anything else. Something like that either breaks you or makes you strong, to learn that side of it. Before I had just thought about the music; I never thought about the mechanics it took to make that stuff work. It really helps to be cognizant of both sides.

My teens were with Basie. I wrote for Basie for twenty years, all the way through the Sinatra days, "Fly Me to the Moon," etc. I played with them for a little while. He was a big model, but I also wrote for them since I was thirteen years old. He was kind of my mentor as a human being too. He was a manager, a brother, a father, he did everything, until the day he died. Sinatra is like that with me, too. Just amazing. I was blessed to have worked with him and played with him. Tina told me after he was gone how serious the friendship was. With somebody that big you're reluctant to accept that—he was such a bigger-than-life person that you didn't want to take it personally and get hurt. But it was a very personal relationship, and I feel it now.

Clarence Avant, Irving Greene, and Steve Ross were three guys I learned from. They said, "We're going to teach you so that you never have fear of corporations as long as you live." I was fortunate that I met Clarence and Irving (at the time he started Mercury Records) and Steve Ross. I saw all the mergers between Time, Warner, and everything. We spent all of our time together, and then eventually had a joint venture with one of the biggest entertainment companies in the world. That was real, because most people don't do that with brothers. The joint venture with Time/Warner in 1990 was pretty strong: magazines, TV stations, films, television production. But I'd had a long association with them. I started my record company with Time/Warner in 1980.

What was your very first job in the music industry, and how did you get it?

My very first job was when I was fourteen. I was in a gospel a cappella quartet called the Challengers with a man named Joseph Powe, who used to be with Wings Over Jordan, the famous black singing group. He had a dance band. I must have been twelve years old, and I used to babysit for him so I could look at his books. He had a Glenn Miller arrangement book and a Frank Skinner book on scoring for films. I always wanted to score for films, before I could even write I wanted to do it. But they didn't have too many black composers doing it, so I didn't think it was realistic.

Seeing the big black bands in the forties come through the Northwest was a big influence. We had lived in Chicago, which is the biggest black ghetto in the America. At ten years old, we moved to the Northwest, which is like the biggest contrast I could ever ask for. Seeing those bands helped me get a fix on who I wanted to be when I grew up as a man. Seeing them unified, dignified, talented, playing together—it was just great. They were my role models.

What was your first big break? The first great thing that ever happened to you . . .

The first time was with Charlie Taylor's band. That was amazing because I got paid seven dollars. I couldn't believe I got paid for doing something I loved so much. We worked at the YMCA in Seattle in 1947, and in 1948 I went with Bumps Blackwell. He was a big guy—he'd found Sam Cooke, Little Richard—from Seattle. He had a junior and a senior band, and we became his junior band. That was another big break because we got to play with Billie Holiday, Billy Eckstine, and Cab Calloway on the same bill. We were fourteen or fifteen then. Then I went with Lionel Hampton when I was eighteen. They wanted me to join him at fifteen, but I was too young, and his wife threw me off the bus—Go back to school!

Then I went to Boston on scholarship to what's now Berklee College of Music. I was there for about six months, and then Hamp called me up and said, "This time it's real if you want to be here." That was my first baby step into the world. That band was at the top of the world, and they worked every night of the year. I played trumpet and piano, and I was an arranger.

What elements of your job make you want to go to work every day?

Passion of discovery. I must admit that it was escape too. My mother was in a mental home when I was seven, and my brother and I had to figure it out ourselves, because my daddy worked all the time. I transferred my need for a mother into my music. I made music my mother; it's that simple. That's what I wrote in my book, and that's what it felt like. I used everything that was negative in my life and tried to transform it. I'd go sit in that closet and try to transform it from that darkness to light through music and creativity. That saved my life.

We were thugs before that. We broke into an armory and had a pie fight. After we ate all the pies and ice cream up, I broke into another room and saw a piano. I was eleven years old and that piano changed my life forever. That was it—you could tell, because all the other stuff started to feel stupid to me then. With music, I could open a door to a big wonderland. I realized I had to go—they say most Americans, especially in jazz, shack up with music, and then they court it later. You play nightclubs first, and then you go study and you go to Nadia Boulanger in Paris to study counterpoint, harmony, and composition. I was lucky to study with Nadia, that turned me around. Same with the Berklee School of Music. You realize you have to understand your craft. Back then, we were lucky because we didn't have any temptation of being rich and famous. That never crossed our mind—not at all! We just wanted to be good.

What qualities most helped you get to where you are today?

Thirst for knowledge. Tremendous determination. As a writer, it was "feel it first," and then figure it out. How does it work? How do they get that sound? How do they get eighteen people to play the same note? How does it work? I've always wanted to know how things work, no matter what it was—a system, harmony, counterpoint—those tools gave me a springboard for my curiosity that was applicable to everything and became a metaphor for life.

It's also about learning to be humble with your creativity, and if you ever have success, to be gracious and have grace with it. That's the bottom line on how I try to live now.

If you knew everything at the beginning of your career that you know now, what would you have done differently?

Probably stayed away from dope. But you have to understand that in those days, the forties, everyone was into dope. All of our idols were into it. I am glad that my encounter was a short one. Some of the others, like Ray Charles, who's my bosom buddy to this day, kept going big time and got caught. It's no joke. He's strong, and he broke through it himself.

What is your greatest lesson learned?

I think the golden rule. You have to build a character that you can love, respect, believe in, and that you can live with. You have to try to keep the humility with each time you go through that creative throng. I really believe—I don't just believe it; it's a fact—that creativity is about a divinity. It's about cause and manifestation. Cause is definitely God's job, and clearly, manifestation is our job. If you can just realize and accept that you are just a terminal to let that creativity, that higher power, come through you, you'll never stop creating. Divinity is the source of our creativity. That's the true truth. If you don't believe it, look at some of these people who get successful who say, "Okay, God, I'll take it from here." I see it every day, thousands of times over fifty years. I've seen the ones that don't and the ones that do. And the ones that do—survive. It's a lack of respect for the source. Don't take it personal because it's coming through you.

What are some of your favorite albums?

Nat Cole

Ray Charles

Kind of Blue was like my orange juice because it had everything in it: Miles Davis, Coltrane, Bill
   Evans, and Cannonball.

Duke Ellington

Count Basie

Joe Pesci has an album out, *Falling in Love,* under the name Joe Doggs, with Joey DeFrancesco.
Joe is a great jazz singer. I've been listening to this record night and day the last few months.
He's an old friend, but I couldn't believe he could sing like that. He's been singing since he was
nine. I've been great friends with him and DeNiro, but I never thought of him seriously as a
singer. But he is a jazz singer personified.

Did you have any posters on your bedroom walls as a kid? Of whom?

I had posters of the bands that came through, like Duke Ellington, Lunceford, Basie, Woody Herman, T-Bone Walker. Jazz at the Philharmonic—those were our Rolling Stones in the forties. It
had as much excitement as rock 'n' roll did. In a funny way, with Lionel Hampton, and the Philharmonic, we were aware very early on how the music really affected a large amount of people.
A lot people talked about my Michael Jackson years almost as if I was selling out. Please! I
played everything from chart issues, to rhythm and blues, to bebop to dinner music by the time
I was twelve years old. Nothing was a stretch, and it's funny when someone who's locked up in
some kind of departmentalized slot thinks you're stepping out of your thing. But that was part
of our breathing apparatus. Debussey, R&B, strip music, bebop, and on and on . . .

What are some great shows you've seen?

My time was seductive with Basie and Sinatra at the Sands. That was probably as good as it
gets. We did "Fly Me to the Moon," and then we went back to Vegas after they played the music *on the moon*—it was just such a symbol. What a great time that was, everybody was at the
top of their game. One key thing for young people to remember is that it's about preparation
and opportunity. When opportunity happens, you'd better be prepared. I was ready for Frank,
man. I was ready for him! I'd been working with Basie, I'd done my homework. He knew it, and
I knew it, too. And we had a good time, until the day he died.

Janet Jackson's show in Hawaii.

Cirque du Soleil's "O" at Bellagio. Steve Wynn is a good friend of mine, and I went opening
night. Just brilliant. Cirque du Soleil is awesome. We'll be working together, too. It's all surre-
alism. It's just art. The guys asked me to hold that pot where the water drips down, and I said,

"Oh my God." Then they pulled me up onstage, rolled up my cuffs, and made me get up on that iceberg. I saw all these frogmen underwater that were giving oxygen to the dancers that had their feet dancing above the water. I couldn't figure out how they were staying down so long. It was a whole city, a whole civilization down underwater. It's just incredible. I'd never seen anything like that before. I was also involved in producing the Clinton inauguration, the millennium celebration, and the Oscars in 1996. I love it all, from structured shows to events that will never happen again. Events like that are so strange.

What are some of your favorite songs?

This is so hard. I've written thousands of arrangements. I would say . . .
"Lush Life" with Billy Strayhorn
"How Do You Keep the Music Playing"
Aretha Franklin's version of "Somewhere" by Leonard Bernstein. That's the song I would leave
  here with . . .

I have worked with every American singer since Louis Armstrong, Ella, Sarah, Billie Holiday, Carmen McRae, Nina Simone, Aretha, Roberta Flack, Diana Ross, everybody. All up to the rappers, to Latifah. All of them: Tony Bennett, Ray Charles, Paul Simon, Luther. I treasure it, and it's a great feeling.

List up to ten things that could be helpful to someone breaking into the business.

The best way to get good at your craft is to walk in the shoes of the giants. Give yourself a chance to grow into your shoes. Copy all of the people you love; copy every note they do. A lot of young people say, "But everybody tells me to be original," and I say you don't even know how to be mediocre! You don't think about being original, you don't know how to be original. You have to copy the greatest people. I played Miles Davis, Ellington, Dizzy, Tadd Demeron, Fats Navarro. And as you do that, then you learn how to walk in shoes that are fifty thousand feet high and then your voice will automatically come after a while and transcend, metamorphose into your own sound. It works for all the arts—painters, writers, everybody. If you're gonna jump out there, you gotta jump into some crazy writers—Dante, Shakespeare, Pushkin. It's not a dirt road—this has all been around a long time. I'd love to dig into the philosophy of da Vinci and Michaelangelo. There's a wisdom that has accumulated over the ages. It's about knowing what you're doing, and loving it. Take your time.

When we were on tour and stranded in Europe in 1959, Nat Cole said if you're chasing success and fame, which we never did because it didn't make sense back then, but if you do, you have to realize you can go all the way up and burn out in a short time. You have to take your time and keep preparing yourself so you can go the long distance. It feels very good to be in this business at age seventy-one and have more work than I can do in the next two hundred years. Anything: movies, film scores, records.

All the young dudes call me every week. I am doing an album as we speak that's a meeting of all of the hip-hop dudes—Dr. Dre, Pharrell, Neptunes, R. Kelly, Jermaine Dupri, Dallas Austin, Ludacris, all these young brothers. They're going to do remixes of my stuff, and I'm going to do big band versions of theirs. It's exciting. I've been around hip-hop for a long time—my daughter was engaged to Tupac, I produced with L.L., Ice Cube. It's just part of my bloodstream. Ludacris was here last week—he's twenty-five years old, and we just feed each other. I love their energy, and their perspective; they listen to mine, stuffed with all of this long-ass history. It's a great feeling. It's the next link. I remember when everyone was saying "rap is dead." That's when I did *Back on the Block,* and they were wrong! In 1987, were they ever wrong. We had the Grammy album of the year when everybody was saying rap was dead. It had everything in it. I've always made my records with the entire family of African-American music. As much as I love 50 Cent and Jay-Z, I'm not giving up Coltrane, Basie, and Duke. It's too much a part of me, and it's all the same stuff. It's gospel music. Jazz is the fashionable music all over the world now. We're having a great time now. We just came back from nine countries in seven weeks, including Baghdad and Kuwait. I've been traveling over there for fifty years, and I feel at home at every place on the planet. It amazes me—Yugoslavia, Estonia, wherever, Latin America, Malaysia—that the entire planet has adopted our music as its Esperanto.

Guess who knows the least about American music? Americans. And if you don't believe it, I was in England as vice-president of Mercury before the Beatles and the Stones happened, while Elvis and Bill Hilly were kicking ass over here. The Stones knew what the real roots were. That's why they had me in the space because they knew what the real shit was all about. Chuck Berry, Bo Diddley, Little Richard, Willie Dixon. Mick and all of them knew that, and that's why they're sixty years old and still kicking everybody's ass. Aren't they? They knock everybody out of the way, because the foundation is based on the real thing. This applies to all of Europe. The idea that jazz and blues has flipped off the radar screens of young kids is crazy. Blues and jazz is the power of music; it's the foundation. Everybody in the world decided to forget about Kabuki in Japan, or bagpipes in Scotland, or German Lieder, and use this music as the expression of their soul. Everywhere on the planet.

Jazz and blues is the music that came from some place so deep after you transport twenty million people out of their country and tear their families apart. They had to go to the bottom, to the depths of their souls to express themselves. No one had ever been down that far before. You had to push them down that far. The only outlet during slavery times was the music in the church. It's powerful shit, obviously. It's all over the planet, and it has been for a long time, since 1910, with Jim Europe and Eubie Blake. It astounds me. I know that as long as I live I want to be involved in something to help Americans understand American music more—the whole, full breadth of American music. It's a powerful, unifying force.

Russell Simmons

FOUNDER OF DEF JAM RECORDS

Did you have a mentor or someone who inspired you? If so, what have you learned from that person?

Quincy Jones and David Geffen. David and Quincy both inspired me to be in the business, and showed me that the creative process requires the embracing of culture. You have to be part of it. You can look corporate, act corporate, and work in worlds where creativity flows. They inspired me to be myself, to be headstrong and independent.

What was your very first job in the music industry, and how did you get it?

I've never had a job. I never worked for anybody.

What was your first big break? The first great thing that ever happened to you . . .

I think when I got off the plane in Amsterdam once, and they called me "Mr. Simmons." They took me to the red-light district, they bought me weed, and they called me "Mr. Simmons." That was in 1979. Nothing since then has happened that was nearly as good as that.

What elements of your job make you want to go to work every day?

All of the philanthropic stuff. You can't help the poor and be one of them, and I think that's really what I enjoy most is doing things that fight elements of poverty. Being able to help open doors for people who are locked out.

What qualities most helped you get to where you are today?

The greatest success that I am having is based on hard work and dedication. When I first had some success, I got nerved out. The second that I wasn't attached, and I wasn't worried, I was able to do some of the greatest things. The fact that I've been conscious of that has really been the greatest business asset. Letting go of my work has allowed me to do great work.

If you knew everything at the beginning of your career that you know now, what would you have done differently?

The anxiety that I had for the first thirty-seven years of my life, the insomnia and those things. I used to think that the anxiety was part of the driving force for me. I thought reassessing things and being nerved out all the time was part of the process. But you have to let go, and not be so attached to the results of your work. You have to enjoy your work. They're never going to pay you enough.

What is your greatest lesson learned?

My greatest lesson learned is that there's nothing they can pay you. I don't care how many chairs you buy, or how many rooms there are in your house, you can only be in one at any time. You may sit in the kitchen all the time, you may hang out in the bedroom. Whether you hang out in the bedroom or in the living room, you can only sit in one chair at a time. You may want a TV, but you don't need fifty of them. I'm not saying it's bad to have them, but worrying about it separates people from doing a good job.

What are some of your favorite albums?

It Takes a Nation of Millions to Hold Us Back, Public Enemy

Raisin' Hell, Public Enemy

Greatest Hits, the Delfonics

Greatest Hits, Al Green

It's Dark and Hell Is Hot, DMX

Did you have any posters on your bedroom walls as a kid? Of whom?

Bruce Lee and James Brown.

What are some great shows you've seen?

Run-D.M.C.

The Forever Tour with Run-D.M.C. and the Beastie Boys

What are some of your favorite songs?

"King of Rock," Run-D.M.C.

"Rebel Without a Pause," Public Enemy

"Touch Me, Tease Me," Case

"Shut 'Em Down," Public Enemy

List up to ten things that could be helpful to someone breaking into the business.

- In hip-hop and black music, where people are more sophisticated in terms of their likes and their tastes, they know exactly what they like. You don't have to spend a long time trying to break a record. A great record you can put out independently—you can throw it out the window and people will get it. All the stars that have made a lot of money in hip-hop have started independently. Even the A&R directors at the major labels are slow to appreciate what's hot.

In hip-hop they're supposed to be young and hip and all that, but they're not as creative as they'd like to think; their ears are not so wide-open. It's the people in the clubs and at the parties and on the street that make you a star in this business—long before you have to deal with the corporations. So my advice would be: go where the action is, where it starts—in the clubs, at the parties, and on the street.

- The most important thing is to focus. You probably have twenty great ideas a week. But you can't put all of them in play at once. Everything takes time. Most people who have ideas are failures because they change their focus so often. You need to have tunnel vision and work toward your goal. You have to be relentless. That's the difference between winners and losers.

- Many people think everything's already happened. But something new is always happening. You just have to find it. Young people always were and always will be about change. You rebel because the things that really affect you become important. Whether it's for the hell of it or there's a reason, they want to change the system, challenge it. That's where all the new culture and ideas and attitudes come from. Go find it!

Joe Smith

CAPITOL RECORDS

Did you have a mentor or someone who inspired you? If so, what have you learned from that person?

From John Hammond—legendary writer, A&R genius (Bille Holiday, Bruce Springsteen, etc.)—I learned the integrity of music.

What was your very first job in the music industry, and how did you get it?

Deejay at Yale radio station, then in Pittsburgh and Boston.

What was your first big break? The first great thing that ever happened to you . . .

Being accepted to Yale after serving with the infantry in the Far East. I joined the Yale station—that set the path.

What elements of your job make you want to go to work every day?

The music industry—the creative side—is seldom static. Next year's Top 10 will have three or four we haven't heard of yet. The thrill of finding one of them . . .

What qualities most helped you get to where you are today?

Easy with people and genuine love of music.

If you knew everything in the beginning of your career that you know now, what would you have done differently?

Started my own label.

What is your greatest lesson learned?

Despite popular perception, success in the entertainment world does not require playing fast and loose with the truth and doing whatever will get you on top regardless of the consequences to others.

What are some of your favorite albums?

Moondance, Van Morrison
Nick of Time, Bonnie Raitt
Jazz Samba, Stan Getz with Gilberto band
Greatest Hits, the Eagles

Sweet Baby James, James Taylor
Greatest Hits, the Grateful Dead
At the Sands with Count Basie, Frank Sinatra

Did you have any posters on your bedroom walls as a kid? Of whom?

Duke Ellington and Count Basie.

What are some great shows you've seen?

Sinatra with Basie, Newport
First time with the Rolling Stones
Elton John

What are some of your favorite songs?

"Moondance"
"Girl from Ipanema"
"You're Right as Rain"
   (Bob James instrumental)
"Summer Wind"

List up to ten things that could be helpful to someone breaking into the business.

■ Love the music.
■ Network with anyone and everyone
   in your company.
■ Learn the ABCs of finance.

■ Stay close to people who work for you.
■ Live the business but have other passions.
■ *Do not be what you do.*

Seymour Stein

FOUNDER OF SIRE RECORDS

Did you have a mentor or someone who inspired you? If so, what have you learned from that person?

I've been lucky enough to have many! In high school in the fifties, I worked part-time at *Billboard*. There I met Paul Ackerman, the legendary music editor, who sent me on various assignments to review early rock 'n' roll gigs. Paul was one of the most knowledgeable men in the music in-dustry, and, although well along in his career when I met him, a very forward and liberal thinker. On his watch, *Billboard* stopped labeling the ethnic charts, "Hillbilly and Race Music," and Paul with Jerry Wexler came up with new categories "Rhythm & Blues" and "Country & Western." Paul was the first to turn me on to country and bluegrass music, and artists like Hank Williams, Jimmie Rodgers, the Carter Family, Lefty Frizzell, Bill Monroe, Ernest Tubb, Bob Wills, and oth-ers. Paul also introduced me to some of the industry's most colorful entrepreneurs, including Syd Nathan, Leonard Chess, Jerry Wexler, Ahmet Ertegun, George Goldner, Morris Levy, Hy Weiss, Morty Craft, and others. Tom Noonan, *Billboard*'s chart editor, brought me into his department, and, together, we worked out the methodology for the original Hot 100, back in the late fifties, when music was all about hit singles.

At *Billboard,* I met my most influential mentor, Syd Nathan, founder of King Records. One of the great R&B indies (along with Chess, Atlantic, Specialty, Imperial, and Vee-Jay), King was different from the rest. Based in Cincinnati, King was home to James Brown, Hank Ballard and the Midnighters, Little Willie John, Billy Ward and the Dominoes, as well as a strong roster of country and western stars like Cowboy Copas, Moon Mullican, Hawkshaw Hawkins, the Stan-ley Bros., and Grandpa Jones. King also had its own distribution outlets in twenty-two cities, a pressing plant, and recording studios in Cincinnati, Chicago, and New York. I learned all as-pects of the business. I spent summers working in Cincinnati while in high school, and, after leaving *Billboard* in late 1961, moved there, where I lived for two years. Working for Syd was the equivalent to my college education.

Soon after moving back to New York, I was approached by George Goldner, arguably the per-son most responsible for bringing the mambo craze to America with his Tico label in the early fifties. He started Rama Records a few years later with "Gee" by the Crows, considered by many to be rock 'n' roll's first hit single. George also started Gee Records and signed Frankie Lymon and the Teenagers, co-founded Roulette Records with Morris Levy, and, after the break-up of that partnership, Goldner started Gone and End Records and enjoyed success with the Flamingos and the Chantels. George was not just a great music man—he was an ace promo man. Back in 1964, George was about to start what would be his last venture, Red Bird Records, with songwriter legends Jerry Leiber and Mike Stoller. I was George's assistant for two years, 1964 to 1966. Red Bird had number-one hits with both the Dixie Cups and Shangri-Las. The company ground to a sudden halt in 1966, and that's when I teamed up with producer Richard Gottehrer to form Sire. During Sire's early years, Syd Nathan, George Goldner, and Paul Ackerman all passed away. My latter-day mentors were Jerry Wexler and Ahmet Ertegun. I'm happy that I remain close friends with both these elder statesmen.

Back in the late fifties and sixties, when I was getting started, it was a much smaller business and, thankfully, a lot easier to get close to people who could be mentors. I don't believe I would have had the same career I've had without the help and support of those mentioned above. I feel badly for young people just entering the business, as it will be hard finding a significant mentor.

What was your first big break? The first great thing that ever happened to you . . .

I've been extremely lucky throughout my career. I'd have to say my biggest break was meeting Syd Nathan. He taught me the business from the ground up.

What elements of your job make you want to go to work every day?

The opportunity to find a new and exciting talent and then to pursue and hopefully sign and help develop it. With few exceptions—Lou Reed and Brian Wilson come to mind—all other artists signed to Sire began their careers on the label. Helping to start and build careers remains pure joy for me.

What qualities most helped you get to where you are today?

Sire started as an independent and I still run it as an independent even though the label has been owned by WB for over twenty years. My earliest associations were with indie labels in the UK and Europe. Dating back to Transatlantic in the late sixties, and later companies like Mute from whom I licensed Depeche Mode & Erasure, Rough Trade (the Smiths, Everything But the Girl, Aztec Camera), Fiction (the Cure), Beggar's Banquet (the Cult/Modern English), Creation (My Bloody Valentine, Primal Scream, Ride), independent labels have been, and continue to be, at the forefront of every important change or trend in new music. I'm an independent at heart. Yesterday, Today, Tomorrow: "Be True to Your School."

If you knew everything at the beginning of your career that you know now, what would you have done differently?

Nothing! I've been wrong more than right, but that's the beauty of this business. I have no regrets. The most important thing to have is the courage to be wrong. You learn from your mistakes. This business is all about taking a chance and having the strength of your convictions! Like the Edith Piaf classic "Non, Je Ne Regrette Rien."

What are some of your favorite albums?

Don't dismiss the importance of singles! It's actually a lot harder to come up with something great in two minutes and forty seconds and a lot easier if you have forty to fifty minutes to work with.

Hank Williams, Fats Domino, Chuck Berry, Jimmie Rodgers (the Singing Brakeman), Elvis Presley, Buddy Holly, Hank Thompson and the Brazos Valley Boys, Johnny Cash, Little Richard, the Five Satins, Nat King Cole, Frankie Lymon & the Teenagers, the Everly Brothers, Marty Robbins, Ray Price, Kitty Wells, LaVern Baker, Ricky Nelson, Del Shannon, Joe Turner, Hank Ballard, Sam Cooke, Little Willie John, the Platters, the Flamingos, the Moonglows, Lee Andrews and the Hearts (and all great doo-wop), Guy Mitchell, Edith Piaf, the Chantels, Marvin Gaye, the Miracles, Bob Dylan, James Brown, the Beach Boys, Ella Fitzgerald, Louis Armstrong, Fats Waller, Them, the Rolling Stones, the Clash, the Ramones, Talking Heads, Depeche Mode, the Pretenders, the Smiths, Madonna, Prince, U2, Bruce Springsteen, Elton John, James Taylor, Cat Stevens, the Replacements, the Byrds, Elmore James, Otis Redding, Dusty Springfield, Mighty Sparrow, Lord Kitchener, Bing Crosby, Russ Colombo, Rudy Vallee, Tino Rossi, Marlene Dietrich, and Lale Andersen

Did you have any posters on your bedroom walls as a kid? Of whom?

LaVern Baker, Ricky Nelson, Elvis, Frankie Lymon, Little Richard, Chuck Berry, Fats Domino, Eddie Cochran, Bessie Smith, Edith Piaf.

What are some great shows you've seen?

All Alan Freed's rock 'n' roll shows at the Brooklyn Fox and Brooklyn Paramount
The Beatles at Shea Stadium
Rolling Stones concerts
Concert for Bangladesh
Live Aid in Philadelphia
The Flamin' Groovies and the Ramones 1976 Bicentennial Concert in London
The Ramones, Talking Heads, Queens Jubilee concert 1977
Depeche Mode's first gig just outside Basildon
Echo and the Bunnymen at London YMCA on Tottenham Court Road

Jimi Hendrix, Middle Earth, London

The Smiths at ICA

Edith Piaf in Paris

Madonna's outdoor gig outside Paris

The Pretenders' first gig at the old Klook's Kleek Pub in West Hampstead

k.d. lang at Calgary Rodeo

The Replacements at the Felt Forum

Depeche Mode at the Rose Bowl in Pasadena

The Clash and the Sex Pistols on Anarchy Tour in Cleethorpes, England

List up to ten things that could be helpful to someone breaking into the business.

- Have no fear of failure, have the courage of your convictions.
- Be steadfast—listen to others but don't let anyone shake your real feelings.
- *Luck is a major factor,* but the harder you work, the better the luck.
- Push yourself to the limits, especially when you're young, and you're only young once.
- Music has no barriers of category or geography. In the end, remember there are only two types of music: good and bad.

Jann Wenner

FOUNDER OF *ROLLING STONE*

Did you have a mentor or someone who inspired you? If so, what have you learned from that person?

I was inspired by Ralph J. Gleason, who was a very well-known jazz critic for the *San Francisco Chronicle* in the fifties and sixties. He was the first jazz critic to recognize what was going on with the new rock 'n' roll. He was the first to start writing about Dylan and the Beatles, and to take these artists seriously because they had a lot to say about society, culture, and the youth of the day. Many people ridiculed him for that position, all of his jazz fans, but he was right. He also went on to be the major defender of rock in the press, leading the crusade to save the San Francisco rock scene, i.e., Bill Graham, from the San Francisco police department.

I met Ralph when I was a student at the University of California, Berkeley. I was writing a column myself and was reading his columns all the time. I finally strolled up to him one day at an early Family Dog dance in San Francisco, with Jefferson Airplane and a bunch of others. I introduced myself, and we became fast friends. Finally, when the time came and I started *Rolling Stone,* I started it with him mentoring me, giving me advice, and putting in some of the money.

One of the principal things I learned from him was the need for accuracy in journalism, in writing and reporting. Get the facts, no matter how small they are—make them all right. Put the extra time into getting the details right. If the person was a mile away, don't say half a mile, or three miles, or a long distance. The other thing was to put it all in perspective. Learn from history. All the things that we see generally have happened before, in some form or another. Slash didn't invent guitar playing. Jerry Garcia wasn't the most brilliant guitar player ever. There were plenty of people who preceded them, like Django Reinhardt, Charlie Christian. So before you start shooting off your mouth, learn history and get perspective.

What was your very first job in the music industry, and how did you get it?

I had been offered to start the Rogers & Cowan rock department, because I had been writing articles for a magazine in San Francisco. They were going to give me a free Porsche—can you imagine what that was like in 1967? I was going to move to L.A., live in Laurel Canyon, and have a Porsche as a company car. I turned them down to start *Rolling Stone*. I turned down some good opportunities, like the Rogers & Cowan thing, because somehow I knew that the other thing is what I wanted to do. I did it by default—I had always been publishing or been around newspapers or journalism. So my knowledge of that field—sketchy as it was as a twenty-year-old—combined with my love of music to start the magazine. Looking back it all makes sense.

What was your first big break? The first great thing that ever happened to you . . .

John and Yoko gave us our first big break for our one-year anniversary issue when they gave us the controversial cover for *Two Virgins.* The album had been banned because of a naked picture they had taken of themselves and used as the cover. At Ralph's suggestion, I sent them a telex and said we would publish it. They agreed, sent it over, and we published it. That got us our first press coverage, our first sell-out issue, the first time I had to go back to press, the first thing that made everybody sit up and pay attention. In the next issue, I wrote an editorial talking about all the things that happened around that super exclusive, ending with the most important lesson of all—"Print a famous foreskin, and the world will beat a path to your door."

What elements of your job make you want to go to work every day?

Enjoying the people I work with. Having a job I love that I can go and do, or walk away from and go travel. I can go back and forth—I'm not locked in.

The opportunity to meet people. In this particular job you can meet almost anybody—politicians, presidents, musicians, actors, businessmen—just a fascinating world of talent.

I still have things to say. I still want to have a voice in what people are thinking, what they're reading about, what they care about. I want to have a voice in the direction the country is headed in, and to have an opportunity to affect that in some way by what we choose to publish, what issues we choose to focus on, and how hard. More than anything, I still have a sense of mission about it, the importance of rock 'n' roll, music, and the importance of certain political beliefs that I have. That sense of mission keeps me going.

Having fun, too . . . If it wasn't fun, I couldn't handle it.

What qualities most helped you get to where you are today?

You have to have an intuitive sense of the job. You have to be able to just feel it and recognize what the right thing to do is. I have a good intuitive sense about what's a good story, what's a good cover, what's a good photograph, or what will appeal to people. Just like a musician knows what music he wants to make. You hear what feels right for you. If you have to second-guess every step that you're making, you're never going to really break through. You're constantly questioning, not sure where you're going, you can't do things as rapidly and effectively. If you can quickly recognize what's right, and act on it, you can get a lot more done. It also means that you're good in that field, that you have talent.

You also need a sense of purpose and mission like I talked about above. You have to love what you do. And you have to be willing to work hard.

If you knew everything at the beginning of your career that you know now, what would you have done differently?

There are all kinds of small things, but those are primarily logistical things I would have done differently. In terms of fundamentally making different choices, no. The only thing I might have changed if I look back would be the drugs. As much fun as they were at some point, they're also an incredible waste of time and energy. I think I could have gotten a lot more done without them.

What is your greatest lesson learned?

Trust your gut. Intuition is about recognizing what is right, but gut is slightly different. You feel it when there are big decisions you have to make, when there are certain roads you should or shouldn't take, about people you should and shouldn't be associated with. Whenever you make a decision, and they can be big ones (particularly in people judgments, strategic judgments, or accepting an offer), and it turns out to be a mistake, nine out of ten times you can look back and say, "I knew it at the time!" It's this feeling in the stomach, that you were doing the wrong thing, or something was not right. Nine or ten out of ten times, your gut will always tell you if something smells good or bad. Of course, you can always override it with ambition, ego, vanity, or any of the other things that get in the way. . . .

What are some of your favorite albums?

To name a few artists—Otis, Howard Tate, all the Motown stuff, the Stax stuff, Sam Cooke is just out of this world, the Beatles, the Stones, Van Morrison, Paul Simon, Dusty Springfield. They're all great artists of a particular time. And the great fucking singing of Bob Dylan. I love his lyrics and the way he sings. He's got the most fascinating voice. Then after that, John Lennon and Mick. The thing I most respond to is R&B, and with the exception of Bob, everyone I mentioned is R&B rooted.

Some favorite albums are . . .

Highway 61 Revisited and *Blonde on Blonde,* Bob Dylan
Moondance, Van Morrison

Sticky Fingers and *Let It Bleed,* the Rolling Stones

Did you have any posters on your bedroom walls as a kid? Of whom?

I was a teenager before they invented posters.

What are some great shows you've seen?

> The Stones. I've seen so many great Stones shows—a couple that really stand out are at Roseland last year, at the old Inglewood Forum in the seventies, and at the San Jose Civic Auditorium in 1965.
> Bruce Springsteen's first New York show after 9/11
> Bob Dylan, Van Morrison, Monterey Pop, and so on. I have been so lucky.

What are some of your favorite songs?

> There are so many great songs I can't even begin. With favorite music you'll find that people like what they heard between the ages of eighteen and twenty-five. Those things stick with them the rest of their life.

List up to ten things that could be helpful to someone breaking into the business.

- Have something you want to say.
- Be good at it.
- Work hard.
- Get it right. Don't be half-assed.
- Do something of real value that's meaningful.
- Be true to yourself and your own vision.
- Look sharp, dress well. And wash your hands . . . seriously.
- Above all, have a good time.

PRODUCERS & SONGWRITERS

Dallas Austin

Did you have a mentor or someone who inspired you? If so, what have you learned from that person?

My first mentor was my brother Claude. He was a drummer. Both of my brothers played in bands, and they always had band equipment set up in the downstairs playroom area so they could rehearse for gigs. At the same time, my mom and my family owned nightclubs and restaurants. In that day, during segregation, Tina Turner, James Brown, anybody, they'd come into my dad's and they'd dance at our place. So it's kind of always been there. I'd go in and mess around with the deejay's records, seeing the bands set up in our club all the time.

Most of all, my stepdad was Jimmy Nolan, who played all the guitar licks in James Brown's band for all those years, all those funk licks. So I was kind of sucked in by the club and Jimmy. I didn't have a choice really.

What was your very first job in the music industry, and how did you get it?

My first real job other than playing in bands was when I moved to Atlanta working with this band, Princess & Starbreeze. I started running lights for the band, doing some of the light rigs. At the same time, I was using the equipment in the daytime to write my songs. The producer they were signed to, Joyce Irving, one day came and heard stuff I was doing, and said, "Whoa, this kid is doing that?" I was like sixteen, seventeen, and all the band members got jealous and stuff. They got pissed off, so I started working at this other little studio called Gold Dog. I was doing whatever they asked me to do, at the same time, I was always making tracks at home.

Debra Killings was the lead singer and bass player of that band. Now, basically, on every record I've done she's done all my singing and backgrounds.

What was your first big break? The first great thing that ever happened to you . . .

It was after I recorded my first song on Joyce Irving, which was a song called "Hey Mr. DJ." It wasn't before that, because while I felt the Princess & Starbreeze stuff, this was the first record. I did two songs on there actually. That was when it was like, wow. Right after I did "Hey Mr. DJ" on Joyce Irving and Dougie Fresh, I was in L.A., sitting up in the hills because I like to go watch the light show from Mulholland. So at the same time I went up there and said, "Wow, look at this city," I'm in this Corolla listening to the AM radio station and the "Mr. DJ" record comes on. It's funny, ever since then, I've noticed that subconsciously or something, after every album I finish I end up in L.A. right on that same path listening to it.

What elements of your job make you want to go to work every day?

The feeling you get when you make a song that you know might be very clever or very good. It's a certain style, and when you hit it, it's a feeling that you just can't pay for. That's why I think for me I've never wanted to have a sound as a producer, because I'm the kind of person who gets bored. I never had a sound. Instead, I would always chase that same feeling. But that feeling never came from reloading the same kicks and snares or guitars—it came from whatever cleverness I had to figure out in that song. And then the fact that somebody else might not like it.

What qualities most helped you get to where you are today?

Songwriting, and the fact that for my era, I was the most universal in a sense. I didn't understand when I got into it that the writer and the producer were different people. I didn't know that you were supposed to make one kind of music. I thought as a producer you were supposed to do whatever you felt for that artist. I like Prince, U2, and Run-D.M.C. Since I liked all of them, I figured out early that if you're working with a rap group, it should sound like a rap record. If you're working with a rock band, it should sound like a rock song. That's been my thing. I've been able to be free.

If you knew everything at the beginning of your career that you know now, what would you have done differently?

Maybe a couple of mistakes . . . but then again, every bad thing I've done, or every business mistake, or getting ripped off . . . it's like being in college. All of those things are lessons for you to learn how to protect and value your work to get it where it needs to be.

What is your greatest lesson learned?

You have to know what you want. It's not about knowing what everybody else or the next person wants, it's about knowing what you want. If you don't know what you want, you get yourself in trouble. You know, if you want a hundred dollars to do four songs, that's your business. You're the one who has to do four songs. So, the most valuable lesson is to know what you want. Know where you want to get to, and then use your mentality, your work, and your relationships to get there.

More important than anything, I've never worked with a person that I really didn't like. A lot of times if you do that, you don't care if you stick 'em or they stick you. It's just a mess. I only really deal with people I like, people who my energy flows good with, and people who like me too.

What are some of your favorite albums?

> A great, clever record is where the meaning is not on the sleeve, but when you understand it, it blows you away.
>
> *Nevermind,* Nirvana
>
> *1999,* Prince
>
> *Blood Sugar Sex Magik,* the Red Hot Chili Peppers. The Chili Peppers are my favorite band of all time. They're an incredible, over-the-top amazing band.
>
> *System of a Down,* System of a Down
>
> *Dark Side of the Moon,* Pink Floyd

Did you have any posters on your bedroom walls as a kid? Of whom?

> KISS, Prince, George Clinton (a big white poster with all this smoke around him), Rick James, Chili Peppers, the Smiths, Ministry.

What are some great shows you've seen?

> Depeche Mode, *101*
>
> Marilyn Manson, the *Dope Show.* I expected it to be a lot less organized. It sounded incredible, and was one of the best sounding concerts I've ever been to, as far as the low end, and the guitars, and the vocals. Everything sounded perfect. His vocals were perfect. I think a lot of people who went to see it were so subdued. This was an act, with the costume changes, and his vocals, everything was perfect. Nobody was idiotic; everybody knew what was happening up there.
>
> U2, *Popmart*
>
> Arrested Development, Masquerade, Atlanta. I felt like people were floating around the room. I'd never seen that energy. It was the most eclectic mix and the most uplifting show I've been to still. I think the kids had never seen anything like it.

What are some of your favorite songs?

> "Money," Pink Floyd
>
> "Genius of Love," Talking Heads
>
> "Smells Like Teen Spirit," Nirvana
>
> "Edge of Seventeen (Just Like the White Winged Dove)," Stevie Nicks. I used to think she was saying, "Just like the one we love." I didn't know the real words until I started working with her. So all these years I was singing, "Just like the one we love," and then when I learned the real lyrics, it just blew me away.

List up to ten things that could be helpful to someone breaking into the business.

- ■ It's important to be unique, but it's also important to show them that you're able to follow right in the cusp of what's happening.
- ■ Don't be afraid to admire other people.
- ■ Don't be afraid to like a song. Don't be afraid to say, "I want to make a song like that," or "I want to make a record that sounds as good as that." I think one thing that happens is that once you "make it," once you're considered one of "them," a lot of people lose respect for other people's work. They stop admiring someone, they stop admiring James Brown or this person or that person, and it becomes "I'm the shit" or special or something. And when you do that, you start to cut yourself off because you're cutting off any influences. There's nothing better than influences that are happening right now around you, not just legendary ones, but ones you could look over to the left and say, "Damn, that shit is really good, I wish I had done that." It keeps you striving. It keeps you inspired.

Glen Ballard

Did you have a mentor or someone who inspired you? If so, what have you learned from that person?

Quincy Jones is both my teacher and my inspiration. His arrangements are always interesting, ever-evolving, very dense but very clear, and always communicate the emotion of the song. His vast musicality and mastery of so many forms always motivated me to be on my game when I was writing for him and when we were in the studio. I always wanted to come in prepared, always wanted to do my best for him. I learned so many things from him, from subtle but important shadings in musical textures to how to feature a vocal in a musical "bed"; but on a macro scale the two most important things were these: (a) the song is the blueprint for failure or success in a record and (b) he showed me how to create a warm and encouraging atmosphere in which creativity could thrive. You always felt you could raise the bar higher than you ever had and get over it with Quincy there.

What was your very first job in the music business, and how did you get it?

My first job was as a gofer for the members of the Elton John band. I tried to make myself useful until they discovered that I was a musician. James Newton Howard was Elton's keyboardist, and heard me playing one day and was sufficiently impressed to recommend me for some session work, and Davey Johnstone was responsible for getting my first *Billboard* chart single as a writer with the artist Kiki Dee. I got the job through an improbable series of events. My uncle knew the golf pro at the Bel Air country club, Eddie Merrons, and gave me his number when I came to California. I called Eddie and he suggested I contact one of his golfing students, a musician and studio owner named Sal "Tutti" Camarata. Tutti generously allowed me to meet with him at Sunset Sound Recorders in Hollywood, where many great records have been made. I discovered we shared a passion for the French composer Erik Satie, and Tutti was in the process of recording some of his work. He subsequently hired me to sing on some of his classical recordings (not Satie). As it happened his studio manager was just going to work for Elton John, and through that connection I found my way to that camp. At the time Elton was the biggest artist in the world, so my great good fortune cannot be overstated!

What elements of your job make you want to go to work every day?

I write almost every day, or make recordings of something I have written. The joy of making music creates that best of all places to be when you're working with inspiration and intent, what Steely Dan called "Time Out of Mind." You look up and it's ten or twelve hours later, and you're exhausted, but you have something (hopefully) beautiful to show for it.

What qualities most helped you get to where you are today?

I'm organized and focused, and music and poetry were things I was interested in and showed some affinity for from an early age. The combination of being disciplined in doing something that comes naturally is probably key.

If you knew everything at the beginning of your career that you know now, what would you have done differently?

I have no regrets.

What is your greatest lesson learned?

A percentage of the net in music means you may actually get paid, whereas in film it means you will not.

What are some of your favorite albums?

Electric Ladyland, Jimi Hendrix

Aja, Steely Dan

If I Could Only Remember My Name, David Crosby

Sgt. Pepper's Lonely Hearts Club Band, the Beatles

It's Only Rock 'n' Roll, the Rolling Stones

Thriller, Michael Jackson

Tanto Tempo, Bebel Gilberto

Music, Madonna

Mellon Collie and the Infinite Sadness, the Smashing Pumpkins

Death Row's Snoop Doggy Dogg Greatest Hits, Snoop Doggy Dogg

Did you have any posters on your bedroom walls as a kid? Of whom?

I was a little strange. I had *National Geographic* maps (they came every issue) all over my room.

What are some great shows you've seen?

Jerry Lee Lewis, Jughead Jones, Vidalia, Louisiana, circa 1960

James Brown and the Famous Flames, Jackson, Mississippi, 1966

Jimi Hendrix Experience, Baton Rouge, Louisiana, 1967 (I actually met him! Blew my mind, as he was and remains my favorite artist.)

Led Zeppelin, New Orleans, 1969

Elton John, fifty times, 1975–76 (Elton *always* gave it up.)

Queen, the Forum, Los Angeles, 1975

Roxy Music, Los Angeles, mid-eighties

Michael Jackson, Madison Square Garden, 1987

What are some of your favorite songs?

"As Time Goes By," Dooley Wilson (Herman Hupfeld)

"Come Fly with Me," Frank Sinatra (Sammy Cahn and Jimmy Van Heusen)

"Julia," the Beatles (John Lennon and Paul McCartney)

"The Thrill Is Gone," B.B. King (Roy Hawkins and Rick Darnell)

"Still Crazy After All These Years," Paul Simon (Paul Simon)

"A Whiter Shade of Pale," Procol Harum (Gary Brooker and Keith Reid)

"One Step Up," Bruce Springsteen (Bruce Springsteen)

"I'm Not in Love," 10cc (Kevin Godley and Lol Crème)

"Silent All These Years," Tori Amos (Tori Amos)

"So Far Away," Carole King (Carole King)

"I Can't Make You Love Me," Bonnie Raitt (Mike Reid and A. Shamblin)

Desmond Child

Did you have a mentor or someone who inspired you? If so, what have you learned from that person?

Laura Nyro and Bob Crewe. Laura inspired me to allow my imagination to flow in a nonlinear way: first the chords, then a melody, then lyrics, then the title . . . which may have nothing to do with lyrics. Bob taught me to write by strict Brill building rules: song title first, the lyrics that lead seamlessly to the title, then the melody, finally the chords. I swim between these two shores.

What was your very first job in the music industry, and how did you get it?

When I was seventeen I had a folk-pop duo called Nightchild with Virgil Night. We sang for our supper (a slice of cheesecake) at the Joyous Lake Café in Woodstock, New York. Our very first night we got discovered by Bernard Stollman, owner of an indie jazz label called ESP Records. He gave me a job packing twelve-inch LPs for shipping in exchange for letting us live free in his country house. He also bought me a big, old, brown upright piano where I wrote night and day.

What was your first big break? The first great thing that ever happened to you . . .

My first break was getting booked into the ultrachic New York cabaret Reno Sweeney by owner Eliot Hubbard as an opening act for cabaret diva Ellen Greene with my singing group Desmond Child & Rouge in 1976. This led to us getting signed by Capitol Records, where we made two albums and appeared as the musical guest on *Saturday Night Live*'s Christmas Show in 1979.

What elements of your job make you want to go to work every day?

I love to sit down and write a song. To me this is my prayer . . . my connection to God. After the song is written . . . the nightmare begins and from demo to final released product the process often becomes a living hell. What keeps me going is remembering the spirit in the song . . . the goose bumps I felt when those magic words stumbled from my lips and I cried out into the night . . ."*Livin' la vida loca!*"

What qualities most helped you get to where you are today?

I grew up poor in the projects of Liberty City in Miami . . . I don't take anything for granted. I start my career over every day. Nothing I ever did before counts. I'm never bored . . . wherever I am I find something to learn.

If you knew everything at the beginning of your career that you know now, what would you have done differently?

What I would have done differently was to really be myself. Looking back I realize that as an artist I was afraid of being judged for being gay, and so I hid not only that part of myself but so much of the beauty of who I am behind a fake macho facade. So I got the opposite effect: instead of being strong I appeared weak. This undermined my self-esteem. This is probably the reason I stayed behind the scenes as a songwriter/producer, which was a safer place where I could be a star vicariously through the artists I work with.

What is your greatest lesson learned?

The greatest lesson I learned is that the truth is either black or white . . . there is no gray about it. This can apply to all aspects of life. Living this way can sometimes make you temporarily unpopular, but in the end you'll be the one everybody respects.

What are some of your favorite albums?

Amoroso, João Gilberto

Love Deluxe, Sade

Christmas and the Beads of Sweat,
   Laura Nyro

Blue, Joni Mitchell

Tumbleweed Connection, Elton John

So Long So Wrong, Alison Krauss

Did you have any posters on your bedroom walls as a kid? Of whom?

When I was thirteen years old I was obsessed with Cher and had her pictures all over my room . . . this is the bobcat-vest-and-bangs Cher. The only problem was trying to figure out if I wanted to have sex with her or *be* her!

What are some great shows you've seen?

Laura Nyro, University of Miami, 1970

Janis Joplin, West Palm Beach Rock
   Festival, 1970

Jimi Hendrix, Gulf Stream Raceway, 1970

Bruce Springsteen, Madison Square
   Garden, 1979

Peter Allen & the Rockets, Radio City Music
   Hall, 1981

Madonna, *Blonde Ambition* tour,
   Los Angeles, 1992

Bon Jovi, Meadowlands, New Year's
   Eve, 1986

Aerosmith, Meadowlands, 1987

Ozzy Osbourne, *Moscow Peace
   Festival,* 1989

What are some of your favorite songs?

"The Look of Love," "Walk On By," and "Alfie," Burt Bacharach and Hal David

"Natural Woman," Carole King, Gerry Goffin, Jerry Wexler

"Emmie," Laura Nyro

"The Way We Were," Marilyn Bergman, Alan Bergman, and Marvin Hamlisch

"To Sir with Love," Don Black and Mark London

"Eleanor Rigby," Paul McCartney and John Lennon

"Because You Love Me," Diane Warren

List up to ten things that could be helpful to someone breaking into the business.

- Choose an aspect of the business or an artistic career that inspires you.
- Move to a music-business city like New York, Los Angeles, London, or Nashville.
- Get to know everyone from the secretaries to the power players.
- Set up your business as you would any business: Invest in your career.
- Have a ball, make it fun. This is your ride!!

Terry Date

Did you have a mentor or someone who inspired you? If so, what have you learned from that person?

I was inspired by underground radio in the early seventies.

What was your very first job in the music industry, and how did you get it?

I was at the University of Idaho when a friend, John Ranlein, from the student radio station asked me to record coffeehouse open mics for broadcast. Instead, I took the gear to the local bars and recorded the cowboy bands that came through town.

What was your first big break? The first great thing that ever happened to you . . .

As an engineer it was when a friend, Paul Speer, set me up with a Seattle, Washington, studio owner, Steve Lawson, to work the night shift. The only question at the job interview was, "Will you steal my mics?" I said, "Probably not." As a producer, Metal Church hired me as an engineer, but gave me production credit on their first record. From that point on I was a producer/engineer.

What elements of your job make you want to go to work every day?

The uncertainty of what will happen. There is always a new sound or a better performance.

What qualities most helped you get to where you are today?

Concentration and patience.

What is your greatest lesson learned?

Never get too high or too low.

What are some of your favorite albums?

Around the Fur, the Deftones

Vulgar Display of Power, Pantera

Badmotorfinger, Soundgarden

Apple, Mother Love Bone

Did you have any posters on your bedroom walls as a kid? Of whom?

Various black-light fuzzy things.

What are some great shows you've seen?

Pink Floyd, 1985

Rush opening for KISS, 1974

The Clash opening for the Who

Limptropolis, Limp Bizkit

What are some of your favorite songs?

I have a hard time thinking of a favorite song. I have always listened to and work on full albums of music.

List up to ten things that could be helpful to someone breaking into the business.

Work hard, work often, work cheap.

Lamont Dozier

Did you have a mentor or someone who inspired you? If so, what have you learned from that person?

I did not have a mentor, but I was inspired by doo-wop groups like Pookie Hudson and the Spaniels, the Flamingos, and the Platters. I was also tremendously inspired by gospel acts like Sam Cooke and the Soul Stirrers. The lead singers of these particular groups were stylists and had distinctive sounds that were recognizable, so very early on I learned that in order to be successful, you had to have a sound and be different.

What was your very first job in the music industry, and how did you get it?

My very first job was in 1960 at Anna Records, where I was hired to pack records and to be a custodian. They needed singers for a group—the Voice Masters—who had lost two of their members, and they had auditions to fill those spaces. I needed to earn a living along with the spot in the Voice Masters, so they gave me that job too.

What was your first big break? The first great thing that ever happened to you . . .

My very first break professionally came when I was fifteen years old in 1957 with a group that I had called the Romeos. We were signed to a small label called Fox Records and had a regional hit with a song called "Fine Fine Baby," which I wrote and produced as well as sang on in the group. Atco bought the group from Fox Records, and we got to position 60 on the national *Billboard* charts with "Fine Fine Baby." That was the first great thing that ever happened to me. Some people would consider this my first job in the music industry, I consider it my first break and the Anna Records job, my first job, even though that came after the Romeos.

What elements of your job make you want to go to work every day?

There are a lot of creative challenges in the business of songwriting that really get my juices flowing: thinking about writing a hit song, being able to express myself, and having the ability to touch people with what I've created is a wonderful feeling. These are the elements that drive me, and I am still a practicing songwriter learning something new each time I sit down at the piano.

What qualities most helped you get to where you are today?

In this business of rejection I found that the quality of persistence is one that a songwriter must have in order to succeed.

If you knew everything at the beginning of your career that you know now, what would you have done differently?

I would have taken the time to learn more about the business side of songwriting to understand the value of copyrights.

What is your greatest lesson learned?

One of the greatest lessons I've learned in this business is never to sign a business document without having it looked over by a competent attorney.

What are some of your favorite albums?

Tapestry, Carole King

A Tramp Shining, Richard Harris

I'm Coming Home, Johnny Mathis

Lady in Satin, Billie Holiday

Thriller, Michael Jackson

Did you have any posters on your bedroom walls as a kid? Of whom?

No, any money I might have spent on posters, which I don't even think that they had at the time, would have gone toward food and bus fare.

What are some great shows you've seen?

Michael Jackson's performance of "Billie Jean" at the *Motown 25* special

Purple Rain tour, Prince

What are some of your favorite songs?

"I Can't Make You Love Me," Bonnie Raitt

"I Hope You Dance," Leanne Womack

"All By Myself," Eric Carmen

"The Christmas Song," Nat King Cole

"This Christmas," Donny Hathaway

"Don't Know Why," Norah Jones

List up to ten things that could be helpful to someone breaking into the business.

- Leave no stone unturned, knock on every door.
- Let rejection be your fuel instead of discouraging you.
- Learn as much about the business as you can and stay current, know who runs the business, who works where, names and places, and their credits in the industry.
- Know your music history.

Jermaine Dupri

Did you have a mentor or someone who inspired you? If so, what have you learned from that person?

Teddy Riley and Herbie Luv Bug were my inspirations. I learned a lot from them by just watching.

What was your very first job in the music industry, and how did you get it?

My first job in the industry was with a group called Silk Tymes Leather. I got them signed to Warner Bros.

What was your first big break? The first great thing that ever happened to you . . .

My first break was with the group called Kris Kross. . . . Major success.

What elements of your job make you want to go to work every day?

The growing of new artists and the excitement of those that hear my music.

What qualities most helped you get to where you are today?

Skill, listening, and hard work.

If you knew everything at the beginning of your career that you know now, what would you have done differently?

A hundred different things. I always believed that when you blow, everything falls into place but that's not true.

What is your greatest lesson learned?

The greatest lesson I learned was to really watch all my business 'cause no one will do it like you will.

What are some of your favorite albums?

Thriller, Michael Jackson

The Chronic, Dr. Dre

My Way, Usher

My first album

Life After Death, the Notorious B.I.G.

Did you have any posters on your bedroom walls as a kid? Of whom?

My room was covered with everybody that was hot.

What are some great shows you've seen?

Can You Feel It and Victory tours, the Jackson 5
Raisin' Hell, Run-D.M.C
Earth, Wind & Fire

What are some of your favorite songs?

"In the Heat of the Night," Phil Collins   "Don't Stop Till You Get Enough,"
"That's the Way Love Goes," Janet Jackson   Michael Jackson
"One More Chance," the Notorious B.I.G.

List up to ten things that could be helpful to someone breaking into the business.

- Listen to others.
- Don't pay attention to negative statements.
- Have somebody you look up to, so you can learn from their mistakes.
- Always work hard and don't try to cut corners.
- Ask questions.

Emilio Estefan Jr.

Did you have a mentor or someone who inspired you? If so, what have you learned from that person?

I've had a lot of mentors, but the main ones that influenced my career were Quincy Jones and Phil Ramone. When you talk about the history of American music, you have to talk about these guys, and I was lucky enough to work with both of them. They combined for me the most talented producers with such incredible creative ability and the most wonderful human beings. In order to be a good producer you have to have some elements of humanity, which they do. Quincy did so much for black music. I learned talking to him that you have to fight for your own sound, no matter what else. That's the only way you can leave a legacy. I think we have a lot of things in common. My background is Latin music, and we were rejected so many times because we had a Latino sound. One thing that I feel proud about is that I didn't let anyone persuade me to change my sound. The most important thing was that I kept my voice; I never forgot where I came from. Having a number-one hit is great, but having a number-one hit with integrity can make your people proud.

What was your very first job in the music industry, and how did you get it?

The first one was my own band. We played at parties and conventions, and then I decided to record our first album. I went to the studio, and I knew that I wanted to be the producer at the time because I wanted to preserve our sound. I didn't want anybody coming in from outside and trying to change it. When I was twenty-four, I was lucky enough to produce my first album, which was half in English, half in Spanish. The single was number-one on the charts for three months.

What was your first big break? The first great thing that ever happened to you . . .

We went to Holland and were promoting the single "Dr. Beat." We had only two songs in English at the time, which we played. The people wanted more, so I turned to Gloria and told her, "Let's do a conga, a typical Cuban conga." We did, and for half an hour, I saw people dancing like you wouldn't believe. I told Gloria, "We definitely have something different from everybody else." I was so happy to see that music had no language. I was convinced that what we were doing was the right thing.

So I went to the studio to record "Conga." When I went to my label, they rejected it. They said it would never work. They said it was not Latino enough and not Anglo enough. I said, it's what we are, so put it out. They did, and it became a huge hit worldwide.

That proved you have to go with your heart and do what you feel is right. You have to do what is good for you and has integrity. Without integrity, it will not translate to sales.

What elements of your job make you want to go to work every day?

The pride. I hope that I can be a role model for a lot of Latinos in this country. I have been lucky enough to do six crossovers—Gloria, Jon Secada, Ricky Martin, Jennifer Lopez, Marc Anthony, Shakira. I am extremely happy. These crossovers have all translated to sales, not only in the States, but worldwide. Doing this, I reinvent my career over and over again, and I get the same excitement that I did the first time many years ago. It's a wonderful feeling, when you've made a record, and you're seeing the same shows, and the crowds—it's an incredible rush, and I love it. Every day is a new day, to me and to my music.

What qualities most helped you get to where you are today?

I create my own sounds. It's the fusion, because we were immigrants from Cuba who grew up in the States. We listened to all kinds of music—from R&B to rock, pop, ballads. I integrated all these sounds into one sound, and that's what makes me different.

Working closely with artists is another thing. As a producer, you have to be open to listening to them. You want to make sure they feel like they have a voice throughout the process. I think that has been my forte as a producer. The people I have produced have come back again and again—we don't just make one album, we make four, five, or six albums. I've been very lucky.

If you knew everything at the beginning of your career that you know now, what would you have done differently?

I wouldn't do anything differently because I stuck to my ground. When they told me "This won't work," I said, "Well, you have to put it out." I took big risks. If it didn't work, at least I tried with integrity and loyalty, to a sound, to my roots, to where I came from. I think that's what was most important. They told me it would never work, and it worked! I think that my career in some way will be a great thing for Latino people, telling them that if you believe in something, don't ever let anyone change your mind. Don't let anybody from A&R or from a record label tell you not to do it. Take a chance. I take full responsibility. If I am going to win, I want to win believing in what I am doing. It is better to lose believing in yourself, than to win without that faith.

What is your greatest lesson learned?

Be persistent. Give it everything you have. Don't be afraid to show your talents. Believe in what you do. Be unique. Don't try to copy anybody's sounds. Make your own trip. Write your own way, because in the end, when you look at your career over many years, you're going to feel proud. I think that's important.

What are some of your favorite albums?

Songs in the Key of Life, Stevie Wonder

Did you have any posters on your bedroom walls as a kid? Of whom?

I was an immigrant kid who had to leave Cuba when I was thirteen. My mind was in a different place. I was more worried about eating and surviving. So I didn't have any posters, but I had a lot of dreams.

I think I came to the United States and fulfilled the American dream. I am proud of this country. I am proud of my career. I will always be thankful to this country.

What are some great shows you've seen?

Tina Turner, Germany, early nineties—amazing
Stevie Wonder, Los Angeles
Santana, at a Grammy party
Celia Cruz—Celia was always someone I admired. When I was first asked whom I'd like to
  work with, I said "Celia Cruz." It was a dream to work with her. I directed her videos. What
  was amazing about her to me was that she didn't age. Whenever you saw her, even when she
  was close to eighty years old, she didn't look like she'd ever aged. She moved people, she
  touched people, and she made people feel. I saw her perform once in Chile, and it was mind-
  blowing. She had the whole crowd going.

What are some of your favorite songs?

"El Dia Que Me Quieras," Carlos Gardel (Carlos Gardel and Alfredo le Pera)

List up to ten things that could be helpful to someone breaking into the business.

- It is definitely harder now to break in as a producer, with everything that is going on in the music business. At the same time, we cannot live without music. If we have to do things with
  smaller budgets, that's okay. Music is the core of our lives.
- Be persistent, be ambitious, and do your own thing. What is most important in producing is to
  create your own sounds. The only way you can translate music into sales is if you're doing
  something nobody's doing. Always do from your heart and with the best quality that you can.
  People are smart. They know when something is made with honesty. You don't have to always
  reinvent yourself. They know when you are working from your heart.

Bob Ezrin

Did you have a mentor or someone who inspired you? If so, what have you learned from that person?

My uncle, Syd, who was a lawyer by occupation but a music fanatic by avocation. He was the first guy in Toronto to have stereo. He had the largest privately owned jazz collection in Toronto (and probably all of Canada). He was also part owner of a coffee house where folk music was played all the time. So I had the great benefit of growing up in my uncle's basement rifling through records, learning the smell of vinyl, playing with tape recorders he had for recording performances, and learning the smell of tape and the feel of a tape recorder and a microphone. I was exposed to all of this—music and the technology of music—at such a young age that it became cellularly ingrained in me. I started discovering things in his basement when I was six or seven, and made my first recording when I was eight. At age eight, I also did TV and radio work as a kid actor/singer, so I got my first exposure to really big studios at the same time.

From Syd, I learned that both music and the media that held it were sacred—to be honored and cared for—and that the privilege of being able to listen to great performances captured in the purest possible way was something that I needed to cherish. I also learned that jazz was beautiful, detailed, deep, articulate, picturesque, intellectual, and emotional, all at the same time. That set the stage for me for all other forms of music. I was trained classically, but the exposure to jazz really informed me, and gave me the intelligence and appreciation necessary to go on and produce rock and pop records.

What was your very first job in the music industry, and how did you get it?

My first paid production was *Love It to Death* with Alice Cooper in 1971. At that time I was working for Nimbus 9 Productions as an assistant to Jack Richardson, who was the producer for the Guess Who. Alice Cooper approached Jack to produce the albums, but Jack was in his forties and didn't understand Alice Cooper at all. I saw them play live and just fell in love, and made all kinds of noise at the office about how we had to do this. Eventually, Jack said, "Enough, already. If you like it so much, you do it." That was the door that opened for me. I was allowed to do four songs with them, to see if I was any good. One of those songs was "Eighteen," which was Alice's first hit.

What was your first big break? The first great thing that ever happened to you . . .

In terms of when I realized something special was happening, I realized that at age eight. I was a really lucky kid and am a really lucky guy. I have been blessed with amazing opportunities and exposure to the most wonderful and varied things from my parents, to my uncle, to the things going on in Toronto when I was growing up. I always knew something special was happening. I never doubted myself at that stage—I only learned to doubt myself later.

My big break was getting hired by Nimbus 9. Everything started happening for me after that. They paid for me to go to school at Eastman School of Music to learn production. My teachers were Phil Ramone and Dave Greene. Phil took a liking to me right off the bat. We formed a relationship that's endured till now. What an amazing opportunity to work with Phil Ramone at nineteen years of age, and to learn the art of remote recording from him. Dave Greene continued to mentor me for years thereafter.

What elements of your job make you want to go to work every day?

I believe that production is essentially the management of artistic people and their ideas toward the creation of a coherent work, whether it's an album, a play, a film, or even sometimes a book. What makes it great to go to work every day is that following that rule, my job is working with creative, unique, and stimulating people on artful projects. What could be more rewarding or fun than that? There are some drier components to production, but they are far outweighed by the excitement of the interaction with special people and special ideas.

Producers are artistic people, too, but our art is primarily the handling of people. Keep in mind that I said *artistic people,* and not *artists*. Not everybody who can sing or play the guitar is an artist. I actually banned that word from the studio. I say, "I'll tell you what—when your name is Rembrandt or Pavarotti, I'll call you an artist. But for now, as far as I am concerned, you're the singer. Or you're the lead guitar player. That's it, and that's good enough." What a great job.

What qualities most helped you get to where you are today?

The most important character trait that got me to where I am today is empathy. I have a special ability to put myself in the other person's place. I am extremely sensitive to what's going on inside the people I am working with. And I am able to be sensitive to numerous people at once while also being sensitive to the music and the process. After that, you have to have vision, and a sense of organization to back that up. You also have to have dogged determination, perseverance, an inhuman level of patience (because otherwise you'd kill people), and in my case, one of the things I've developed that has been among the greatest aids to me as a producer is a loss of ego. As a kid, I had the same ego as any upstart kid has, but I learned pretty quickly that what was going on and what people were doing around me was not necessarily all about me. As soon as I got that straight, things didn't bug me as much, and I wasn't so nervous all the time. In the beginning, I wasn't nervous because I had stupid teenage bravado. As I got to realize the level of responsibility I had, I started to worry about it and then came to the conclusion that that in itself was egotistical. It suggested that everybody else was thinking about what I was doing. That's just not true—everybody else is thinking about what they're doing, and they're all worried about getting their jobs done. When you can accept that, you realize that somebody's burst of anger or depression or irritation isn't about you at all. It's about them, and when you realize that, you can be much less sensitive and more empathetic.

If you knew everything at the beginning of your career that you know now, what would you have done differently?

I would have managed my money more wisely. I approached my life exactly the way I approached the art, which was kind of always in the present. I urge anybody who's breathing to try to discipline themselves, or get somebody who'll be disciplined for them, to take care of those details. It sure makes a difference later on in life.

What is your greatest lesson learned?

The most important lesson that I've learned in life is the lesson of NOW—an acronym that came to me when I was preparing a lecture. It stands for:

No ego or expectations.

Open ears, eyes, and heart (empathize).

Wonder and be willing.

You'll get out of your own way, and you'll allow yourself to be what you can be. If you get out of your own way, you can be anything and do anything.

What are some of your favorite albums?

Nelson Eddy's *Willie the Whale*—a profoundly dramatic story set to operatic music . . . my first eyelid movie.

In Spooktacular Stereo, Spike Jones and the Band that Plays for Fun

Rubber Soul and *Revolver*—the latter was a life-altering experience—it made me listen to rock music in a completely different way, and see it as theatrical, and almost cinematic.

The Moody Blues' *In Search of the Lost Chord*—listen to that album, with its brilliant narration and unbelievable orchestration, yet it's rock music with a rock band playing—I think all of that had a huge impact on me, pushing me toward a concept of rock grandeur.

The O'Jays' *Ship Ahoy* gave me a whole new sense of how to marry funk with drama.

Le Mystère des Voix Bulgares, the Bulgarian Women's Choir—otherworldly harmonies and magnificent voices.

Led Zeppelin II gave me a new way of looking at heavy music.

Dark Side of the Moon, Pink Floyd

Who's Next, The Who—the most powerful rock of its time.

Sketches of Spain, Miles Davis

Remain in the Light, the Talking Heads

The Joshua Tree, U2

Three Feet High and Rising, De La Soul—unbelievably inventive, the prototypical hip-hop album.

So, Peter Gabriel—one of the great writers of our time and one of the best voices of any time.

Pet Sounds, the Beach Boys—just plain genius.

The Gray Album, Danger Mouse—the greatest album that never was.

Did you have any posters on your bedroom walls as a kid? Of whom?

No posters. I lived in kind of a garret—it was more of an Indian prayer room than it was a little North American kid's room. I was really into all of that, and back then I liked the paisley, tie-dye, and hippy stuff. I went from beat to hippie, then folkie, then rocker. By that time, I had art on the walls.

What are some great shows you've seen?

The Who, Cow Palace, Toronto, 1968. It's a very small venue. It was unbelievable.

Alice Cooper, Max's Kansas City, 1970. This show changed my life.

Pink Floyd performing *The Wall,* Nassau Coliseum, 1980. I think it was the best rock show ever.

Nusrat Fateh Ali Khan, Universal Amphitheatre, 1996. Transcendant. I was there with Paddy Moloney who pulled out his penny whistle and played along.

Tony Bennett and k.d. lang, 9/15/01, Greek Theatre, Los Angeles. Four days after 9/11. It was a gathering of wounded souls looking for communion. A completely uplifting experience. There wasn't a dry eye in the house.

U2, *Elevation,* Staples Center, 2003. All heart and balls. A wonderfully emotional experience.

Cirque du Soleil, Las Vegas, 2001. Not a concert but the most visually spectacular live show I have ever seen.

What are some of your favorite songs?

"Roundabout," Yes

"Won't Get Fooled Again," the Who

"School's Out," Alice Cooper

"Purple Haze," Jimi Hendrix

"The Times They Are a-Changin'," Bob Dylan

"I Will Always Love You," Dolly Parton

"Reach Out," Four Tops

"Fly Like an Eagle," the Steve Miller Band

"Hotel California," the Eagles

"Doctor Doctor," Thompson Twins

"Cars," Gary Numan

"Wish You Were Here," Pink Floyd

"Mountain Song," Jane's Addiction

"Smells Like Teen Spirit," Nirvana

"Head Like a Hole," Nine Inch Nails

"Do You Know the Way to San Jose" and "Alfie," Dionne Warwick—check out the lyric writing on these songs. Hal David may be the greatest lyricist of all time.

"Strawberry Fields," the Beatles. That song does it all. Listen to it and see how many bars until they repeat themselves. It's eighteen bars! The way we write today, you get four bars and then start repeating yourself. It's an unbelievable song.

List up to ten things that could be helpful to someone breaking into the business.

■ The best way to break into the business right now is to make your own music, or to make your own recordings. Don't try to break in through a major label. Don't try to break in through getting a publishing deal. That's where you go once you've already got something going for yourself. If you start there, you will die there. But if you start out in the real world—making your own music, building your own fan base, creating your own reality—when you get *there,* all you need them for is an assist. If you rely entirely upon a major label, publisher, producer, or manager to create who you are, you'll only last as long as they're interested in you.

■ Don't be jealous of an idea. It suggests that you may never have another.

■ Be open to opportunity. If there is a chance to play, record, listen, or watch—take it. Don't think twice.

■ This whole thing is about a song. Without a song, there is nothing to sing or say. There are no musical parts that matter and there is no production or mixing technique that has any relevance. It all begins there. If you are a writer, then you must concentrate on the song before worrying or wondering about anything else in the process. Too many people start producing a record before the song they are working on is actually finished. Technology makes it easy for everyone to get into production, and it is dangerously seductive. It takes real discipline to finish the song before getting hung up on the details. How many records sound great but have no lasting value because they have no enduring songs?

David Foster

Did you have a mentor or someone who inspired you? If so, what have you learned from that person?

Firstly, my father: not only by teaching me to play the piano, but teaching me, by example, how to be a decent person. Secondly, Tommy Banks—a great musician from Canada. He showed me that a piano player can be more than just a piano player. Take your talent and maximize it. He is now a Canadian senator. Doug Morris, Clive Davis, Jimmy Iovine, and Tommy Mottola, also, for being such great role models. And, finally, B.J. Cooke, a great Canadian singer, and Ric Reynolds, for turning me on to all the different kinds of music.

What was your very first job in the music business, and how did you get it?

I had a dance band when I was thirteen—we would play gigs on the weekends. I was the leader, and I got the jobs by hustling.

What was your first big break? The first great thing that ever happened to you . . .

I thought I would say my band Skylark's hit record "Wildflower" in 1973. But I think the bigger one would be getting the job as the piano player in the *Rocky Horror Show* at the Roxy. That's where I met the musicians that would eventually take me into session work, arranging, writing, and producing.

What elements of your job make you want to go to work every day?

I love music. I love a challenge. I love winning. I hate losing. I love singers. I love this business. I love the chase. I get to do it all. When you stop chasing, you're screwed.

What qualities most helped you get to where you are today?

Being respectful.
Listening—God gave us two ears and only one mouth.
Not getting involved in drugs or drinking.
Talent??
Never forgetting that I came from nothing.

If you knew everything at the beginning of your career that you know now, what would you have done differently?

Not sold my publishing in the eighties.
Built ownership at an earlier age.

My answer was going to be "nothing" because all the successes and failures are who I am today. I probably learned more from my "misses" than from my "hits."

What is your greatest lesson learned?

Do everything from your heart. Whenever I made a move purely for money it always seemed to screw up in some way. The times I ignored the financial gain usually had much greater rewards in every way. Examples: 1. Josh Groban. 2. Natalie Cole and Nat King Cole. 3. *Quest for Camelot*—animated feature which the song "The Prayer" (Celine/Bocelli) came from. 4. Michael Buble and, lately, my charity work, where I constantly have a platform for showcasing new artists.

What are some of your favorite albums?

Blood, Sweat & Tears, Blood, Sweat & Tears   *Revolver,* the Beatles
Greatest Hits, Def Leppard   *West Side Story,* Oscar Peterson
The Nightfly, Donald Fagen

Did you have any posters on your bedroom walls as a kid? Of whom?

My bedroom was the laundry room. Six sisters. Three-bedroom house. No other place for me. I was thrilled to have my own space (three-by-ten feet). But no room for posters.

What are some great shows you've seen?

Yes (the group), Bryan Adams, *A Chorus Line, Lion King,* Alice Cooper.

What are some of your favorite songs?

"Yesterday," the Beatles   "Close to You," the Carpenters
"Send in the Clowns," Stephen Sondheim,   "Photograph," Def Leppard
   from *A Little Night Music*   "Breaking Up Is Hard to Do," Neil Sedaka
"Broken Vow," Lara Fabian & Josh Groban   "The Living Years," Mike and the Mechanics

List up to ten things that could be helpful to someone breaking into the business.

■ The most important: Be prepared. You never know when you'll get a chance to sing for someone or give them a CD. The Boy Scouts got it right!!!
■ Be confident, but be humble.
■ Never forget where you came from.

- Work 24/7 to reach your goals and dreams. And put blinders on.

- Don't do drugs. Sorry about this bit of preaching, but I never did and it became a very powerful weapon to be the only one in the crowd that didn't. It doesn't make me a better person, but it sure gave me the edge.

- Learn about the people who came before you in your profession. If you're a musician, listen to Earth, Wind & Fire or Beethoven's Fifth. If you're an actor, study old scripts like *Citizen Kane* or *On the Waterfront*. Rent all of Marlon Brando's movies. If you're a director, know everything you can about Billy Wilder.

- That saying, "You meet the same people on your way down as you do on the way up" is not bullshit. It's 100 percent true. Be respectful to everyone and I mean *everyone*.

- Give until it hurts. Be charitable. If you don't have money, give your time. If you have both, give both, not just money. Whenever possible, try to do it anonymously. In the end, it feels better.

- Take any job while you're starting out—there's great dignity in flipping burgers, especially when you know that one day you'll own the place.

- Save your money. The sooner you learn that when you earn a dollar you only get to keep fifty cents of it (after taxes), the better off you'll be. Every time you get a check, mentally cut it in half right away—you'll thank me on this one. And finally, always live beneath your means. Don't ever talk about how much money you have once you start becoming successful. Be proud, but don't be braggadocious.

Nellee Hooper

Did you have a mentor or someone who inspired you? If so, what have you learned from that person?

Not so much a mentor but a partner. I had Jazzy in the beginning, later Bono and Björk for the openness of listening, and later Puffy for his work ethic.

What was your very first job in the music industry, and how did you get it?

Playing drums and deejaying. For me it has been a strange journey from being a young punk-rocker playing drums in Bristol to the Grammys!! I guess it started after being a teenage punk, which introduced me to reggae, which then led to funk, and beyond. I then started deejaying with the guys I grew up with under the name the Wild Bunch. We were the cool guys . . . far too cool for school, fearless, we would mix up early rap with dub reggae and punk and funk, all this people later decided to call "trip hop." We had a huge cult following and soon outgrew Bristol, so I left with my partner in crime, DJ Milo, and moved to London; the other guys stayed in Bristol and became Massive Attack and Tricky.

What was your first big break? The first great thing that ever happened to you . . .

In London I started deejaying with Soul II Soul, but the twist happened when Jazzy B and I met Howie B, who was working in the film composer Hans Zimmer's recording studio as a tape operator. Hans Zimmer was recording the movie score to Bertolucci's *The Last Emperor.* We saw our break when Hans and the musicians would leave at midnight. We would sneak into the studio to record our own tracks while they were sleeping and the result was Soul II Soul's "Back to Life." We started playing it at the peak of our deejay set . . . the crowd loved it, and we knew it was our track. Virgin records picked it up, and it went on to be number-one all over the world.

Some really great moments were:

Leaving the studio with the finished version of "Back to Life" and playing it fresh in a club. When my first solo production, Sinéad O'Connor's "Nothing Compares 2 U," was number one. Going to New York City for the first time to play the Palladium with Soul II Soul and half of lower Manhattan was cut off . . . roadblocked.

What elements of your job make you want to go to work every day?

Not having a formula, so every day is like the first day.

What qualities most helped you get to where you are today?

The same ones that stopped me being much more successful. I'm a musical snob and have turned down lots of productions with major artists that I thought weren't cool enough. I guess that's kept some kind of longevity.

Not having formal musical training has helped more than hindered me. I see a "record producer" having the same role as the director of a movie in that you have to see the bigger picture and tell the story. I try to approach every track as a short movie.

Lots of producers (and great producers at that!) have a formula or sound, Jam & Lewis, Trevor Horn, Prince, the Neptunes, etc., but for me every time it's like the first time I've ever seen a recording studio—scary yet challenging. My thing is the challenge, a different genre everytime. The journey is the destination—Soul II Soul, Sinéad O'Connor, Massive Attack, Björk, Madonna, U2, Smashing Pumpkins, No Doubt, P. Diddy . . . where next??!!

I'm the one at the back . . . but it makes it worth it when I hear "hip new record producer" after fifteen years of work.

If you knew everything at the beginning of your career that you know now, what would you have done differently?

I would have done more writing.

What is your greatest lesson learned?

Stick to your instincts. If I would have ever produced anything I didn't like for the money I couldn't have lived with myself.

What are some of your favorite albums?

Innervisions, Stevie Wonder   *Achtung Baby,* U2
What's Going On, Marvin Gaye   *King Tubby Meets Rockers Uptown,*
Pink Flag, Wire   Augustus Pablo
Cut, the Slits

Did you have any posters on your bedroom walls as a kid? Of whom?

Sex Pistols, the Slits, and Big Youth.

What are some great shows you've seen?

U2, *Zooropa,* Wembley Arena   Radiohead, Troubador, Los Angeles

List up to ten things that could be helpful to someone breaking into the business.

Program, but never lose sight of storytelling through the medium of music.

Daniel Lanois

Did you have a mentor or someone who inspired you? If so, what have you learned from that person?

From my brother Bob and Brian Eno . . .

Master a few tools. Maintain the ability to be excited. Always challenge the usual regulations.

What was your very first job in the music industry, and how did you get it?

I started my own recording studio for fun and because I love music. All kinds of music came my way in a natural manner. People started paying me for my work. I was never formally employed.

What was your first big break? The first great thing that ever happened to you . . .

Quite early on in my mom's basement I was lucky enough to record a lot of great people including Rick James and Ian & Sylvia. In the presence of these people my education escalated quickly.

What elements of your job make you want to go to work every day?

My job is ongoingly mysterious to me. I never know where the magic is going to come from. It keeps me on my toes.

What qualities most helped you get to where you are today?

I am a naive spirit. I believe that everybody has something great about them. I also have flashes of inspiration; it's almost a sort of channeling energy. I still don't know exactly where it comes from.

If you knew everything at the beginning of your career that you know now, what would you have done differently?

If I could go back I would study the great songwriting forms of our time. I would make myself an expert in rhyming scheme, song structure, and subject matter.

What is your greatest lesson learned?

Know how to celebrate. Fight the fight that you can win.

What are some of your favorite albums?

Are You Experienced?, Jimi Hendrix   *Got to Give It Up*, Marvin Gaye
    Experience   *Fresh*, Sly & the Family Stone
Kind of Blue, Miles Davis

Did you have any posters on your bedroom walls as a kid? Of whom?

I didn't have any posters in my bedroom. I had lots of vinyl covers that were artistically in-spiring. Like the T. Rex—him in a hat, background out of focus. That blown-out look kept me in-terested.

What are some great shows you've seen?

Sly & the Family Stone in my hometown skating rink around 1970
Sam & Dave (Sam Moore and Dave Prater) in a small club in Toronto
Muddy Waters in Toronto

What are some of your favorite songs?

"Sad-Eyed Lady of the Lowlands," Bob Dylan
"Reach Out," the Four Tops, written by Holland-Dozier-Holland
"Suzanne," Leonard Cohen

List up to ten things that could be helpful to someone breaking into the business.

■ Find out what it is you are most passionate about, work very hard at it, and try to be the best at it.
■ Look for a window of opportunity—for example, figure out a way of making records for cheap while everybody else is spending too much money.

Arif Mardin

Did you have a mentor or someone who inspired you? If so, what have you learned from that person?

Herb Pomeroy, my arranging teacher at Berklee College of Music in Boston and a big band leader. And then I had Tom Dowd, who recently passed away. I think he was maybe my most important mentor because I learned almost everything from him, especially in the field of technical engineering, editing, and things like that. And then of course I had sort of a big brother: Quincy Jones. Actually, I'm a year older than he is! Dizzy Gillespie, Ahmet and Nesuhi Ertegun, and of course Jerry Wexler. I learned so much from these people.

What was your very first job in the music business, and how did you get it?

I became an assistant to Nesuhi Ertegun at Atlantic Records in 1963. That's how I got into Atlantic Records.

What was your first big break? The first great thing that ever happened to you . . .

My first break was to work with the Young Rascals. Both Tom Dowd and myself were assigned to them as staff producers at Atlantic Records. We had a number-one record with "Good Lovin'."

Another first break was when I met Quincy Jones in 1956. He was a member of the Dizzy Gillespie Band, which gave concerts in Istanbul. I wrote four original pieces, orchestrating them for an imaginary band, and sent them to a friend who gave them to Quincy. Voice of America financed this recording session, and my four compositions ended up at Berklee College. Quincy sent the tape to them, and I ended up getting the Quincy Jones scholarship! The band that Quincy selected to play my arrangements was the A-team of 1956. We're talking about Phil Woods, Art Farmer, Hank Jones, you name it. The playing was incredible, and at one point I asked myself, "Did I write this?"

When I got the scholarship to Berklee College of Music in 1958, I was just six months married, working for my dad in Istanbul. I said, "Dad, I'm going." "Where?" "To Boston, to be a big band arranger." He thought I was going to Mars! My son always says, "If he'd been a reader, he would have said, 'But son, big bands are dead!'" But I had this crazy notion, and I was burning with music fever. So I left behind a very comfortable life and arrived in Boston to live in a cold-water room in a boarding house. The period of riches to rags had started. From security in Istanbul to a tough but idealistic existence in Boston. My wife, Latife, followed me a few months later. She has been, and still is, my main pillar of strength. At one point she found a job at the United Nations. She was supporting me, and I was trying to peddle my songs and arrangements before I joined Atlantic Records. So it was quite a journey that we made together.

What elements of your job make you want to go to work every day?

The excitement of creating something. And also to hear . . . I'm a sucker for great voices, and I was very, very fortunate to have worked with the great voices: like Aretha, like Patti LaBelle, Bette Midler. There is no end to it. Jewel! Then lately, Norah Jones. It's just the pleasure of hearing someone perform in the studio and being privy to it, and coming home and telling my wife, "You know, these vocals were incredible!"

Creating something. I look at production as making a small film, a mini film. I get excited about visual aspects of a song. Like Bette Midler, I like singers who enter the character depicted in the lyrics. At present my son Joe and I are co-producing a new album with Queen Latifah, and she is singing up a storm. She (also being a great actress) knows how to get into character of the person mentioned in the song.

What qualities most helped you get to where you are today?

I guess my knowledge of music and orchestration, together with the desire for my music to be sincere. I don't like fake productions, so whomever I work with, be it with Willie Nelson, or John Prine from the old days up to Norah Jones today—their music is sincere. When I use the word "fake," what I really mean is, "trendy." I am not a person who thinks "the good old days" were better than the present. I use cutting-edge technology whenever it is called for.

If you knew everything at the beginning of your career that you know now, what would you have done differently?

No . . . I've evolved. With each artist I've worked with, I've learned. You go to college with Aretha in the field of gospel and soul. With Bette, you enter the field of interpreting a song. She would use different voices until she settled on one character. From Norah, I learned less is more. I don't have any regrets, I just kept on learning. I was fortunate to have learned from the best.

What is your greatest lesson learned?

There are so many. For example, I was working with the great stage actress Irene Worth, who passed away three years ago. I wrote orchestral soundscapes for a project we were doing, a Women of Shakespeare in which she recited all the famous Shakespeare women's speeches. We were working on Lady Macbeth's famous "Sleepwalking" scene, which I felt needed Scottish bagpipe music. I said, "Irene, I found a Scottish bagpipe player in New York, and I recorded him playing a sixteenth-century song. I would like to use that." She said, "Oh darling, that's too 'on.'" I didn't understand what she meant! I said, "Okay, let me orchestrate the bagpipe solo for a string section." So I transcribed it. The cellos played the drone, and the top strings played the melody. So I learned something—that yes, you don't use the obvious, you go one step beyond. . . .

What are some of your favorite albums?

> *Main Course,* the Bee Gees
> *I Feel for You,* Chaka Khan
> *A Night in Tunisia,* Chaka Khan with Dizzy Gillespie (track)
> *Young Gifted and Black,* Aretha Franklin (and many more)
> *Some People's Lives* and *Beaches,* Bette Midler
> *Come Away with Me* and *Feels Like Home,* Norah Jones

> Also, I like very much a Christmas album I made with Jewel a few years ago.

> There are so many other albums. Donny Hathaway, a lot of Average White Band albums, the list goes on!

Did you have any posters on your bedroom walls as a kid? Of whom?

> *No!* I grew up in Istanbul. If I had any posters, it would be the local soccer team! I was a science fiction fan, reading all the American comics and things like that.

What are some great shows you've seen?

> One of the most memorable evenings was catching Duke Ellington's band in 1961, I think, in the middle of an incredible snowstorm in Boston. At that time I was a teacher at Berklee College of Music, and I told my wife, Latife, "We have to go see Ellington's band. My hero is in town!" All right, so we brave the elements, and we end up at a hotel in downtown Boston. There were only two tables: ours and a friend of Duke's. Instead of canceling, the band played to two tables. To us! So it was like a command performance. The other table were his friends, so he would tell them, "I love you madly." All the patter, everything was intact. The soloists were marvelous. They played for us!

What are some of your favorite songs?

> So many. I love a song that has not just a story, but the essence contains a meaningful message, say, of hope.

List up to ten things that could be helpful to someone breaking into the business.

> ■ Honesty is very important. If an artist or a producer says, "I can do this because it's the latest fad," he or she won't go far. Honesty in creativity and your art is paramount.

■ Other qualities are: patience and perseverance because doors don't open up just like that—you have to have the burning desire. First you have to have that burning desire, then you mustn't be discouraged, and then of course there's also something called talent. Maybe some person has a burning desire but doesn't have the talent. Other people have to judge that and say, "Kid, you don't have it. Don't lose your day job." Burning desire, perseverance, not be disappointed, and honesty.

Sir George Martin

Did you have a mentor or someone who inspired you? If so, what have you learned from that person?

I had a Fairy Godfather. When I came out of the Royal Navy after World War Two, I was twenty-one years of age and had no career. As a kid I had been a self-taught musician and ran a dance band as a hobby, but really all I could do after four years in the Fleet Air Arm was to fight the enemy in a plane. Purely by chance I met Sidney Harrison, a brilliant pianist and teacher, a professor of music at the Guildhall in London. He urged me to take up music as a career, and he arranged for me to study composition, harmony and counterpoint, conducting and orchestration at his college.

What was your very first job in the music business, and how did you get it?

Out of the blue I was invited to produce classical music for a small record label. I learned later that I had been recommended for the job by my Sidney Harrison. To begin with I handled a group called the London Baroque Ensemble, but as time went by I was asked to record all kinds of fine musicians, and I got hooked.

What was your first big break? The first great thing that ever happened to you . . .

Surprisingly for me I was made head of the Parlophone label in 1955, when I was just twenty-nine years old. A double-edged sword, because I had to make this small and ailing company pay. I took a gamble and started to produce comedy records with Peter Sellers and other greats like Dudley Moore and Peter Cook, and I had my first number-one in England with a zany jazz group called the Temperance Seven. They took the name because there were nine of them, and they all drank like fishes.

What elements of your job make you want to go to work every day?

Being able to create something that gives immense pleasure to many people is an enormous privilege.

What qualities most helped you get to where you are today?

Natural musical talent, courage to follow my own path, and a firm determination to succeed.

If you knew everything at the beginning of your career that you know now, what would you have done differently?

I would have left EMI to start my own company long before I did. I am not really a company man, towing the company line.

What is your greatest lesson learned?

Humility and the necessity for understanding and tact when producing great artistes.

What are some of your favorite albums?

Pet Sounds, the Beach Boys

Rubber Soul, Revolver, and *Abbey Road,*
   the Beatles

Like Blue, Andre Previn and David Rose

Come Fly with Me, Frank Sinatra

Apocalypse, Mahavishnu Orchestra

Icarus, Paul Winter Consort

Blow by Blow, Jeff Beck

Did you have any posters on your bedroom walls as a kid? Of whom?

Art Tatum, Glenn Miller, Gary Cooper, and Ingrid Bergman.

What are some great shows you've seen?

My Fair Lady when it opened in New York.

The Music for Montserrat Charity Concert in the Royal Albert Hall—a fantastic line-up with a band which included Sting on bass guitar, Eric Clapton and Mark Knopfler on electrics, Phil Collins on drums, and Paul McCartney and Elton John on keyboards and vocals. Unforgettable!

Elton John and Billy Joel

The last Paul McCartney tour

What are some of your favorite songs?

Too many to mention, but let us say lots by Paul and John, Elton, Dylan, Bacharach, Paul Simon, Stevie Wonder, Joni Mitchell, Tchaikovsky, Cole Porter, and Fauré.

List up to ten things that could be helpful to someone breaking into the business.

- You have to be sure to know what you really want to do.
- You then have to pursue that aim without deflection, learning all you can.
- Do not give up too easily. There will be many put-downs, many rejections, but they are all part of getting there.
- Love your work, but above all love your fellow men.

Giorgio Moroder

Did you have a mentor or someone who inspired you? If so, what have you learned from that person?

From the Beatles I learned that the melody of a song is the most important part of music.

What was your very first job in the music industry, and how did you get it?

My first job in the industry was an engineering post at a publishing company, and I got it by sending them some of my recordings I had done.

What was your first big break? The first great thing that ever happened to you . . .

My first break was a song I did for a singer called Ricky Shane. My first worldwide hit was "Love to Love You Baby" with Donna Summer.

What elements of your job make you want to go to work every day?

Basically the whole production of a song—the composing, recording, and mixing.

What qualities most helped you get to where you are today?

A lot of transpiration and a lot of inspiration.

What is your greatest lesson learned?

Don't give up on a good idea.

What are some of your favorite albums?

I like some of the Beatles, Pink Floyd, and the good old albums.

What are some great shows you've seen?

The Rolling Stones, Wembley Stadium.

What are some of your favorite songs?

Most of the Beatles.

List up to ten things that could be helpful to someone breaking into the business.

Take the job seriously, work hard, and one day luck will be with you.

Alan Moulder

Did you have a mentor or someone who inspired you? If so, what have you learned from that person?

At the studio that I trained at, all the house engineers were kind of mentors. They taught you your job and more importantly how to behave on sessions, when to speak and when to shut up and the general politics and protocol of studio life.

What was your very first job in the music industry, and how did you get it?

I managed to get a job as a tea boy as they were called in England, or a runner as they are better known now. I got the job straight from leaving school by sending a letter asking for a job and being lucky enough to be seen. This was at Trident Studios in London, which was a very big studio at the time. I worked there for a month and decided I wasn't ready—having just left school—to completely abandon any hope of a social life, so I quit and got a job four years later at the same studio as an assistant. . . . How I pulled that one off I don't know but am eternally grateful to Stephen Stewart Short, who owned the studio and gave me the chance!

What was your first big break? The first great thing that ever happened to you . . .

Whilst being a house engineer at Trident I got to work with the Smiths and recorded and mixed a single called "Shoplifters of the World." They were one of my favorite bands at the time, and one of the reasons I decided against pursuing a career as a guitar player was I thought Johnny Marr was much better than I would ever be.

What elements of your job make you want to go to work every day?

The fact that I still don't really think of it as a job, just a hobby where you get to play with lots of expensive toys!

What qualities most helped you get to where you are today?

Patience!

If you knew everything at the beginning of your career that you know now, what would you have done differently?

I can't really think of anything I would change, but I would have bought a lot of the valve compressors and microphones that were not valued that much when I was an assistant and now cost a fortune.

What is your greatest lesson learned?

I'm not always right. When I was producing an album with Shakespear's Sister there was a song on the album called "Stay." I didn't really like it and thought we should think about leaving it off the album. It went on to be the biggest single on the album and was number-one in the British single charts for eight weeks. Funnily enough, I like the song now!

What are some of your favorite albums?

Dark Side of the Moon, Pink Floyd
Physical Graffiti, Led Zeppelin
Violator, Depeche Mode

Did you have any posters on your bedroom walls as a kid? Of whom?

Raquel Welch, Brigitte Bardot, and Georgie Best.

What are some great shows you've seen?

The Tubes at Leicester De Montford Hall. Fee Waybill broke his leg.

What are some of your favorite songs?

"California Love," 2Pac featuring Dr. Dre
"Get It On," T. Rex
"The Ace of Spades," Motörhead

List up to ten things that could be helpful to someone breaking into the business.

- Always try to do more than is expected of you.
- People like it when you make them cups of tea and coffee.

Linda Perry

Did you have a mentor or someone who inspired you? If so, what have you learned from that person?

Bill Botrell inspired me to become a producer. I learned that there was no right or wrong, to EQ, compress, move microphones around until it sounded good to my ears.

What was your very first job in the music industry, and how did you get it?

Being signed to Interscope Records with 4 Non Blondes was my introduction to the music industry.

What was your first big break? The first great thing that ever happened to you . . .

I have had two big breaks. First was 4 Non Blondes getting signed. Second big break was having Pink call me up to produce her record.

What elements of your job make you want to go to work every day?

Music.

What qualities most helped you get to where you are today?

I'm a dreamer, very motivated, and always get what I want.

If you knew everything at the beginning of your career that you know now, what would you have done differently?

I wouldn't change a thing. Every mistake made in the past benefits your future.

What is your greatest lesson learned?

Do be more diplomatic.
You are only as good as the people you surround yourself with.

What are some of your favorite albums?

Dark Side of the Moon, Pink Floyd
All Led Zeppelin

Tapestry, Carole King
Jesus Christ Superstar sound track

Did you have any posters on your bedroom walls as a kid? Of whom?

Never had that luxury.

What are some great shows you've seen?

The Who, Neil Young, Annie Lennox, Sade.

List up to ten things that could be helpful to someone breaking into the business.

Envision what you want, and don't stop until you get it.

Rick Rubin

Did you have a mentor or someone who inspired you? If so, what have you learned from that person?

There was a person named Ed Bahlman at 99 Records store on Macdougal Street in Greenwich Village. He ran a little indie label out of the store, he walked me through the record making process from finding a good inexpensive studio, where to have vinyl pressed, who pressed sleeves, what indie distributors to contact. He was there to answer questions as they came up.

What was your very first job in the music industry, and how did you get it?

I never really had a job in the music industry. I produced twelve-inch singles while at NYU and created Def Jam Records to put them out. It was always a hobby—never an intended profession. It's still amazing to me that my job is to listen to music all day and discuss how it makes me feel.

What was your first big break? The first great thing that ever happened to you . . .

The first dream I had while still at NYU was producing Run-D.M.C. They were my favorite group in the world at the time, and it was a great honor when it came to pass.

What elements of your job make you want to go to work every day?

The magic moment when a new song appears, or when a performance is so good it's worthy of being recorded for history.

What qualities most helped you get to where you are today?

I think one of the things that had the biggest impact on my life was learning to meditate at a young age. That practice has really enhanced my ability to stay focused for long stretches and look deeply and clearly into things.

If you knew everything at the beginning of your career that you know now, what would you have done differently?

Everything happens exactly as it's supposed to, to get you where you are now.

What is your greatest lesson learned?

All you can do is your very best. If you keep your standards high and are willing to do whatever it takes to reach them, you will feel good with the results. Hard work pays off.

What are some of your favorite albums?

White Album, the Beatles, and every other Beatles album
Highway to Hell, AC/DC
Full Moon Fever, Tom Petty
After the Gold Rush, Neil Young
First four Dylan albums
All Simon & Garfunkel
All Doors
Greatest Hits, the Mamas and the Papas
Hot August Night, Neil Diamond
Debussy, Satie, Bach
Gurdjief/De Hartmann (original recording)
Greatest Hits, Donovan
Original Greatest Hits, the Everly Brothers
Albums by Jimmy Rogers, Mississippi John Hurt, the Monkees, No More Shall We Part, Nick Cave
The Bends, Radiohead
Henry Mancini box set

Did you have any posters on your bedroom walls as a kid? Of whom?

Yes. Ramones, Devo, AC/DC, Aerosmith, Ted Nugent, Plasmatics, Steve Martin, and the Beatles.

What are some great shows you've seen?

U2, *Elevation,* 2001
AC/DC with Bon Scott, Madison Square Garden
Rage Against the Machine, *Tibetan Freedom Concert*
Radiohead, 9:30 Club, Washington, D.C.
Black Flag, Peppermint Lounge, San Francisco
The Ramones, New York Palladium, New Year's Eve, 1979
Nine Inch Nails, first headline tour, Hammerstein Ball Room in New York
James Brown, Boston, 1980
Devo, 1980

What are some of your favorite songs?

"Across the Universe" and "Strawberry Fields Forever," the Beatles

"Imagine," John Lennon

"Rockaway Beach," the Ramones

"One," U2

"Keep on Dancin'," the Gentrys

"I Believe in You," Neil Young

"You Were on My Mind," We Five

"Baby I'm Yours," Barbara Lewis

"To Sir with Love," Lulu

"Just a Little," the Beau Brummels

"Sally Go 'Round the Roses," the Jaynetts

"Sealed with a Kiss," Brian Hyland

"I'll Never Find Another You," the Seekers

"California Dreamin'," the Mamas and the Papas

"Moonlight Drive," the Doors

"Hurdy Gurdy Man," Donovan

"My Sweet Lord," George Harrison

"Look Out (Here Comes Tomorrow)," the Monkees

"I Say a Little Prayer," Bacharach/Warwick

"Cherish," the Association

"Blowin' in the Wind," Bob Dylan

"Black Sabbath," Black Sabbath

"Since I Don't Have You," the Skyliners

List up to ten things that could be helpful to someone breaking into the business.

- Ignore deadlines. It's done when it's done.
- Do it because you love it, not because you think someone else will like it.
- Take your work seriously and study your craft. Practice, practice, practice. There is no substitute for hard work.
- Do it yourself. Don't wait to get signed or wait for a job to come up. Work at your craft now, for free if need be. Talent rises very quickly. Start anywhere you can, but start now!!

John Shanks

Did you have a mentor or someone who inspired you? If so, what have you learned from that person?

Besides my parents, it would be my music teachers. They taught me the joy of learning and that to practice is to learn. I learned to listen, to be open, willing, humble, and teachable. With those qualities, you will always grow and continue to enjoy listening, playing, and making music forever.

My parents taught me to be the best that I could be.

What was your very first job in the music industry, and how did you get it?

I had a band in high school, and we played every club in town a thousand times. That taught discipline—moving gear, practicing, and getting paid nothing to do it. You had to love it. My first paid gig was playing guitar for Teena Marie—I was sixteen, and it was a blast. White boy on funk . . .

What was your first big break? The first great thing that ever happened to you . . .

There are always things that you can track that led you to where you wanted to be, but one big one for me was getting the gig with Melissa Etheridge. I toured the world from the ground up, saw what it took to break an artist, and played every kind of venue, from the Roxy to Wembley, Woodstock, etc.

What elements of your job make you want to go to work every day?

The joy of music. And everything from trying to make great records, to getting to write, play, and discover the secrets that keep me inspired to dare to suck.

What qualities most helped you get to where you are today?

Listening, compassion, and being open-minded.

If you knew everything at the beginning of your career that you know now, what would you have done differently?

The small, little thoughts count. I would have trusted my instincts more and trusted that I did not need to medicate myself to get through the fear.

What is your greatest lesson learned?

There's room for everybody. Don't be afraid to ask. Trust your heart. Listen.

What are some of your favorite albums?

Innervisions, Talking Book, and *Fulfillingness'*
  First Finale, Stevie Wonder
Kind of Blue, Miles Davis
Houses of the Holy, Led Zeppelin
Are You Experienced?, Jimi Hendrix
  Experience

Avalon, Roxy Music
Let It Bleed and *Sticky Fingers,*
  the Rolling Stones
Wish You Were Here, Pink Floyd
What's Going On, Marvin Gaye
Imperial Bedroom, Elvis Costello

Did you have any posters on your bedroom walls as a kid? Of whom?

Pink Floyd, Led Zeppelin, Cream, Peter Frampton, Jimi Hendrix, and Stevie Nicks.

What are some great shows you've seen?

James Brown—when I was five years old in Baltimore
Early U2
Chuck Berry, Madison Square Garden, in the round
Pink Floyd, Madison Square Garden, second row
Led Zeppelin, four nights at Madison Square Garden
Shows by the Rolling Stones, KISS, Bruce Springsteen, the Police, the Allman Brothers, Stevie
  Ray Vaughan, Jeff Beck, AC/DC, the Clash

What are some of your favorite songs?

"In My Life" and "Because," the Beatles
"Love Is Everything," Jane Siberry
"God Only Knows," the Beach Boys
"What's Going On," Marvin Gaye
"Father and Son," Cat Stevens
"Fragile," Sting
"I Will," Wendy and Lisa

"Dear God," XTC
"Shoot Into the Night," Peter Gabriel
"Ain't No Sunshine," Bill Withers
"Castles Made of Sand" and "The Wind
  Cries Mary," Jimi Hendrix
"Day After Day," Badfinger

List up to ten things that could be helpful to someone breaking into the business.

- Don't look at your watch.
- Be in it for the right reasons.

- Think long-term.
- You can be nice and succeed.

Billy Steinberg

Did you have a mentor or someone who inspired you? If so, what have you learned from that person?

My favorite songwriters have inspired me. They include Lennon and McCartney, Bob Dylan, Chuck Berry, Jagger and Richards, Roy Orbison, Smokey Robinson, Van Morrison, Bacharach and David, Holland-Dozier-Holland, and Laura Nyro. They taught me to hunt everywhere for songs: the unconscious, hurt, lust, and love, and to recognize and worship a beautiful melody.

What was your very first job in the music industry, and how did you get it?

In the late seventies, Richard Perry signed my band, Billy Thermal, to Planet Records. I wrote the songs and was the lead singer.

What was your first big break? The first great thing that ever happened to you . . .

I was working in my father's table-grape vineyards in Thermal, California. In my spare time, I would record demos of songs I was writing. Craig Hull played electric guitar on those demos. He knew Linda Ronstadt. Unknown to me, Craig gave a copy of our demos to Linda. She loved a song I wrote called "How Do I Make You." She cut it, and it was a Top 10 hit in 1980. That was unbelievably exciting for me!

What elements of your job make you want to go to work every day?

I have loved songs since I was a child listening to the Everly Brothers sing "All I Have to Do Is Dream." The magic of writing a song is irresistible. I like the idea that on any given day I might write my best one ever—a song that might move someone the way "All I Have to Do Is Dream" moved me.

What qualities most helped you get to where you are today?

Passion for music. Determination. Love of words and poetry. The ability to be motivated by, instead of destroyed, by rejection. The ability to collaborate. Converting personal angst into creative expression.

If you knew everything at the beginning of your career that you know now, what would you have done differently?

In 1992, I sold the publishing rights to my early songs. I regret it more than I can express.

What is your greatest lesson learned?

My greatest lesson learned is to believe in myself and my creations. The music business can be incredibly cold. I don't let that cold extinguish my creative spark.

What are some of your favorite albums?

Blonde on Blonde, Bob Dylan

Rubber Soul, the Beatles

Are You Experienced?, Jimi Hendrix
   Experience

A Beard of Stars, T. Rex

Eli and the Thirteenth Confession,
   Laura Nyro

Greatest Hits, Smokey Robinson &
   the Miracles

A Man and His Soul, Ray Charles

The Real Folk Blues, Muddy Waters

Did you have any posters on your bedroom walls as a kid? Of whom?

The Beatles and the Rolling Stones.

What are some great shows you've seen?

Ray Charles in '64 or '65 (my first concert)

The Jimi Hendrix Experience, Greenwich
   Village, summer of 1967

Laura Nyro, Carnegie Hall, 1969

Roy Orbison, the Hop, Orange County, 1987

John Fogerty, UCLA, 2000

What are some of your favorite songs?

"Like a Rolling Stone," Bob Dylan

"Gloria," Them, featuring Van Morrison

"Spoonful," Howlin' Wolf

"Cathy's Clown," the Everly Brothers

"Pretty Ballerina," Left Banke

"Money Won't Change You," James Brown

"I Am the Walrus," the Beatles

List up to ten things that could be helpful to someone breaking into the business.

- There is no "formula."
- If it's not fun, it's probably not good.
- Be realistic in assessing your own skills. If necessary, seek collaborators who can provide what you lack.
- Work hard. Most successful people I know have strong work ethics.

Diane Warren

Did you have a mentor or someone who inspired you? If so, what have you learned from that person?

I didn't have one mentor, really. The radio was my mentor. I grew up with an ear glued to the radio and learned how to write songs by osmosis. I listened to Top 40 radio, to nothing but hits, so that influenced me. I grew up in Van Nuys, California, so I listened to Boss Radio KHJ, KFWB, and KRLA. I also had older sisters who had a lot of hit records, and when I was little, I remember checking out their 45s and seeing who wrote things. Even when I was little that interested me for some crazy reason.

What was your very first job in the music industry, and how did you get it?

This is the job I've always had, even though it took a while to actually get paid for it. It started when I was signed to a guy named Jack White, who produced Laura Branigan. She was pretty big in the early eighties, and she did a couple songs of mine through Jack.

Jack was administered through Arista publishing at the time, so they were working my songs, too. They got "Rhythm of the Night" to DeBarge, which was the first huge, international hit that I had written by myself.

What was your first big break? The first great thing that ever happened to you . . .

I had had a Top 10 hit with a song called "Solitaire" with Laura Branigan, but I didn't write that all myself. When "Rhythm of the Night" went Top 10, I got a real taste of success, and I wanted more. That was really exciting for me.

What elements of your job make you want to go to work every day?

I'm in love with writing songs. I love my work. I can't wait to get to the office every day to create. I love getting to work every day and not knowing what is going to happen, not knowing what I am going to write. The only plan I have in mind is that I want to accomplish writing something great. I am excited as well by the prospect of becoming better at what I do, always trying to write a better song than what I just wrote.

I never really talk about my process—it's something magical, but I generally just start with an idea. It's always different—it could be a beat, it could be hitting a sound on the keyboard.

What qualities most helped you get to where you are today?

Tenacity, stubbornness, drive, resilience, and my obsessive-compulsive disorder are a few qualities that have helped me along the way. I'm as obsessed today as I ever was. But it starts out with talent, because all the tenacity, luck, and perseverance in the world won't get you anywhere if what you're doing isn't quality. It starts with having something of substance and quality (which I think I have) and then it's having the vision to see it come to life and have a life.

If you knew everything at the beginning of your career that you know now, what would you have done differently?

In my life, even the pitfalls have turned out okay. For example, I was signed to a terrible publishing deal with Jack White. But if I hadn't been signed to a terrible publishing deal, I wouldn't have had "Rhythm of the Night." I also wouldn't have had a lawsuit with him that forced me to keep my publishing. I wasn't able to sign with anyone while we were in litigation, which forced me to own my own songs from 1986 on, when things really exploded. So I write these songs myself, and I own them. In hindsight, that pitfall was an amazing blessing. No one starts out being able to get any deal they want, so it's about being smart about what you do.

What is your greatest lesson learned?

I'm not going to name names, but I always thought when you get to the top, everyone's going to be a lot smarter. Everyone thinks that when they're starting out, but then I found out that it's almost the opposite sometimes. There are some smart people, but, oh my God, I have had the stupidest things happen to me, and people have said the stupidest things. Someday I'll have to write them all down in a book, or at least a good chapter of dumb things people have done or said to me.

I don't know if I have great lessons to teach anybody, but if I were to give advice, it would be that in anything you do, you have to work really hard at it to be great. It comes down to the time, passion, and love you put into what you do. If you don't have that, you should be doing something else. If you wouldn't die without doing it, don't do it. I was and I am very lucky to have figured out what it was for me, but I think everybody has something they are great at.

What are some of your favorite albums?

I have a lot of favorites for many reasons . . .

Songs in the Key of Life, Stevie Wonder
Sgt. Pepper's Lonely Hearts Club Band and
 Revolver, the Beatles
Purple Rain, Prince

Dusty in Memphis, Dusty Springfield
The Very Best of Burt Bacharach,
 Burt Bacharach
Aretha Franklin's Greatest Hits

Did you have any posters on your bedroom walls as a kid? Of whom?

I clearly remember the Beatles posters. Maybe I shouldn't admit to the Bobby Sherman ones, but now it's too late! His mother lived near my junior high school. He's a cop or a highway patrol man now. Could you imagine being pulled over by Bobby Sherman?

I can't remember what other posters I had, but I remember when my dad ripped them all off the wall when I got kicked out of school. He was pissed off because I got expelled. Oh, well.

What are some great shows you've seen?

My older sisters took me to see the Beatles when I was really little. I still remember how exciting that was. Another that sticks in my mind was seeing Prince at the beginning of his career. It was an amazing concert.

Springsteen puts on a great show.
Led Zeppelin

What are some of your favorite songs?

When you think back on the sixties, they're just so fucking great. All those great Motown songs—Ashford & Simpson, Holland-Dozier-Holland, the Supremes—they're just great.

I have such weird taste. I love everything from "Welcome to the Jungle" to "Some Enchanted Evening" and everything in between, but I'd have to mention everything on *Songs in the Key of Life*.

"Here, There, and Everywhere," the Beatles

"Up on the Roof," the Drifters

"You've Lost That Loving Feeling," the Righteous Brothers

All Holland-Dozier-Holland

All Burt Bacharach

List up to ten things that could be helpful to someone breaking into the business.

- Persistence
- Love of your job
- Understanding and education of the business
- Professionalism
- Thick skin
- Ultimate belief in yourself and your songs
- Be good at what you do and work hard at it!

A&R WIZARDS AND EXECUTIVES

Lyor Cohen

Did you have a mentor or someone who inspired you? If so, what have you learned from that person?

Russell Simmons—Energy and love. Dreams can become reality.

Rick Rubin—detail to art and its relationship to the fan. Art is the most important thing . . . period.

What was your very first job in the music industry and how did you get started?

Road manager for Run-D.M.C. The Run-D.M.C. road manager, Jeff Flood, lost his passport. The band was waiting at the airport to go to England for the first time. I was the only one they knew who had a passport. The rest is history.

What elements of your job make you want to go to work every day?

The chance that on any given day I could meet someone whose feet don't touch the ground and radically change my life.

What qualities most helped you to get where you are today?

Respect for talent and staying focused on the important aspects, not allowing myself to drift into unnecessary bullshit.

If you knew everything at the beginning of your career that you know now, what would you have done differently?

Enjoy the early days more.

What is your greatest lesson learned?

Life is fragile—RIP Jam Master Jay.

What are some of your favorite albums?

Bum Rush the Show, Public Enemy

Johnny Cash

What are some great shows you've seen?

Slayer at the Olympic Auditorium   Public Enemy at the Briton Academy

Run-D.M.C. in Detroit and at   Jay-Z at Madison Square Garden

    Madison Square Garden

List up to ten things that could be helpful to someone breaking into the business.

■ Sign stars.

■ Don't dust bums off.

Jason Flom

Did you have a mentor or someone who inspired you? If so, what have you learned from that person?

Ahmet Ertegun and Doug Morris. Ahmet—for showing me that talented artists and hit records solve all problems. Doug—for teaching me everything else. Most importantly, that my opinion of a record is secondary to those who spend their money on them, the consumers.

What was your very first job in the music industry, and how did you get it?

In 1979, I started as a trainee at Atlantic Records putting up posters in record stores.

What was your first big break? The first great thing that ever happened to you . . .

I discovered a band named Zebra who was being played on WBAB in Long Island and was able to convince Atlantic to take a shot with it. The record went gold, and I had the break I needed.

What elements of your job make you want to go to work every day?

I love the music, the people I work with, and the joy of discovering and helping to break tomorrow's stars.

What qualities most helped you get to where you are today?

Persistence, loyalty, and belief in myself.

If you knew everything at the beginning of your career that you know now, what would you have done differently?

I would have signed all the hit acts that I passed on.

What is your greatest lesson learned?

That you can win while maintaining your integrity and that you can be firm without raising your voice.

What are some of your favorite albums?

Welcome to the Pleasuredome,
   Frankie Goes to Hollywood

Purple Rain, Prince

Rocks, Aerosmith

Appetite for Destruction, Guns N' Roses

Highway 61 Revisted, Bob Dylan

Sgt. Pepper's Lonely Hearts Club Band,
   the Beatles

Led Zeppelin II, Led Zeppelin

Night at the Opera, Queen

Ziggy Stardust, David Bowie

Devil Without a Cause, Kid Rock

Little Earthquakes, Tori Amos

Highway to Hell, AC/DC

Goodbye Yellow Brick Road, Elton John

Did you have any posters on your bedroom walls as a kid? Of whom?

Almost all of the aforementioned bands. My room was a shrine to rock 'n' roll.

What are some great shows you've seen?

Led Zeppelin, Madison Square Garden, 1977

Prince, the Bottom Line, 1981

Kid Rock at SIR, 1999

What are some of your favorite songs?

"Nobody's Fault," Aerosmith

"Sgt. Pepper's Lonely Hearts Club Band,"
   the Beatles

"Honky Tonk Women," the Rolling Stones

"Whole Lotta Love," Led Zeppelin

"Monkey Business," Skid Row

"If You Want Me to Stay," Sly & the
   Family Stone

"Sign O' the Times," Prince

"Evenflow," Pearl Jam

"Devil Without a Cause," Kid Rock

"We Will Rock You," Queen

"War," Frankie Goes to Hollywood

"All Right Now," Free

"Rock Candy," Montrose

"Rock n' Roll Hoochie Coo," Rick Derringer

"Superstition," Stevie Wonder

"Pour Some Sugar on Me," Def Leppard

List up to ten things that could be helpful to someone breaking into the business.

- Just get your foot in the door any way you can.
- Stand up for what you believe in.
- Never say, "I told you so."
- Return every phone call.
- Don't take your own opinion too seriously.
- Remember that the feet you step on today may be connected to the ass you'll kiss tomorrow.
- Do something for someone less fortunate than you.

Michael Goldstone

Did you have a mentor or someone who inspired you? If so, what have you learned from that person?

Steve Moir. Always, whenever possible, try to succeed or fail with your own instincts. There is never something that you can't do given the opportunity. Remain true to yourself.

What was your very first job in the music industry, and how did you get it?

While finishing high school, I got a part-time job at Chrysalis Records in Los Angeles. My friend Arlen saw the job listing on a board at school and, because of my passion for music, stole it and gave it to me. I wasn't the only one who was interviewed, but I'm sure it helped.

What was your first big break? The first great thing that ever happened to you . . .

After cleaning up dog shit in West L.A. (no shit or pun intended) for an executive at Chrysalis, I was rescued into a marketing job. That led me to A&R eventually at PolyGram, where I signed a band called Mother Love Bone. Then with Michele Anthony's help, we all landed at Epic, where we signed Pearl Jam.

What elements of your job make you want to go to work every day?

The chance that at any given moment you can discover talent that could actually influence pop culture. Play in the traffic and hopefully find talented artists. Help those artists reach an audience. Have a job where arrested development is a must and an asset.

What qualities most helped you get to where you are today?

Resilience and conviction. The resilience is a must because it's a long arduous process. The conviction is imperative because all along the way, people will question you. Most importantly, that it's more important to win than to be right.

If you knew everything at the beginning of your career that you know now, what would you have done differently?

I started at sixteen. If I had the choice to take a different path, I would have found a partner and started our own label/business. Having an entrepreneurial sprit is paramount to certain freedoms. I would never regret my journey. There have been moments where not knowing information led to mistakes that helped me grow as an A&R man and a human being.

What is your greatest lesson learned?

See above: it's better to win than to be right!

What are some of your favorite albums?

In no particular order:

Never Mind the Bollocks, the Sex Pistols	*Legend,* Bob Marley
A Rush of Blood to the Head, Coldplay	*London Calling,* the Clash
Marshall Mathers LP, Eminem	*Quintessential Catalogue,* Billie Holiday
(What's the Story) Morning Glory?, Oasis	*Paul's Boutique,* the Beastie Boys
Sublime, Sublime	*Turn On the Bright Lights,* Interpol
Weezer (Blue Album), Weezer	*Blue Note/Capitol Recordings,* Miles Davis
Nevermind, Nirvana	*Nothing's Shocking,* Jane's Addiction
Very Good Years, Frank Sinatra	*Millennium,* Robbie Williams

Did you have any posters on your bedroom walls as a kid? Of whom?

Sex Pistols, Clash, Springsteen, Led Zeppelin, and N.Y. Giants Football.

What are some great shows you've seen?

Nirvana, Roseland, New York City

U2—Croke Park, Dublin (*Joshua Tree*)

Robbie Williams, Bowery Ballroom, New York City (First U.S. Show)

Jam, Santa Monica Civic Auditorium (*All Mod Cons*)

Springsteen—Santa Monica Civic (*Born to Run*)

Rage Against the Machine, Pinkpop Festival, Landgraaf, The Netherlands

Jane's Addiction, John Anson Ford Theatre, Hollywood (*Nothing's Shocking*)

The Clash, Hollywood Palladium, Hollywood (*London Calling*)

Pearl Jam, Limelight, New York City (*Ten*)

Elton John, Troubadour, Los Angeles (*Captain Fantastic*)

What are some of your favorite songs?

In no particular order:

"Smells Like Teen Spirit," Nirvana	"Who We Be," DMX
"Where Is the Love?", Black Eyed Peas	"Just a Girl," No Doubt
"I Want It That Way," the Backstreet Boys	"Loser," Beck
"Tangled Up in Blue," Bob Dylan	"One," U2
"In Da Club," 50 Cent	"Take On Me," a-ha

"Be My Baby," the Ronettes

"White Riot," the Clash

"Living on a Prayer," Bon Jovi

"New York, New York," Frank Sinatra

"Creep," Radiohead

List up to ten things that could be helpful to someone breaking into the business.

If you want an A&R job . . .

1. Find talent.
2. Stay in the traffic . . . according to Ahmet Ertegun . . . if you stay in the traffic you're likely to bump into a genius.
3. Reputation—treat people with respect . . . you never know who will go where.
4. Conviction—having it will get you to the front of the pack.
5. Taste—don't be afraid to go out on a limb. Some of the greatest signings nobody ever wanted.
6. Family—don't lose yourself and forget the important things.
7. Success—the minute you think you're somewhere you're nowhere.
8. Humility—people will root for your success and help you along the way.
9. Gratitude—you can't succeed by yourself.
10. Sense of humor—don't lose it. We have to be able to laugh and sometimes at ourselves.

Ron Handler

Did you have a mentor or someone who inspired you? If so, what have you learned from that person?

I was working at BMG Publishing when my old boss was let go. My new boss came in and said to me, "Get your shit together, or get the hell out of here." Since that day, I've taken my working life more serious and haven't looked back. David Geffen and Mo Ostin are my bosses now. They both are most inspiring.

What was your very first job in the music industry, and how did you get it?

I was delivering alcohol for a liquor store in college. One of our accounts was Arista Records. I walked in those doors, and said to myself, "This is it! This is where I want to be." My first job was working for Arista in that very building.

What was your first big break? The first great thing that ever happened to you . . .

I signed my first songwriter at my first job, BMG Publishing. He was writing and producing a new artist named Mariah Carey. Next thing I know we were printing money.

What elements of your job make you want to go to work every day?

Simply working with talented artists—and the chance that they may become stars. Hearing a demo and later hearing it on the radio and seeing it on MTV.

What qualities most helped you get to where you are today?

Being competitive with myself only.
Always being humble.
Being true and nice to people around me.
Always changing and adapting.

If you knew everything at the beginning of your career that you know now, what would you have done differently?

I would have started my own label early in my career.

What is your greatest lesson learned?

Be respectful towards others and it will come back to you with great rewards.

What are some of your favorite albums?

Greatest Hits, Bob Marley

London Calling, the Clash

2001 and *The Chronic,* Dr. Dre

Fear of a Black Planet, Public Enemy

Grace, Jeff Buckley

The Bends, Radiohead

Appetite for Destruction, Guns N' Roses

Did you have any posters on your bedroom walls as a kid? Of whom?

The Clash, the Jam, the Who, Marley and spliff.

What are some great shows you've seen?

Early L.A. punk shows

The Clash opening for the Who

Radiohead at the Troubadour

What are some of your favorite songs?

Well, there are too many to answer, but I like most one-hit wonders from the eighties.

List up to ten things that could be helpful to someone breaking into the business.

- Don't be fearful.
- Set your mind to something you would like to accomplish.
- Carry that thing through.
- If a door closes, bust another door open.
- No matter what someone says, never give up, keep pursuing your dream. It will come true with hard work, dedication, and persistence.

Andre Harrell

Did you have a mentor or someone who inspired you? If so, what have you learned from that person?

No.

What was your very first job in the music business, and how did you get it?

I was a rapper! I was Dr. Jeckyll of Dr. Jeckyll and Mr. Hyde.

What was your first big break? The first great thing that ever happened to you . . .

I made a record called *Genius Rap*.

What elements of your job make you want to go to work every day?

Trying to uplift the culture. Making music that empowers people to feel good about themselves, makes them want to celebrate, man fall in love with a woman, or feel comfortable about loving their fellow man. Doing music that inspires fashion styles so people look better and feel more beautiful.

What qualities most helped you get to where you are today?

I'm interested in life and the trends of life. Music, people from different cultures.

If you knew everything at the beginning of your career that you know now, what would you have done differently?

I probably would have been more patient.

What is your greatest lesson learned?

If you have an original thought, an original voice, don't get distracted, don't get impatient, don't get bored, stay in that place till it's fully grown. Like when I started with Mary J. Blige, I knew that she was going to be a big star. I didn't know necessarily that she was going to be the voice of her generation, I just knew it was a great voice, and I pursued that.

What are some of your favorite albums?

What's the 411, Mary J. Blige

What's Going On, Marvin Gaye

Life After Death, the Notorious B.I.G.

The Chronic, Dr. Dre

Albums by Stevie Wonder

What are some great shows you've seen?

Hammer and Puff Daddy.

What are some of your favorite songs?

"Ain't Nobody," Chaka Kahn

"Love Without a Limit," Mary J. Blige

"My, My, My," Johnny Gill

"Whip Appeal," Babyface

"Got to Give It Up," Marvin Gaye

List up to ten things that could be helpful to someone breaking into the business.

1. Pick a good mentor.
2. Work for a company that has music you like.
3. Get to know the interns and assistants.
4. Be helpful.
5. Be hardworking and focused.
6. Look like and live your point of view.
7. Have an opinion.
8. Make sure your "timing" is appropriate in giving your opinion.
9. Don't work *for* someone . . . work *with* someone; it's your career . . . you're on the team.
10. Be a team player.

Craig Kallman

Did you have a mentor or someone who inspired you? If so, what have you learned from that person?

Ahmet Ertegun.

I've been fortunate enough to have the man who was a great inspiration to me when I started my label later become my mentor. For over fifty years, Ahmet has been a model of impeccable taste. He has a pioneer spirit, a passionate love of music, and a deep understanding of it. On top of all that, he's managed to maintain respectful and nurturing relationships with his artists. Over the last decade, with a lot of gracious encouragement, he's been a day-to-day example of how to be the best partner to the artists.

What was your very first job in the music industry, and how did you get it?

My first job was a deejay gig at a nightclub, the Mansion, in New York City, and I got it by dropping off a mixtape in 1981. That led to weekly spots at the Palladium, Danceteria, the Cat Club, Area, the Tunnel, the Choice, and Mars.

What was your first big break? The first great thing that ever happened to you . . .

In 1987, I was in a store called Downtown Records when I heard a demo tape that suddenly made me want to start my own record company. Just like that. The demo was "Join Hands" by Taravhonty and was the start of Big Beat's run in house music. I had no idea that simply selling a series of twelve-inches out of my bedroom would give my label almost instant street credibility. It all just happened spontaneously.

What elements of your job make you want to go to work every day?

Many. The chance to discover something new: a new artist, a new sound, a new genre. The opportunity to help established talents stretch themselves in unexpected ways. To be one of the authors of a new chapter in the history of a great label. I love the fact that every record we put out has the potential of moving music forward in a significant way.

What qualities most helped you get to where you are today?

I think, more than anything, it's been acting on my inner compulsion to devour every kind of music, new and old, and study the origin and history of it all. That's been my foundation for assessing talent, contributing musical ideas, and guiding careers. Passion is crucial, but it's not enough. It's also acting on your passions and what your expertise adds to the mix that makes you key to the process.

Then, given the enormous quantity of pop culture today and the speed with which it's being disseminated and consumed and, often, instantly discarded, it's a job to stay on top of everything. In a way, it's the most critical job to me.

I try to be tapped into what's on the cutting edge—whatever's urgently trying to surface—in music, fashion, movies, art, and also in demographics and changing lifestyles.

If you knew everything at the beginning of your career that you know now, what would you have done differently?

I would have fought even harder to sign Def Jam when they left Columbia. In addition, I would have bought each and every Trojan and Studio One single when they were released for seventy-five cents.

What is your greatest lesson learned?

Follow your instincts: they are probably right. Still, you have to challenge your assumptions every day. Music and the marketplace move so fast that staying ahead of the curve is a nonstop task. When you get complacent, or stay too wedded to a particular viewpoint or a specific way of doing things, you inevitably fall behind.

What are some of your favorite albums?

Veedon Fleece, Van Morrison

Forca Bruta, Jorge Ben

Electric Ladyland, Jimi Hendrix Experience

Catch a Fire, Bob Marley and the Wailers

The Smiths, the Smiths

Paid in Full, Eric B. & Rakim

Whatever's for Us, Joan Armatrading

Harvest, Neil Young

Physical Graffiti, Led Zeppelin

What's Going On, Marvin Gaye

L'Histoire de Melody Nelson,
  Serge Gainsbourg

Back in Black, AC/DC

Sour Times, Portishead

Kind of Blue, Miles Davis

The River, Ali Farka Toure

Did you have any posters on your bedroom walls as a kid? Of whom?

KISS and Led Zeppelin.

What are some great shows you've seen?

The Clash, Bond's International Casino, New York, June 1981

Black Uhuru, Lupo's, Providence, Rhode Island, October 1983

Led Zeppelin, Madison Square Garden, New York, June 1977

New Order, Paradise Garage, New York, July 1983

What are some of your favorite songs?

"I Choose You," Willie Hutch

"Another Girl, Another Planet,"
the Only Ones

"If You Want Me to Stay," Sly &
the Family Stone

"Desperado," the Eagles

"Back Stabbers," the O'Jays

"Wonderwall," Oasis

"Ms. Jackson," Outkast

"What Can I Do for You?," Labelle

"Beautiful Child," Fleetwood Mac

"Maggot Brain," Funkadelic

"Strictly Business," EPMD

"Dream On," Aerosmith

List up to ten things that could be helpful to someone breaking into the business.

■ Be a student. And never stop being one. Be so totally informed you can talk about any kind of music with anyone. And then learn more.

■ Meet everyone you possibly can. And make sure you have something to say when you meet them.

■ Keep your word. You'll never have to tell anyone you're trustworthy: they'll say it for you.

■ Ask for help and accept criticism, but don't ever be talked out of your own style, or into any decision—business or music—that isn't true for you.

■ When it starts to feel like work, change careers.

John Kalodner

Did you have a mentor or someone who inspired you? If so, what have you learned from that person?

Ahmet Ertegun, David Geffen, Clive Davis.

Ahmet for his wild artistic persona and his ability to sign and get along with great artists. David because he is the smartest person I've ever met, both in the music business or not, and for his ability to let people do their own thing and succeed or fail on their own. Clive for his great song sense and ability to make hit records.

What was your very first job in the music industry, and how did you get it?

Working in a record store in 1969. A hippie record store called Hassle Records in Philadelphia. I just walked in off the street and asked for a job, and fifteen minutes later I was working in a record store.

What was your first big break? The first great thing that ever happened to you . . .

Walking by the desk of Jerry Greenberg, president of Atlantic Records in 1976, and picking up a tape that turned out to be Foreigner's demo tape, and then going to see them and having Jerry Greenberg allow me to sign them.

What elements of your job make you want to go to work every day?

Great songs and superstar performers. When I heard everything from "I Wanna Hold Your Hand" by the Beatles in 1964 to "Take It Easy" by the Eagles in 1972 to "Livin' on a Prayer" by Bon Jovi in 1986 to "Closing Time" by SemiSonic in 1998 to "A Thousand Miles" by Vanessa Carlton in 2002. Songs like that make me want to go to work every day.

What qualities most helped you get to where you are today?

Great ears. A big ego. Not giving a shit what anyone thinks about me. Having no fear. And most importantly always being able to spot people with great talent.

If you knew everything at the beginning of your career that you know now, what would you have done differently?

I would have insisted, over David Geffen's objections (the only time he objected to anything I did), to sign Phil Collins for his first solo record, even though he was only the drummer of Genesis.

What is your greatest lesson learned?

You never know what's going to happen, no matter how talented you are—that rap would still be meaningful fifteen years after it began, that I could possibly get thyroid cancer, and that most people aged twelve to thirty now think that music is for free.

What are some of your favorite albums?

Court and Spark, Joni Mitchell

Eli and the Thirteenth Confession, Laura Nyro

Boston, Boston

Slippery When Wet, Bon Jovi

Pump, Aerosmith

Jagged Little Pill, Alanis Morissette

Cracked Rear View, Hootie & the Blowfish

Pyromania, Def Leppard

Rubber Soul, the Beatles

Did you have any posters on your bedroom walls as a kid? Of whom?

The Beatles, of course.

What are some great shows you've seen?

The Who, Madison Square Garden, 1975

Led Zeppelin, Madison Square Garden, 1975

Joni Mitchell, the Academy of Music, Philadelphia, 1974

The Eagles, Dallas, Texas, 1975, 1979, and 2001

Journey, Tacoma, Washington, 1984

Aerosmith, Dallas, Texas, 1990

Bon Jovi in Columbus, Ohio, 2001

Jimi Hendrix, Electric Factory, Philadelphia, 1969

What are some of your favorite songs?

"Take Me to the Other Side," Aerosmith

"Rock of Ages," Def Leppard

"Help Me," Joni Mitchell

"Don't Look Back," Boston

"Here I Go Again," Whitesnake

"Livin' on a Prayer," Bon Jovi

"Runnin' with the Devil," Van Halen

"What a Fool Believes," Doobie Brothers

"Game of Love," Michelle Branch

"Highway to Hell," AC/DC

List up to ten things that could be helpful to someone breaking into the business.

- Wise up. Don't think you know everything.
- Try to learn from people who know more than you.

- Be honest, and not a liar like many people in the music business.
- Don't be a pussy! Say what you think, and do what you think.
- Don't ever care what anybody thinks about you, except maybe your mother.
- The music comes first.
- Without musicians you wouldn't have a job.
- Most things matter more than money.

Bruce Lundvall

Did you have a mentor or someone who inspired you? If so, what have you learned from that person?

A major mentor for me was John Hammond. Probably the best talent scout in the history of the business. And obviously Goddard Lieberson, the president of Columbia in the sixties, the first record company I worked for. He was an inspiration. Ken Glancy. Clive Davis. Bill Gallagher, the vice president of marketing and distribution, who hired me at Columbia. Key people who set the tone for me when I was in my formative years. The most important lesson came from John Hammond in regard to signing talent. He always believed that when you sign an artist who is original, you end up with a career. Among his legendary signings were Billie Holiday, Count Basie, Lester Young, Charlie Christian, Aretha Franklin, Bruce Springsteen, Bob Dylan, George Benson, Pete Seeger, and Stevie Ray Vaughan.

What was your very first job in the music business, and how did you get it?

I always wanted to be in the music business. I graduated from college in 1957. Walked the streets knocking on doors at Blue Note, Columbia, Capitol Records. But since I hadn't done my military service, there was no point in anyone hiring me. I got a job in the mailroom of an advertising agency and I got a call from a musician I knew called Teddy Charles. He wanted me to come on the road with him as his roadie. Within two or three days, I got my draft notice, so that was the end of that! When I got out of the army in 1960, my old college roommate Mike Berniker was a trainee at Columbia Records, and he got me an interview. And the first thing they asked me was, could you sit down with Leonard Bernstein and read a score? I said, well, I don't really think I'm up to that, so they said, well, we think you belong in marketing, so they sent me up to marketing with Bill Gallagher. I told them, "I'll work for nothing if you'll pay my bus fare into New York to show you I can do the job." And they said, "We'll call you tonight at home." I get home, six o'clock the phone rings: "You start Monday morning." They actually paid me eighty-five dollars a week. The happiest moment of my entire life. July 1960.

What elements of your job make you want to go to work every day?

Hearing something you haven't heard before, or to read a great review of one of your artists. We have Norah Jones right now. What I love best about this business is that it's a constant adventure. If you like people, hearing something new, signing an artist you believe in, or planning a marketing campaign—it's exciting to be part of an artist's career.

What qualities most helped you get to where you are today?

A deep love of music. And curiosity. And hard work, of course.

What is your greatest lesson learned?

To follow your instincts when it comes to signing new talent, as opposed to rationalizing, having meetings with a bunch of other people. You have to go with what your gut tells you. When I follow my gut instinct, I make the right decision more times than not. When I had to make joint decisions with a bunch of people, I've often ended up losing artists by waffling around, or making a marketing judgment rather than a "musical" decision.

What are some of your favorite albums?

I'd rather list artists than specific albums. Mostly jazz artists: Bud Powell, Charlie Parker, Lester Young, Clifford Brown, Nat Cole, Sinatra, pop artists like the Stones, Dylan, Tom Waits, and Joni Mitchell, and of course the artists currently on Blue Note.

What are some great shows you've seen?

I used to hang out at clubs when I was sixteen. I went to Birdland, Café Bohemia, the Downbeat Club, the Open Door, and clubs up in Harlem. Seeing Art Tatum was one of the great moments of my life. I was sitting right by the piano. Also hearing Segovia, Bernstein, Vladimir Horowitz, Willie Nelson, Aretha. The great ones are the great ones. Sinatra, Nat King Cole.

What are some of your favorite songs?

I'm a fanatic for obscure standards. I used to carry a little notebook where I wrote down every standard that came into my head and refer to it when I was looking for material for an artist.

List up to ten things that could be helpful to someone breaking into the business.

The first thing I would say to someone trying to get a job in a record company is to take any job they offer. Because it's very hard to get in the door. Once you're in the door, then you can show your stuff and move forward into different areas of a company. Don't hold out for the job you want! I wanted to be in A&R, but what the hell did I know about that? Nothing!

I had a business degree, but I was a huge fan. I ended up getting pushed into the marketing department. I ended up being vice president of marketing under Clive Davis. And later I became the general manager of the Columbia label, a newly created position. Phoebe Snow was my first signing. And then Willie Nelson, Herbie Hancock, Return to Forever, Toto, and many others. My advice is to be prepared to work long hours and late hours and to always remember that the artists and the music are what drive the business, not *you*. You are simply a middle-man (woman) between the artist and the public, and that's a pretty important position to be in. So check your ego at the door!

Guy Oseary

Did you have a mentor or someone who inspired you? If so, what have you learned from that person?

I've had a lot of mentors in my life, beginning with my father and on through many good friends who have been there for me through the years. But in the music business, I can think of two people—Madonna and David Geffen—who made the most impact on me. It's no coincidence that I became close with both of them very early in my career, starting with Madonna in my teens. I said in the introduction to this book that she held my hand and showed me the world. She was very patient with me and very supportive of me. Madonna turned me on to art, music, new places, new people, the theater, cinema and much more, taking the time to educate me on a whole other world I didn't know existed and could only imagine. Her friendship has had an incredible impact on my life and who I am today.

From the moment I met him, David was extremely good to me. He took the time to explain things to me and gave me the best advice. To this day I am often reminded of the things he has taught me. He has so many one-liners that apply daily to my life and my business. David has been an example for what one can do and where one can go in this business. He's also taught me about relationships. David has so many strong relationships, and people really respect his opinion. Even when he knows you're not going to like what he's going to tell you, even if it hurts you, he will tell you the truth. David doesn't beat around the bush, which is something he and Madonna both have in common. They both tell it like they see it, and that's a big reason why they've achieved everything they have.

David has a wealth of relationships and friendships, and everyone knows that if you have a problem and call David, he'll give you the best advice. I've really tried to emulate that in my world, with my peer group and with the people I've grown up with. I've tried to make as many connections with the talent pool of people growing up around me, and I've tried to advise as many of my peers as possible. Down the road, I'd like to be a guy who people come to because I truly get enjoyment out of being there for my friends.

What was your very first job in the music industry, and how did you get it?

My first job in the music industry was when I started managing bands. How did I get it? I created it. I didn't know I was going to start managing bands—I just knew I wanted to be in the music business. I knew that I would have to find talent, so I would go out and look for it. Pretty early I realized that a lot of talent didn't have anyone representing them or helping them, so I said, "Hey, I'll manage you," even though I was about fifteen at the time. That was my first job, trying to get record deals for my bands.

What was your first big break? The first great thing that ever happened to you . . .

There were really three "big breaks." One was when Freddy DeMann and Madonna started Maverick, and I was brought in to search for talent. It was a real opportunity. Then my second break was signing my first rock band, Candlebox. They ended up selling over three million records. That was a pretty big break for me, to immediately have that sort of success. The biggest break was signing Alanis Morissette, which took Maverick and me to a whole other level.

What elements of your job make you want to go to work every day?

What I love about what I do is the ability to do something different, to not have a set day. I walked into my office one day and said, "I want to write a book about the music business," and now you're reading this book. It was just an idea, and I did it. That's just an example of how I like to do or to try something different, sometimes weekly, sometimes even daily. I am always trying to come up with things to stay inspired and to be excited.

What qualities most helped you get to where you are today?

What helped me get to where I am today is that I didn't really have a choice. I didn't really have any money, but I went to Beverly Hills High School. I was a kid who pretended to live in Beverly Hills and had to use a fake address to get into that and so much opportunity. Knowing where I came from, it pushed me to prove something to myself—that I too could do something with my life, that I too could have some of the things that other kids had. It really pushed me early on to focus on a career and to just go for it. I was too scared of losing, and I couldn't afford to. Not wanting to be a failure was my biggest helper in getting to where I am today.

If you knew everything at the beginning of your career that you know now, what would you have done differently?

You should really understand the contracts that you sign. Always get a second opinion if you're worried or concerned. Another thing is to not believe what you're told by the people you deal with. You have to get it in writing.

If I could go back in time knowing what I know now, I would have signed every great band that I either passed on or didn't go after. That would be great!!

What is your greatest lesson learned?

It's a really hard lesson, but my greatest lesson learned is that even your failures end up being blessings. It's a hard lesson to learn because when you're in those moments of failure, you don't see the possibility of it being a positive turn. But somehow, even failures can end up being great for you. So never give up and never underestimate your potential to take something bad and turn it into something good.

What are some of your favorite albums?

Every Beatles album

Every Bob Marley album

Some Great Reward, Depeche Mode

The Queen Is Dead, the Smiths

Galore, the Cure

Did you have any posters on your bedroom walls as a kid? Of whom?

The Smiths, Prince, Billy Idol, Depeche Mode.

What are some great shows you've seen?

Jane's Addiction on the first *Lollapalooza* tour. Everything about the first *Lollapalooza* was great.

The Red Hot Chili Peppers at the Forum in Los Angeles

Rage Against the Machine (I saw them early on; they were always amazing.)

U2 at the Forum in Los Angeles

Elton John in Las Vegas

What are some of your favorite songs?

"Under Pressure," Queen & Bowie

"I Could Have Lied," the Red Hot
    Chili Peppers

"Across the Universe," the Beatles

"Kiss Me Deadly," Generation X

"Perfect Day," Lou Reed

"Summertime Rolls," Jane's Addiction

"Your Song," Elton John

"Imagine" and "Woman," John Lennon

"Redemption Song" and "Bad Card,"
    Bob Marley

"One More Try," George Michael

List up to ten things that could be helpful to someone breaking into the business.

- Get a great attorney and have them look at your contract. If it's a major deal, have a second attorney look at it and get a second opinion.
- Surround yourself with the smartest people possible.
- Set goals and have a six-month plan.
- Be a good listener.
- Be an honest person.

- Don't spend time with people who have negative energy.
- Write your ideas down on paper as much as possible. You should have a paper and pen next to your bed and in your bathroom for all those spontaneous thoughts.
- Working out helps with focus.
- Make sure everyone knows who you are. The odds of you getting something great or finding an incredible opportunity are much greater the more people who know you. Meet everyone. When I first started out I was everywhere, something I still try to do a bit of now.
- Save your money. Don't rush to spend it. Most people lose all the money they make initially. It's like some sort of process that everyone goes through—they succeed, they make money, they lose it (because they spend it on the wrong stuff), and then they learn their lesson and move on from there. So maybe whoever is reading this book, remember when I tell you that when you start making money—save it. *Just save it.* Sit on it for two years, and don't do anything with it. There's no rush. If you want to buy your first house, then do that—it's always a good investment. Other than that, just put your money away, and instead of spending, write down all the things you want to do with it. Two years later, if you still want to do those things, then go ahead. But I have a feeling that two years later you'll be very thrilled that you didn't waste your money.
- Don't limit yourself. You can do so much. People will try to brand you as the guy who does this or the guy who does that. Don't allow yourself to be boxed into a corner. Continue to grow, continue to try new things, continue to expand your mind, be more creative, and do more than what your title may be. If you're a musician, always work on your art. Be involved in everything, even if it's the design of your band's shirts. Or maybe direct a short—you could even get a little money together and direct your own video, just to see what that's like. Get creative. Dig in. Go deeper.
- If you're an artist, I can't recommend enough that you need to get a *real* manager. I see so many artists with managers who don't understand the business. Therefore, they're learning it while you're learning it. You don't want your manager learning the business. You need a good manager. It's a really big part of your career.
- Never give up. Remember that no matter what you do, you will continually be tested. You might have four, five, or six amazing consecutive years, but in anything that you do, no matter what field you're in, you will inevitably have that down period and be tested again. It doesn't matter. Don't allow yourself to give up. Don't lose faith in yourself. Remember that you can do it. Stay strong.
- Educate yourself as much as possible about the area you want to get into. I highly recommend reading every page from this book. See what all these stories have in common. Learn it! Read magazines. See what's going on. Learn about music. Learn about the history of music. Learn about new ideas. Get out and research.
- Lastly, don't ever forget the hunger. The hunger is what is going to get you to a certain point, and it's what's going to keep you there. Stay hungry to learn, hungry to grow, hungry to win.

Antonio "L.A." Reid

Did you have a mentor or someone who inspired you? If so, what have you learned from that person?

I've gained inspiration from many sources. I can't really say I had one person who really inspired me. I'm a student of the business, and a student of music. I tend to like many things about many people, and I try to pull it all together and gain my inspiration from that. If I had to narrow it down to one inspiration, it would be James Brown.

When I was a teenager, I focused only on the music, and at that point, I loved James Brown, Sly Stone, Jimi Hendrix, and John Bonham from Led Zeppelin because I was a drummer. More than anything, though, I loved songs.

What was your very first job in the music industry, and how did you get it?

I came up playing in bands. The first time I got paid was when I was fourteen or fifteen years old, and I was hired as the drummer to play behind a singing group called the Mysticks. I came about it because I was in school, probably a freshman at the time, and my music teacher was the singer. He needed a drummer, he heard me play, and I went out and made a few dollars.

I also had a band prior to that which played some clubs, but we made very little money.

What was your first big break? The first great thing that ever happened to you . . .

When I was about eighteen years old in Cincinnati, Ohio, I was hired to play on a record with a local act. They never had national acclaim, but locally they had a lot of success. It was a guy and a girl singing duet, and they called themselves simply Larry and Vicky. The record became a Top 10 record on the local R&B station, WCIN. At the same time, I had my own band, Essence, and we made a funk/rock record that was released at the same time to the FM rock station. So at eighteen, nineteen years old, I had two songs in the Top 10 on each station—one in the R&B format, one in the rock format—that I was a part of. At that point, I saw it all right there. That was a sign.

What elements of your job make you want to go to work every day?

The excitement of helping artists achieve their goals by providing them a platform of artistic freedom while giving guidance and direction gives me great pleasure. I also love the magic of teamwork, whether it be guiding the team of executives at Island Def Jam Music Group or the combination of record label and artist working together to achieve the common goal of winning. All of those things give me the energy to look forward to going to work each day.

What qualities most helped you get to where you are today?

On a professional level, I am very honest about music. I don't put out records that I don't believe in. Even if people don't like it, or even if it drives artists or producers crazy, that really doesn't matter to me. I need to feel that everything we do is special; that everything that every artist does is special. I stick to that, no matter what, and I have many fights because of it. I have many torn relationships because of it, but it's the one thing that I stick to. I believe in my ears. I believe in my gut and my intuition about songs and about music. It's the one thing that I count on that has served me well over the years.

If you knew everything at the beginning of your career that you know now, what would you have done differently?

Had I known where I was headed, I may have taken a job in a record company before becoming a label head. My first job in the record business, that somebody hired me to do as an executive, was to be the head of Arista Records. I'd never had a job before that, so it might have been nice to have a job for a couple years and then take the position as head of the label. I might have learned a lot of things. I might have been better prepared. And it might have been a little bit of a smoother ride.

What is your greatest lesson learned?

Be straight with people, no matter how difficult. People may not like what you say, but no one can get mad at you when you're being honest and straight with people.

What are some of your favorite albums?

The Art of Tea, Michael Franks
Captain Fantastic & the Brown Dirt Cowboy, Elton John
Are You Experienced?, Jimi Hendrix Experience
Chapter Two, Roberta Flack
CrazySexyCool, TLC
I Want You, Let's Get It On, and *What's Going On,* Marvin Gaye
Birth of the Cool, Miles Davis
The Chronic, Dr. Dre

Jagged Little Pill, Alanis Morissette
Off the Wall and *Thriller,* Michael Jackson
Aja, Steely Dan
Songs in the Key of Life and *Talking Book,* Stevie Wonder
Nevermind, Nirvana
College Dropout, Kanye West
The Blueprint, Jay-Z
Dirty Mind, Purple Rain, and *Sign O' the Times,* Prince

Did you have any posters on your bedroom walls as a kid? Of whom?

I had Sly & the Family Stone, the Beatles, Jimi Hendrix. I don't think I had any famous women on the wall, but I may have had the centerfolds from *Jet* magazine.

What are some great shows you've seen?

I've seen some amazing live performances:

Earth, Wind & Fire, Cincinnati

Yes, Cincinnati

The Jackson 5, Cincinnati

The Time & Prince, Indianapolis

The Eagles, Cincinnati

Weather Report, Cincinnati

James Brown, Cincinnati, when I was ten or twelve years old. It was the first concert I ever watched, and I was just blown away. It was amazing.

I watched a jazz fusion show from Return to Forever that was really good. I didn't think it could be topped until I saw Weather Report. It was topped.

What are some of your favorite songs?

This is such a difficult question. I have 3,500 songs on my iPod, and they're all my favorite songs.

"Poetry Man," Phoebe Snow

"Me and Mrs. Jones," Billy Paul

"Babylon Sisters," Steely Dan

"Your Song," Elton John

"When Doves Cry," Prince

"Hotel California," the Eagles

"Thank You (Falettinme Be Mice Elf Agin)," Sly & the Family Stone

"Little Red Corvette," Prince

"If It Isn't Love," New Edition

"Never Knew Love Like This," Alexander O'Neal & Cherrelle

"Human Nature," Michael Jackson

"Don't Speak," No Doubt

"As," Stevie Wonder

"G-Thang," Dr. Dre & Snoop

"Stairway to Heaven," Led Zeppelin

"You Oughta Know," Alanis Morissette

"Jesus Walks," Kanye West

"Glamorous Life," Sheila E.

List up to ten things that could be helpful to someone breaking into the business.

■ If you're a talented musician, then chances are you have the talent to learn most instruments. You should learn as many instruments as possible.

■ Listen to all music. Don't listen to any one genre of music. Listen to all music because you'll gain great influences from anywhere. You should listen to rock, jazz, classical, soul, dance, hip-hop.

As a musician, you have to experience it all because you never know where your great inspirations may come from.

- As sexy as it is to be on the road and be on stage, education is absolutely vital. Go to college, no matter what. Even if you have a million-dollar record contract staring you in the face, go to college. That contract will still be there if you're really talented.
- Learn as much about the business as you can learn about music, but if you're an artist, maintain your artistry and don't get too heavy.
- Enjoy the process, don't take yourself too seriously, and don't let anybody take the thrill away from you when you do have success.

Steve Rifkind

Did you have a mentor or someone who inspired you? If so, what have you learned from that person?

My father who owned a small record company called Spring Records. Not to be afraid to take chances. Stay focused and always give respect to the person who nobody knows: You will never know where that person will end up.

What was your very first job in the music industry, and how did you get it?

Interning at A&M Records for Charlie Minor and Al Cafaro.

What was your first big break? The first great thing that ever happened to you . . .

My first break was when Hiriam Hicks introduced me to Mike Bivens, and we started to manage New Edition.

What elements of your job make you want to go to work every day?

The love of music and sitting down with the most creative people in the world and just being amazed how they take an idea, help get it executed, and watch it grow.

What qualities most helped you get to where you are today?

My gut, a great dream, and not taking the word *no* for an answer.

If you knew everything at the beginning of your career that you know now, what would you have done differently?

Nothing because then you would not learn and grow.

What is your greatest lesson learned?

When my gut said something and everybody else told me I was crazy, I kept on it while everybody else put it to bed. And then the album broke.

What are some of your favorite albums?

Paid in Full, Eric B. & Rakim
License to Ill, the Beastie Boys
Raisin' Hell, Run-D.M.C.

Fear of a Black Planet, Public Enemy
Enter the Wu-Tang (36 Chambers),
 Wu-Tang Clan

Gamble & Huff boxed set

All Eyez on Me, 2Pac

Ready to Die, the Notorious B.I.G.

What are some great shows you've seen?

Led Zeppelin, Madison Square Garden, 1976

Eddie Murphy, *Raw,* the Forum, Los Angeles

Live Aid in Philadelphia

What are some of your favorite songs?

"Free Bird," Lynyrd Skynyrd

"Superstition," Stevie Wonder

"Papa Was a Rolling Stone," the Temptations

List up to ten things that could be helpful to someone breaking into the business.

- Have a plan.
- Stay true to the plan.
- Have a call sheet the night before so you are prepared for the next day.
- Execution is key.
- Network, get out, and meet as many people as you can.
- Live by your word.
- Know who your real friends are.
- Stay away from people who are jealous.
- Try to always be one step ahead of the person you are trying to get in to see.
- Trust your gut.

Tom Whalley

Did you have a mentor or someone who inspired you? If so, what have you learned from that person?

There are two people who I feel have been an inspiration. The first inspired me through his music. I grew up in New Jersey. I spent many nights going out to see bands. One place in particular was the Stone Pony. It was there I saw Bruce Springsteen. His music had a tremendous impact on me. The second happened years later when I met Lenny Waronker. He was working for Warner Bros. Records as a staff producer and eventually became the president.

Bruce Springsteen made me realize how much I loved music. I eventually moved to California to get a job in the business. Years later I met Lenny while I was working in the mailroom at Warner Bros. Records. He loved the whole creative process. He was amazing at discovering talent and then developing his artists' careers. He was also a wonderful person. In a business filled with characters, he was a breath of fresh air. He proved to me you could be a decent, truthful person and still succeed.

What was your first job in the music industry, and how did you get it.

In 1979, I started in the mailroom at Warner Bros. Records. I applied for the job.

What was your first break? The first great thing that ever happened to you . . .

My first break came when I was given the task of listening to demo tapes for the A&R department at Warner Bros. Records. At that time companies still listened to unsolicited demo tapes. My job was to listen to those tapes.

What elements of your job make you want to go to work every day?

I have a passionate love for music. I especially enjoy discovering new talent and developing their careers. I believe in longevity and building futures.

What qualities most helped you get to where you are today?

Honesty, integrity, and determination.

If you knew everything at the beginning of your career that you know now, what would you have done differently?

I would have started my own record company years ago.

What is your greatest lesson learned?

Belief in creativity and talent should always come before business decisions.

What are you some of your favorite albums?

Born to Run, Bruce Springsteen

Graceland, Paul Simon

Avalon, Roxy Music

White Album, the Beatles

Did you have any posters on your bedroom walls as a kid? Of whom?

Jimi Hendrix, Led Zeppelin, and Bruce Springsteen.

What are some great shows you've seen?

Jimi Hendrix, Led Zeppelin, Bruce Springsteen, AC/DC, Pink Floyd, Nine Inch Nails.

What are some of your favorite songs?

"Rosalita," Bruce Springsteen

"Don't Dream It's Over,"
 Crowded House

"Sittin' on the Dock of the Bay,"
 Otis Redding

"No Woman No Cry," Bob Marley

List up to ten things that could be helpful to someone breaking into the business.

Commitment, honesty, determination, perseverance, a passion for music, and independence.

MANAGERS

Irving Azoff

Did you have a mentor or someone who inspired you? If so, what have you learned from that person?

David Geffen. He told me in 1972 it would be a great business without artists. I revised this to "I resent artists for taking 85 percent of my money." Seriously, he was the first great manager.

What was your very first job in the music industry, and how did you get it?

I hired myself to book and promote local bands as a senior in high school. My drumming was too awful to be in the band.

What was your first big break? The first great thing that ever happened to you . . .

Dan Fogelberg walked into my office and played me an amazing tape. He became one of my first management clients. His bicycle was stolen while we met. We were hardly old enough to drive.

What elements of your job make you want to go to work every day?

I am the Dennis the Menace of the music business—and it's all for a good cause, to protect artists from the wolves out there.

What qualities most helped you get to where you are today?

I give great phone. I return every call. There is no mountain I won't scale for a client.

If you knew everything at the beginning of your career that you know now, what would you have done differently?

Absolutely nothing. I have been a manager, merchandiser, record company head, record company owner, publisher, agent, movie producer, etc., and I've had fun every time.

What is your greatest lesson learned?

In this business, no good deed goes unpunished. Keep a sense of humor—it's not brain surgery what we are doing here.

What are some of your favorite albums?

Meet the Beatles, the Beatles
Hotel California, The Long Run,
   and *One of These Nights,* the Eagles

The Best of Van Morrison
Aja, Steely Dan

Did you have any posters on your bedroom walls as a kid? Of whom?

Muhammad Ali with the Beatles.

What are some great shows you've seen?

The Beatles, the Hollywood Bowl
The Eagles, Lucca, Italy
The Eagles, Elton, and the Beach Boys at Wembley Stadium

What are some of your favorite songs?

"All My Loving," the Beatles
"Hotel California," the Eagles
"Tupelo Honey," Van Morrison

"Deacon Blues," Steely Dan
"Lookin' for Love," Johnny Lee
"Lowdown," Boz Scoggs

List up to ten things that could be helpful to someone breaking into the business.

- Be on time.
- Return every phone call.
- Don't bullshit a bullshitter.

Caresse Henry

Did you have a mentor or someone who inspired you? If so, what have you learned from that person?

My first mentor was Freddy DeMann—he gave me an introduction to the music business and to a certain degree reminded me of Colonel Parker, who I was always intrigued by. I have been inspired by so many people from Madonna to Liz Rosenberg (Madonna's press agent) to the success of Judy McGrath and Oprah Winfrey. Being a woman in this business is a challenge, and I feel that I have had the privilege of working with or meeting some of the most inspiring and successful people who work in entertainment.

What was your very first job in the music industry, and how did you get it?

Working at a business management firm and was hired via my roommate who worked there. I enjoyed learning about the financial and business side of the entertainment business. I was in the right place at the right time. My original goal was to be a news anchor—so I totally veered off course.

What was your first big break? The first great thing that ever happened to you . . .

I feel like I have had so many breaks in life and breakthroughs in this industry. I would say that my very first break was meeting Madonna. That was the beginning of my career, which has been and continues to be fantastic. The greatest thing that has ever happened to me is having two beautiful and healthy girls and being with my soul mate.

What elements of your job make you want to go to work every day?

I love what I do. There are so many challenges that come up daily in the ever-changing entertainment business. No one can predict success, and there are no solid answers to what is right or what is wrong to do. Sometimes you have to take risks or go outside your comfort zone and things end up being better than you expect. I am gracious to be in the position I have, and the fact that I am able to work with such a true genius artist like Madonna makes me feel extremely grateful and constantly inspired.

What qualities most helped you get to where you are today?

I never give up. I don't believe in ever stopping. Life is too short, and I try to not let negativity permeate my existence. Also, it's very important to be inspired and to surround yourself with people who are smart and trustworthy. Having a family also helps me maintain a balance and perspective on what is truly important in life.

If you knew everything at the beginning of your career that you know now, what would you have done differently?

I would have invested more in Starbucks!

What is your greatest lesson learned?

That hard work really does pay off; it's not just a cliché.

What are some of your favorite albums?

Café del Mar series

KCRW's *Sounds Eclectic* CDs

Master Sessions, Cachao

All Brian Eno albums

The Mission, Ennio Morricone

Best of Cesaria Evora, Cesaria Evora

Dummy, Portishead

London Calling, the Clash

Pieces in a Modern Style, William Orbit

American Life and *Music,* Madonna

Did you have any posters on your bedroom walls as a kid? Of whom?

Lee Majors's *Six Million Dollar Man*!

What are some great shows you've seen?

Madonna's *Blonde Ambition*

U2's *Elevation* tour

Cirque du Soleil—especially *O*

Lollapalooza, 1992

What are some of your favorite songs?

Any Beatles tune

Any Stevie Wonder song

"Hallelujah," Jeff Buckley

"Nothing Fails," Madonna

"I Still Haven't Found What I'm
    Looking For," U2

"Little Red Corvette," Prince

"Who Are You," the Who

"Your Song," Elton John

"Mercy Mercy Me," Marvin Gaye

There's so many more it's too hard
    to list them all!

List up to ten things that could be helpful to someone breaking into the business.

- Stamina.
- Do not get discouraged.
- Do not get sidetracked.
- Follow your heart and your gut.
- Treat everyone with respect.
- Always remember to give back.
- And most of all, do it for the right reason.

Jon Landau

Did you have a mentor or someone who inspired you? If so, what have you learned from that person?

Among them were Jerry Wexler and David Geffen. Jerry really was the first one to teach me the inside of the record world and encouraged me to become a young producer. David taught me how to be a manager.

What was your very first job in the music industry, and how did you get it?

I started as a critic while I was still in high school. From my journalism I got noticed within the industry and got some of my early opportunities.

What was your first big break? The first great thing that ever happened to you . . .

One of them was meeting the MC5 and getting to produce their *Back in the U.S.A*. It was a crash course in all the skills I would find I needed later in my career.

What elements of your job make you want to go to work every day?

The people I work with and the people I work for. I've worked for Bruce [Springsteen] in one way or another for almost thirty years and words could not begin to describe what a wonderful and satisfying experience that has been.

What qualities most helped you get to where you are today?

My ability to understand artistry and to make a contribution to the larger talents of the artists themselves, whether in the studio or in their careers.

If you knew everything at the beginning of your career that you know now, what would you have done differently?

I would have hired Allen [Grubman] and Artie [Indusrky] sooner.

What is your greatest lesson learned?

Jerry Wexler told me thirty-five years ago that the most talented producer, manager—what have you—in the world is the man with the new Beatles album under his arm. Recognizing artistry is the single most important part of this work.

What are some of your favorite albums?

Dictionary of Soul, Otis Redding

England's Newest Hitmakers, the Rolling Stones

God and Me, Marion Williams

What are some great shows you've seen?

I saw Pete Seeger give a children's concert when I was five years old, and it started a lifelong love of music. Bruce [Springsteen] is the greatest performer I've ever seen, and the first time I saw him certainly changed my life.

List up to ten things that could be helpful to someone breaking into the business.

- You can't love music too much.
- You have got to be a self-starter and capable of creating your own opportunities because when you're starting out no one creates them for you.
- And you have to find ways to always maintain your dignity in a universe where that can sometimes be hard to do.

Chris Lighty

Did you have a mentor or someone who inspired you? If so, what have you learned from that person?

I have a few mentors in the business. The first is my dear friend Red Alert who allowed me to carry crates into the great hip-hop parties that he deejayed. The most profound mentor in my life has been Lyor Cohen who showed me the business inside and out.

What was your very first job in the music industry, and how did you get it?

My very first job was carrying crates for Red Alert in and out of the clubs. I got the job by being a pest; persistence overcomes resistance.

What was your first big break? The first great thing that ever happened to you . . .

My first break was being a part of the Jungle Bros. As a slash road manager/deejay/garbage collector, we traveled the world five times. The first great thing was being able to be a part of Rush Management and work with Russell Simmons and Lyor Cohen.

What elements of your job make you want to go to work every day?

The love of music . . . finding and creating new stars, and making the dreams and aspirations of my clients come to reality. I am fortunate to work with so many talented people from Busta Rhymes to Mobb Deep. It's all different spectrums of the musical rainbow.

What qualities most helped you get to where you are today?

Persistence, patience, and the thirst to learn how the business works and how I can master it. The ability to understand that "slow and steady" will win the marathon.

If you knew everything at the beginning of your career that you know now, what would you have done differently?

Nothing. I have no true regrets on how my career has evolved. We all make mistakes on signings and passing over stars. I'm just glad to have worked with so many talented people.

What is your greatest lesson learned?

Crawl, walk, run. Do not rush to keep up with the Joneses. Build a career; sell ten million records over ten years (a million at a time) versus selling ten million at one time and no career thereafter.

What are some of your favorite albums?

Criminal Minded, Boogie Down Productions

The Low End Theory, A Tribe Called Quest

Love Deluxe, Sade

Off the Wall, Michael Jackson

Portishead, Portishead

Mama Said Knock You Out, LL Cool J

Did you have any posters on your bedroom walls as a kid? Of whom?

None. I was following after the Zulu Nation movement. Growing up in the Bronx, I would say . . . my first inspiration every day was when I saw my mother leave for work.

What are some great shows you've seen?

The Fresh Fest and *Raisin' Hell* tours

A Tribe Called Quest on *Lollapalooza*

Busta Rhymes on *Smoking Grooves* tour

Sade, Madison Square Garden

What are some of your favorite songs?

Anything by Sade

Anything on the *Off the Wall*
   and *Thriller* LPs

"Criminal Minded," Boogie Down Productions

"Doin' It," LL Cool J

List up to ten things that could be helpful to someone breaking into the business.

■ Adopt a philosophy and follow it . . . "Crawl, walk, run" is our mantra at Violator.

■ Learn patience.

■ Pick a mentor and follow his/her footsteps and then create your own.

■ Read the *48 Laws of Power* and adapt it to your own life.

■ Embrace your failures with the same dignity as you embrace your victories.

■ Love what you do so it's not a job but a life.

Terry McBride

Did you have a mentor or someone who inspired you? If so, what have you learned from that person?

Roy Lott, current president of Virgin U.S., taught me a lot during his days at Arista. Deane Cameron, president of EMI Canada, taught me to express my passion for music.

What was your very first job in the music industry, and how did you get it?

Deejay at college radio (CITR, Vancouver, B.C.); first paid gig was at record retail.

What was your first big break? The first great thing that ever happened to you . . .

A local band let me manage them and release their first album. I lost a good portion of my savings but learned some valuable lessons.

What elements of your job make you want to go to work every day?

Music.

What qualities most helped you get to where you are today?

Honesty: As hard as it can be when dealing with an artist, best to just say it as you think it.

Passion: Don't yell, scream, just say it with heart, and laugh at those who doubt.

If you knew everything at the beginning of your career that you know now, what would you have done differently?

I would never have gone on the road in a van for years on end.

What is your greatest lesson learned?

That you can have the same partners for twenty-plus years and remain great friends.

What are some of your favorite albums?

Closer, Joy Division

Fumbling Towards Ecstasy, Sarah McLachlan

A Rush of Blood to the Head, Coldplay

Singles Going Steady, the Buzzcocks

Rumours, Fleetwood Mac

Magical Mystery Tour and *Sgt. Pepper's Lonely Hearts Club Band*, the Beatles

Led Zeppelin IV, Led Zeppelin

Harvest, Neil Young

Nevermind, Nirvana

Bridge Over Troubled Water,
  Simon & Garfunkel

Dark Side of the Moon, Pink Floyd

Did you have any posters on your bedroom walls as a kid? Of whom?

No band posters, but I had some weird-ass black-light poster.

What are some great shows you've seen?

U2, Slane Castle

Coldplay, Vancouver, 2001

Avril Lavigne's first concert ever. It was a free show in Vancouver. Simply no fear . . .

Sum 41, summer 2002

Barenaked Ladies, *Stunt* tour

Lilith Fair—the very first and very last concerts . . . spine-tingling

What are some of your favorite songs?

"Seasons in the Sun," Terry Jacks

"Angel," Sarah McLachlan

"Trouble," Coldplay

"Song 2," Blur

"Nothing Compares 2 U," Sinéad O'Connor

"The Boxer," Simon & Garfunkel

"Roxanne," Police

"Smells Like Teen Spirit," Nirvana

List up to ten things that could be helpful to someone breaking into the business.

- Keep a few part-time jobs until you make some $.
- Be passionate.
- Work 24/7 while you're young.

Paul McGuinness

Did you have a mentor or someone who inspired you? If so, what have you learned from that person?

Chris Blackwell, Frank Barsalona, Ian Flooks, Barbara Skydel, Jimmy Iovine, and Arthur Fogel.

What was your very first job in the music industry, and how did you get it?

I promoted a concert in Dublin with Donovan in 1970.

What was your first big break? The first great thing that ever happened to you . . .

Donovan performed free.

What elements of your job make you want to go to work every day?

No assholes—colleague or client—and seeing all the great cities of the world every time U2 tours.

What qualities most helped you get to where you are today?

The qualities of my clients were extremely important.

If you knew everything at the beginning of your career that you know now, what would you have done differently?

Never to deal with someone who is always too busy.

What is your greatest lesson learned?

The management business is a high overhead business, not a low overhead business.

What are some of your favorite albums?

Exile on Main Street, the Rolling Stones
Zooropa, U2
Stabat Mater, Pergolesi

Did you have any posters on your bedroom walls as a kid? Of whom?

Charlotte Rampling in *The Night Porter.*

What are some great shows you've seen?

U2, Madison Square Garden, 1997

U2, Madison Square Garden, 2001

David Bowie, Montreux, Switzerland, 2002

What are some of your favorite songs?

"One," U2

"Born to Run," Bruce Springsteen

"Da Doo Ron Ron," the Crystals

"Moonlight Mile," the Rolling Stones

List up to ten things that could be helpful to someone breaking into the business.

- Luggage—Tumi is good
- Constitution of an ox
- Taste
- Discrimination
- Very talented client who hasn't made any bad deals yet
- Lawyers
- Guns
- Money

Benny Medina

Did you have a mentor or someone who inspired you? If so, what have you learned from that person?

The only two guys that I ever worked for were Berry Gordy at Motown and Mo Ostin at Warner Bros. Records. From Berry Gordy, I learned that the song itself was the key, that melody was king and that presentation was everything. From Mo Ostin, I learned that you should always only sign and get involved with artists that you truly believe in. Seek out visionaries with integrity.

What was your very first job in the music business, and how did you get it?

What I consider my first job in the music industry was taking care of Berry Gordy's pets— deer, llamas, and koi at his estate. I went from pet care to security to a sort-of assistant type to a writer/producer/artist/executive at Motown Records. It all went from one stage to the next. And I thank God for the experience. I was exposed to a world of creativity populated by people of color who were color-blind.

What was your first big break? The first great thing that ever happened to you . . .

I consider my first break to be growing up in a place called St. Elmo's Village, which led to moving from East Los Angeles to a garage in Beverly Hills where I was allowed to go to Beverly Hills High School. I already had the entertainment bug, but then I became surrounded by so many people whose lives, successes, and homes were built out of entertainment. The break was when I connected the art with the commerce in a totally new environment. I was fifteen.

What elements of your job make you want to go to work every day?

That I am actually going to create something that's going to incite reaction, positive or whatever, and that it all just comes from an idea. Every day there's a new piece of clay to be shaped in any way that I, or the creative people that I am involved with, want to shape it. I love the idea that every day you can create some form of permanent art, whether it's a record, or a television show, or a film, something that will hopefully stand the test of time.

What qualities most helped you get to where you are today?

My faith and my instincts. My ability to communicate. My passion and love for creating and being a part of the process. My motivation. My patience and my impatience. Being a team player.

If you knew everything at the beginning of your career that you know now, what would you have done differently?

I don't know if I would have *done* anything differently because I feel so grateful to be where I am today. I wish that I had known that only a very small percentage of the advice you get is actually worth anything. I probably wouldn't have taken as much advice as I did from other people about things that I wanted to do. I would have followed my own instincts earlier . . . maybe!

What is your greatest lesson learned?

Over the years what I have learned is that you have to do it for love, but it's great to own what you create. When I say "own what you create," I mean not only in terms of the copyright, the intellectual property library, but also in terms of owning the idea/creative space that you exist in. It's about making sure that a great business structure exists behind you that is going to support whatever you generate; that there is an infrastructure in place to handle the business properly. It is entertainment business after all.

What are some of your favorite albums?

What's Going On, Marvin Gaye
Innervisions or *Songs in the Key of Life,* Stevie Wonder
Joshua Tree, U2
The Song Remains the Same, Led Zeppelin
Sgt. Pepper's Lonely Hearts Club Band, the Beatles
Gratitude or *That's the Way of the World,* Earth, Wind & Fire
Born in the USA, Bruce Springsteen
Kind of Blue, Miles Davis
Are You Experienced?, Jimi Hendrix Experience
Hotel California, the Eagles
Off the Wall and *Thriller,* Michael Jackson

I believe that the most significant music you'll hear is in your teen years, and that that becomes indelibly etched into your psyche. I'm forty-five years old, and those are the records I grew up with, and every time I listen to them, they take me there.

I believe the music being produced today will have the same effect on younger generations of music listeners, and I think that the newer art forms that have come along are completely and totally viable. While a lot of stuff today is hot, it's not timeless. That's just my own opinion about music today. But I do believe when I came up there was an opportunity to experience a greater variety, and that there's something lost when you're not open to all kinds of music— from pop music, to urban music, to rock music, to rap music, to alternative music, to classical music and jazz. I mean jazz is America's classical music. I think that what will be indelibly etched into the psyches of modern youth is more limited today, although I still think it's valid—you can't sample forever.

Did you have any posters on your bedroom walls as a kid? Of whom?

There weren't a lot of posters to get. But I remember having the Guess Who, Led Zeppelin, Bad Company, Supertramp, Marvin Gaye, the Jackson 5, Earth, Wind & Fire, Al Green, the Temptations, and, of course, Martin Luther King and Malcolm X.

What are some great shows you've seen?

Earth, Wind & Fire at the Forum in Los Angeles during the *That's the Way of the World* tour, which became a live album and took the idea of a big production for a black, urban group to a whole different level.
U2's *Zoo TV* in Los Angeles, Paris, London, Germany—I followed it around the world.
Bruce Springsteen at the Roxy on Sunset Boulevard
Boz Scaggs at the Roxy before the *Here's the Low Down* album came out
David Bowie at the Hollywood Palladium in the seventies and at the Santa Monica Civic
KISS at the Santa Monica Civic
Led Zeppelin at the Los Angeles Forum
Elton John with the *Candle in the Wind* tour at the Greek Theater

What are some of your favorite songs?

"When Doves Cry," and "Sign O' the Times" Prince
"The Breaks," Kurtis Blow
"Peter Piper," Run-D.M.C.
"What's Going On," Marvin Gaye
"Living for the City," Stevie Wonder
"With or Without You," "In the Name of Love," "Where the Streets Have No Name," U2
"Imagine," John Lennon
"My Philosophy," Boogie Down Productions
"Fight the Power," Public Enemy
"What the World Needs Now"

"People"
"One More Chance," the Notorious B.I.G.
"Stairway to Heaven," Led Zeppelin
"Owner of a Lonely Heart," Yes
"I'm Bad," LL Cool J
"All I Need," Method Man and Mary J. Blige
"I'll Be There," the Spinners
"Ain't No Stopping Us Now," McFadden & Whitehead
"Reminisce," Pete Rock and C.L. Smooth
"Paid in Full," Eric B & Rakim
"If I Were Your Girlfriend"

List up to ten things that could be helpful to someone breaking into the business.

■ I believe that if you're going to be in the music business, you really should know music, either from a player's perspective and/or a historical perspective, to have that as a reference. At the same time, your individuality as an executive, your point of view as a musician, and your point of view as a producer or a writer is the actual key to your success and how you're going to carve a path. Individuality and originality are so important.

■ You should be really careful about how to listen and process advice, but hang on to your own instincts.

■ It's ride or die. It's not about what appears to be a super glamorous business today by virtue of music videos and what they exploit about the business. Instead, it's about the passion that you need to have to be a creative entity. That's what really makes it fun, and ultimately, those rewards last. When you think about where people start, and then hopefully have this huge and successful arc, they invariably end up back where they started, in the best of ways. Whether they're multimillionaires or not, they still gotta play. Bruce, the Stones, Earth, Wind & Fire, David Bowie, U2—everybody's still gotta play. So my big piece of advice is that you gotta play— and not that many people do today, which is why there is no touring business for a lot of acts out there. You have to take it to another visual and/or aural level. It's that indelible connection beyond opening the record for the first time and playing it that carves your creativity into my existence. When Zoo TV did that Martin Luther King "I Have a Dream" speech in the middle of *In the Name of Love,* and then they did it with Salman Rushdie in Paris—it was just amazing!

Peter Mensch

Did you have a mentor or someone who inspired you? If so, what have you learned from that person?

My mentor was and is my partner, Cliff. I met him when he promoted my college radio station at Brandeis. We became friends, and all we talked about (mostly long distance) was the music business. I learned nearly everything about all of it. And then what I did not learn from him, I picked up in my first job with Aerosmith on the road. The guy who hired me for that job, David Krebs, was a bit of a mentor as well.

What was your very first job in the music industry, and how did you get it?

First job out of graduate school was working for my eventual partner, Cliff Burnstein. Cliff was an A&R man for Mercury Records in Chicago, and he had persuaded the powers that be to give him a small alternative label he had named Blank Records (logo was the mathematical symbol for the null set). Blank had a budget for one employee living in New York City. We signed two acts: Pere Ubu and the Suicide Commandos. I was the label manager, and my outstanding memory of that period was that I spent a lot of time at CBGB watching acts. I got the job because he was my friend (see the first question).

What was your first big break? The first great thing that ever happened to you . . .

First break was meeting Cliff. Second break was getting this job with Aerosmith as their tour accountant. It was on the *Draw the Line* tour where I met AC/DC. I became friends with them through 1978 and through a byzantine set of circumstances became their manager in 1979.

What elements of your job make you want to go to work every day?

The desire to be involved in music on all levels. Also being a competitive fuck.

What qualities most helped you get to where you are today?

Doggedness. Perseverance. Being driven. Being smart. Desire not to lose.

If you knew everything at the beginning of your career that you know now, what would you have done differently?

You know, that's a good question. Besides an act or two I missed as a manager (Linkin Park springs to mind), not a lot. Perhaps a bit quicker on the uptake as to what Nirvana would do to all of the eighties acts I managed. Better life advice to my friend Steve Clark from Def Leppard. I have had a pretty charmed life to be honest.

What is your greatest lesson learned?

You cannot lose if you are on the side of the artist.
Own the moral high ground.

Don't do it for money.
Do it because it is the right thing to do

What are some of your favorite albums?

Too many to name. And I go back and forth between the past, like Jethro Tull's *Benefit,* to the present, such as Gillian Welch's *The Revelator Collection.*

Did you have any posters on your bedroom walls as a kid? Of whom?

Trotsky, Einstein, a poster from Georges Santayana: "Those who do not study history are condemned to repeat it," and an Escher poster.

What are some great shows you've seen?

The Who performing *Tommy*
Steeleye Span playing support to Procul Harum
Guns 'N Roses supporting the Rolling Stones in L.A
Creedence Clearwater Revival at the Fillmore East
Hole in Columbus, Ohio
Metallica in Bristol, UK
Def Leppard on the *Hysteria* tour at the Meadowlands
The Red Hots headlining in Holland during the summer of 2001
AC/DC at Le Bourget, Paris, on the *Back in Black* tour
Emerson, Lake & Palmer and Yes playing together at the Auditorium Theatre in Chicago
The Rolling Stones in rehearsal for the *Steel Wheels* tour at Nassau Coliseum in '89
The list is endless.

What are some of your favorite songs?

Impossible to list. It changes every day.

List up to ten things that could be helpful to someone breaking into the business.

- Pure dumb luck. And then like a running back hitting a hole, when the luck happens, drive a truck right through it.
- Thinking a couple of steps ahead and *always* thinking like the audience thinks.

Sharon Osbourne

Did you have a mentor or someone who inspired you? If so, what have you learned from that person?

I never had a mentor.

What was your very first job in the music industry, and how did you get it?

I was a receptionist in my father's management company when I was fifteen.

What was your first big break? The first great thing that ever happened to you . . .

It was when my dad said I was now capable of doing day-to-day management on bands.

What elements of your job make you want to go to work every day?

Just knowing that you were right either about an artist that's talented or about a project that you believe will be successful and then it comes to fruition.

What qualities most helped you get to where you are today?

Knowledge and being lucky enough to work with talented people.

If you knew everything at the beginning of your career that you know now, what would you have done differently?

I know now that you should always keep hold of an artist's publishing.

What is your greatest lesson learned?

To be nice to people on the way up because you're going to need them on the way down.

What are some of your favorite albums?

Imagine, John Lennon
Night at the Opera, Queen
No More Tears, Ozzy Osbourne

Did you have any posters on your bedroom walls as a kid? Of whom?

John Lennon.

What are some great shows you've seen?

When I was a kid I was lucky enough to see so many amazing shows: Sam Cooke, Ike & Tina Turner, the Everly Brothers, Jerry Lee Lewis, Gene Vincent, the Righteous Brothers, Chuck Berry, the Rolling Stones, Barbra Streisand on Broadway, and Julie Andrews.

What are some of your favorite songs?

"Imagine," John Lennon

"Bohemian Rhapsody," Queen

"Stairway to Heaven," Led Zeppelin

"Respect," Aretha Franklin

"Crazy Train" and "Mama I'm Coming Home," Ozzy Osbourne

"Bridge Over Troubled Water," Simon and Garfunkel

List up to ten things that could be helpful to someone breaking into the business.

- Never take no for an answer.
- Take less money up front and more royalties.
- Don't take on a project unless you 100 percent believe in it, otherwise it shows.
- If you don't know something, *shut the fuck up!*

Scott Welch

Did you have a mentor or someone who inspired you? If so, what have you learned from that person?

I was fortunate enough to have several throughout my life. They all taught me different things about not only the "business" but more importantly about life. The main things were be patient, respect the art and the artists, treat other people as you expect to be treated, and find enjoyment on the darkest days.

What was your very first job in the music industry, and how did you get it?

I was the student body president in high school and was chairman of the entertainment committee. I auditioned bands for all the dances at my school.

What was your first big break? The first great thing that ever happened to you . . .

Upon graduation my grandfather loaned me fifteen thousand dollars to buy into a recording studio. This allowed me to earn a living in the business and still pursue management of artists.

What elements of your job make you want to go to work every day?

It is very rewarding and fulfilling to work alongside artists and be a part of their creations. The most incredible thing is to hear a song that the artist has just written before anyone else and help it to be shared with the world.

What qualities most helped you get to where you are today?

The most important quality you can possess is a strong work ethic. Be self-motivated and be humble in your successes and lean on your integrity in your failures.

If you knew everything at the beginning of your career that you know now, what would you have done differently?

Gone to law school? Nothing!! I am so fortunate to work in a great partnership, have amazing clients, employees, and the most supportive family you could ask for.

What is your greatest lesson learned?

I never forget that the reason any of us have a job is because of the artists. We have a sacred responsibility to preserve, protect, and nurture the artists and the art they create.

What are some of your favorite albums?

Abbey Road, the Beatles

Physical Graffiti, Led Zeppelin

Joshua Tree, U2

Jagged Little Pill, Alanis Morissette

Did you have any posters on your bedroom walls as a kid? Of whom?

Jimi Hendrix, peace symbol, marijuana reform, and the *Easy Rider* movie poster.

What are some great shows you've seen?

Lynyrd Skynyrd, club show, 1972

Guns N' Roses

Prince

U2

Crosby, Stills, Nash & Young, 1974

Bruce Springsteen, 1976

What are some of your favorite songs?

"With or Without You," U2

"You Shook Me All Night Long," AC/DC

"Smells Like Teen Spirit," Nirvana

"Imagine," John Lennon

List up to ten things that could be helpful to someone breaking into the business.

- Respect the art and artists first and foremost.
- Be humble.
- Prepare to fail more than you succeed.
- Educate yourself on the history of music and its evolution. It will provide you with a foundation of love and respect for the music.
- Read as many psychology books as possible. You will spend more time on the couch with your clients than you can imagine.
- Listen, listen, listen to your gut!!

ATTORNEYS

John Branca

Did you have a mentor or someone who inspired you? If so, what have you learned from that person?

There was an article in *Los Angeles* magazine in the late seventies when I was a very young lawyer listing the most powerful attorneys in the music business. I worked with one of them, David Braun. That article motivated me. I wanted to go to the top of that list. Also, I was inspired by Professor of Political Science Raymond McKelvey of Occidental College, and by Dean Susan Prager of UCLA Law School. Most of all, I was inspired by great music, the first being Elvis Presley.

What was your very first job in the music industry, and how did you get it?

In ninth grade, I formed a band called the Other Half, which was signed to GNP/Crescendo Records. I was too young to tour with the group, and then while still in school formed another band which was signed to Original Sound Records after performing at Gazzari's and other Sunset Strip clubs.

What was your first big break? The first great thing that ever happened to you . . .

I was hired by David Braun and began representing Neil Diamond and Bob Dylan in the late seventies. My first major break was representing my first major client, the Beach Boys, and then Michael Jackson, following the release of the *Off the Wall* album. I renegotiated Michael's contract with Epic Records at that time, which set up the release of the *Thriller* album. Upon the release of "Beat It," Michael decided to go without management for the duration of the *Thriller* album. That placed me in the unique position at a young age to work in a legal and management capacity with one of the industry's all-time greatest artists and to help him market the biggest-selling worldwide album of all time. Thereafter, we bought the Beatles catalog and made other precedent-setting deals.

What elements of your job make you want to go to work every day?

The most exciting element is creative problem-solving—what we do is a puzzle on one level or another—and helping my clients capitalize on their success. I am also motivated by a love of music and adding to the fact that I've had the opportunity to represent, so far, twenty-eight members of the Rock and Roll Hall of Fame.

What qualities most helped you get to where you are today?

Intelligence, judgment, ambition, flexibility, and creativity.

If you knew everything at the beginning of your career that you know now, what would you have done differently?

I would have played lead guitar for Bad Company.

What is your greatest lesson learned?

Still learning. Some people do things for money. Others for power. I love both, but ultimately I make decisions based on what's right to me. This has put me at odds with many people in the business, but at the end of the day, it's what makes the most sense to me.

What are some of your favorite albums?

Thriller, Michael Jackson

Supernatural, Carlos Santana

For LP Fans Only, Elvis Presley

Pet Sounds, the Beach Boys

Sgt. Pepper's Lonely Hearts Club Band, the Beatles

Let It Bleed, the Rolling Stones

The Doors, the Doors

Bad Company, Bad Company

Hotel California, the Eagles

Permanent Vacation, Aerosmith

Shake Your Money Maker, the Black Crowes

Live at Mr. Kelly's, Muddy Waters

Goin' Back to New Orleans, Dr. John

That's All, Bobby Darin

Did you have any posters on your bedroom walls as a kid? Of whom?

Elvis Presley, Jim Morrison, Mickey Mantle, and Dr. Martin Luther King Jr.

What are some great shows you've seen?

Michael Jackson, *Victory*

U2, *Zoo TV*

The Rolling Stones, Long Beach Arena

The Doors, Whiskey A-Go-Go

Led Zeppelin, Cal State Northridge

Muddy Waters, Troubador

Wilson Pickett, 5-4 Club

Camelot with Richard Burton

What are some of your favorite songs?

"Turn Back the Hands of Time" and "Turning Point," Tyrone Davis

"Stubborn Kind of Fellow," Marvin Gaye

"Sweet Little 16," Chuck Berry

"California Girls," the Beach Boys

"One Love," Bob Marley

"In the Ghetto," Donnie Hathaway

"Isn't She Lovely," Stevie Wonder

"Black or White," Michael Jackson

"Can't Get Enough of Your Love," Bad Company

"Walk This Way," Aerosmith

"All Right Now," Free

"Don't Be Cruel," Elvis Presley

"It's Not My Cross to Bear,"
  the Allman Brothers

"Volare," Domenico Modugno

"Beyond the Sea," Bobby Darin

List up to ten things that could be helpful to someone breaking into the business.

"The only thing to do with good advice is to pass it on; it is never of any use to one's self."
Oscar Wilde

- Do what you love, combine your passion with your vocation.
- Have single-minded focus and dedication.
- Set goals.
- Don't get discouraged.

- Re-evaluate your game plan.
- Periodically take time out for perspective.
- Balance your life with recreation, passion, and family.
- Good luck!

Jay Cooper

Did you have a mentor or someone who inspired you? If so, what have you learned from that person?

Thanks to an autobiography by Clarence Darrow, *My Life and Times,* which exemplified his dedication, belief, and passion for his cases and his clients, I was taught to love the law. Adlai Stevenson, from his speeches and writing, I learned about caring and integrity. From a neurosurgeon, Kenneth Richland, I observed and learned about dedication, focus, and thoroughness.

What was your very first job in the music industry, and how did you get it?

I was a musician in a big band that brought me to California. I arrived with a saxophone, clarinet, flute, and a law degree. I later opened a small office on my own, and my first clients were the musicians, singers, and dancers that I had worked with.

What was your first big break? The first great thing that ever happened to you . . .

I received a call one day from a New York attorney by the name of Andy Feinman, saying that Phil Spector was coming to California, and he needed an attorney to negotiate a record contract with two young guys from Orange County . . . the Righteous Brothers.

What elements of your job make you want to go to work every day?

I represent very interesting and creative people who present fascinating challenges which allow me to be creative in finding solutions to whatever their problems or desires may be.

What qualities most helped you get to where you are today?

My willingness to learn, to be thorough, and expend whatever effort it takes to do the best possible job for my clients.

If you knew everything at the beginning of your career that you know now, what would you have done differently?

Maybe spending a few more years as a musician before making the transition to law.

What is your greatest lesson learned?

Your time and your reputation are really the only assets you can truly possess. Therefore, guard them jealously.

What are some of your favorite albums?

Only the Lonely, Frank Sinatra

Tommy, the Who

The *Red Album* and the *Blue Album,* the Beatles

Atomic Basie and *Basie Plays Hefti,* Count Basie and Neal Hefti

Miles Ahead, Miles Davis

Did you have any posters on your bedroom walls as a kid? Of whom?

My room wasn't big enough for posters, but I had a lot of Benny Goodman, Stan Kenton, Count Basie, and Woody Herman records stashed around the apartment.

What are some great shows you've seen?

Other than clients . . .

Frank Sinatra at the Mocambo
  (I was in the band)

Elton John with Ray Cooper,
  the Hollywood Bowl

Sting, the Forum

Bruce Springsteen, the Forum

What are some of your favorite songs?

Again, clients aside . . .

"Fame," David Bowie

"Waltz for Debbie," Bill Evans

"Is That All There Is," Leiber
  and Stoller

"Sophisticated Lady," Duke Ellington

"Summertime," George Gershwin

"Just the Way You Are" and "My Life,"
  Billy Joel

"Candle in the Wind," Elton John

List up to ten things that could be helpful to someone breaking into the business.

- Listen, listen, listen.
- Immerse yourself in the business, that is, be around the places, restaurants, bars, seminars, clubs, concerts where the people in the business are.
- Treat people fairly. If you don't, it's a very small business and that will become your reputation.
- If you don't know, don't pretend.
- Seek out quality people for advice and mentoring.
- Read everything about the business.
- Learn, learn, learn. There's always more to learn.

Ronnie Dashev

Did you have a mentor or someone who inspired you? If so, what have you learned from that person?

Jay Cooper was my first mentor in the music business. He gave me a real sense of ethics in deal making and representing clients. He always operated under the principle that a good deal is one in which both sides feel like they got what they needed, even if neither side necessarily got what they originally wanted. When you subscribe to this philosophy, both sides walk away from a negotiation having left something on the table which allows room for continuing discussions and an ongoing relationship.

What was your very first job in the music industry, and how did you get it?

I got a job fresh out of law school as an associate attorney in the law firm of Cooper, Epstein & Hurewitz. Due to my interest in music, I knew I wanted to represent recording artists, so I applied for jobs at several Los Angeles law firms with substantial music practices and was fortunate to have been hired by Jay Cooper.

What was your first big break? The first great thing that ever happened to you . . .

I was representing Lionel Richie in the late eighties when he happened to be looking for a personal manager. Freddy DeMann, who was managing Madonna at the time, was interested in managing him, and I negotiated Lionel's personal management agreement with Freddy's lawyer. In early 1990 Freddy asked me if I would be interested in leaving my law practice to help him and Madonna start a multimedia entertainment company focusing on recorded music, music publishing, film, and television. We formed Maverick in 1992. Working at a record company is so much more enjoyable for me than working in a law firm because I am involved in all aspects of the business, not just the deal making.

What elements of your job make you want to go to work every day?

The best part of my job is being involved with young, creative people. I'm not referring only to the artists, although it's wonderful to play even a small part in fostering their careers. I'm also talking about all the young people who work at Maverick, and whose creativity, passion, and loyalty are instrumental in advancing the careers of our artists. They make me proud every day.

What qualities most helped you get to where you are today?

My greatest assets have been my focus and my self-confidence. I knew what I wanted, and I went after it. First I realized I wanted to be financially self-sufficient, which led me to go to law school. Once I graduated and decided that I wanted to work as a music lawyer, I interviewed until I finally found a job in a music firm. When I realized I was becoming bored with the practice of law, I had enough faith in myself to leave a successful practice to help start a new company with a minimum of financial backing and without any guarantees that it would have any future. Each step of the way it was about keeping my eye on the ball and betting on myself.

If you knew everything at the beginning of your career that you know now, what would you have done differently?

I wouldn't have spent twelve years practicing law and would have been more entrepreneurial at an earlier age. I knew after just a few years of practice that I was not really happy in a law firm and wanted to do something more entrepreneurial. Both fortunately and unfortunately, I was juggling my career with motherhood which diverted some of my attention from the fact that I was unhappy practicing law.

What is your greatest lesson learned?

That you can't please everyone and you can't control what other people say and do. All you can do is what you believe is right and hope it works out for the best.

What are some of your favorite albums?

Let It Bleed, Rolling Stones

Abbey Road, the Beatles

No Count Sarah, Sarah Vaughan

Moondance, Van Morrison

What's Going On, Marvin Gaye

Gaucho, Steely Dan

Did you have any posters on your bedroom walls as a kid? Of whom?

The Rolling Stones.

What are some of your favorite songs?

"Like a Rolling Stone," Bob Dylan

"Gimme Shelter," the Rolling Stones

"In My Life," the Beatles

"What's Going On," Marvin Gaye

"Crying," Roy Orbison

"Take It to the Limit," the Eagles

"Nessun Dorma," Puccini

List up to ten things that could be helpful to someone breaking into the business.

- Believe in yourself. If you don't, no one else will.
- Think long term, not short term.

- Never take anything for granted.
- In deal making, there should be no losers.
- Always follow up.
- The devil is in the details.
- Network. The more people you know, the better your chances of success.

Fred Davis

Did you have a mentor or someone who inspired you? If so, what have you learned from that person?

The best mentor anyone can ever have is one's father. I was blessed with a father with tremendous experience and success in the music industry. The rest is easy to understand.

What was your very first job in the music industry, and how did you get it?

My first job was working for a small mom-and-pop record store, Stereo Stop, in New York City. I applied for it the same way any other sixteen-year-old gets a job. After that, I worked for Paul Marshall directly after law school.

What was your first big break? The first great thing that ever happened to you . . .

As a young attorney in 1985, I elected to develop my own business by searching for new talent and "shopping" record deals for them. In 1989–90, I had a great run by finding young/unsigned bands such as White Zombie, Live, and Chris Whitley.

What elements of your job make you want to go to work every day?

Although I love the intrigue of problem solving, what is most exciting is not knowing every day what will happen—good or bad. I believe that I have the best job in the music business—our playing field is so broad.

What qualities most helped you get to where you are today?

I return every phone call, realize I am in the personal service industry, and listen.

If you knew everything at the beginning of your career that you know now, what would you have done differently?

I would have been an English major in college. Reading and writing are the two most important skills that any person can sharpen in life. Other majors are good, but very few are actually relevant later in life. Not so for English—it applies to everything one does.

What is your greatest lesson learned?

Return every phone call!
One gets paid for results, not just effort.

What are some of your favorite albums?

Live at the Fillmore East,
   the Allman Brothers Band
11-17-70 [live], Elton John

Piano Man, Billy Joel
Born to Run, Bruce Springsteen

Did you have any posters on your bedroom walls as a kid? Of whom?

Mickey Mantle.

What are some great shows you've seen?

Lynyrd Skynyrd and the Outlaws, the Beacon Theater
Bruce Springsteen, the Bottom Line
Billy Joel, the Bottom Line

List up to ten things that could be helpful to someone breaking into the business.

- Learn if you are better at "selling" or "buying."
- Be a "specialist" not a "generalist."
- Entrepreneurs are greatly needed in the music industry.

- Network.
- Listen.
- Don't be lazy.
- Be patient.

Fred Goldring

Did you have a mentor or someone who inspired you? If so, what have you learned from that person?

My father gave me great inspiration at three critical points during my career. The first was when I was in college and had the epiphany that I wanted to be a music lawyer, then had the paralyzing realization that (1) I didn't actually know anybody in the music business, and (2) there were only a handful of music lawyers in the world who actually represented the major artists. His analysis: "Well somebody's got to do it—it might as well be you." The second was when I was working the first couple years making next to nothing in my first jobs and getting depressed. His inspiration: "Don't worry, if you love what you do, work hard, and become the best at what you do, the money will show up all by itself, and you'll make it back in a day." The third time was when I was struggling to figure out if I should go into my own business. His advice: "Go for it. You can always get another job if it doesn't work out." Looking back, he was right on all fronts.

What was your very first job in the music industry, and how did you get it?

I was a student usher for campus concerts at Duke University in the late seventies. I did whatever I could to work my way up through the concert committee (including actively lobbying for jobs) and was made chairperson in my junior year. I also played a lot of gigs as a guitarist/singer alone and in various bands starting in high school and once opened for Roger McGuinn.

What was your first big break? The first great thing that ever happened to you . . .

My first big break was getting a job with Allen Grubman's law firm in New York as the youngest lawyer they had ever hired, where I then worked for five years. The first great thing that happened in my own practice was getting the opportunity to represent a band from my hometown of Philly when they had just released their first album, who went on to become one of the biggest selling acts of all time (Boyz II Men).

What elements of your job make you want to go to work every day?

The unexpected things that might happen. You never know what artist or project might come into your life that you could end up becoming a part of that ends up impacting the lives of millions of people in a positive way. Also, the creative challenge of constantly having to make things happen and keeping things moving forward.

What qualities most helped you get to where you are today?

I became interested in this business because of my passion for music and creative people. Since I'm also a musician, it's really helped me relate to and bond with my clients in a special way and feel I can really understand things from both business and artistic perspectives. I'm also doggedly determined and focused in my pursuit of things that I'm passionate about and that includes our clients' careers.

If you knew everything at the beginning of your career that you know now, what would you have done differently?

In the end analysis, nothing, since with each step or misstep along the path of the journey I've learned something which has later proved to be an invaluable part of my development. The only regrets are that I might have gone into my own business earlier or gone more into the creative side of things instead of leaning toward the business side. But luckily we've been able to meld things pretty well the way we set up our practice.

What is your greatest lesson learned?

Luck is what happens to you after you've done everything you can to try to make something happen. It rarely happens on its own.

What are some of your favorite albums?

Sweet Baby James, James Taylor
  (It inspired me to be a guitarist.)
Are You Experienced?, Jimi Hendrix
  Experience
Led Zeppelin II, Led Zeppelin

Tommy, the Who
On the Border, the Eagles
Piano Man, Billy Joel
Any Police, Sting, Steely Dan,
  or Beatles

Did you have any posters on your bedroom walls as a kid? Of whom?

James Taylor, Eagles, Beach Boys, Stan Smith (I'm a tennis player from way back).

What are some great shows you've seen?

Live Aid, Philadelphia, 1985 (I actually ended up onstage at the end singing "We Are the World.")
The first and second Rock and Roll Hall of Fame dinners (amazing jams—and my wife and I had
  our second date at the second one!)
Sting's three nights at the Ritz in New York, where he rehearsed before recording his first
  solo LP
Carole King opening for James Taylor in Philadelphia before *Tapestry* was released
Bruce Springsteen opening for Hall & Oates at Villanova

Billy Joel opening for the Doobie Brothers

The Eagles opening for Linda Rondstadt

What are some of your favorite songs?

Of course, every song by our clients! Actually, it really depends on my mood. I love so many songs for so many different reasons that, like albums, it's hard to pick just a few as favorites.

List up to ten things that could be helpful to someone breaking into the business.

■ Trust your instincts. If you're passionate about something, and no one seems to get it, you're probably on to something special.

■ Don't take no for an answer—take it as a challenge.

■ Read the trades religiously so you know who people are, what they do, and what is going on at any given minute in the business so you can talk intelligently when you need to.

■ When you're starting out, go to the opening of an envelope. You never know who you'll meet or what might come out of it that could end up being huge for you.

■ Get as much advice from people in the business who are actually doing what you want to do and stay in contact with them.

■ Meet and get to know as many people as possible. You can't know too many people, and they are your biggest resource in a people-driven business.

■ Be honest. People can smell bullshit a mile away. And if you always tell the truth, you never need to remember who you told what to.

■ Get whatever experience you can even if it is only remotely related to your goal. It'll come in handy later even though it might not seem like it at the time.

■ If you only want to get into the business because it seems fun and sexy (which, of course, at times it is) or because you are bored with whatever else you are doing, don't bother. There are zillions of other people right behind trying to get in for all the right reasons who won't eat or sleep until they do.

Eric Greenspan

Did you have a mentor or someone who inspired you? If so, what have you learned from that person?

Unfortunately I never had a mentor. I wish that I had had one. I did not have an opportunity to work with a great music lawyer early in my career and had I done so I think it would have inured to my benefit.

What was your very first job in the music industry, and how did you get it?

I was given the opportunity to promote concerts at Cameron Indoor Stadium at Duke University. It was an incredible opportunity and, in the two years that I booked shows for the school, I was lucky enough to work with the Grateful Dead, the Allman Brothers, Ten Years After, Yes, Janis Joplin, Leon Russell, the Moody Blues, and numerous other bands.

What was your first big break? The first great thing that ever happened to you . . .

My first break was being accepted to Duke University. I was a native New Yorker and the school exposed me to people from all over the country. In my career, my first break occurred in 1982. I was introduced to a young band that had just begun to play in clubs. Unfortunately two of the members of the group had an opportunity to sign a record deal with another band. They elected to leave the band. The two remaining musicians, Anthony Kiedis and Flea, found two other musicians to join them. I often wonder how my career would have been different had I represented the other two leaving members and not Anthony and Flea.

What elements of your job make you want to go to work every day?

I love having the opportunity to work with young artists and help them throughout their careers. I've always enjoyed the art of negotiating, and the ability to marry those two passions—both music and business—is priceless.

What qualities most helped you get to where you are today?

My single-mindedness. It is remarkable to me how many successful executives don't take care of the basics: returning phone calls and treating each client the way you would like to be treated yourself. I never forget that the first recording agreement an artist signs is the most important thing in their life, and it is tragic to not remember that fact at all times.

If you knew everything at the beginning of your career that you know now, what would you have done differently?

I cannot think of anything I would have done differently. The past may have been different had I turned left instead of right at particular junctures of my life, but it all worked out in the end.

What is your greatest lesson learned?

Try to see as far down the chessboard as you possibly can. Try to avoid making short-term decisions without thinking of the ultimate consequence of those decisions.

What are some of your favorite albums?

Electric Ladyland, Jimi Hendrix
Songs for Swingin' Lovers, Frank Sinatra
American Beauty, the Grateful Dead
Blood on the Tracks, Bob Dylan
Californication, the Red Hot Chili Peppers

Abbey Road, the Beatles
More Songs About Buildings and Food,
Talking Heads
Derek and the Dominos
Any and all Bob Marley albums

Did you have any posters on your bedroom walls as a kid? Of whom?

Elvis Presley and the Beatles.

What are some great shows you've seen?

The Grateful Dead, the Allman Brothers,
and the Band, Watkins Glen
The Who performing *Tommy,* Metropolitan
Opera House
Jane's Addiction, Hollywood Palladium

The Rolling Stones, Madison Square
Garden, 1972
Bob Marley, the Roxy
The Red Hot Chili Peppers, Woodstock

List up to ten things that could be helpful to someone breaking into the business.

- Return everyone's calls.
- Be nice to everyone you meet—you never know when they will become a star.
- Don't try to cover up a lack of knowledge with bravado—it is okay not to know an answer.
- Play golf well.

Allen Grubman

Did you have a mentor or someone who inspired you? If so, what have you learned from that person?

I learned from and was inspired by several people. One of the first was Henry Stone. He owned a company in the early seventies called TK Records which had artists like KC & the Sunshine Band and George McCrae. As my career progressed there were a lot of very important record executives who I looked up to and admired, such as Mo Ostin and Joe Smith.

What was your very first job in the music industry, and how did you get it?

When I was in law school I wanted to be an entertainment lawyer, so during my first year I worked in the messenger room at the William Morris Agency in New York. In my second and third years I was a page at CBS. While there I worked on *The Ed Sullivan Show* and the game shows *What's My Line?* and *I've Got a Secret*. Those experiences gave me a feel for the business before I got my first job as an entertainment lawyer in 1969. It was with Walter Hofer, whose specialty was music and who had represented the Beatles in the early sixties.

What was your first big break? The first great thing that ever happened to you . . .

The first break was taking that job with Walter Hofer. It was my entrance into the music business, and my first big opportunity. I stayed with Walter until 1974 and then decided to go out on my own. About two months after I opened my firm, Henry Stone called me and said, "I have a present for you. It's a record called *Rock Your Baby* by George McCrae." It was a big hit and it jump-started my practice. Shortly after that I began to represent Henri Belolo and Jacques Morali, who had just formed the Village People. And then Hall & Oates happened.

During the seventies I was very involved with disco music. We represented all these disco record companies. There was Boardwalk Records, TK Records, Delite Records with Kool & the Gang, and Salsoul Records with the Salsoul Orchestra. So, as disco took off during the seventies, so did the firm. I really loved disco music. I got a charge out of Donna Summer and all those great disco acts. It was a very enjoyable time.

What elements of your job make you want to go to work every day?

Now what challenges me is being able to do something unique. I love structuring deals that are innovative, that are truly different from anything that has been done before.

I also take pleasure from representing really great artists, artists that have basically changed modern culture, whether it's an Elton John, Bono, Bruce Springsteen, or Madonna. I also do a lot of corporate work, which I enjoy as well.

What qualities most helped you get to where you are today?

Being very candid with people. Being very honest with people. Working very hard and, of course, being very lucky.

If you knew everything at the beginning of your career that you know now, what would you have done differently?

I was never interested in representing people in the sports world. If I had known then what I know now, we also would be representing a lot of athletes. It has become such an interesting field. I totally missed the boat on that.

What is your greatest lesson learned?

Being totally honest with everybody you deal with is critically important. If you try to tell Person A one story and Person B another story (which happens in this business), you end up trapping yourself, stepping on your toes, and getting into trouble. The key to being successful in the music business, particularly if you are in a service role, is being very candid, very direct, and very honest. It is extremely important. Talking through two sides of your mouth is a recipe for disaster. Unfortunately, too many people do that.

What are some of your favorite albums?

One of my favorite albums, believe it or not, is *Dr. Buzzard's Original Savannah Band.*

My favorite albums are usually those of people I represent. *Saturday Night Fever* was fabulous. I love disco music . . . KC & the Sunshine Band, Kool & the Gang, and the Village People. I have always had a tremendous admiration for Elton's music and Madonna's as well. I like the entire body of their work.

Did you have any posters on your bedroom walls as a kid? Of whom?

I never put posters up in my room. My whole life I've been a Frank Sinatra fan. I never had a poster of Frank Sinatra, but if you asked me whom I idolized as a kid, it would be the same person I idolize today—Frank Sinatra.

What are some great shows you've seen?

One of my favorite shows—I wasn't a music lawyer yet—was Creedence Clearwater Revival. The first and only time the Village People ever played in Madison Square Garden was exciting.

The first time I saw Bruce Springsteen was great. That was at Madison Square Garden, probably in 1982.

Elton—I always love his performances.

We represent James Taylor now. I think he's fabulous. I love to watch him.

What are some of your favorite songs?

It would be difficult for me to name a lot of particular songs, but "The Lady Is a Tramp" sticks
out in my mind. I'm also very fond of Cole Porter, Rodgers & Hammerstein, and music of the forties and fifties.

List up to ten things that could be helpful to someone breaking into the business.

Take any job you can get. Don't be proud. Work for free, or for less than free if you have to. Your
first job in the entertainment business is critically important. Just get your foot in the door.
Whatever you are offered that gets your foot in the door you do it. Because once your foot is in
the door you can show people what you have and go from there. There are certain people who
say, well, unless I have this kind of job or this opportunity, I'm not gonna do that. It's a huge
mistake.

Ken Hertz

Did you have a mentor or someone who inspired you? If so, what have you learned from that person?

I worked for a Federal Court Judge once, and he taught me that being good at your job means taking pride in what you do; that what you think about yourself—your integrity, honesty, self-respect, and self-esteem—are the keys to success, and that success is not measured by any external yardstick.

What was your very first job in the music industry, and how did you get it?

I worked at Capitol Records, working for the head of business affairs, Vic Rappaport. I also worked with Picture Music International, one of the first music video production companies working on videos by Springsteen, Bowie, Michael Jackson, and Phil Collins, among others.

What was your first big break? The first great thing that ever happened to you . . .

That first big break was probably being hired to be the head of music business and legal affairs at Walt Disney in 1985.

What elements of your job make you want to go to work every day?

Because we represent primarily artists, once in a rare while, we get to work with someone from the time no one has ever heard of them until they've become a household name. Helping an artist find an audience is extraordinarily gratifying. Also, since some artists are not particularly good businesspeople, helping to protect their interests can be quite rewarding.

What qualities most helped you get to where you are today?

I'd like to think I'm tenacious and resourceful. I am passionate about the things I do, and I don't give up easily. I try to be creative in the way I approach difficult problems, and I believe that creativity has been rewarded for us and for our clients.

If you knew everything at the beginning of your career that you know now, what would you have done differently?

I wouldn't do anything differently, because every choice I might make differently would come with its own set of unanticipated consequences. If I've learned anything, it is that happiness isn't about getting what you want, it's about wanting what you get.

What is your greatest lesson learned?

You can never underestimate people's ability to do the right thing and their willingness to do the wrong thing. Surprises abound, and the only people who can betray you are people you trust, but if you don't trust anyone, no one will ever trust you.

What are some of your favorite albums?

Toots Thielman's *Brazil Project I* and *II*

White Album, the Beatles

Déjà vu, Crosby, Stills, Nash & Young

Crime of the Century, Supertramp

Head Hunters, Herbie Hancock

Mellon Collie and the Infinite Sadness, Smashing Pumpkins

Stop Making Sense, Talking Heads

Did you have any posters on your bedroom walls as a kid? Of whom?

A poster of that little old lady sitting in a rocking chair flipping you off. And a McGovern '72 poster.

What are some great shows you've seen?

Miles Davis, Hollywood Bowl

Taping of the Fleetwood Mac reunion show for MTV

Guns N' Roses opening for the Rolling Stones at L.A. Coliseum

The Police opening for the Knack at the Forum in 1980

The free Talking Heads shows at Berkeley

Carlos Jobim Tribute in Rio

What are some of your favorite songs?

There are so many. I don't really think about favorite songs, but I do have many favorite lyrics. Just about anything Randy Newman, Suzanne Vega, Jill Sobule, or Jude Christodal writes. The New Radicals song "Someday We'll Know" convinced me we had to represent Gregg Alexander, and I could listen to B.B. King read the phone book.

List up to ten things that could be helpful to someone breaking into the business.

- Rule No. 1 is, tell the truth (not getting caught in a lie is not the same as telling the truth). This is a *very* small business.
- Don't worry about what others think of you—they are too busy thinking about themselves.
- Be kind to everyone—you never get a second chance to make a first impression (see rule No. 1).
- Don't be afraid to admit what you don't know, or to tell people what you really think.
- You can't overthink anything; you might not be smart enough to know how stupid you are.
- Don't ever expect anyone to tell the truth, and don't ever ask anyone to lie.
- Don't expect anyone to keep a secret.

- You can't be too tenacious, too cynical, or too optimistic.
- Return every phone call.
- Don't forget rule No. 1.

Joel Katz

Did you have a mentor or someone who inspired you? If so, what have you learned from that person?

Early in my career, I was inspired and mentored by the artist James Brown, my first client in the entertainment business. He taught me the fine line between patience and aggressiveness.

What was your very first job in the music industry, and how did you get it?

My first job was in 1971, representing James Brown. I got that job and client because a student of mine at Georgia State University recommended me to him.

What was your first big break? The first great thing that ever happened to you . . .

After meeting and servicing James Brown as a client, I met Willie Nelson. He became a client and introduced me to Tammy Wynette, Waylon Jennings, Merle Haggard, Kris Kristofferson, and David Alan Coe. They all became clients.

What elements of your job make you want to go to work every day?

The excitement that each day will be different and no situation will be the same.

What qualities most helped you get to where you are today?

Patience and aggressiveness. Never giving up on a situation and a human being!

What is your greatest lesson learned?

The "creative mind" is totally unpredictable. You never can predict failure. There is in "creativity" always a chance for great success.

What are some of your favorite albums?

Red Headed Stranger, Willie Nelson
Thriller, Michael Jackson
Sounds of Silence, Simon & Garfunkel

Did you have any posters on your bedroom walls as a kid? Of whom?

Posters were New York Yankees baseball stars Joe DiMaggio, Mickey Mantle, Whitey Ford, and Yogi Berra.

What are some great shows you've seen?

Jackson's *Victory* tour
Live Aid
Farm Aid

List up to ten things that could be helpful to someone breaking into the business.

- Be patient and aggressive.
- Look at each situation. There are potential benefits hiding within.
- Perception becomes reality.
- In chaos is opportunity.
- *Never* give up!

Tim Mandelbaum

Did you have a mentor or someone who inspired you? If so, what have you learned from that person?

Frankly, my wife, Elisa, has always been the person who has best understood me and has encouraged me to follow my passions and to not be limited in my goals. She continues to be a source of great strength for me and is someone who constantly forces me to be honest with myself in confronting my weaknesses and shortcomings.

What was your very first job in the music industry, and how did you get it?

Celluloid Records, just out of law school. My then-girlfriend's (now wife) boss's boyfriend owned the label and introduced us over a weekend in the Hamptons. He realized that he could have an inexpensive, in-house lawyer, rather than paying a law firm for their counsel. Big mistake on his part. Big break for me. I spent a year at Celluloid being a lawyer/jack-of-all-trades.

What was your first big break? The first great thing that ever happened to you . . .

In late 1988, at thirty-one years old, I had been the director of Business Affairs at EMI Manhattan Records approximately ten months when my boss, the head of the department, abruptly left the label. After watching several more experienced attorneys interview to be my new boss, I decided I should get the position. I approached the CEO and asked for the job. It was as if he had been waiting for that moment as he promptly promoted me. The new title and position leapfrogged me several notches in terms of career advancement. I was immediately drawn into all sorts of difficult situations and negotiations which were tremendously challenging but which exposed me to the highest levels of deal making and company strategy.

What elements of your job make you want to go to work every day?

The love of music and the opportunity to make dreams come true (and make a difference) for my clients. Just when everything feels dull and boring, I'll hear a great new song or demo and will remember why I'm in the music business and not a corporate lawyer.

What qualities most helped you get to where you are today?

Being honest, trustworthy, and perseverant. It's a very cut-throat business played very hard by a lot of not-so-nice people. I've distinguished myself by being straightforward and dedicated to my clients but still aggressive in pursuit of their goals.

If you knew everything at the beginning of your career that you know now, what would you have done differently?

That's a tough one. I could go with "nothing" or write a treatise. I think I'll stick with "nothing" and move on to the next question, hastening my return to my clients.

What is your greatest lesson learned?

Don't be reckless. Think everything through. The mistakes I've made have occurred when, to mask insecurity, I've made rash decisions which have not necessarily been in the best interest of my client because I didn't want to appear unknowledgeable. It's better to say "let me think about it and get back to you" than to make an on-the-spot decision about which you are uncertain.

What are some of your favorite albums?

Physical Graffitti and *Houses of the Holy,*
   Led Zeppelin
Exile on Main Street, the Rolling Stones
All That You Can't Leave Behind, U2
August and Everything After,
   Counting Crows
Jagged Little Pill, Alanis Morissette

Gaucho, Steely Dan
Third Eye Blind, Third Eye Blind
Blood on the Tracks, Bob Dylan
Live at the Fillmore East, the Allman
   Brothers Band
Feats Don't Fail Me Now, Little Feat

Did you have any posters on your bedroom walls as a kid? Of whom?

Led Zeppelin in concert
The Who, *Live at Leeds*
Hot Tuna

What are some great shows you've seen?

Many Grateful Dead shows
Many Allman Brothers shows
Little Feat, New York Academy of Music
J. Geils Band, New York Academy of Music

Two U2 shows post 9/11, Madison
   Square Garden
Earth, Wind & Fire, Duke University, 1978

List up to ten things that could be helpful to someone breaking into the business.

There is no question in my mind that the people who successfully break into the business do so because they are hungry and aggressive and don't take no for an answer. These people, all of us who have succeeded, keep banging down the doors until they're inside the hallowed pearly gates. Don't give up on your dreams!!

Don Passman

Did you have a mentor or someone who inspired you? If so, what have you learned from that person?

My mentors were my partners, Payson Wolff and Bruce Ramer, consummate gentlemen and extraordinary lawyers.

What was your very first job in the music industry, and how did you get it?

My first job in the music industry was playing in a band in college, where I made more money (on an hourly rate) than my first year practicing law.

What was your first big break? The first great thing that ever happened to you . . .

My first break was a client who came in at age nineteen, with no deal and no shirt, through a friend of a cousin of somebody, and ended up selling platinum.

What elements of your job make you want to go to work every day?

I love the intersection of business and art. They've always been at odds with each other, but neither can exist without the other. I like explaining business concepts to creative people, as well as advocating creative concepts to business people.

What qualities most helped you get to where you are today?

I think it was the passion for what I do. It may sound strange to creative people, but I love my profession as much as creative people love theirs.

If you knew everything at the beginning of your career that you know now, what would you have done differently?

I'm pleased to say that I wouldn't have done anything differently. I would have liked to have "happened" faster than I did, but in retrospect it was important for me to build a solid foundation for what I do, as a lot of the fast burners have faded away.

What is your greatest lesson learned?

That there are no secrets to success in this or any other business—it's a matter of setting goals, solid planning, and hard work.

What are some of your favorite albums?

Sgt. Pepper's Lonely Hearts Club Band
   and *Abbey Road,* the Beatles
Led Zeppelin I and *Led Zeppelin II,*
   Led Zeppelin
Songs, Leonard Cohen

Rain Dogs, Tom Waits
In Search of the Lost Chord,
   the Moody Blues
Surrealistic Pillow, Jefferson Airplane

Did you have any posters on your bedroom walls as a kid? Of whom?

Ham radio QSL cards.

What are some great shows you've seen?

The Beatles at the Hollywood Bowl
Led Zeppelin, Tina Turner, Paul McCartney, Cat Stevens, Donovan

What are some of your favorite songs?

"Suzanne," Leonard Cohen
"Diamonds & Rust," Joan Baez
"Lady in Red," Chris De Burgh

"White Rabbit," Jefferson Airplane
"Driving Wheel," Tom Rush
"Hey Jude," the Beatles

List up to ten things that could be helpful to someone breaking into the business.

- Passion
- Keep going no matter what.
- Make music from your soul, not to conform to what might "be happening."
- Build a solid team of people around you.

Peter Paterno

Did you have a mentor or someone who inspired you? If so, what have you learned from that person?

Lee Phillips. I learned that if you want to represent an artist properly as a lawyer, it's not enough to hang out in clubs. You have to hone your skills, both with respect to transactional matters *and* litigation. Most music lawyers never do this, and do an amazingly poor job of representing their clients when it comes to anything outside the standard recording contract.

What was your very first job in the music industry, and how did you get it?

My first job in the music industry was as a lawyer at what was then Manatt, Phelps, Rothenberg & Tunney. I got it when a friend of mine from law school called and said, "Do you know anyone who wants a job as a music lawyer, 'cause I'm quitting. I can't stand working for that bitch." The "bitch" was Debbie Reinberg, a good friend of mine from law school and an excellent lawyer (but harsh taskmaster) who later ran business affairs at Elektra/Asylum Records. I interviewed for the job and eventually got hired. The friend who bailed from the job is my current partner and scourge of Napster, Howard King.

What was your first big break? The first great thing that ever happened to you . . .

My first break was getting hired away from my three-person, general-practice law firm to work at Manatt, Phelps. I was handling general dog-bite law—probates, drunk driving, avocado grove purchases, personal injury, divorces ("It's four A.M., my ex-husband has a gun, and he wants the furniture. Didn't I get the furniture in the property settlement?" "If he's got a gun, I don't think it really matters."). I then got to do real music law, getting to work for Jackson Browne, Prince, Linda Ronstadt, and other artists I loved. My first big break as a music lawyer was getting hired by Metallica.

What elements of your job make you want to go to work every day?

I get to work with great artists like Metallica, Dr. Dre, Pearl Jam, Chris Cornell, Rancid, Brian Setzer, and a host of others. They're not only talented artists, they're great people. I also really enjoy the managers I work with, although they all hate each other.

What qualities most helped you get to where you are today?

It's pretty much the cliché—hard work and luck. It also doesn't hurt being at least as smart as the average bear.

If you knew everything at the beginning of your career that you know now, what would you have done differently?

The music business seduces you when you're young and can make you look really silly when you're old. So I guess you should try not to get old.

What is your greatest lesson learned?

There are a lot of them. Be honest, avoid screaming psychopaths where possible (not always possible in the music business), and get your artist a good manager are some.

What are some of your favorite albums?

Any Beatles noncompilation album
The Eminem Show, Eminem
2001, Dr. Dre
The Doors
A bunch of Beach Boys compilations
Marshall Crenshaw, Marshall Crenshaw
Court and Spark, Joni Michtell

Classic Queen, Queen
Exile on Main Street or *Forty Licks,*
  the Rolling Stones
The Best of Wham! Wham (really)
Sweet Baby James, James Taylor
Appetite for Destruction, Guns N' Roses

Did you have any posters on your bedroom walls as a kid? Of whom?

The only one I remember is George Harrison from the *White Album.*

What are some great shows you've seen?

The Doors at the Hollywood Bowl
Altamont
Jackson Browne, Linda Ronstadt,
  and the Eagles at the Aladdin
Woodstock 1999 (especially Metallica)
Metallica at the Palladium
Springsteen at the Roxy
Up in Smoke, especially the Seattle
  Experience Museum show
The Jacksons' *Victory* tour
Prince at Flippers
Metallica at the Country Club

Alice in Chains at the Palace
Soundgarden at the Lingerie
Stevie Wonder at Long Beach
Van Morrison at Long Beach
James Taylor at the Greek
The Pixies at the Roxy
Paul McCartney and U2, both at the Pond
Public Enemy at the Palace
The Brian Setzer Orchestra at the Greek
Pearl Jam at San Jose State
Guns N' Roses and Aerosmith at Costa Mesa
I could go on awhile, but that's enough.

What are some of your favorite songs?

"Don't Worry Baby," the Beach Boys

"Do You Believe in Magic?," the Lovin'
 Spoonful

"Every Little Thing She Does Is Magic,"
 the Police

"Everlong," the Foo Fighters

"Revolution," the Beatles

"Enter Sandman," Metallica

"Nuthin' but a 'G' Thang," Dr. Dre

"Ticket to Ride," the Beatles

"Photograph," Def Leppard—Ringo's
 is good, too

"Bad," MU2

"Badge," Cream

"American Girl," Tom Petty

"Jeremy," Pearl Jam

"My Cherie Amour," Stevie Wonder

"Golden Lady," Stevie Wonder

"Straight Outta Compton," N.W.A.

"Born to Run," Bruce Springsteen

"Houses of the Holy," Led Zeppelin

"In the Shape of a Heart," Jackson Browne

List up to ten things that could be helpful to someone breaking into the business.

- Associate yourself with talented artists.
- Do a good job for them.
- Remember they're the stars. You're not.

TELEVISION & FILM

Danny Bramson

Did you have a mentor or someone who inspired you? If so, what have you learned from that person?

The Beatles, Lew Wasserman and Sid Sheinberg, Ned Tanen, Neil Young, David Geffen, Stanley Kubrick, Tom Cruise, and Cameron Crowe, all of whom inspired me profoundly and in turn gave me something to aspire to, dream, and reach for as a fan, and along the way gave me their wisdom, friendship, patience, and trust. Most significantly, I took from them their unflagging joy and relentless passion for the work at hand. They will forever remain my heroes.

What was your very first job in the music industry, and how did you get it?

The music industry? I was a stagehand/production assistant at what later became the Universal Amphitheatre in 1973 after pressing the next-door neighbor to spend ten grand and book the Grateful Dead to "sound check" the venue as an outdoor concert venue. I passed the audition with the Dead selling out both nights and even closing down the Hollywood freeway. Lew Wasserman hired me at a hundred bucks a week to get through UCLA film school with the understanding that I was being groomed to take a significant role in the place one day. That concept accelerated big-time, and after a couple lackluster attempts to mount a few compelling concert lineups, the big job was available. That same week, I graduated UCLA, in May of 1975, I also turned twenty-one and was officially hired full time as the director of the Univeral Amphitheatre in charge of all the concert bookings and promotions for MCA/Universal. We started off with about forty-five shows that summer, with artists ranging from James Taylor and Linda Ronstadt to a week of David Bowie's legendary *Diamond Dogs* tour. Within five years, the concert series grew to over a hundred concerts booked across a nonstop three-month period with celebrated shows and engagements ranging from Frank Sinatra to Fleetwood Mac, Bob Dylan, and Joni Mitchell. Then, at twenty-five in 1979, Lew and Sid Sheinberg indulged my aspirations and let me start my own label, Backstreet Records. I got lucky, in the right place at the right time once again, and landed Tom Petty and the Heartbreakers as my first and most significant signing. The first Backstreet release was Tom's *Damn the Torpedoes,* and I "learned" the record business behind that amazing album that cut so deep both artistically and commercially. Most significantly to me, Tom and that album represented the breakthrough of a major artist that I treasured. In the decades since that loose Grateful Dead show with their psychedelic painted P.A. in those part-time stunt show bleachers in the summer of 1972, MCA

Inc. and Lew Wasserman have developed and built the now landmark City Walk and twenty movie theatres, making it one of Los Angeles's prime tourist destinations.

What was your first big break? The first great thing that ever happened to you . . .

I returned to my folks' house one fall day to wash my clothes and car and get a hot dinner, and the next-door neighbor, Jay Stein, pulls up to me. Mind you, I look like a Breck ad now with hair halfway down my back, and he pulls up and asks me to come over after dinner and talk to him about that idea I had about rock concerts and Universal's bleachers for their stunt show. He gave me the production job immediately, and it got me through UCLA and film school at one hundred bucks a week . . . and free records! Being in the right place at the right time and being able to hit that inside slider . . . basically, good old luck to get that shot at the plate and then the good fortune to connect just to get in the door.

What elements of your job make you want to go to work every day?

I love music and I love movies. The luxury to have a job in such creative environments as cutting rooms, screening rooms, recording studios, and scoring stages is the job of the century if you can get it. I start every movie as if it were my first and savor every project as if it were my last. I am passionate in what I do and continue to learn, explore, risk, challenge, and most significantly . . . continue to have fun and feel that creative rush.

If you knew everything in the beginning of your career that you know now, what would you have done differently?

I truly have few regrets. I was so fortunate to apprentice and grow up fast in the shadow of Lew Wasserman's MCA/Universal. If anything, I would have had a lawyer represent me in the creation of my record label, Backstreet Records. Then I would have left with more than the gold and platinum albums and the stationery. I shook hands on the concept and deal with the masters of the game, Lew Wasserman and Sidney Sheinberg, across an impromptu, forty-five-minute discussion on my future with them. I got my dream, and they got me to continue the success of the Universal concert division, building the amphitheatre into an enclosed, year-round internationally acclaimed venue and landing concert rights to the legendary Dodger Stadium. More than a fair return for indulging my aspirations. I didn't get monetarily rich, but they gave me their trust and an unlimited playground with concerts, records, publishing, and, as importantly, film and a front seat to the video explosion. I wouldn't have changed that experience growing up on the Universal lot and the world of Wasserman's MCA Inc. for anything. It truly broke my heart when I left at thirty, but in the end, it taught me that successful independence can be even sweeter and more rewarding.

What is your greatest lesson learned?

Never look over your shoulder, you will always fall off your bicycle . . . the future is more exciting.

What are some of your favorite albums?

All Beatles albums

Neil Young, After the Goldrush, Harvest, Tonight's the Night, On the Beach, Rust Never Sleeps, and *Comes a Time,* Neil Young

Blue, Ladies of the Canyon, and *Miles of Aisles* (my first gold album), Joni Mitchell

Imagine, John Lennon

All Things Must Pass (reissue with alternate takes), George Harrison

Damn the Torpedoes, Tom Petty and the Heartbreakers, on Backstreet Records

Blood on the Tracks, Blonde on Blonde, and *Highway 61,* Bob Dylan

Beggar's Banquet, Get Yer Ya-Ya's Out, Sticky Fingers, and *Exile on Main Street,* the Rolling Stones

London Calling and *Sandinista!,* the Clash

Born to Run and *Darkness on the Edge of Town,* Bruce Springsteen

What's Going On and *Let's Get It On,* Marvin Gaye

Electric Ladyland and *Axis: Bold As Love,* Jimi Hendrix

Joshua Tree and *Achtung Baby,* U2

Live at the Fillmore East, the Allman Brothers Band

Cameron Crowe's road tapes

Elton John and *Tumbleweed Connection,* Elton John

All Bob Marley

If I Could Only Remember My Name, David Crosby

Led Zeppelin box set

Ziggy Stardust and *Station to Station,* David Bowie

Grievous Angels, Gram Parsons

Murmur, R.E.M.

Ritual de lo Habitual, Jane's Addiction

Vanilla Sky sound track

OK Computer and *Kid A,* live acoustic bootlegs, Radiohead

Citizen Dick

Farrington Road, Stillwater

Did you have any posters on your bedroom walls as a kid? Of whom?

The Beatles (definitely those four eight-by-tens from the *White Album*), Neil Young and Joni Mitchell, Cassius Clay and Muhammed Ali, Jimi Hendrix, Cream.

I am sure David Crosby was somewhere up on that wall, Buffalo Springfield, Lennon's *Rolling Stone* covers, and the *Life* magazine cover of JFK and his brother Bobby.

What are some great shows you've seen?

Crosby, Stills, Nash & Young with Joni Mitchell, Greek Theatre, August, 1969

David Bowie, Hollywood Palladium, with the *Ziggy Stardust* tour and Mick Ronson

David Bowie, *Diamond Dogs* tour at the Universal Amphitheatre

Jimi Hendrix, Hollywood Bowl

Janis Joplin, Hollywood Bowl

Rolling Stones with Mick Taylor, Inglewood Forum, 1969, with Ike and Tina opening and Terry
   Reid as warm-up

Crosby, Stills, Nash & Young at UCSB outdoors and at the old Balboa Stadium in San Diego

Neil Young solo at UCLA's Royce Hall

The *Last Waltz* concert on Thanksgiving Day in San Francisco at the Winterland

Tom Petty and the Heartbreakers, Whiskey A-Go-Go

Joni Mitchell and the Eagles, Royce Hall, UCLA

Frank Sinatra, Universal Amphitheatre, 1977

James Taylor and Joni Mitchell, Doug Weston's Troubadour, 1973

Neil Young, *Tonight's the Night* with Cheech and Chong, the Roxy opening, 1974

Jimi Hendrix and Steve Stills jamming at the Experience Club, Hollywood, 1968

Paul McCartney in the studio, Spring, 2002

Pearl Jam, Soundgarden, Alice in Chains, and Heart, at the *Singles'* film wrap party, Seattle 1992

Nancy Wilson, Topanga, 2003

Led Zeppelin and Jethro Tull, Rose Palace, Pasadena, 1968

The Band, Long Beach Auditorium, 1970

Bob Dylan, Universal Amphitheatre, 1978

Elton John with Nigel Olsen and Dee Murray, Royce Hall, UCLA, 1970

The Blues Brothers debut opening for Steve Martin, Universal Amphitheatre, 1978

The Doors and Jefferson Airplane opening the Birmingham High School Football Stadium, Van
   Nuys, California, 1967

The Buffalo Springfield, the Valley Music Theatre, 1967

List up to ten things that could be helpful to someone breaking into the business.

■ My dad dropped me off at the curb of the Universal tour center on the day of my first taxable job in the summer of 1969. I had just turned sixteen, cut my hair off, and was hired for a buck ninety-five an hour to be a custodian in a starch-white, itchy uniform. He turns to me and tells me, "Never bullshit in this town, you will always be labeled a bullshit artist, and if you steal . . . steal so big that you never come home." That is what he left me with on that curb.

■ Don't ever take the first no for an answer unless it is a date.

- Patience. You must love what you do and/or choose to do it with insatiable passion or you begin ten steps back each day. And regardless of the project and genre, always keep your eye on the ball. Focus on the work, because the work is king. The process is everything and take nothing for granted. Never assume or presume regardless of the whos, wheres, and whys. Nothing can bite one in the ass with more consequence.

- A brief note, when MCA gave me full reign and made me the director of the Amphitheatre in 1976, the opening-night celebration featured Frank Sinatra. The legendary producer Jerry Weintraub, who at the time managed the careers of John Denver, Bob Dylan, and was consulting with Sinatra, asked me to put down four folding chairs in the orchestra pit for some dignitary or icon. It was opening night, my first night at the theater which I had all but dreamt up . . . and although I didn't actually speak, the look of disappointment registered with Weintraub. About twenty minutes later, with the show up and running, he took me aside . . . lit a cigar, and said, "Kid, let's take a walk." He told me, "Kid, there are two types of people in this world, stars and ushers. You and me, my friend, are ushers." I can't tell you how many times— whether backstage, in a dressing room, and especially on a movie set—I've taken that walk with the new guy or girl.

- My last piece of advice . . . when asked how I have had such a long run in the business of show, I tell them no photo ops and no interviews; the work is king!

Carson Daly

What was your very first job in the music industry, and how did you get it?

I interned at Palm Springs, California, in radio with Jimmy Kimmel in 1991. He was a pal and offered it to me.

What was your first big break? The first great thing that ever happened to you . . .

My ankle, when the training wheels finally came off.

What elements of your job make you want to go to work every day?

The new music on my desk, the friends and coworkers I have here at MTV, NBC, and 456 Entertainment, my love for New York, working on the studio 8-H, and good times.

What qualities most helped you get to where you are today?

Two-thirds of a cup of luck and 1 heaping tablespoon of Jimmy Kimmel.

If you knew everything at the beginning of your career that you know now, what would you have done differently?

I would have kidnapped Tiger Woods when we were kids, drugged him, told him I was his father, and all checks would come to me.

What is your greatest lesson learned?

Jägermeister really *does* taste like shit.

What are some of your favorite albums?

What real music fan could even start to just jot a few down? Okay—I started to . . .

White Pony, the Deftones   *Straight Outta Compton*, N.W.A.

True Democracy, Steel Pulse

Did you have any posters on your bedroom walls as a kid? Of whom?

No posters . . . but I did have an Incredible Hulk night-light.

What are some great shows you've seen?

Damien Rice, Troubadour, Los Angeles

Ben Harper, Elbow Room, San Francisco

Stevie Wonder, New York City

Country Bears, Chuck E. Cheese, USA

What are some of your favorite songs?

"3 Libras," A Perfect Circle

"Fall at Your Feet," Crowded House

"March of the Pigs," Nine Inch Nails

"Ring of Fire," Johnny Cash

"Burn Hollywood Burn," Public Enemy

"Know Your Enemy," Rage Against
  the Machine

"Wasting My Hate," Metallica

"Perfect People," Pennywise

List up to ten things that could be helpful to someone breaking into the business.

■ Learn to read.

■ Intern anywhere (work for free).

■ Start your own TV/movie studio.

■ Move to Iraq and open a Hard Rock chain.

■ Partner with Madonna.

Danny Elfman

Did you have a mentor or someone who inspired you? If so, what have you learned from that person?

For me as a child, a magical combination for a great successful film was Ray Harryhausen and Bernard Herrmann. I think of Herrmann as my mentor, though he's really more of an inspiration since I never met him. Before Herrmann, I had assumed music was just there, in the film itself. Maybe it was made by magic or in a factory, I just never really thought about it. I was around ten or eleven when I started to notice music as a separate part of filmmaking, when I saw a re-release of *The Day the Earth Stood Still.* This was the era of all the Ray Harryhausen sci-fis, a time when I saw what were to become the favorite movies of my childhood, such as *The 7th Voyage of Sinbad, Jason and the Argonauts,* and *Journey to the Center of the Earth.* Bernard Herrmann's name began to mean something special to me. It meant something extra had gone into the movie I was about to see, so when I'd see his name come up in the titles, I would say, "Oh boy!"

As a young adult, I became more of a serious film buff. The seventies were a great era for that, because not only were there really interesting films being made, there were also two retrospective theaters in Los Angeles, the Nu-Art and the Fox Venice, that played a different double feature every night of the week. It only cost a dollar to get in (at some point it became two) and for a starving musician, or in my case, a starving street performer, it was great. They played everything from all eras—one night it would be Kurosawa, the next Polanski, then Alfred Hitchcock. During that period, I rediscovered backwards all of Bernard Herrmann's work, and I learned that the science fictions I had grown up on in the mid-sixties were only one part of him. There was also all of his Hitchcock work that I was too young to have seen. So I went backwards and discovered *Psycho, North by Northwest,* and all the other great scores he did, back to *Citizen Kane,* developing a much deeper appreciation of Herrmann and what he brought to film music. It got me more into film music in general, to the point that I could watch a movie on television, hear a score, and I might recognize the composer. I was still years away from ever doing a film score, but I would play a little "who scored that?" game with myself watching old movies. Was it Franz Waxman, Erich Korngold, Max Steiner? Steiner did interesting things that nobody else did which I connected to. His music had a great energy and use of melody.

As I learned more, what always put me over the top would be the juxtaposition of a composer's diverse work. I was a huge Fellini fan, but when I heard *The Godfather* it really killed me. Anyone who could write these Fellini scores and *The Godfather* is genius. Anybody who could write *Jason and the Argonauts* and *The Day the Earth Stood Still* and *Citizen Kane* and *North by Northwest*—wow! They don't do just *one* thing great; they build and cross bridges.

What was your very first job in the music industry, and how did you get it?

I started with the street theater group that my brother founded, which evolved over the years into a multimedia musical theatrical troupe. I'll refer to them as the Mystic Knights even though technically they were called the Mystic Knights of the Oingo Boingo. I had a band called Oingo Boingo later, and I don't like to confuse them. The Mystic Knights was a twelve-piece ensemble, and everybody had to play three instruments in addition to our homemade percussion. We didn't necessarily play every instrument perfectly, but we worked really, really hard at it. I played violin, trombone, and guitar. When my brother did an underground cult film called *The Forbidden Zone,* he had us do the music. It wasn't a traditional film score. It was to be played by this twelve-piece, ragtag ensemble. So even though I wasn't timing it super-accurately to the screen, the way I would later, I was creating the music for a film.

What was your first big break? The first great thing that ever happened to you . . .

The music for *The Forbidden Zone* didn't lead to anything immediately. We did it around 1978–79 . . . just before we broke up as a troupe. About that time, I became reinspired by ska music coming out of England, such as Selecter, Madness, and XTC, and I decided to start Oingo Boingo. It wasn't until 1985 that I got my first call to do a more traditional film score, for *Pee-Wee's Big Adventure.* Paul Reubens (Pee-Wee Herman) and Tim Burton both had a voice in who was going to do music for the movie, and they each knew me from two different incarnations of my work. Paul was a big fan of my work from *The Forbidden Zone,* and Tim knew of Oingo Boingo. It was enough to get me a surprise call and a meeting. I had not initiated any of this and was shocked to receive the call.

What elements of your job make you want to go to work every day?

What makes it interesting and what keeps me going are two different questions. What keeps me going every day is really simple—deadlines. If it weren't for deadlines, I'd still be working on *Pee-Wee's Big Adventure.* I never get to the point when I think I am really done, but in film, you don't have the luxury of time. You get intense, brutal deadlines, and the only reason I've survived all these years is that, for whatever reason, I learned early on that I am able to work well under pressure. I think that if you can't handle that, you're not going to have much of an extended career in film music. It's all-consuming, to the point that when I start a film, I have what is almost a going-away party. I know I'm not going to go out to dinner, see my friends, or do almost anything for the next two to three months.

What gets me through each day is the knowledge that I have to write at least two minutes (more or less) of music that day—whether I'm sick or have other things happening in my life is irrelevant. I simply have to write close to two minutes of music that day before I go to sleep. That may not sound like a lot of music, but it is, even more so when you're on an active movie, or you write in a style like I do which sometimes gets chaotic and isn't quick and easy to write down.

As for what inspires me each day, I couldn't begin to guess. It's just a desire to do something really good.

What qualities most helped you get to where you are today?

As I had mentioned, the ability to function under fire. Often, on a big, difficult film, there's a war going on, and as composer, you're right in the middle of it. Everything has been plugging along at a certain pace in a certain way, for a year perhaps, and then suddenly, there's the preview. The composer works very closely (and often only) with the director, but the director is moving in a certain direction and very often gets derailed. I've seen humongous battles go down around me that were so emotional and so intense. Since the composer is the last guy on the film, we're very often right in the most intense part, so I'd say the ability to hunker down, stay calm, and hold your end together is a very important quality.

There are several things that can make a movie difficult. A movie can be radically changed in the eleventh hour—it's not uncommon for me to work forty-eight hours straight on a complicated queue only to find out just when I finish it that that scene has been totally recut, and I have to start from scratch. Sound effects, dialogue, and music are all working simultaneously at the end. If you lift twenty frames from the beginning of a scene and add a couple seconds a little later, sound effects and dialogue can quickly adjust all of their work, because everything is disconnected—each line of dialogue is a separate line of dialogue; each sound effect is a separate sound effect. Music, however, works in meter in time. So when you have a pulse going, when you have a melody that's working in four-bar phrases and suddenly you lose time, you can't just conform it without making everything sound completely fucked up. It may sound truncated and incomplete, because the meter has been broken. So we are under a unique problem of having to conform after the fact, conforming to an edit which can change at any time.

Some movies are really difficult just because of the internal nature of the movie. *Big Fish*, which I loved, was a really difficult movie (most of Tim's movies are) but not because of any battles or wars. The studio was behind it, and the producers seemed to be in synch with Tim. It was a harmonious production, but for me, it was still really difficult because the balance was so delicate. Film music is often a real tightrope balancing act to find the tone, to capture the heart of the film, and to figure out how far to go and in what direction as you follow the emotion.

If you knew everything at the beginning of your career that you know now, what would you have done differently?

When you're only going to do a couple movies a year, you have to make choices—you may take on a movie and wish later when you're in the middle of hell that you hadn't, or maybe you passed on something that you didn't know was going to turn into the fascinating project that it evolved into.

So much of it is luck, but what you do with luck is up to each individual. My path is uniquely my own—I got my first film without any idea that I was going to be a film composer. I survived because I worked super, super hard at it when I got those first few films, but I was lucky that the first film I got was a hit. The music that I did for it was unusual enough that it established my name. It was a quirky comedy, and at that point, nobody had any idea what to do musically with quirky comedies. I wasn't aware I was doing anything unique, but it was different enough that instantly I was offered almost every offbeat comedy made in Hollywood.

I don't know what advice to give to someone at the beginning of their career other than to stick to one's guns. Always stick with your instincts. I have rarely passed a point that I felt I was losing the identity of my work, and when I did, I always regretted it. At the same time, that could be bad advice, because that might cause somebody to lose work. Sometimes not caring about one's career is a great luxury. In hindsight, I never cared if I got another movie—I enjoyed doing them, but I always looked at it as an interesting fluke. And I knew that there would always be other movies, so if somebody didn't like what I was doing, I was already prepared to take a hike. I think being in a rock band for years was helpful. It made it easy for me to have that kind of idealistic view. I draw my line in the sand, and that's that. I don't consider myself to be arrogant when I am working on a film, insofar as I really do try to bend over backwards to get the director what they want, but, if I am not providing what they want, I will be the first one to suggest that they find another composer. Rather than imitate someone else or adopt their style, I'd move off. Dozens of times, if I felt like the director was really attached to the temp score, I would suggest he hire that composer, whoever it is, because I am not going to do it. At the end of the day, I've got to live with myself, and if I feel like they just want me to rip somebody off, I'd be pretty miserable.

What is your greatest lesson learned?

That's a tough one. For me there wasn't a *single greatest lesson,* but a long agonizing lesson of how to find a balance as an artist in a weird, difficult profession. I think that for anybody starting out, there's a big decision to be made. What are your objectives and what are your expectations? If you're content to be a hack, it's an easy one. A hack can do very well in this business. The hack says, "Give me the temp score, and I'll re-create it or even duplicate it for you."

Or, do you want to be a craftsman? That's no easy feat and a good craftsman can gain much respect. They'll say, "I understand what you're looking for, and I've got enough technique to produce any style you want." There's nothing wrong with that.

If you want to be an artist, it's going to be really tough. You have to transcend technique and create your own voice, find your own unique instincts and set out on a difficult, uncertain path. I know that sounds super corny, and you've heard it a million times, but it's true. The pressures to imitate become stronger and stronger, even to imitate yourself.

The problem is this: in film composing, if you want to do really well, if you're lucky enough to get your start at all, you have to keep working. Not only to hone your skills, but to keep your name present and alive in directors' minds, and to hope that just maybe, one of your projects will become that rare "gem" that will allow you to really show what you're capable of.

That means, as you plug away, you're going to have a harder and harder time keeping original and not feeling like you're becoming a prostitute. I can testify. Over the course of my career, I've been a whore, and I've striven to be an artist. The problem for me is that when I do fall into the strong gravitational pull of "prostitution mode," after it's done I'll beat myself up for it.

Almost nobody's immune to the whore side of the business because at a certain point, you're offering your services for money and you're going to try to please them and give them what they want. The question is, how do you feel in the end? For me, that's the whole struggle working in film. For many of us, writers, composers, actors, and even directors, the line between art and prostitution can get very, very blurry. The biggest ongoing lesson for me is to learn how to find that balance.

What are some of your favorite albums?

Requiem, Fauré

Il Casanova, Nino Rota, sound track
  to *Fellini's Casanova*

Romeo and Juliet and *Piano Concerto No. 3,*
  Sergey Prokofiev

String Quartets, Dmitri Shostakovich

Taraf de Haidouks, Taraf de Haidouks
  (a Gypsy band)

Buena Vista Social Club

Underground, Goran Bregovic sound track
  to *Underground*

L'Histoire du Soldat, Igor Stravinsky

The Okeh Ellington, Duke Ellington

Best of Django Reinhardt

The best of Geeta Dutt
  (Old Indian film music)

Did you have any posters on your bedroom walls as a kid? Of whom?

A shitload of cutouts from *Famous Monsters in Filmland,* which gradually got replaced by Jimi Hendrix, the Doors, the Beatles, Grateful Dead, and Zeppelin.

The beauty of my generation is that we all had the same posters. It's not like it was when I watched my kids growing up. All of my daughter's friends were into different kinds of music.

What are some great shows you've seen?

I haven't really heard a lot of live classical music. I might as well have grown up in a little town in the middle of nowhere for all the concerts I've seen in my life. I did see a great performance of *L'Histoire du Soldat* that was really inspiring to me. It was at a tavern in Los Angeles.

Fanfare Ciocarlia also performed at my birthday last year on a rooftop in Hollywood. I was fortunate enough to catch them on a world tour and hired them to perform at my party for the night. That was one of my favorite live concerts.

Jimi Hendrix's last concert on the Isle of Wight

Mozart's *Magic Flute*

What are some of your favorite songs?

I don't use albums anymore—I use playlists in Apple iTunes.

Going back to my early theater days, the first music I ever wrote down was Duke Ellington transcriptions. The Mystic Knights were playing a lot of thirties jazz, and even though I'd never had any music lessons, I had to learn to notate stuff we were playing. I owe this tremendous debt to Ellington even though I don't consider him a composer who is very present in my work. Django Reinhardt is also some of my favorite music to listen to. Prokofiev and Stravinsky are my two great inspirations in terms of orchestral music. If you create a playlist with *Romeo and Juliet,* one or two of his piano concertos, some of his film music (for example, *Aleksandr Nevsky* or *Lieutenant Kizhe*), you'll have everything you ever need to know about orchestra, orchestration, nuance, and the dynamics and subtlety of film music. He is the greatest melodic, emotional composer to me, and can effortlessly switch between something witty to something playful to something tragic. It can be immensely powerful or purely emotional.

List up to ten things that could be helpful to someone breaking into the business.

If I wanted them to succeed in the business the way it is now, I would tell someone to learn to imitate and provide, because that's the direction (more and more) the business is working toward. If they want to take the riskier route, I would advise the opposite—to do whatever it takes to create and develop your own sound and stick to it. However, you may not get work, so that may not be the best advice on how to be a successful composer anymore. I feel that Hollywood, more and more each year for the last fifteen years, has been embracing the derivative. I think it's encouraged to write music that sounds like something that the people who are hiring you or the audience in their minds already know. If one could lose oneself and just dive into other people's personalities and styles for the producers or directors who are hiring them, that would probably serve them best in their career, in terms of getting work. The other question is, can the individual be content with that? That is up to each person.

I don't know how to give advice anymore. I am very cynical as to the whole world of film and film music right now and where it's going. I see the celebration of mediocrity all the time. The Academy celebrates it. The award-givers celebrate it. I think the only part of film music and filmmaking that I'm not cynical about is that while the audiences will buy into the worst, most derivative stuff imaginable, they'll also buy into things that are completely unique. The movie-going audience doesn't sit there and think, "Wow, this is something I've never heard before" or "this sounds like a movie I heard two years ago." To them, it either works or doesn't. Because composers are kind of invisible to the audience, they don't necessarily know who they're listening to. The audience can be very forgiving. They have the capacity to hear things that are really new and fresh, and enjoy them. The hard part is getting something new and fresh into a film score in the first place. That takes the courage of a director and/or studio, which gets harder all the time in Hollywood.

Tom Freston

Did you have a mentor or someone who inspired you? If so, what have you learned from that person?

I never really had a formal mentor who used to look after me. But I did look at, study, and talk to a lot of the legendary record men, who began with great talent relationships and built very successful businesses—David Geffen, Chris Blackwell, Ahmet Ertegun, Mo Ostin, and so on. All of them understood that this is first and foremost a creative-based business. Also, looking at many of these guys, you learned that hiring great people was the second best thing that you could do as an executive, as well as building a culture where people do well, have fun, thrive, and want to stick around.

These guys all had good instincts and followed them. They were their own guys. Emotionally connected to the music, great with talent, they built those relationships into thriving businesses. They set up healthy and creative cultures. Importantly, people at those companies loved it and worked like they were on a mission.

They were all also tight with a dime when they needed to be.

What was your very first job in the music industry, and how did you get it?

My first job in music, really, was at MTV. Before that, I lived and ran an import/export business in Afghanistan and India for eight years. We used to design and make clothes and sell them around the world. It was a whole other life and very enjoyable. I had a major love affair with Asia. Things in that business went bust in 1979 (I made and lost a lot of money) so I sold the company and came back to New York. I wanted to do something that really turned me on and got me excited. I had had that when I was working in Asia, and I didn't want to settle for "just a job."

Having a job you love puts you ahead of 90 percent of the other people in the world. Music was my main passion and interest. I was a big fan. I also knew a lot of people who were in the music industry at that time, including my brother, who was at CBS records. With luck and research I ended up at MTV Networks (before it was even called that) and talked my way into being part of a small team that was to develop the idea of a "music channel for cable TV." I convinced them to hire me based on my enthusiasm for music and this new idea, along with the fact that I had been an entrepreneur in my last business and this was certainly going to be an entrepreneurial undertaking.

Back then they wouldn't hire anyone from the traditional television world, so I was certainly qualified. At that time, they were hiring anyone—former school teachers, people from the record business, beatniks, anybody offbeat and interesting. It was a pretty eclectic mix and a blast.

A lot in life is about luck and timing, and I clearly had come along for this job at exactly the right time. Had it been a week later, I probably wouldn't have gotten it. Back then I was just thinking I'd be lucky to get a job anywhere when people asked me what the hell I had been doing in Afghanistan for eight years.

What was your first big break? The first great thing that ever happened to you . . .

I came onto the team as the marketing guy. After a while there was a general manager, who wasn't very popular. He alienated everyone and got fired. So my boss at the time, Bob Pittman, promoted me to general manager at MTV and VH1. It was a real break as it moved me from being kind of on the periphery to dead-center at the networks. That allowed me to broaden my experience, credibility, and usefulness. It was an exciting move and, years later, I'm still here.

What elements of your job make you want to go to work every day?

Mainly, passion and empowerment. I love what I do, and we are left to run the company pretty much as we see fit. I am surrounded by creative people. All the things that I love are here. It isn't just MTV—we also have Nickelodeon, VH1, Country Music Television, Spike. It's also global. I am even back in India with MTV India. Music, film, animation, the Internet—all of that is a real turn-on to me. I feel very energized and very lucky.

What qualities most helped you get to where you are today?

Passion for the job, hard work, and a sense of humor. It's also good to keep an open mind, an appreciation for the offbeat, and a strong sense of curiosity. All of these things have played into it. You never know where or when you're going to find something great, so a willingness to listen to almost anything or anyone has paid off. I also haven't let my own ego dominate what I do. I'm very open and eager to have people under me take stuff, run with it, and get credit for it. That keeps them here, and that keeps them happy.

If you knew everything at the beginning of your career that you know now, what would you have done differently?

Well, I never really had a big career focus. And it's not like everything's been perfect, but there's very little that jumps out at me that says "You would have been here if you had done that." Things have gone a lot better than I had expected.

I can't think of any long-term, big decisions that have really turned out to be shit. This is not to say that I've done everything right, and there have been plenty of bad, smaller-time decisions—

you learn from those. I don't want to name names, but there are probably a few people I wouldn't have hired, and a few people I should have fired sooner.

The worst mistake I ever made at MTV was I promoted the wrong guy to general manager. Not somebody who came from the creative side, not somebody with any passion or knowledge about music, but a person to whom this job was like any other job. He never saw that there was a kind of magic to the place, and he did a lot of damage to the culture. A lot of that happened before I realized it.

I learned that the best way to run a creative business is to put a real creative person at the top. Someone who can be seen by the people who work there as a champion of ideas, openness, and creativity. If it is just a dollars-and-cents businessman, bad things can happen. We see this happening all over the entertainment business nowadays. I learned that you can actually have a good business led by nontraditional people. You can always get business people to support them, and partner with them, but a leader for a creative business needs good creative instincts and passion.

What is your greatest lesson learned?

Hiring great people and trying to make a real team that goes after a common goal and strategy. And to have a sense of humor under all circumstances.

What are some of your favorite albums?

In a Silent Way and *Kind of Blue,* Miles Davis
Blood on the Tracks and *Pat Garrett*
   and Billy the Kid, Bob Dylan
What's Going On, Marvin Gaye
Stan Getz and João Gilberto
Exodus, Bob Marley

For the Beauty of Wynona, Daniel Lanois
Blue Train, John Coltrane
Tales from Urban Bohemia,
   the Dandy Warhols
Almost anything by the Jayhawks, Steve Earle,
   U2, R.E.M., Emmylou Harris

I also listen to a ton of world music. Some of my favorites are . . .

The River, Ali Farka Toure
Tropicália 2, Caetano Veloso

Specialist in All Styles, Orchestra Baobab
Buenos Hermanos, Ibrahim Ferrer

Did you have any posters on your bedroom walls as a kid? Of whom?

I just had one that I remember . . . I had Allen Ginsberg walking around with a sign that said "Pot is fun."

What are some great shows you've seen?

Best show I've ever seen was U2 with Pearl Jam in Rome at an outside amphitheater on a summer night in about 1993. The audience was right off the ground. It was eighty thousand Italians.

I was at Bruce Springsteen's at the Bottom Line in '75 when they did the *Born to Run* showcase. That blew me away.

Live Aid

The *Unplugged* with Eric Clapton outside of London in 1991 that went on to sell 23 million copies worldwide. "Tears in Heaven" was on that.

Last summer I went to see Orchestra Baobab in Central Park. They lit up the place.

What are some of your favorite songs?

> "Like a Rolling Stone," Bob Dylan
> "Redemption Song," Bob Marley
> "Who Let the Dogs Out?," Baha Men

List up to ten things that could be helpful to someone breaking into the business.

■ Study before your interview! I interview people all the time, and I am always amazed at how many people know nothing about the company. If you just know three things about what this company has done you'd be ahead of 95 percent of the other people. Know what they're building, what their challenges are, and show some emotion about what they're doing. That's how to get in the door. . . .

■ You have to follow your heart. Particularly if you're young—in your twenties or thirties—you really shouldn't be giving up on your dreams easily. You should figure out how you can find a job doing something you actually really love and are passionate about.

■ Be open-minded. In this business, it's quite often that the thing that becomes the runaway, breakaway hit is something that people laughed at or said would never work. Trying to look at new things from different angles can be a handy trade. And, of course, the perennial tip— "Don't be an asshole."

Paul Hunter

Did you have a mentor or someone who inspired you? If so, what have you learned from that person?

Joe Pyka inspired me to direct. It was my first time on a film set. I watched him shoot a commercial for Pepsi.

What was your very first job in the music industry, and how did you get it?

My first job I was as a PA on a music video for free. I told the producer of the video that I would do anything on set. I just wanted to be around anybody who was filming.

What was your first big break? The first great thing that ever happened to you . . .

My friend in high school was starting a rap group. He gave me three thousand dollars to shoot a video for him. From there, I started showing every record label the video. They all said I sucked and I would never work.

What elements of your job make you want to go to work every day?

I love thinking about ideas and seeing them come into existence.

What qualities most helped you get to where you are today?

Persistence. Working with people. Being ready with ideas when any chance came around.

What is your greatest lesson learned?

Being prepared. Never quitting even though I wanted to so many times.

What are some of your favorite albums?

Earth, Wind & Fire, Earth, Wind & Fire
Innervisions, Stevie Wonder

On & On, Erykah Badu
No Left Turn, Pat Metheny Group

Did you have any posters on your bedroom walls as a kid? Of whom?

Bruce Lee from *Enter the Dragon*.

What are some great shows you've seen?

Prince and the Revolution's *Sign O' the Times*

Miles Davis

List up to ten things that could be helpful to someone breaking into the business.

- Study the trends of the business.
- Know music from marketing and advertising.
- Work for free.

- Smile.
- Have a point of view.
- Know that the business is always looking for new ideas.

McG

Did you have a mentor or someone who inspired you? If so, what have you learned from that person?

Without a doubt Rick Rubin is the reason I got into the music business. Here was this guy in an NYU dorm room connecting with Russell Simmons, plugging into what was happening on the street and doing it all with his own style and panache.

What was your very first job in the music business, and how did you get it?

I started my own label called G Recordings. The music scene in Orange County was happening—No Doubt, Stone Temple Pilots, Rage Against the Machine, and my best friends were the guys in Sugar Ray. They didn't have any great songs at the time, but Mark was an incredibly charismatic performer so we decided to make a video. I scraped up $3,500, we shot it on 35mm, stole all the locations, and just overcame the odds with determination and enthusiasm. The video was for a song called "Caboose." It had quantifiable energy. Doug Morris saw it, said "Get those guys on Atlantic," and it all started from there.

What was your first big break? The first great thing that ever happened to you . . .

My friend Paul Pontius had just signed Korn, and I knew they were very special. I kicked open the door to his office and begged him for ten thousand dollars to shoot a video for "Blind." He agreed and then proceeded to help me pick up the camera gear in his Ford F150. Jonathan worked so hard performing he collapsed on set. People responded to the authenticity of this great band's voice. I had my foot in the door.

What elements of your job make you want to go to work every day?

I love exploring my three favorite things—music, film, and television. I never take it for granted.

What qualities most helped you get to where you are today?

I never thought about failure. I am so focused on the warm elixir of successfully completing a record or a film. I waste very little energy about worrying if it's going to work or not. This quality does however make me a terrible gambler.

If you knew everything at the beginning of your career that you know now, what would you have done differently?

The first thing I did when I got a couple of bucks was build a recording studio. I figured I could record all my favorite acts and never have to shell out big dough for the expensive Hollywood studios. Turns out I am a shitty engineer—I sold the gear at ten cents on the dollar and basically lost it all. Thank God for film.

What is your greatest lesson learned?

When things are going your way, don't buy into your own bullshit. Every great songwriter, every great filmmaker, only had a limited period of greatness.

What are some of your favorite albums?

Paul's Boutique, the Beastie Boys
Never Mind the Bollocks, the Sex Pistols
Jazz, Queen

Did you have any posters on your bedroom walls as a kid? Of whom?

Morris Day and the Time. I truly aspired to be Morris Day. I bought Stacy Adams shoes and emulated his every move.

What are some great shows you've seen?

Rage Against the Machine at the Santa Monica Civic opening for House of Pain ruined me—an absolute emotional explosion.
The Red Hot Chili Peppers at Nightmoves in 1988. I wanted to be like Flea.

What are some of your favorite songs?

"Bigmouth Strikes Again," the Smiths
"In Only Seven Days," Queen
"She Sells Sanctuary," the Cult

List up to ten things that could be helpful to someone breaking into the business.

You have to be willing to endure an immeasurable amount of resistance. This is a subjective world where nothing is fair and very little sense can be made of the way things pan out. It's a pursuit for those who truly love the way music makes you feel in the middle of the night, by yourself, alone in your bun huggers.

Judy McGrath

Did you have a mentor or someone who inspired you? If so, what have you learned from that person?

Two thoughts. I take my inspiration from musicians, who remind me that everyone has something to say, that we should all champion free thought, weirdness, individuality, honesty, art, originality, creativity, and the right to speak your mind.

I've also learned that short of full-frontal nudity, almost anything should go in a work environment.

What was your very first job in the music industry, and how did you get it?

My first job in a music-related industry was writing promo copy for MTV, two months after it launched. I still hadn't seen the network, because you had to live in New Jersey to get it. I wrote a piece about waiting for MTV, and made the analogy that it was like waiting for Godot. I believe they were so new and so desperate for help, I got the job. My goal was to write Random Notes for *Rolling Stone.* I believe I will still get there.

What was your first big break? The first great thing that ever happened to you . . .

I had a waitressing job in high school, and that taught me I needed to get an education and move out of my town. ASAP. I had a job at a radio station writing copy for an alcoholic deejay, who taught me that you could love music and earn money doing it. But the first great thing that ever happened to me was that my father played Duke Ellington records every day when I was a child. Who could go wrong after that? As for real work, I made a painfully naive but "dummy" magazine layout for a job at Conde Nast. I got hired to type recipes at *Mademoiselle* magazine, and I don't cook. Ever. But it introduced me to some great people and new ideas. I've been lucky.

What elements of your job make you want to go to work every day?

Definitely not the free soda. But the freewheeling atmosphere, the creative people, the challenging people, the diversity . . . the artists, managers, and label people . . . the chance that someone in the music group or on the air promos will tip me off to a new artist or a new idea . . . the fact that for twenty-plus years my musical horizons have been continually expanded by the people I work with . . . political activism as part of the programming market . . . meeting Johnny Knoxville.

Seriously, I have excellent colleagues who raise the creative bar very high . . . I've met Beavis and Butthead . . . and for those of us who've been together a very long time, it is definitely family.

What qualities most helped you get to where you are today?

An open mind. Lack of an ironclad plan for myself. Associating with interesting people. Championing those who work along with, and for me. Appreciating my boss.

If you knew everything at the beginning of your career that you know now, what would you have done differently?

Gotten out a bit more. Wasted less time in meetings, or at least butting heads in meetings. It's soul-sucking. Brought more people into my world from the outside.

What is your greatest lesson learned?

That there is always something more to learn. And music usually provides it.

What are some of your favorite albums?

White Album, the Beatles
Fables of the Reconstruction, R.E.M.
Songs in the Key of Life, Stevie Wonder
Gold
Any and all albums by: Neil Young, Nirvana, Beck, Lauryn Hill, Whiskeytown, Ryan Adams, Lucinda Williams, Mary J. Blige, the Black Eyed Peas, the Beatles, Tom Waits, Radiohead, the Roots, the Vines, Steve Earle, Duke Ellington, PJ Harvey, the Beastie Boys, sound track to *Dead Man Walking,* and, especially, *Play* by Moby

Did you have any posters on your bedroom walls as a kid? Of whom?

John Lennon. The Chicago Seven. Jimi Hendrix. The Brontë Sisters. All my friends (I'm an only child). Covers from *Cream, Crawdaddy,* and *Rolling Stone* magazines. Covers from *National Lampoon.*

What are some great shows you've seen?

Nirvana *Unplugged*
Nirvana at Roseland
Zoo TV in Dublin
Neil Young at the Beacon Theater
Willie Nelson at the Beacon Theater
Ryan Adams at Irving Plaza
The Hives and Mooney Suzuki at the
   Bowery Ballroom

Traffic at the University of Scranton
Bruce, opening *Born in the USA*
   in Philadelphia
Live Aid
Eminem in Barcelona
Madonna in Houston
Wyclef Jean at Roseland
The Strokes and the White Stripes

Tom Waits on Broadway

The Band, at the Syria Mosque
in Pittsburgh, late seventies

R.E.M. and the Feelies at the Felt Forum

The Clash at Bond's

Pearl Jam at the Garden

What are some of your favorite songs?

"Blackbird"

"Take the A Train"

"A Bar Is a Beautiful Place"

"Anna" (my daughter's name)

"Forever Young"

"London Calling"

List up to ten things that could be helpful to someone breaking into the business.

- Don't wear a suit.
- Don't do *all* the talking.
- Don't be scared.

Kathy Nelson

Did you have a mentor or someone who inspired you? If so, what have you learned from that person?

I think I've had a few on different levels. First of all, my father for being inspiring and incredibly creative. He's an artist himself. Musician, writer, painter, photographer—he does it all. I think because he was a very young parent and such a bohemian kind of guy. He encouraged me and gave me a lot of freedom. And my tendency was to explore a lot of things and be artistic and emulate him a little bit. And he encouraged it. So in the early years I think that had a huge influence on who I turned into as a person. On a larger scale, my entire family. Because I came from a family in which everybody worked together and lived together and took the work very, very seriously. Yet the structure was fairly strict, and manners and morals were incredibly important to have. When you're a kid, whatever deck you're dealt, you think that is the norm. You don't have any frame of reference. I only realized it and appreciated it when I grew up and looked around me, and saw it was actually kind of unique.

In terms of works, I would say . . . Irving Azoff, who, basically, in observing who I was and where I came from, and having his own agenda—as Irving always did—decided that I would do movie sound tracks. It wasn't my idea at all! And Irving was a pretty scary guy, a pretty demanding guy, and I thought, "Oh my God, I better figure this out or he'll kill me." So off I went.

What was your very first job in the music business, and how did you get it?

In terms of taking it to the next level, it was probably Joe Roth. I think I was at MCA for eleven years, and in negotiating with them I'd kind of hit a wall. I think people realized and appreciated the job that I did, but I don't think they really thought that there was much more I could do. After I did *Dangerous Minds,* which was an MCA sound track and a Disney/Touchstone film, Joe turned around and realized how important the music was to the success of that film—and pretty much on the spot offered me the job of running music for his own studio. So for five years, that's where I was. Joe left the year before I left, and I stayed till the very last day of my contract, and then I wanted to do something at least a little new, a little different—which brought me to where I am now. I'd already worked on the music side, I'd already worked on just the film side. So I figured why don't I try to create a situation where I can oversee both sides, and where I can have greater control and greater insight into both of these worlds, which are both definitely connected but definitely operate separately. And a lot of times they don't take advantage of opportunities because they don't really understand each other's wants and needs. So I thought I'd try to connect the dots better than anybody's been able to because I literally am part of both worlds. And at that time I got to be maybe the only person who has this position at a major studio that has movies and music. In some ways it's fantastic, and in some ways it's a nightmare.

What was your first big break? The first great thing that ever happened to you . . .

Well, the first lion's den that Irving Azoff threw me into was Don Simpson and Jerry Bruckheimer, who were making *Beverly Hills Cop*. Jerry is still part of my continuing education, and Don taught me so much—and he enjoyed it. He enjoyed mentoring and taking me under his wing, being very protective and incredibly supportive of me. Not necessarily to my face—because he was very tough on me, like he was with everybody. But, to the outside community, he had much bigger opinions of my ability than were warranted at the time! I don't know if it was something he saw about me that made him realize I would do well at this, or whether it was his own ego! Whatever the reason, it gave me a lot of courage to forge my way through a business that certainly at times was so small and unique that I couldn't have gotten a job anywhere else. No other company would ever have cared about having a person who did movie sound tracks. In fact, Irving was the only person at a record company to have a position like that.

What elements of your job make you want to go to work every day?

The creative part!

What qualities most helped you get to where you are today?

I love being challenged to come up with creative ideas, and ways that music, whether it's on a marketing side or purely a creative side helps a director fulfill his vision and gets him what he wants. All of it, to me, is motivating! I love music, I love movies, and I love the combination of the two and how they make each other different and better. And I'm also interested in how they can screw each other up. Like I was sitting in a movie once with my father, and I said, "I hate this; let's go," and he said, "No, no. It's just as important to see why a movie doesn't work."

If you knew everything at the beginning of your career that you know now, what would you have done differently?

Hmm . . . Nothing! Intellectually, I might say I probably should have spent more time in school, I probably should have actually gotten a college degree instead of just taking two-and-a-half-years' worth of classes that I wanted to take. But maybe not! Would it have made me more successful? Some of the things that I pooh-poohed and didn't have much interest in—like educating myself—now it's interesting to me. Then I can say, "Oh, I probably should have gotten married and had kids and the picket fence, but the truth is I can't honestly say that either. I guess I like where I'm at! The road I took to get here seems almost inevitable. Everything just kind of happened! It wasn't like I had any big design.

And I still want to know what I'm going to be when I grow up!

What is your greatest lesson learned?

I think the lesson I still learn all the time is the importance of listening. Listening and observing as opposed to going, going, going all the time. It's a lesson I'm still learning: how to listen and pay attention. It's not that easy. Like if somebody starts to talk and you think you know what they're going to say, rather than letting them finish the sentence, you finish it for them. I think that happens on a lot of levels!

What are some of your favorite albums?

Freewheelin', Bob Dylan. My dad was such a fan, so I was exposed to a lot of early Bob Dylan. Also, I loved Tom Petty, Miles Davis, U2, the Clash, Elvis Costello, and the Rolling Stones.

Did you have any posters on your bedroom walls as a kid? Of whom?

I had a Thelonius Monk poster, a Japanese one! It was great looking. To be honest with you, it was my dad's, and I loved it for the design of it. I was familiar with Thelonius Monk, my dad knew him and had photographed him and stuff, but it was just a great poster. What else did I have? The Clash.

What are some great shows you've seen?

Prince, Universal Amphitheatre, 1999

Bob Dylan at the Shrine in Santa Monica when he first played electric. My dad said to me, "This won't mean anything to you yet, but you're sitting next to Marlon Brando." I was about seven years old! It was one of my favorite concerts not because of Bob Dylan's music but because as a kid, the excitement in the room, the intensity of him coming out. . . . I don't really remember any of the songs per se, but I remember what he had on, and I remember that the crowd was really electric.

Also when I young, my father took me to see Miles Davis at the Troubadour. I remember, because he faced the wall, saying to my dad, "Why doesn't he turn around?" That was another favorite concert.

U2 anytime

What are some of your favorite songs?

I loved the Doors. I loved the Police. I loved Billy Idol. I loved Stevie Wonder. He could be one of my favorite artists of all time and almost every one of his songs! And Prince. Early Prince! I love *Purple Rain,* oh my God! He's remarkable. And U2. And Mose Allison's version of "Seventh Son."

List up to ten things that could be helpful to someone breaking into the business.

- Learn how to observe and listen and pay attention.
- Learn to recognize what you really love and what you're good at. If you're lucky enough to figure out those things, you have a much better chance, and it'll be a lot smoother ride!
- The ability to recognize what is your natural talent and what you really have a passion for.
- Don't be so concerned about what the other guy is doing or how well the other guy is doing. Just focus on yourself.

Brett Ratner

Did you have a mentor or someone who inspired you? If so, what have you learned from that person?

Russell Simmons was my mentor. I watched him build Def Jam Records, Def Comedy Jam, Phat Farm, and various other companies from scratch. He allowed me to be around him during his negotiations with Sony, Polygram, HBO, and all the other companies that he dealt with. Because I was privy to all these meetings, I took what I could from it and applied it to being a filmmaker. Russell mentored me by allowing me to shadow him, and I learned a great deal from him and used that knowledge on my path to achievement. In particular, he showed me that perseverance and not being afraid to fail were key factors in achieving his success. I felt very lucky being around Russell, but I also remember what Robert Evans has said, "Luck is when opportunity meets preparation," and I am always prepared.

What was your very first job in the music industry, and how did you get it?

I was continually talking to Russell about my dream of being a movie director. Russell was hopeful, but he didn't have the relationships in the movie industry to help me at the time; however, while I was at film school he had a screening of my film *Whatever Happened to Mason Reese*. We had the screening and the only people that Russell invited happened to be rappers. A few months later, Russell and I are backstage at the U2/Public Enemy concert in Miami. Chuck D of Public Enemy said to Russell while I stood beside him, "I want Brett to do our next video." Russell said, "Brett who?" Chuck pointed at me and said, "Your man, Brett, white man Brett." Russell turned to me with a smile on his face and asked me if I wanted to do it. I said, of course, and the rest is history. Russell was so proud that one of his artists had asked for me to direct one of his videos without him having to force me on them. My first job was directing the Public Enemy video "Louder Than a Bomb." Which leads to question three . . .

What was your first big break? The first great thing that ever happened to you . . .

The day "Louder Than a Bomb" aired was the first day the director's name was included on the video on MTV. When other artists started seeing my name on such a good video, they called Russell to see if I could do their next video. I was prepared. Music videos were like another film school to me. I was getting paid to learn.

What elements of your job make you want to go to work every day?

I love my job. I literally don't know how to do anything else. I would have to work at McDonald's if I didn't do this. I would have paid for the opportunity to watch a film like *Rush Hour* get made!

What qualities most helped you get to where you are today?

I think the qualities that have helped me get to where I am today are perseverance, a tremendous passion for my work, and a need to tell stories. I never quit until I complete my vision, and I never compare myself to anybody else. If I compared myself, I'd never be happy. I try to focus on one project at a time and do the best I can.

If you knew everything at the beginning of your career that you know now, what would you have done differently?

I would have saved every penny I ever made. Instead of buying a big house and a lot of cars, I would have put a lot of money away in the bank for my future.

What is your greatest lesson learned?

Never be afraid to fail. Even if I didn't make it as a director, my mom was still going to love me, and my true friends were still going to be my friends.

What are some of your favorite albums?

The Best of the Delfonics, the Delfonics
All Jodeci albums
Raisin' Hell, Run-D.M.C.
Ready to Die, the Notorious B.I.G.
All Time Greatest Hits, Barry White
The Ultimate Collection,
    the Commodores
The score album to *Enter the Dragon*
    by Lalo Schifrin

Imagine, John Lennon
Le Freak, Chic
Thriller, Michael Jackson
Any greatest hits album
    by the Stylistics, the Chi-Lites,
    Curtis Mayfield, and Blue Magic

Did you have any posters on your bedroom walls as a kid? Of whom?

Bruce Lee and Farrah Fawcett.

What are some great shows you've seen?

Run-D.M.C. and the Beastie Boys at Madison Square Garden in 1986.

What are some of your favorite songs?

"Freek 'N U (remix) featuring Ghost
Face and Raekwon," Jodeci

"La-La Means I Love You," the Delfonics

"PYT," Michael Jackson

"Just to Be Close to You," the Commodores

"Betcha by Golly, Wow," the Stylistics

"If I Was Your Girlfriend," Prince

"The Rain," Oran Juice Jones

List up to ten things that could be helpful to someone breaking into the business.

- Find a mentor/role model that you can ask advice from.
- Ask questions, especially to the people who are doing what you want to be doing.
- Do whatever you can to find a job in the industry, even if you have to start at the bottom.
- If you want to be a record producer, go make a record. If you want to make films, get a camera and go and shoot a film. Learn from just doing it. Remember never give up. If you give up, you'll never know if you would have made it.

Mark Romanek

Did you have a mentor or someone who inspired you? If so, what have you learned from that person?

When I was a teenager, I didn't plan to make music videos. There was no MTV back then and no sense of the medium as an art form. I wanted to be a feature filmmaker and was immersed in learning about the films of Stanley Kubrick, Roman Polanski, Ingmar Bergman, Federico Fellini, Orson Welles, Sidney Lumet, Robert Bresson, Hal Ashby, Robert Altman, etc.

Later, when the chance to make music videos arose, I was inspired by the Polish short-filmmaker Zbiegnew Rybzcinski, who had made this amazing short film called *Tango*—which had won an Oscar. The video for Peter Gabriel's "Shock the Monkey" really impressed me. Also, Tim Pope (who directed all of the videos for the Cure) taught me that you had to be a little bit crazy to succeed in this job. That, in fact, it was considered a real plus.

Later still, I discovered the work of Jean-Baptiste Mondino and David Fincher. When I began working at Propaganda, I was lucky enough to hang around with Fincher and Mondino, and to watch them work. Both of those guys were very patient with me and taught me a lot. From Mondino, I learned about obsessive perfectionism and making things from the heart and soul—even if the piece was silly or strongly visual. Mondino taught me how to turn jobs down. To only do work that you felt really passionate about.

From Fincher, I learned about not selling the medium short, about thinking grandly, and how to navigate your vision through the political minefield of the music business of that time. Fincher had (and still has) a take-no-prisoners approach that was very inspiring. Both of these directors' work had an elegance and a level of craft that was not only far beyond other video directors' work, but surpassed most of what was going on in world cinema in general.

What was your very first job in the music industry, and how did you get it?

I became friends with Matt Johnson of the British group The The, and he asked me to do a music video for him. This was about 1987. I was busy trying to make various feature films, but wasn't getting any big breaks, so I figured why not? The The was one of my favorite bands at the time, so it seemed like a cool thing to do.

I used to carry this notebook all around New York, which I was filling up with a lot of stray ideas, sequences, and imagery that were too weird for any normal narrative use. So, I strung a few of them together and presented it to Matt. The video cost about thirty-five thousand pounds, which seemed quite a lot to me at the time.

The video's crap. It's terribly embarrassing now. Though I think it won a prize in some obscure Scandinavian film festival somewhere. There was one very good image of Matt screaming full-force into the lens in extreme slo-motion. They made a poster of that image, I think.

What was your first big break? The first great thing that ever happened to you . . .

I think the first real music-video break was when Jeff Gold at A&M offered me a tiny video for Robyn Hitchcock. This video's budget was only thirty-five thousand dollars, but I was a huge fan of Robyn's music at the time and was very excited to work with him.

Robyn wasn't so comfortable with the whole music video process, the phoniness, the lip-synching, giving up his song to some pipsqueak director's "vision." But, the video was odd and quirky and MTV loved it. It was one of the first big MTV "Buzz Clips." I think that video really helped sell quite a few records.

What elements of your job make you want to go to work every day?

Well, I don't usually want to go to work. I still don't enjoy the shooting process. It seems fraught with too many time pressures, stresses, and compromises. I much prefer the relative peace of the writing and editing process.

But, there are certainly times when things are going smoothly, when everyone's work and working relationships are flowing, and you know you're capturing something exciting and iconic on film. It's in these moments that the process can be very exciting.

I am also inspired by my love of music. It's always been a gigantic part of my life, and I feel privileged to work with music every day.

I can't deny that it's very cool to work with artists you have always admired. I've gotten to meet and to work with several idols of mine and/or really iconic figures in the pop world. I'm not so jaded that it isn't still a thrill for me.

Also, the fact that these artists entrust me to create a visual depiction of what are sometimes very personal songs is a source of real pride. I take seriously my responsibility to not let them down by doing sloppy or substandard work. I try to make every one of them special and to handcraft them in every detail. This detail work is something I enjoy quite a lot.

What qualities most helped you get to where you are today?

I was just lucky in a lot of ways. I had a love of music, and a love of cinema, and an oddly innate knack for filmmaking. This coincided with my coming-of-age in the mid-seventies when the most exciting filmmaking in the world exploded in a sort of golden age. On top of that, I went to a very progressive public high school north of Chicago that had a four-year cinema production and theory program. This was (and still is) unheard of! The teachers for this department were all procured from the Art Institute of Chicago and decided to teach us the history of non-narrative experimental cinema. They exposed our impressionable minds to the films of Stan Brakhage, Jonas Mekas, Michael Snow, Andy Warhol, Maya Deren, Kenneth Anger, and others. So, I was watching all this weird, exciting, subversive stuff in the classroom. Then, on the weekends, I'd go to see *Nashville* or *The Godfather II* or *Dog Day Afternoon* or *Barry Lyndon*. I think it was the confluence of all these lucky factors that "got me where I am today."

That, and being blessed with supportive parents, who let their movie-nut son explore all this stuff with impunity.

After these formative experiences, I would say that the qualities that most helped me were having the sense to listen to my inner voice about what to do at any given juncture, a certain self-confidence/fearlessness, and the clichés of old-fashioned hard work, perseverance, and a lot of stubbornness.

If you knew everything at the beginning of your career that you know now, what would you have done differently?

As far as music videos go, I would've skipped a few jobs that I did for the wrong reasons. Early in my career—because I was eager and hungry to work and needed the money—I took some video jobs for music that wasn't any good, thinking that the video could somehow elevate the music. It didn't work. Instead, the bad music was like a lead weight that didn't allow the video to soar. To this day, I'm embarrassed by these pieces. The lesson I learned was this: Wait for good tracks, no matter how long it takes. Only associate your work with good music.

What is your greatest lesson learned?

Professionally and personally, I'd say that the greatest lesson I've learned is to listen very closely to your intuition—that inner voice that tells you what to do. Even when all those around you are telling you that it's got to be one way, and your intuition is telling you (sometimes only whispering to you) that it should be the other way. You must go the other way—and deal with the consequences. Always stay tuned in to this inner voice. It will never steer you wrong.

What are some of your favorite albums?

Blood on the Tracks, Desire,
   and *The Basement Tapes,* Bob Dylan
Songs of Leonard Cohen, Leonard Cohen
Kind of Blue, Miles Davis
Hunky Dory, David Bowie

Mutations, Beck
Elliott Smith, Either/Or, and *XO,* Elliott Smith
All Things Must Pass, George Harrison
OK Computer, Amnesiac, and *Kid A,*
   Radiohead

The Velvet Underground & Nico,
    The Velvet Underground
White Album, Abbey Road, and *Rubber*
    Soul, the Beatles
Parachutes, Coldplay
Goat's Head Soup, the Rolling Stones
Pink Moon, Nick Drake

Bridge Over Troubled Water,
    Simon & Garfunkel
Songs in the Key of Life, Stevie Wonder
Electric Warrior, T. Rex
Rain Dogs, Frank's Wild Years,
    and *Swordfish Trombones,* Tom Waits

Did you have any posters on your bedroom walls as a kid? Of whom?

When I was a kid, the walls of my bedroom were floor-to-ceiling Stanley Kubrick stuff. My room was wallpapered with cork, so the entire space was a giant bulletin board. I had every poster, every still, and every photo of Kubrick at work. It was virtually a shrine. I just thought he was the coolest guy ever.

What are some great shows you've seen?

I've been lucky to see a lot of great concerts.

The first show I ever saw was Cat Stevens at Chicago Stadium. I was fourteen.

Perhaps the most memorable show was when I was in a tiny audience for U2's first-ever gig in London in 1979. It was in a small pub venue called the Nashville in West Kensington next to the tube station. I swear, there were only twenty people there. (Bono remembers it as being more, but he's wrong.) There were so few people that if they decided to pack it in, no one would've blamed them. Instead, they played like they were at Madison Square Garden. They were astounding even then.

I saw the Clash twice at Bonds on Broadway.

I saw Leonard Cohen at the Hammersmith Odeon for the *Recent Songs* tour, where he was backed by Gypsies. That was very beautiful.

I saw Bruce Springsteen's solo guitar-only "Ghost of Tom Joad" show at the Wiltern in L.A. This was an extremely powerful and moving experience. (And, incidentally, the most I've ever paid for a scalped ticket in my life.)

The Waterboys gave a fantastic show at the Wiltern a few years back. I recall that it went on and on.

I used to see Tom Waits every New Year's Eve at the Wiltern, until he stopped that tradition. I've seen him many, many times and love it in a different way each time.

Elliott Smith gave a sweet, quiet concert at Town Hall in New York a few years back. I've seen him at Largo too, which was super intimate.

There've been great R.E.M. concerts, great Radiohead concerts, Jane's Addiction at the Hammerstein Ballroom, Nina Simone, Mazzy Star, Bob Dylan.

I saw Nine Inch Nails in a minuscule club. They used the same PA they use for stadium shows. My ears rang for two days.

What are some of your favorite songs?

"The Bewlay Brothers," David Bowie

"The Passenger," Iggy Pop

"Tomorrow," Elliott Smith

"Mrs. Robinson," Simon & Garfunkel

"If It's Magic," Stevie Wonder

"A Kiss to Build a Dream On,"
   Louis Armstrong

"Don't Cry No Tears," Neil Young

"I Wish I Knew How It Would Feel to
   be Free," Nina Simone

"Hey Jude," the Beatles

"Nobody's Fault But My Own," Beck

"Every Grain of Sand," Bob Dylan

"Hot Love," T. Rex

"How Can We Hang on to a Dream,"
   Tim Hardin

"You Got the Silver," the Rolling Stones

"Spinning Away," Brian Eno and John Cale

"Perfect Day," Lou Reed

"Everybody's Talkin'," Harry Nilsson

"Fire and Rain," James Taylor

"I Walk the Line," Johnny Cash

"The Sire of Sorrow (Job's Sad Song),"
   Joni Mitchell

"Sisters of Mercy," Leonard Cohen

"It Never Entered My Mind," Miles Davis

"Which Will," Nick Drake

"All the World Is Green," Tom Waits

"Me and Julio Down by the Schoolyard,"
   Paul Simon

"Wish You Were Here," Pink Floyd

"Electrolite," R.E.M.

"Exit Music (for a Film)," Radiohead

"Pale Blue Eyes," the Velvet Underground

List up to ten things that could be helpful to someone breaking into the business.

- *Be flexible:* You must have a clear vision of the film—every frame, every rhythm, every nuance, every sound. However, you must also remain open. You must be ready to embrace surprising opportunities, the happy (or unhappy) accidents and be extremely collaborative. If that sounds like a bit of a contradiction, it is. Sometimes, you must "bend like a reed in the wind" or you'll snap. Sometimes when something appears to be going wrong, it's actually going right and you don't know it. Have a strong vision, but be sensitive to the flow of events. It may be pointing you in the right direction.

- *Don't forget your original inspiration:* Keep things around that remind you of the idea or feeling that originally sparked your excitement about making the film: a photo, a sentence, an object, etc. As the difficulties and near-constant crisis-management of production wear on, often these original sparks of inspiration can become lost in a miasma of compromise and fatigue. It's easy to forget why you wanted to subject yourself to this nightmare in the first place.

- *Listen to your intuition:* Always listen to your intuition—that inner voice that's telling you what to do. Sometimes you have to be the "enemy of the people" and do what you know in your heart is right, even when all those around you are telling you you're mistaken. That said, never act rashly.

- *Don't take the easy way out:* Filmmaking is hard. Sometimes things seem so difficult that you want to take the easy way out. Don't. Often the labor-intensive way is the best way. It's nice to be nice, but you're not there to make friends and be social. You're there to try and do something original and interesting. You can sleep when you're dead. Also, it's the producer's job to make your job easier. Not the other way around.

- *Ask for advice:* Seek the advice of those who know more than you.

- *Be even tempered:* "Work for the work's sake only. Do not work for the fruits of your labor. Be even-tempered in success and failure, for this evenness of temper is what is known as yoga."—Bhagavad Gita

John Sykes

Did you have a mentor or someone who inspired you? If so, what have you learned from that person?

I'm fortunate to have had many mentors in my career. I've tried to learn from everyone around me: family, friends, and business associates. To me, a mentor doesn't have to be a boss or an employer. It can be anyone who achieves great success while treating others with respect.

What was your very first job in the music industry, and how did you get it?

I played the drums in a not-so-great rock band from junior high through high school. But we actually made money! I realized during that time that although I loved music, I was a better manager for the band than I was a drummer. That experience taught me that if I was going to have any real success in entertainment, I had better give up my drumsticks and go off to college.

What was your first big break? The first great thing that ever happened to you . . .

In 1980, there was talk in the industry that Bob Pittman had been hired by Warner/Amex to develop music ideas for cable television. I called Bob every day for two months to try and get an interview. We hit it off, and he hired me on the spot. I became part of the team that ten months later launched MTV.

What elements of your job make you want to go to work every day?

I love that I can make a living being involved in the creative process with creative people. I am in awe of artists, musicians, actors, writers, and directors and their ability to create a place for people to escape to. I'm never tired of hearing great new ideas.

What qualities most helped you get to where you are today?

Besides good luck, having a true passion and love for what I do and surrounding myself with people who are smarter than I am.

If you knew everything at the beginning of your career that you know now, what would you have done differently?

I've taken many risks in my career and I have no regrets. Life is an adventure. I've learned equally from winning and losing.

What is your greatest lesson learned?

Never do anything solely for the money.

What are some of your favorite albums?

Revolver, the Beatles

Let It Bleed, the Rolling Stones

Who's Next, the Who

Disraeli Gears, Cream

Blonde on Blonde, Bob Dylan

Stand!, Sly & the Family Stone

Rumours, Fleetwood Mac

Ghost in the Machine, the Police

Scarecrow, John Mellencamp

The River, Bruce Springsteen

Joshua Tree, U2

End of the Innocence, Don Henley

Tuesday Night Music Club, Sheryl Crow

Crash, Dave Matthews Band

Counting Crows

Stone Temple Pilots

Pet Sounds, the Beach Boys

Did you have any posters on your bedroom walls as a kid? Of whom?

Mitch Mitchell, Cozy Powell, Pete Townshend, Keith and Mick, Grace Slick, Roy Haynes, Ginger Baker, Keith Moon, and Whitey Ford.

What are some great shows you've seen?

The Who

Jethro Tull and It's a Beautiful Day, Tanglewood Music Fair, 1970

The Band, the Allman Brothers, and Grateful Dead, Watkins Glen, 1972

The Rolling Stones, Soldier Field, 1978

U2, *Zoo TV* tour, Giants Stadium, 1992

Cream Reunion, Rock and Roll Hall of Fame dinner, 1993

Bruce Springsteen, John Mellencamp, Sheryl Crow, or Dave Matthews anywhere, anytime, but above all the greatest music experience was the Concert for New York City on October 20, 2001—five and a half hours, and no one sat down.

What are some of your favorite songs?

Anything from the albums listed above.

List up to ten things that could be helpful to someone breaking into the business.

- If you're looking to get into the business side . . . get a great education. Read everything you can get your hands on. Don't be afraid to ask what you don't know. Treat the job you currently have like it is the most important one in the world. Treat others with respect. Above all, listen to everyone, then follow your own instincts.
- If you want to be an artist . . . never give up.

Hans Zimmer

Did you have a mentor or someone who inspired you? If so, what have you learned from that person?

The way I got into film music wasn't by going to music school. My formal musical education was two weeks of piano lessons. I basically worked as an assistant to another film composer in London named Stanley Myers who'd written *Deer Hunter*. I was the apprentice, so between making coffee and stuff like that he would very gently explain to me how to do things in a good way. He would explain the orchestra to me, and he just let me write right away, gently steering me away from complete disasters. I was in my twenties.

The whole music thing I got into because I had to. When I was a kid I started playing piano for myself when I was about four. I just loved it, there was nothing else I could do. There was nothing else I was good at. And there was nothing else I wanted to do. One of the things about being a musician is that we don't keep regular hours. The weekend is a great time to work because the phone rings less, but we don't take any time off and we're obsessed with it. That goes hand in hand with finding someone who believes in you and tries to help you learn some things and have a career.

I also loved spaghetti westerns when I was in my teens, so Ennio Morricone was absolutely my hero. He probably still is. I've got to know him a little bit over the years. His work ethic is tremendous. He's really strict with himself, and he just does excellent work. An enormous amount of soul and heart goes into it, and he's incredibly inventive. All those spaghetti-western sound tracks were great . . . they were like crazy remixes.

What was your very first job in the music industry, and how did you get it?

My first job in the music industry was playing bad synthesizer stuff on commercials in England. I got that job through a company called AIR Studios, which was Sir George Martin's company. I was in a band, and a recording engineer in the studio suggested me to them. Within two days I'd left the band and was working on commercials and suddenly people were actually paying me money, on top of having a lot of fun. Working with George as my first boss was pretty amazing. I learned a lot from him. All the really good guys are very generous with giving you their knowledge.

What was your first big break? The first great thing that ever happened to you . . .

Probably this small movie called *A World Apart,* which I did in England and Barry Levinson's wife saw. She bought him the CD, and he loved it so much that he gave me *Rain Man.* That was pretty cool. There's a period until you have your first success where you're just knocking your head against the wall, and everybody tells you how terrible your stuff is. Then suddenly, and I don't know how it quite happens, the same stuff written by the same guy finds general acceptance, and what was horrible yesterday suddenly turns into a hit today.

That really kicked my career off over here in the United States. The unimaginable, for a European to be able to have a career in Hollywood, that all happened through *Rain Man.*

What elements of your job make you want to go to work every day?

I love the collaborative process between the director and the composer, more so than the collaboration I used to feel when I was in a band—all anybody ever talked about was music. What I like is working with people who talk about music in a different language. They try to describe a piece of music by describing a painting, or showing you a painting, or showing you a bit of footage from a film. They're as passionate about their thing as I am about mine, but at the same time they give me freedom and autonomy. That makes such a difference. It's never dull. I love doing this. I have this rule that every morning when I wake up—and I've done this now for ten years—I check with myself if I want to go to the studio and write some music. The day I decide I don't want to do that anymore, I'll quit, and go do something else. It's quite good to occasionally check with yourself, and make sure, "Is this really the thing?" For me, it truly is. I put all my heart and soul into music.

What qualities most helped you get to where you are today?

Having a point of view. Not being a musical secretary. I always believed in the fact that you just have to sit down and listen to what the director is saying, and then you need to do something that he can't even imagine. Because that's the job, otherwise he'd be writing the music himself. In my case, I think I may be a better filmmaker than I am a composer. I try to understand and grapple with a film as much as possible, on a sort of subtextual level. I still don't know why some music works in film and why some doesn't. I think as long as I keep asking the question, it won't get boring.

If you knew everything at the beginning of your career that you know now, what would you have done differently?

I don't really know how I would have done it differently, but I would really have liked to leave out the part when I was poor, bouncing checks and not able to pay my rent. That's the crazy thing. As a musician you just have to play music. It's not often very practical, because it's very hard to make a living at it. I don't ever want to go back to those years. I don't think I learned anything from squalor and poverty, or living in flats with the roof leaking. I don't think that is character-forming or anything. I think it's just tiring, debilitating, and a bore. And you start getting a bit desperate. The only thing that saved me from becoming a lunatic was going to play some music. The great thing about music is that you can lose yourself in it. And all those walls with the bad wallpaper go away. I was living in Brighton, in England, which in winter is about as ghastly as it can get, especially if you don't have enough money to stick into the gas meter. But the cold would just recede if you played music, it kept me warm.

The other thing I learned very quickly is to never be at the mercy of anybody else. Learn how to record your own stuff. Learn a little bit about engineering. Learn enough about the business. I think of all those stories about how bands get ripped off. Go and find out about the business. You are responsible for your own career; your manager isn't really going to do it. Whatever horrible things happen are usually self-inflicted through ignorance, or not spending the time doing your homework. It's your piece of music—why do you want to be at the mercy of some recording engineer who you're desperately trying to explain how it is supposed to sound.

What is your greatest lesson learned?

That I still don't know anything. After working on all those films, I recently had an epiphany. I realized "I have learned nothing." Every movie is like starting from scratch. Your drawers are empty. And that's how it should be, otherwise you just repeat yourself. My problem with being in a band on the record side of things was that as soon as you had a hit, everyone expected you to follow it up with something that sounded similar. But look, in the film world, I'm the guy who wrote *Driving Miss Daisy*. I'm the guy who wrote *Gladiator*. Even if you just look at the stuff I did with Ridley Scott—*Thelma and Louise, Gladiator,* and the comedy *Matchstick Men* . . . I get to skate around, wherever it takes me, to try new things, which gives me a lot of freedom.

With *Matchstick Men,* we wanted to preview it with Ridley's name on it, because everyone expected car chases and guns, or the *Blade Runner*–type epic. But it's a small comedy. I think the other thing that's important is to not let them type-cast you.

What are some of your favorite albums?

That's really tough because it depends on my mood. There's a recording of the Berlioz *Symphonie Fantastique* that really rocks. They play it like a rock 'n' roll piece.

Let It Bleed, the Rolling Stones
Sonny Boy Williamson and the Yardbirds
China, Vangelis
Midnight Express, Giorgio Moroder
Blade Runner (both the album and the movie—I feel lucky that I get to work with one of my heroes)

Selling England by the Pound, Genesis

London Calling, the Clash. The most influential album for me. *Black Hawk Down* is very much me approaching the orchestra a little bit like the way I hope the Clash would approach them. Actually what I wanted to do on that movie was to work with Joe Strummer, and we finally got him in to do some stuff.

Also, Abba. I just love their well-crafted pop songs and their productions. From them I learned if you have a happy tune, write some sad chords underneath, or vice versa. That conflict makes great pop songs happen.

Did you have any posters on your bedroom walls as a kid? Of whom?

Damn right I did. I had the Rolling Stones, Janis Joplin, the Clash.

What are some great shows you've seen?

I was thinking the other day, if you only listened to the composers starting with the letter *B,* you could probably get a complete musical education, because you get Bach, Alban Berg, the Beatles, Brahms, Berlioz, Bartok.

I think the greatest live show I ever saw was *Live Aid.* I so didn't want to go, I was being grumpy about it. Queen, who I never really liked, just blew me away.

Arturo Sandoval. This was still when he was living in Cuba, no one had ever heard of him. There was a moment when I thought of just giving up playing because he was so amazing. There was such heat to his playing, and in the audience as well, it was that amazing level of communication.

What are some of your favorite songs?

"Yesterday," the Beatles. I think it has amazing structure.

"Broken Wing," Chet Baker

"Unfinished Sympathy," Massive Attack

"Two Tribes," Frankie Goes to Hollywood

List up to ten things that could be helpful to someone breaking into the business.

■ Ask for help. Don't be like the guy driving round and round and being too embarrassed to ask for directions at a gas station. I've found people are really forthcoming with help, assistance, and giving you tips on how to do things. When I first came to Hollywood I had never really worked with an orchestra, but the first time I met John Williams I must have bored the poor man to death because I was asking him all sorts of questions—how did you record this, how did you do that? And he was great—he would answer all this stuff for me.

■ On a personal level, you have to be forthright with your friends because you're going to live this crazy life where they might not see you for months and months because you're stuck in the studio (out of your own free will, of course). It's a strange existence.

FOR THE RECORD

A very big thank-you to Steven Tyler for writing the foreword to this book. I couldn't have a better frontman.

On the Record is a collection of shared wisdom, and it is only possible because so many remarkable individuals far wiser than I took the time to pass on some of what they have learned along the way. Without any questions asked, you all answered my questions and gave of yourself to the next generation. Your sincere and inspirational responses are the heart and the soul of this book.

This book would not have been possible without the support and enthusiasm of literally hundreds of people throughout the music business.

Thank you to the *On the Record* team . . .

Jennifer Ehmann

David Vigliano

Ken Hertz

Bill Vuylsteke and Shelley Venemann

Philip Burke for the amazing cover

Miles Donovan, and his agent Stephanie Pesakoff, for his inspired artwork

Holly Adams for coming up with the title

Jann Wenner and David Wild. Thanks for your creative input.

Brandon Panaligan and Sara Zambreno. I appreciate your tireless efforts.

Special thanks to my father, Yossi, my mother, Gila, and my sweet Michelle.

Lastly, on the record, I'd like to thank everyone whose support has made my career—and my life—possible.